THE
REPEAL
OF
RETICENCE

THE
REPEAL
OF
RETICENCE

*A History of America's Cultural and Legal Struggles
over Free Speech, Obscenity, Sexual Liberation,
and Modern Art*

ROCHELLE
GURSTEIN

HILL AND WANG
A division of Farrar, Straus and Giroux
New York

LIBRARY OF CONGRESS CATALOGING-IN-PUBLICATION DATA
Gurstein, Rochelle.
The repeal of reticence: a history of America's cultural and
legal struggles over free speech, obscenity, sexual liberation,
and modern art / Rochelle Gurstein. — 1st ed.
p.   cm.
Includes bibliographical references and index.
1. Freedom of speech—United States.   2. Obscenity (Law)—United
States.   3. Privacy, Right of—United States.   I. Title.
JC599.U5G87   1996   323.44'3'0973—dc20   95-47259 CIP

Excerpts from *Selected Writings 1950–1990*,
copyright © by Irving Howe, reprinted by permission
of Harcourt Brace & Company.

ACKNOWLEDGMENTS

My first debt is to Christopher Lasch and Robert Westbrook, both of whom devoted an enormous amount of time to carefully reading and criticizing this study when it was a dissertation. I am also grateful to Thomas Bender, Richard Wrightman Fox, and Thomas Haskell, who offered me encouragement and criticism at that delicate moment when a dissertation is about to become a book. I had the good luck to have a friend and patient computer master, Bruce Lebowitz, who made the physical manuscript possible. I am fortunate to have a number of friends who are also formidable intellectuals who read parts or all of this book at various moments in its long development—Marc Aronson, Vivian Heller, Jerome Kohn, Colin Morris, Richard Tristman, and Catherine Tumber. And I was also fortunate to have a forceful yet reticent editor, Elisabeth Sifton. But without the criticism, guidance, and extraordinary example of my great teacher Christopher Lasch, and the forbearance, magnanimity, intellectual spark, imagination, and radiance of my husband, Jack Barth, this book simply would not exist, and it is with the deepest gratitude that I dedicate it to the living memory of the one and to the living spirit of the other.

CONTENTS

THE
REPEAL
OF
RETICENCE

TASTE AND THE COMMON WORLD

"The activity of taste," Hannah Arendt once observed, "decides how this world, independent of its utility and our vital interests in it, is to look and sound, what men will see and what they will hear in it."[1] In our own time, however, taste has no public resonance at all; rather, it has been drastically reduced to mean little more than individual whim or consumer preference. In consequence, judgments about which things should appear in public, speculation about the common good, as well as deliberation about moral and aesthetic matters, have increasingly been relegated to the obscurity of the private realm, leaving everyone to his or her own devices. And in the absence of considered debate about the meaning of democracy, freedom, equality, and justice, or about the good, the beautiful, and the true, the public sphere has degenerated into a stage for sensational displays of matters that people formerly would have considered unfit for public appearance.

It has become a cliché to notice that our common world is flooded with lurid discussions, representations, and images of sex and violence. And it is not just the old culprits—movies, television, radio, journalism, best-sellers, advertising, rock and roll, and, more recently, rap music—that shamelessly exploit these subjects. Sex in its most obscene form—pornography—now appears in the most unlikely public places: not only is it an unregulated, multibillion-dollar industry, it has also become a litmus test of the First Amendment, a badge of sexual liberation, a tried-and-true strategy of "advanced" artists, a divisive feminist issue, and a subject of serious academic study.

The other remarkable quality of our common domain is its sheer triviality: we are persistently bombarded by reports of people's most intimate affairs by way of celebrity gossip and human-interest stories, confessional talk shows and soul-baring interviews, and by omnipresent television series and movies that treat the most banal incidents of ordinary life with the utmost gravity. Our public sphere, which should have displayed and preserved the grandeur and beauty of our civic ideals and moral excellences, is instead inane and vacuous when it is not utterly mean, ugly, or indecent.

To render this judgment, so plain to common sense, is to invite the inevitable charge of elitism. For, in contemporary America, to judge at all is to be "judgmental." To hold out the hope that commercial entertainment might occasionally rise above a puerile, sniggering adolescent level, for instance, is evidence of snobbery or, worse yet, of attempting to inculcate middle-class or "highbrow" values in others. Critics are scolded time after time: "No one is forcing you to consume popular culture, but don't interfere with others who have a right to do as they please and are entitled to their tastes." It is a sign of our time that this ready-made plea for freedom of choice, and the dismissal of standards as a form of cultural imperialism, is automatically offered not only on behalf of commercial entertainment but also for obscene art and pornography; and it is offered with equal gusto by Hollywood, Broadway, and Madison Avenue as well as by postmodern academics, liberal arts administrators, "advanced" artists, record companies, and First Amendment lawyers.

Personal taste is also typically presented as a justification for sensational and invasive journalism. If we are troubled by the quick cut of the camera to the horrified faces of the families of a space-shuttle crew at the moment the shuttle bursts into flames, by grisly confessions of murderers and rapists on local television news, by diagrams of President Reagan's colon as he is operated on for cancer, by photographs of the mangled corpses of the latest victims of "tribal massacre" on the front pages of newspapers, we are supposed to be mollified by some combination of the following: such news satisfies the public's right to know; it is protected by the First Amendment; it is reality, so we must face up to it. Rare protests that public decency has been violated are dismissed as signs of prudery or neurosis; in the same way, complaints that privacy has been invaded are treated as proof that the person must have something to hide.

This propensity for name-calling is even more pronounced in the occasional dispute that erupts over "avant-garde" art. As every student of modernism has dutifully been taught, today's acclaimed masters once suffered the taunts and jeers of the public and the academy; in the cases of James Joyce and D. H. Lawrence, they suffered the iniquity of having their novels banned. Everybody also knows that history vindicated these same figures—often in their own lifetimes—with the once-maligned works finding their rightful place in the museum or literary canon and their critics consequently unmasked as philistines and prudes. Thus, to raise objections to so-called free expression—no matter how graphically violent, sexually explicit, perverse, or morbid—is to invite the epithet "puritan." On the one hand, objections to the moral content of flagrantly obscene images are interpreted as a lack of aesthetic sophistication; on the other, they are treated as a squeamish refusal to confront reality in all its variety and intractability. In the logic that rules this argument, the next move is inevitable: to question the value of the work of any self-proclaimed artist is to endorse censorship, and censorship is the first step toward fascism.

These resorts to ad hominem attack make it difficult to think critically about these pressing matters, since no right-thinking person wants to be on the side of puritans, philistines, censors, and fascists. And this form of personal abuse, which has replaced vigorous disputation about what should appear in public, has received strong ideological support from the law. Even sensitive and searching liberal legal thinkers now interpret the principle of liberty in such minimal terms that they find themselves defending pornographers. Thus, while Ronald Dworkin is willing to grant that pornography is "often grotesquely offensive," he nonetheless contends that it cannot be banned for that reason "without destroying the principle that the speech we hate is as much entitled to protection as any other." Where John Stuart Mill valued liberty as vital to the development of individuality and to the pursuit of truth, Dworkin insists, "The essence of negative liberty is freedom to offend, and that applies to the tawdry as well as the heroic."[2] Many modern liberals and radicals are now in the sorry predicament in which they can no longer discriminate between the essential circulation of ideas, which is the cornerstone of liberal democracy, and the commercial exploitation of news, entertainment, and sex as commodities; likewise, they can no longer distinguish between the expression of unorthodox ideas in the pursuit of truth, which is the lifeblood of art, and the desire to publicize anything that springs to mind in the name of artistic genius.

With the powerful weapons of rights-talk and personal ridicule at the command of all forward-looking people today, anyone who tries to criticize anything that can be formulated as a free-speech issue— and free speech has been so overextended that it now encompasses not only pornography but cross-burning—is forced to acquit himself or herself of these charges in advance. This is impossible, of course, since to be critical of these liberal pieties is to be a self-confessed traitor to the liberal cause. All of this results in the interminable quality and fruitlessness of our most important controversies over our public life. If we are ever to move beyond these stalemates, we shall need to pose a more fundamental question: How and why have puritan-baiting, which focuses narrowly on a person's alleged sexual liberation or aesthetic sophistication, and rights talk, which makes the individual right to free expression the only issue, displaced principled debate about the quality and character of our common world?

The burden of this study, then, is to recover the origins of what was once a vital debate about what belongs in public and trace how it has degenerated into its current predictable form. The history I relate is the story of how the "moderns" of a century ago succeeded in discrediting their Victorian forebears and in opening the public sphere to matters previously believed to be private and therefore unfit for public display. I shall focus on arguments made for and against three agencies of exposure that first came to prominence during the last quarter of the nineteenth century and whose legitimacy is still in dispute today. The most aggressive was mass-circulation newspapers specializing in invasive and sensational reports; they anticipated what we now call mass or, more favorably, "popular" culture. Social reformers' insistence that information about sexual hygiene be made widely available introduced another powerful form of exposure; it anticipated both public sex education and the sexual-liberation movement of the 1960s. And, finally, a new literary style, realism, which depicted intimate life in a serious and candid fashion was the third threat; it was an early manifestation of the avant-garde.

This return to the past will be a rigorous examination of the terms of these long-forgotten debates to see if there is anything worth recovering in them, especially from the losing side. Now that our rare disputes about art concern *only* photographs or live performances—as in the cases of Robert Mapplethorpe and Karen Finley, respectively, where actual instances of sexual torture, degradation, or humiliation are publicly displayed—it is worthwhile to reconsider whether the old defenses of modernist novels such as *Ulysses* or *Lady Chatterley's Lover* should continue to receive automatic endorsement. This re-evaluation is even more urgent when it comes to violent pornographic movies that record the actual rape and mutilation of women. By now it should be obvious that there is something fraudulent, if not perverse, in the endless rehearsal of arguments that were developed to destroy nineteenth-century Victorians in a world where Victorians have been long extinct. Even Senator Jesse Helms is willing and able to distinguish between censorship of Mapplethorpe's photographs and NEA sponsorship of them.[3] And in the recent obscenity trials—of Mapplethorpe and the rap group 2 Live Crew—we see that yesterday's stirring calls to arms have deteriorated into today's tired clichés: in both trials, ordinary people—who are supposed to be censors and philistines—found on behalf of the defendants. One juror in the 2 Live Crew trial construed the issue exclusively in terms of free speech: "You take away one freedom and pretty soon they're all gone." And a juror in the Mapplethorpe trial expressed the common wisdom that because of the checkered history of the avant-garde, one must refrain from passing judgments and instead defer to expert opinion: "It's like Picasso. Picasso, from what everybody tells me, was an artist. It's not my cup of tea, I don't understand it, but if people say it's art, then I have to go along with it."[4]

While the democratization of culture, sexual emancipation, and the triumph of the avant-garde are usually presented as signs of progress —and there are good reasons for doing so—that story is only a partial one. For there have been unexpected consequences of these victories. One of the most surprising and devastating is the way that intimacy —which, for moderns, is supposed to provide the deepest meanings —has been stripped of the privacy it needs in order to flourish. The torrent of clinical, sterile public talk about sex—whether it be the language of "safe sex," condom distribution, "date rape," sexual ha-rassment, or fetuses and trimesters—coupled with the realist imper-ative to speak the language of the street in art, mass entertainment, and journalism, not to mention the growth of "gender" and "queer" studies as academic disciplines, have made it increasingly difficult to speak the old poetic languages of love, for now they sound evasive, sentimental, platitudinous, or naïve.

An equally unexpected and disastrous outcome of the victory of the party of exposure is that we no longer understand debates about the things that occupy our common space as matters of taste and judgment susceptible to public deliberation and speculation. Instead, when they are not simply banished to the private sphere of "lifestyle" choice, they are formulated as legal disputes, in which courts balance and weigh the relative rights and interests of the individual against those of society. This resort to the law has made it impossible to address many vital issues that fall outside its narrow precincts, and thus urgent differences over political, moral, and aesthetic matters are all but impossible to articulate. It is the contention of this book that with the defeat of the party of reticence in the twentieth century, the faculties of taste and judgment—along with the sense of the sacred and the shameful—have become utterly vacant; yet, without them, it is now clear that disputes about the character of our common world can only be trivial, if not altogether meaningless.

1

⚜

THE TOPOGRAPHY
OF THE HUMAN CONDITION:
PUBLIC AND PRIVATE

To understand how our common world has become home to discussions and images of matters earlier generations would have thought beyond representation if not imagination itself, we must begin with an account of what "public" and "private" mean. Taking Hannah Arendt's *The Human Condition* (1958) as my starting point, I am going to argue that public and private are actual, physical spaces of the human condition and, though it may be unfashionable to speak of universals, can be found in one form or another in all societies, ancient and modern, "primitive" and "advanced." The public is the physical space we share with others: "Everything that appears in public can be seen and heard by everybody and has the widest possible publicity," according to Arendt. "For us, appearance—something that is being seen and heard by others as well as by ourselves —constitutes reality." Not only does this physical public space constitute our only reliable reality but in its temporal dimension it offers the hope of transcendence: "It cannot be erected for one generation and planned for the living only; it must transcend the lifespan of mortal men." The public sphere, or what Arendt also calls "the common world," gives us the possibility of making a home of the earth, a world constructed of durable things, artistic achievements, cultural practices, and actions commemorated in history, preserved and passed down through time, linking generations of the past to the present and the present generation to future ones. "The common world," as Arendt put it in one of her most poignant formulations, "is what we enter when we are born and what we leave behind when we die."[1]

The private, in contrast, is the physical space in which we are alone. And it has an even more fundamental purpose. "From the beginning of history to our own time," observed Arendt, "it has always been the bodily part of human existence that needed to be hidden in privacy, all things connected with the necessity of the life process itself, which prior to the modern age comprehended all activities serving the subsistence of the individual and the survival of the species." Because the private sphere shelters the activities and experiences pertaining to the body, it can never acquire the durability or transcendence of the public sphere; those who dwell there are relegated to the futile cycle of biological necessity. For this reason, the ancient Greeks viewed the private sphere with contempt. For them, the women, children, and slaves who were confined to the household existed, in Arendt's words, as "specimens of the human species" and not as individuals distinguished in the eyes of others by their various excellences. At the same time, however, they regarded the private realm as a sanctuary for deeply venerated mysteries; indeed, they believed "the realm of birth and death must be hidden from the public realm because it harbors things hidden from human eyes and impenetrable to human knowledge."[2]

THE UNIVERSALITY OF EXPOSURE
AND CONCEALMENT

This contradictory assessment of the private sphere recalls the discovery made by modern anthropologists that tribal societies often regard the same set of experiences as both sacred and dirty or "polluting." "The sacred," according to Mary Douglas, "is recognisable [by] its dangerousness. Because of the contagion it emanates the sacred is hedged by protective rules." In her pathbreaking study *Purity and Danger, an Analysis of the Concepts of Pollution and Taboo* (1966), she speculated that activities and things which a society designates as dirty or polluting are typically phenomena that cannot be fit into that society's given order. Dirt, then, is best understood as "a compendium category for all events which blur, smudge, contradict, or otherwise confuse accepted classifications. The underlying feeling is that a system of values which is habitually expressed in a given arrangement of things has been violated."[3] It is in these classifications, Douglas argued, that social order, hierarchies, and ultimately meaning reside.

Anthropologists also found that primitive societies drew strict boundaries between what could be seen and what must be hidden, and developed elaborate ritual practices around this distinction. Douglas discovered that "pollution rules in essence prohibit physical contact. They tend to be applied to products or functions of human physiology." In this same vein, Bronislaw Malinowski observed: "It is characteristic that sexual activities, sleep, and excretion are surrounded by protective taboos and mechanisms of concealment and isolation in every society." The greatest theorist of the idea of taboo, Franz Steiner, also pointed to this configuration: "The greater number of taboos are indeed concerned with the various delimitations of our spheres and boundaries, our time spans and our experiences. Taboos are concerned with the passage of things into the body and out of it; they guard the body's orifices."[4]

Bearing this anthropological perspective in mind, I am going to argue that privacy, in its most fundamental and timeless function, serves as a social container for bodily experiences associated with shame. "Experiences of shame," according to the sociologist Helen Merrell Lynd, "appear to embody the root meaning of the word—to uncover, to expose, to wound. They are experiences of exposure, exposure of peculiarly sensitive, intimate, vulnerable aspects of the self."[5] In the most literal way, the physical condition of nakedness leaves us exposed and defenseless to the exigencies of nature. The age-old commerce between shame and nakedness is preserved in Genesis, where shame enters human experience at the moment Adam and Eve eat from the tree of knowledge and discover that they have all along been naked. It is also preserved in the etymology of the word "shame." Both the German *Scham* and the French *pudeur* are related to nakedness (literally, genitals) as is the English euphemism "private parts." Consider, too, the physical vulnerability of the person asleep, in pain, or in rapture. These activities leave us defenseless precisely because we are not our usual selves at those moments: a person asleep, like a person lost in pleasure or pain, surrenders normal consciousness.[6] These activities, because they leave the body vulnerable, require a safe haven from the outside world.

It is not only the literal exposure of the physical vulnerability of the body that is liable to produce feelings of shame. Shame also threatens to engulf us at moments when our biological reality—our "animal" nature, as it is commonly called—overwhelms our "civilized" self; that is, when we are too directly confronted with the body in its most physical aspects. Norbert Elias's pioneering study *The Civilizing Process* (1939) traces the way "people, in the course of the civilizing process, seek to suppress in themselves every characteristic that they feel to be 'animal.' "[7] The work of Clifford Geertz on the Balinese illustrates that this suppression belongs to non-Western societies as well, suggesting both its deep roots in consciousness and the variety of ways public and private are delineated by different societies:

The Balinese revulsion against any behavior regarded as animal-like can hardly be overstressed. Babies are not allowed to crawl for that reason. . . . The main puberty rite consists in filing the child's teeth so they will not look like animal fangs. . . . Not only defecation but eating is regarded as a disgusting, close to obscene activity, to be conducted hurriedly and privately, because of its association with animality. Even falling down or any form of clumsiness is considered to be bad for these reasons.[8]

Douglas's work on the Lele tribe reveals the same pattern. She emphasized "the constant reiteration in daily social intercourse of the basic distinction, the opposition between mankind and animal kind." This distinction is most fully realized in the Lele value of "*buhonyi*, which is shame, shyness, or modesty," the feeling for propriety which is present in humans but absent in animals. *Buhonyi* "is nothing less than the reaction of the nicely cultivated person to any improper behavior."

At its strongest *buhonyi* is sexual shame. All sexual intercourse is embarrassing and should be hidden. . . . All natural functions are embarrassing and should be performed in private. Eating is embarrassing, so men and women eat apart. If an infant defecates in the presence of its elders, its father will call a child to remove the dirt, commenting on his own confusions and *buhonyi*.[9]

Privacy, in its most fundamental function, shelters bodily experiences from the kinds of exposure that evoke shame, the feeling of degradation or dehumanization that comes from having too much attention drawn to what we all share by virtue of existing in biological time, the feeling of dread or mortification that overwhelms us whenever we experience the self reduced to the one-dimensionality of the body. This meaning of privacy, however, is all but absent from discussions today about what should be said or shown in public. In fact, this fundamental meaning of privacy, not to mention the significance of shame, if they are approached at all, are usually dismissed as bourgeois values not worthy of serious consideration, or belittled as laughable relics of the overfastidious, prudish, and hypocritical age of Puritans or Victorians. Sophisticated moderns, breaking with the wisdom of all previous ages, typically pride themselves on their ability to live without such "sentimental" or "romantic" illusions. What makes the modern understanding of privacy modern is this scorn for the very idea of the sacred. Yet the work of anthropologists suggests that this passion for exposure with its mantra that nothing is sacred is actually an aberration. Virtually all known civilizations and societies have maintained distinct boundaries between those things that must be hidden and those that are fit to appear before others. Mary Douglas warns of the absolute necessity of maintaining such classifications because they form the foundation not only of social order but of meaning itself:

> An unstructured society leaves us prey to every dread. As all the veils are successively ripped away, there is no right or wrong. Relativism is the order of the day. . . . This is the invitation to full self-consciousness that is offered in our time. We must accept it. But we should do so knowing that the price is William Burroughs's *Naked Lunch*. The day when everyone can see exactly what it is on the end of everyone's fork, on that day there is no pollution and no purity and nothing edible or inedible, credible, or incredible, because the classifications of social life are gone. There is no more meaning.[10]

THE RISE OF THE SOCIAL

Although modern American society is consumed with a passion for openness and publicity, it has also been animated by an opposite ideal—that of privacy—since its founding. One of the most striking characteristics of modern American life is that a cult of privacy exists side by side with a zeal for exposure. While liberated moderns often suspect privacy as the source of wrongdoing and repression, it is simultaneously glorified as the site of individual freedom and autonomy—so essential to individual and social well-being that it deserves state protection. Justice Louis Brandeis declared it "the most comprehensive of rights and the right most valued by civilized men."[11] While the idea of privacy as a protective container for vulnerable experiences has been rendered fatally incomprehensible for reasons that will become clear in the course of this study, a new, rights-bounded notion of privacy has grown up along with liberal society. Freedom from government intervention, the right to be let alone—these are the most familiar notions of privacy in our time.

This attempt to make privacy the foundation of liberal democratic politics is unprecedented. The traditional focus of classical republicanism was the advancement of the public good; the pursuit of private interest was considered tantamount to corruption. One way of getting at the novelty of the liberal project is to contrast its view of privacy as a cherished right with the ancients' disdain for it. The modern perspective, as Hannah Arendt has taught us, turns out to be an astonishing reversal. The ancient Greeks' concern for the body is why, as we have just seen, they revered the household as a sanctuary for the venerated mysteries of birth and death. Their word for the privacy of one's own, *idion*, is etymologically linked to our word "idiot," reminding us that the condition of privacy meant exclusion from the world of full reason and that privacy was connected to *privation*. They located the potential for freedom in the public sphere. There and there alone, citizens could actively exercise civic liberty by participating in self-rule among equals. The polis was also the reserve of individuality, where peers displayed a "fiercely agonal spirit," attempting to distinguish themselves from all others through heroic actions, excellent works, or eloquent oratory, in hopes of fixing their names in history, and in so doing, winning eternal fame.[12]

The conundrum that needs to be unraveled is how moderns reversed this ancient valuation, elevating privacy from its lowly status as the sphere in which people are least individuated to the locus of freedom and individuality. This conceptual shift can be traced to the eighteenth century, when ideas about commercial society, the cultivated individual, and personal freedom first began to take their modern shape. In the eighteenth century, for the first time in history, activities once associated only with the private sphere of labor appeared in public. It is this momentous shift in the locus of labor and of new kinds of activity that would take place in public which Arendt described as "the rise of the social." "We see the body of peoples and political communities in the image of a family whose everyday affairs have to be taken care of by a gigantic nationwide administration of housekeeping." Society was "the form in which the fact of mutual dependence for the sake of life and nothing else assumes significance and where the activities concerned with sheer survival are permitted to appear in public."[13]

Once the processes of labor emerged from their shadowy existence in the private household, the character of the public sphere was decisively changed. While the division of labor introduced by the factory system degraded craftsmen by placing creativity and thinking under the control of managers, leaving only the monotonous tasks of execution to workers,[14] it also elevated the work process by dramatically increasing productivity. With the growth of these new social relations of production, politics increasingly came to be identified with government, and government with the administration of social and economic life, the primary aim being to protect and promote, in Arendt's words, "an undisturbed development of the life process of society as a whole."[15]

While public and private as the topography of the human condition—the places where activities take place—cannot literally collapse into one another, the kinds of pursuits, the things that appear in each sphere, and the languages used to describe them did begin to blur. Arendt suggests that the social and the intimate eventually replaced public and private respectively as a hazy in-between realm, but it is probably more helpful to think of these terms not so much as new topographical spaces but as part of a new sensibility, the key terms of which included sociability and intimacy. What is distinctive about this sensibility is that the happiness of the self in its encounters with people and things began to eclipse the older humanist concern for the world as the home of history and culture. The rise of the social coincided with a gradual receding of the common world and of common sense—in short, of reality outside the ever-growing subjectivity of the self in pursuit of individual happiness.

The consequences of this new state of affairs were first articulated when Scottish Enlightenment philosophers such as Adam Smith, David Hume, and John Millar addressed the nature of this burgeoning commercial society and considered the role and locus of liberty in it.[16] They were the first to create that body of thought called political economy, a pairing of ideas that vividly expresses the confounding of public and private realms: from the ancient Greek point of view, the phrase would have been a contradiction in terms, since what was economic was necessarily related to the household (the *oikos*) and, therefore, was nonpolitical by definition. Although these thinkers were generally sanguine that the division and diversification of labor would bring greater wealth for nations and a higher standard of living, widespread refinement, and a new cosmopolitanism for entire populations, they were at the same time acutely aware of the long-standing tension between wealth and virtue, which threatened the well-being of republics and could prove just as deadly to a commercial society.[17] Formulating this conflict as an argument with the ancients, these moderns challenged the classical ideal of the "austere," "virtuous," "unspecialized" republican citizen with that of the "commercial and cultivated," "social and sentimental" individual. In self-conscious opposition to the classical definition of civic liberty—the active virtue of a citizen exercising equal deference—they posited the liberal idea of freedom as freedom *from* political participation: the modern individual would pay others to perform what had previously been understood to be his own civic duties of military and public service so as to be free to pursue the private goods of wealth and leisure. Not only did they deem personal freedom to trade and make contracts more important than civic liberty; they also redefined the proper aim of politics by replacing the public-spiritedness of civic virtue with a liberal conception of government as ensuring security through the judicious administration of law—especially state protection of private property.

Once the establishment of security became the primary aim of politics, nothing less than a complete reconceptualization of the self and the conditions it required to flourish had been accomplished. This was a first step in enhancing the concept of liberty outside of the strictly political sphere. "The social psychology of the age," according to J.G.A. Pocock, "declared that encounters with things and persons evoked passions and refined them into manners; it was preeminently the function of commerce to refine the passions and polish the manners." The pursuit of civility through the exercise of good manners became an alternative to the pursuit of civic virtue. Accordingly, from the perspective of the moderns, the locus of virtue shifted from the civic to the civil, replacing the *polis* by politeness and *oikos* by political economy. "The political image of man," observes Pocock, "was replaced by a social and transactional image of man and politics." The philosophers of the Scottish Enlightenment, then, emerge as the first writers to posit the rich possibilities for individual freedom and self-culture in commercial society. *La douce commerce*, as it was commonly called, gave people occasions for polishing manners and refining passions, and spectatorial clubs, associations, and coffeehouses afforded further opportunities for practicing the social arts of friendship, sympathy, and conversation. Diversification of personality, refinement, sociability, and culture were the rewards of commercial society; they would more than compensate for the loss of civic virtue and classical republican understanding of politics.[18]

The Scottish Enlightenment hope of a commercial society at once polite and refined was quickly dashed: "A wedge was driven through this burgeoning universe," according to Pocock, "and rather suddenly we begin to hear denunciations of commerce as founded upon soullessly rational calculation and the cold, mechanical philosophy of Bacon, Hobbes, Locke, and Newton."[19] The daunting task of civilizing commercial society was undertaken by a number of nineteenth-century critics, including John Stuart Mill, Thomas Carlyle, John Ruskin, and Matthew Arnold in England and their counterparts, Charles Eliot Norton, E. L. Godkin, and William Dean Howells, in America. Whereas eighteenth-century liberals had believed that a wide diffusion of sociability, politeness, and cultivation would be the great benefit bestowed by commercial society, their nineteenth-century successors drew the opposite conclusion: the division and diversification of labor had failed to enrich the personality; instead, it was homogenizing experience and fostering a "herd mentality." Similarly, commerce failed to polish manners and refine passions; instead, the practice of politeness was degenerating into empty forms, encouraging hypocrisy and quashing authentic individuality. Against the growing social demands for conformity and the unrelenting pressures of the marketplace, these critics argued, the individual required a protected private space.

Arendt identified Jean-Jacques Rousseau and the Romantics as the first explorers of the uncharted territory of intimacy; she characterized them as locked in rebellion against "the levelling demands of the social, against what we would call today the conformism inherent in every society."[20] John Stuart Mill, too, can be counted as an early and influential explorer of this terrain. Mill feared that mass democracy was leveling society, leading to what his contemporary Alexis de Tocqueville called "the tyranny of the majority." With this danger in mind, he devoted much energy to the task of understanding "how to make the fitting adjustment between individual independence and social control." In *On Liberty* (1859), Mill advanced his famous argument that the sole end for state interference with an individual's liberty of action was to prevent harm to others: "The only freedom which deserves the name is that of pursuing our own good in our own way so long as we do not deprive others of theirs, or impede their efforts to obtain it."[21] For Mill, the cumulative weight of traditions, customs, and religious dogma threatened to crush the individual; but this was not all: the "moral coercion of public opinion" might be more than any nonconformist could withstand.

It was this idea of society as an enemy to individuality that led Mill to insist on the importance of privacy as a necessary condition of liberty: "The appropriate region of human liberty," he declared, is "the inward domain of consciousness," the domain of thought and feeling, opinion and sentiment, tastes and pursuits.[22] Liberty, for Mill, meant more than simply doing as one likes; it also meant the freedom to think and choose for oneself, and it was the only means by which self-culture, autonomy, individuality, creativity, originality could flourish—values which by Mill's lights could be realized only in private. In both versions of liberalism, the private realm was the locus of liberty. For Scottish Enlightenment thinkers, it was a prerequisite for economic liberty; for Mill, the essential condition for the fulfillment of an individual's potential. By the second half of the nineteenth century, the more the private realm became entwined with personal freedom and individuality, the more it shed its privative aspects.

Yet a discussion of privacy as such—unconnected to either political economy or individual liberty—simply did not occur until the final decades of the nineteenth century, and then it was in the context of reactions to invasive journalism. When a doctrine of privacy was finally articulated, it typically depicted privacy as the crowning achievement of polite, liberal society. The influential essay "The Rights of the Citizen—to his own Reputation" (1890) by E. L. Godkin, the respected founding editor of *The Nation* and longtime editor of the *New York Evening Post*, exemplifies this perspective. Giving pride of place to private property, Godkin recited Sir Edward Coke's well-known dictum: "A man's house is his castle and fortress as well as his defense against injury and violence as for his repose." The existence of a secure private place, according to Godkin, gave a person the opportunity to "draw the line between his life as an individual and his life as a citizen, or in other words, the power of deciding how much or how little the community shall see of him, or know of him, beyond which is necessary for the proper discharge of all his duties to his neighbors and to the state."[23]

Godkin's analysis clearly presumed two spheres in commercial society: a public one, the stage for the diligent rendering of services owed to business associates or employees, neighbors, and the state; and a private one, furnishing space for the inner world of the individual, his personal thoughts and feelings, tastes and habits, activities and affairs. Although the company and good opinion of others were key components of this formulation of the good life, the life lived in the presence of others provided not so much the occasion for freedom as the opportunity to enact already scripted roles. The private sphere, in contrast, was represented as the arena in which a person reveals and realizes his or her authentic self. Echoing Mill, Godkin insisted that the legal recognition of a man's house as his place of repose was "but the outward and visible sign of the law's respect for his personality as an individual, for that kingdom of the mind, that inner world of personal thought and feeling."[24]

In addition to drawing from Mill in his picture of privacy, Godkin also borrowed from the Scottish Enlightenment, particularly their notions of politeness and cultivation. Respect for privacy, from this standpoint, marked the pinnacle of civilized life and progress: "Privacy is a distinctly modern product, one of the luxuries of civilization, which is not only unsought for but unknown in primitive or barbarous societies." Along these same lines, the novelist Elizabeth Stuart Phelps observed: "Civilization implies personal modesty. The lack of personal modesty betokens the savage." In their seminal law-review essay "The Right to Privacy" (1890), which literally invented that right, Louis Brandeis and his law partner at the time, Samuel Warren, also drew out the connection between the refining influences of culture and the recognition of the value of privacy: "The intensity and complexity of life attendant upon advancing civilization have rendered necessary some retreat from the world, and man, under the refining influence of culture, has become more sensitive to publicity, so that solitude and privacy have become essential to the individual." This connection between a well-developed sense of privacy, delicacy, and refinement was a commonplace in nineteenth-century America. As Phelps declared: "Increased delicacy is the ready proof of increased civilization. We may almost say that civilization *is* delicacy."[25]

Charles Eliot Norton: "The Social Spirit and the Cosmopolite Ideal"

Perhaps more than any other figure in late-nineteenth-century America, Charles Eliot Norton exemplifies the sensibility of politeness and sociability. Norton was respected and admired by virtually all the leading lights of his era, for his writings crystalized their shared ideals for society. He counted among his friends such stellar figures as Emerson, Holmes, Lowell, and Longfellow, and was also an intimate of many of the most influential men of his generation—E. L. Godkin, William Dean Howells, Henry and William James, Frederick Law Olmsted, and Samuel G. Ward. His acquaintances stretched across the Atlantic and included Matthew Arnold, Charles Darwin, Charles Dickens, George Eliot, Elizabeth Gaskell, Rudyard Kipling, John Stuart Mill, William Morris, and Dante Gabriel Rossetti; his close friends included Edward Burne-Jones, Thomas Carlyle, John Ruskin, and Leslie Stephen. Norton's standing as the preeminent American cultural figure was attested to by one of his former students, the respected newspaper editor Oswald Garrison Villard: "We knew that, outside the college, he was regarded as the outstanding celebrity on Harvard's faculty. He . . . wore the mantle of the last of the Cambridge Immortals. We knew that . . . [influential] English writers regarded him as the leading American thinker, the greatest American scholar, the most cultured figure in American life."[26]

According to Henry James, Norton's letters were "truly animated by the social spirit and the cosmopolite ideal." And, as those letters reveal, for Norton, the only life worth living was one spent in sociable pursuits. The greatest service a man could render his fellows (and Norton is speaking only of men here) "consists in the influence, direct and indirect, which he may exert by force of character." It was not enough for a man to possess "the common moral virtues of industry and integrity"; he would also need to develop virtues that foster sociability—"open-mindedness, independence of judgment, generosity, elevation of purpose in his dealings with men." As Norton once counseled a young friend, the good man would need to practice what amounted to an ethos of friendship: he must "keep himself simple, pure, tenderhearted, and sympathetic in relations with those nearest to him." If he succeeded, Norton was convinced that "whether he be businessman or clergyman, he will be doing the best service to his kind." A true believer in the refining influences of domesticity, he was quick to add "that the service which a man may render to his fellows will depend largely upon the woman whom he loves. A true wife more than doubles her husband's virtues and powers. Love is the fulfilling of life."[27] While it is this aspect of Norton's thinking that moderns have found saccharine, we need to keep in mind that sweetness was not yet the exclusive property of women, and the vocabulary of sociability, like that of intimacy, was abundant in expressions of delicacy and tenderness.

Women, too, had a special service to perform by setting the highest example of cultivation for the rest of society. In his commencement address to the graduating class of Radcliffe College in 1900, Norton told the young women that "with the rapid rise in the social order of great masses of men and women who till very lately have had little share of civility . . . it is for you, the gentle and well-bred, to conform in nothing to the vulgar standard, and, in the crowd, to set the example of refinement, elegance, and propriety." Women acted as cultivators and civilizers, elevating the moral and aesthetic tone of both the family and society at large, while men, through the practices of friendship and the arts, had the occasion to disclose their individuality and, in so doing, leave a distinctive mark on the world and set new standards:

> It is the achievements of good men that give shape to our own ideals, and the little which any one of us can do for his fellows (that is, the true end of life) consists in his attainment of such relations to them as may enable him to contribute his mite of individuality to the improvement of the common ideals. It is the poets who help us most, through the arts; their contribution is the largest and the best.[28]

The value of "society"—what Norton defined as "the very rarest and best thing that our modern materialism is largely killing out—

that is, in its highest form, the society that bears witness to leisure and culture, and good breeding, made up of men who though versed in affairs are still idealists and lovers of poetry; not all *novi homines*, but men with traditions and independence"—is repeatedly insisted on in Norton's letters of the last decades of his life, when he realized that the world he had cherished was disappearing with the deaths of his friends. In 1899, he confided to his lifelong friend Godkin that it was becoming harder to enjoy the pleasures of friendship and conversation—what he called "society in the higher sense"—even in Cambridge:

> Half the pleasantness of a companion lies in the common stock of things taken for granted, the broad basis of natural understanding. The lack of this among people who move in the same circles in America is what makes society in the higher sense impossible. Not even in Cambridge can I now get together half a dozen men or women round a table, who have a large common background for their thoughts, their wit, their humour.

Significantly, Norton immediately added that "literature in the best sense used to supply a great deal of it [a common background], but does so no longer," reflecting the Victorian expectation that culture would expand the sympathies of a people.[29]

Representative of this melancholy mood was a letter he wrote to Edward Lee-Childe a few years earlier. In his lamentation of the disappearance of "the social art" in the new age of democracy, Norton clearly articulated its content:

> Brimmer's death is a great loss to me. He leaves no one like him in Boston; few like him anywhere. The true gentleman is as rare as the true genius, and democracy in its present stage is not favourable to the existence of either. There are many excellent and worthy men, but very few who care for, or are capable of practicing, the social art, that finest of the dramatic arts, in which the individual nature expresses itself in modes of ideal pleasantness and refinement.[30]

In this passage we have a crystal-clear expression of the ideals of sociability, politeness, and culture. What links the "true gentleman" with the "true genius" is each one's capacity for expressing his "individual nature." This vision differs significantly from Mill's notion of individuality as emerging through inevitable struggle against society. For Norton, it is through the "social art"—the theatricality of the self revealing its essence before friends or in the larger community of the arts—that genuine individuality appears. This observation suggests the central role that appreciation for the arts was to play in enlivening one's capacity for sociability. But at the same time, these remarks inadvertently reveal the limitations of sociability and intimacy: while friendships both delight and console by joining us sympathetically with others, they are wholly reliant on particular living persons, whom one holds dear, but whose existence is at the mercy of contingent events and bounded by death. The civic humanist conception of the public sphere, in contrast, is of a durable world that will outlast particular individuals; it is concerned with taking care of the traces of excellence inscribed in culture and the consequences of actions commemorated by history.

Democracy vs. Distinction

As his letters reveal, Norton, like other leading nineteenth-century liberals such as Tocqueville, Mill, and Arnold, was anguished by the prospect that democracy was at odds with distinction and individuality which the ideals of the "true gentleman" and the "true genius" embodied.[31] During his last years, in his private correspondence and published essays alike, Norton grappled with this paradox, for it threatened to dash his lifelong hopes for democracy and excellence in America; he despaired at the idea that material progress—as measured by an improved standard of living, by technological innovations and scientific discoveries, and by the growth of democracy—had brought about a general deterioration of morals and manners. To be able to formulate the matter in this way was to rock the very foundations of commercial society, whose legitimacy had been predicated on the promise that *la douce commerce* would soften passions and polish manners. Norton's concerns about the paradoxical relation between material and moral progress anticipate the debate about mass culture that was to contend with these very same issues in the 1940s and 1950s.

Standing at the close of the nineteenth century, Norton was one of the last explorers to remember the source of these ever-deepening fissures, and one of the last to employ the language of the original argument to survey the broken terrain. "I wonder," he queried his old friend Samuel Ward in 1900, "whether you feel the doubt which often assails me as to the advance of mankind—whether the increase in knowledge and the mastery of nature is to be counted as true progress." Setting out the tensions between wealth and virtue, material progress and moral improvement, Norton observed,

> There can be no question that in our time a greater proportion of mankind are physically comfortable, than has ever been the case in the

past, but even this is not unmixed blessing. Is there a moral advance at all in proportion to the material? There is a wider diffusion of virtue, morality has become more democratic, more men and women are controlled by right principles, but better men and even women than there were two thousand years ago are not easy to find.[32]

In a letter to Sir Mountstuart Grant-Duff in 1896—representative of many he wrote at the time—Norton expressed his dismay at the apparent miscarriage of the forces of material progress. "Our generation has been too hopeful," he thought. "We gave too much credit to the influence of material things in securing a better order of society. . . . The Democracy has been a disappointment in its incapacity to rise morally in proportion to its rise in material welfare and in power."[33]

During 1896, in one of his darkest moments, Norton confessed to Samuel Ward his disillusionment with mass democracy. He was especially alarmed by "the scorn of wisdom, the rejection of authority," telling signs that democracy had vitiated respect for anything other than an individual's limited experience. He pointed to the popular mood of "extravagant self-confidence" that is disposed "to make self-will the rule of conduct." This self-congratulatory attitude, he observed, set the stage for "an increase of lawlessness and of public folly." Nevertheless, he continued to hope that "the calamities resulting from these conditions are to be the hammers by which better dispositions and better conditions are to be slowly beaten out on the anvils of time." In the end, Norton blamed the enfeebled condition of the American republic not only on the old conflict between wealth and virtue, which had brought about material progress at the price of corrupt morals and rude manners, but also on the erosion of civic virtue—upon which republics are founded—by selfish, private interests:

> Democracy, ideally, means universal public spirit; practically it exhibits itself in its actual phase as general selfishness and private spirit. . . . Men are not worse than they were, but they are exposed in larger numbers to temptations which they are not prepared to resist, and which are threatening to the public welfare.[34]

No matter how deeply and frequently Norton lamented the "vulgarity" of the age to his correspondents—"the disregard of beauty, the decline in personal distinction, the falling off in manners . . . the absence of high culture, of generous ideals and of imaginative life"[35]—he always tried to soften this assessment by considering the benefits of widespread material comforts. In his attempt to offset moral losses with material gains—and ward off his own personal despair—he initiated a balance-sheet approach to progress, which soon became a habit of mind of apologists for the many failings of American society and culture. In another letter to Samuel Ward exemplifying this style of cultural accounting, Norton first recited the deficits of modern life, then pointed to the

> one consoling reflection, that there are far more human beings materially well off today than ever before in the history of the world; and if you and I could have the choice, there is no period at which we would have rather lived, and none in which we could have lived with so much satisfaction in the condition of the generality of our fellows.[36]

Typically he added a caveat: "All life is made up of a series of compensations for which there is no quantitative balance."[37]

In published essays Norton continued to articulate the extent of the unexpected corrosive effects of material progress and widespread democracy (as well as increases in immigration and of "adventurers" and "pioneers" in the West) on individual and social standards of morality and courtesy. In "The Intellectual Life of America" (1888), he left no doubt as to the grave challenges facing American civilization as "democratic forms of society" took root everywhere. He asked his audience to consider

> whether the highest results attained by the civilization of the past . . . can be preserved, diffused, and made the foundation of a social order in which all advantages shall be more equally shared; or whether the establishment of democratic forms of society will involve a loss which such gains in human conditions as may result from the new system cannot make good, however much they may outweigh it in their sum.

Almost a decade later, in perhaps his best-known essay, "Some Aspects of Civilization in America" (1896), he spelled out, in even starker language, "the grave problem which the next century is to solve," again raising doubts about the material promises offered by commercial society in exchange for civic virtue.[38]

Norton also deplored the crass temper of his times, focusing his readers' attention upon the general atrophy of the faculties of taste and judgment. Repeatedly he denounced the "ascendant power of mediocrity which is a characteristic feature of our actual civilization" as well as the "increase in vulgarity, by which I mean a predominance of taste and standards of judgment of the uneducated and unrefined masses, over those of the more enlightened and better instructed few." A primary cause for this, he thought, was the overextension of "the principle of equality . . . into regions where it has no proper validity." Literature, churches, amusements, politics, he feared, were bowing "to the crowd . . . to popular demands." The lowered standards made for an ugly and inhospitable common world, and also cheapened the tone of public conversation; even more disastrously, it corrupted politics. In a thoroughgoing indictment of mass-circulation newspapers, Norton suggested that their enormous popularity revealed "a people not likely to be shocked by coarse means adopted to promote personal or party success," which was deplorable, for he believed that people should defer to men who, "by superior character, intelligence, and education, are more competent to deal with [public interests]."[39]

To vanquish or at least subdue the many forces arrayed against excellence and distinction in America, Norton continued to uphold education and self-culture as antidotes. His definition of liberal education encompassed all aspects of character building. In its personal dimension, it "enlarges the scope of mental vision, invigorates the understanding, confirms the reason, [and] quickens and disciplines the imagination." It would prepare young people for a life of service, in which they would set and maintain standards of excellence, thereby ensuring an elevated and durable public domain. It would, moreover, "instill into the soul of youth the sense of proportion between the things of the spirit and the things of sense"; it would strengthen

> it against the multiform temptations to worldliness, which means selfishness, and to acceptation of popular standards of judgment, which means superficiality, inspiring it with the love of what is best in thought, and in those arts which are the expressions of the ideal conceptions and aims of men.

And he chastised the privileged and educated elite of America for not exerting enough influence in "rais[ing] the general standards of character and of conduct." He thought the consequent "prevalence of vulgarity . . . a national disgrace."[40]

As one can see, Norton's relationship to mass democracy was, at best, extremely ambivalent. For him, like all liberals of the time, the well-being of the self-possessed personality—guaranteed by privacy— was essential to the flourishing of democracy; it was "the more enlightened and better instructed few" who would stand firm against the rising tide of mediocrity and, in so doing, guide and elevate society. He wholeheartedly subscribed to Mill's doctrine that the majority must be tempered by "respect for the personality of the individual, and deference to the superiority of cultivated intelligence." In his endeavors to establish an elite to guide and elevate American society, Norton's "more enlightened and better instructed few" resembles not only Mill's "wisest" but also Coleridge's clerisy and Arnold's remnant. That these thinkers each tried to imagine new ways of distinguishing a cultural elect, which they invariably identified with "the best," indicates a general uncertainty about authority that plagued thinkers coming to terms with the increasingly egalitarian conditions of the nineteenth century. In America and Britain alike, there was a widespread sense, as Raymond Williams put it, "that there [had] been a breakdown in old ways of distinguishing the best fitted to govern or exercise influence by rank and heredity, and a failure to find new ways of distinguishing such persons by formal (parliamentary or democratic) election." In the United States this uncertainty was acute, for republican habits of mind had long taught Americans to be suspicious of "aristocratic" manners, which many of them interpreted not as refinement and cultivation but as a sign of social snobbery.[41]

In order to check what they feared was the end of civilized life and at the same time reestablish their own cultural and moral authority, Norton and his circle attempted to assert culture over rampant materialism and selfish individualism by putting into place a vast array of cultural institutions—public parks and gardens, art museums and galleries, orchestras and libraries. They looked to these new institutions as means of cultivating taste, habits of discipline, and an ethic of deference to the best, convinced as they were that culture was the best antidote to chaos, "as much needed for human beings," declared Norton, "as for the products of the earth." For Norton, the well-being and safekeeping of American civilization depended on widespread dissemination of the fine arts, because "nowhere in the civilized world are the practical concerns of life more engrossing; nowhere are the conditions of life more prosaic; nowhere is the poetic spirit less evident, and the love of beauty less diffused."[42]

Here, Norton—like the Romantic poets, Mill, Carlyle, Ruskin, and Morris—was giving voice to a despair about the dismal situation in which labor had been wrenched apart from its craft ideal by the new industrialism. As the manual arts became ever more remote from any values other than economic or functional ones, the fine arts not only became equated with the idea of culture but also were increasingly perceived as the last refuge for all the noncommercial, nonutilitarian values and ideals that had made life worth living before the nineteenth century.[43]

This overriding faith in culture as the antidote to the ills wrought by industrialism and mass democracy raises two related questions:

Why did Norton and his circle attribute seemingly inordinate powers of reform to culture in the first place? And what moved them to seek solutions not in the political realm, which they might have construed as the appropriate place for discussing the quality of public life, but rather in the realm of culture and society? To answer these questions, we need to turn once again to the eighteenth century, when concern about how to live in a world of commerce, in a world where the distribution and administration of things predominated, led to a redefinition of virtue in terms of manners: "A right to things," according to Pocock, "could become a way to the practice of virtue, so long as virtue could be defined as the practice and refinement of manners." Since commercial society required a large number of strangers to interact in complicated transactions, it depended for its success upon mutual goodwill, kindliness, and cooperation. Good manners operating within a fixed and reliable code of politeness became indispensable. In addition, we need to recall that eighteenth-century thinkers prided themselves on their civility and refinement, self-consciously defending the polite and gentle manners of the commercial man against what, from their perspective, was the rude and militant virtue of the warrior-citizen of ancient republics.[44]

The transformation of civic virtue into the practice of politeness had deep-reaching consequences for the public sphere and accordingly, for the meaning of politics. Whereas politics had traditionally been understood as the statecraft which deals with innovating forces that create disorder, in commercial society politics became fixed on the distribution and administration of rights and things. The ideal of public service was still alive, as we have seen, for liberals of Norton's generation: laissez-faire liberalism and welfare liberalism alike, with their emphasis on individual rights and interests, would slowly dissolve this long-standing tension between commerce and virtue; in fact, self-interest, previously regarded as the height of corruption, would gradually be reconstrued with the aid of the theory of the invisible hand as the means to positive good for both individuals and society, though for civic-minded liberals like Norton, it continued to represent a threat to the commonweal.

While the public good never entirely disappeared from the liberal lexicon, by Norton's time there was a great deal of emphasis on politeness and cultivation as means of tempering the excesses of self-interest in industrial society. And it is precisely this emphasis, inherited from the Scottish Enlightenment, that transferred what had once been regarded as the fundamental concern of politics to the realm of culture. The age-old tension between order and chaos, which had characterized political theory throughout history, was transferred to discussions about culture; Matthew Arnold's *Culture and Anarchy* was an important signpost in this development. This new dialectic expressed tensions between politeness and rudeness, refinement and vulgarity, cosmopolitanism and provincialism.[45] And Norton's practice of sociability turns out to be the final expression of the culture of politeness that had begun to take shape a century earlier.

The nineteenth-century liberal gentleman, like his eighteenth-century counterpart, praised politeness for encouraging sociability, smoothing interactions between friends, acquaintances, business associates, and strangers. Where he differed from his predecessor was in his creed of self-culture, his conviction that appreciation of the fine arts would elevate a society that had become philistine not only because of the want of culture on the part of the poor but also because of the utilitarian mentality of the middle classes who insisted that the arts must have a functional, economic, or social value. The less the language of liberal politics could address concerns about the moral and aesthetic qualities of the common world and public life, the more culture as a repository of values banished from everyday life became a kind of surrogate for politics. If politics no longer concerned the public, then culture, as if by default, would have to do.

INTIMACY AND THE PROMISE OF HAPPINESS

People in the modern age have elevated private life to unprecedented heights by infusing it with the manifold qualities of what we have come to call intimacy. Intimacy as an innovative social practice came to prominence during the nineteenth century in what historians today call "the cult of domesticity," which venerated a set of intense relations in the conjugal family. With the decline of both church and state authority, and with the movement of productive labor out of the household, the home came to be viewed as the chief agency of moral education, especially the fostering of the all-important and largely secular conscience. Whereas the outside world of enterprise was conceived as a dangerous competitive arena for the manly pursuit of wealth and the furtherance of self-interest, the household and with it, the institutions of marriage and the family, particularly the role of wife and mother, were celebrated as civilizing, moralizing forces, working to good effect on the character not only of individual family members but of society as a whole.[46]

The household, once it was emptied of its productive functions, became a refuge for emotion and self-disclosure. Through intense love relations, family involvement, and friendships, the self was supposed to find its fullest expression.[47] This heightened consideration of the private realm inadvertently transformed the emotions and virtues that had been housed there: the new emphasis on love, affection, tenderness, fidelity, trust, gratitude, and the mutual baring of souls—in short, intimacy—endowed private activities and experiences with unexpected emotional depth. Yet, as Arendt suggested in one of her most penetrating observations, "the intimate is not a very reliable substitute" for loss of privacy. The trouble with placing so much weight on intimacy as the locus of meaning and the promise of happiness is that this most fragile of edifices is overburdened with expectations it cannot possibly support. A small circle of family and friends furnishes good company, security, warmth, and comfort, but it can never provide the grand scope or the permanence which can arise only in connection with appearance and action in public. "Compared with the reality which comes from being seen and heard," Arendt pointed out, "even the greatest forces of intimate life—the passions of the heart, the thoughts of the mind, the delights of the senses— lead an uncertain, shadowy kind of existence unless and until they are transformed, deprivatized and deindividualized, as it were, into a shape to fit them for public appearance."[48]

By 1903, feminists like Charlotte Perkins Gilman were suffocating in the claustrophobic atmosphere of intimacy. For many early feminists, the sphere of the household, once it became wholly associated with the "sentiments of sanctity, privacy, and sex-seclusion," in Gilman's words, held out little hope of individuality and freedom. She scornfully described the ideal of the home as an attractive trap:

> A beautiful, comfortable house meeting all physical needs; a happy family, profoundly enjoying each other's society; a father, devotedly spending his life in obtaining the wherewithal to maintain this little heaven; a mother, completely wrapped up in her children and devotedly spending her life in their service, working miracles of advantage to them in so doing; children, happy in the home and growing up beautifully under its benign influence—everybody, healthy, happy, and satisfied with the whole thing.[49]

The Victorians, who were the first to attempt to find the deepest meanings within the intimate circle of the family, were also the first to incessantly worry out loud about the rules of proper sexual conduct, upon which the well-being of the household depended. It is, of course, during this time that morality became synonymous with sexual morality. For the Victorians, sex was never conceived of as a neutral category; its moral dimensions were implicit in the only words available to describe it—love and lust. Nineteenth-century moral language was saturated with sexual connotations: a "woman's virtue" was her chastity, and a woman of "weak" or "loose" morals or "easy virtue" was either a prostitute or an adulteress. In the same way, the boy with a "secret vice" partook in solitary pleasures. The many societies that flourished during this period for the "suppression of vice" were intended to rid the world of prostitutes and to reform the men who patronized them, along with gamblers and drunkards. Surely it is significant that these reformers defined vice not as injustice, cowardice, or dishonesty but as intemperance.

It is also significant that sexual obscenity as a legal category simply did not exist before this time. In England, from the sixteenth to the eighteenth century, obscenity was usually a term applied to heretical or seditious works. Controls on expression emphasized the need to protect the religious and political fiber of society rather than sexual morality. Sexual offenses instead fell under the jurisdiction of ecclesiastical courts, though acts of indecency were indictable at common law. In colonial New England, the strict moral code associated with Puritanism succeeded in keeping materials relating to or representing sex out of the public domain, and no obscenity trials occurred in America during the colonial period. By the beginning of the twentieth century, this older understanding of obscenity as words uttered against the church or the state was so outdated that plaintiffs who pursued justice in matters centering on political slurs and verbal attacks upon clergymen were advised by their respective courts to try their cases as libel.[50]

The emphasis on the sphere of intimacy as the locus of meaning provides a number of clues about the narrowing of obscenity law to sex and, more generally, the larger cultural habit linking sex and morality. As church and state became more tolerant and liberal, the need to suppress what they both had once regarded as threats and therefore obscene lessened; at the same time, the more the household was sanctified as the wellspring of morality, indiscriminate speech about it began to qualify as obscene. If sexual morality was equated with virtue and respectability, then to speak openly of it was to violate propriety. But even as this new emphasis upon domesticity gave rise to a richer private life, a greater degree of individuality, and allowed for a more profound experience of intimacy than any time before in history, the private sphere still retained its essential function, about which Victorians were acutely sensitive: to shelter activities concerned with the maintenance and well-being of the life process. Because of their inherent fragility and vulnerability, bodily activities needed to be clothed in moral language that gave them a deeper meaning and content, making them worthy of the new importance attached to the household. And because the household furnished the physical and emotional space for marital intimacy and the nurturing of children, public exposure of matters relating to it was perceived as a threat to its authority. Consequently, such material—pamphlets and lectures about sexual hygiene, for example—was refused entry into the public sphere through the formulation of the legal category of sexual obscenity.

2

THE RETICENT
SENSIBILITY AND THE
VALUE OF PRIVACY

Throughout the nineteenth century, privacy was understood both as a social container for experiences associated with shame and as the physical and spiritual locus of individuality and freedom. But its meanings were not exhausted there; privacy was also closely associated with domesticity as the wellspring of intimacy and with the related concept of private property. All of these connotations were taken for granted and embodied in the reticent sensibility. By the last part of the century, however, they were put into question with the appearance of three agencies of aggressive exposure. The first arose from technological innovations that fueled mass-circulation newspapers, photographs, and advertising which gave publicity to subjects once treated with circumspection and with lowered voice. The second emerged when sex reformers attacked what they called a "conspiracy of silence," demanding that the private mysteries of sex be made public through lectures and pamphlets about sexual hygiene and morality. The third appeared in the form of the realist novel: in its Continental (usually French) inflection, private dramas having to do with adultery and prostitution were depicted in unsparing detail; in the United States, the trials and tribulations of everyday domestic life were given a full airing.

Confronted by these new forces of exposure, the party of reticence was forced to become self-conscious and articulate their principles and ideals. In articles, essays, novels, published letters, speeches, debates, legal reviews, and in the courts, they vigorously attacked enthusiasts of exposure for flooding the world with material they believed "polluted" the public sphere; in so doing, they developed a sustained defense of privacy, articulating the threats posed to the "sanctity" of private life and to the "high-mindedness" of public conversation. So extreme were these dangers that the party of reticence turned to the law to rein in their opponents, resulting in the cases of invasive journalism, instant photographs, and exploitative advertising techniques, in the invention of a new legal right, "the right to privacy"; and in the cases of sex education and the realist novel, in a redefinition of obscenity to encompass matters relating to sex.

What is most remarkable about these developments is that the various critics of intrusive journalism, of public discussions about sexual hygiene, and of realist novels voiced their objections to these apparently unrelated concerns in precisely the same terms—invasions of privacy and obscenity amounted to the same thing—and their opponents, making their respective cases for exposure, also mounted virtually the same arguments. That these three disputes were conducted quite apart from one another makes their similarities all the more striking from our contemporary perspective, since we no longer can detect any connection between invasive journalism, sex education, and realist art.

"The Devouring Publicity
of Life"

In "The Décolleté in Modern Life" (1890), the novelist Elizabeth Stuart Phelps lamented that modern young women were openly speaking to their male acquaintances about subjects their mothers barely mentioned to their husbands. She spread the blame widely for this general waning of modesty: "Certain associations for the advancement of moral purity have wrought mischief by relaxing the strict rule of reserve in speech. Anything which does that, whether it come from the moralist or the scientist, the sick room or the ball room, is doing a harm less easy to rectify because it is so difficult to define and so easy to defend." While controversy over realist fiction engaged the literary world in a ferocious battle during the 1880s and 1890s, and the dispute over public discussions of sexual hygiene took place primarily in courts, denunciations of invasive and sensational journalism were heard everywhere. Disparagement of the new journalism was so pervasive that critics typically began with apologies for speaking of it once again. As Charles Dudley Warner, editor of *Harper's New Monthly Magazine*, observed in 1897: "In any intelligent circle you may happen to drop into, the common talk is about the depravity and unworthiness of the newspapers. This is an old topic, a worn-out subject of talk."[1]

Techniques of journalism had become so brazen that Louis Brandeis and Samuel Warren felt compelled to do something—hence their famous formulation of "The Right to Privacy," published in the *Harvard Law Review* (1890). While their essay marks the first sustained effort to control prying journalists legally, it is better understood as the culmination of a fully developed criticism of mass-circulation newspapers that first gained momentum after the Civil War but the beginnings of which can be traced to the 1830s, with the birth of the penny press and the notorious New York papers of James Gordon Bennett. People of a later generation were convinced, however, that journalism had never before degenerated to such a pass. In 1890, E. L. Godkin issued what had become a common warning about newspapers: "It is not too much to say that they are, and have been for the last half century, exerting more influence on the popular mind and the popular morals than either the pulpit or the book press has exerted in five hundred years."[2] By 1893, in one of the many special magazine issues devoted entirely to this problem, a writer presented empirical evidence "proving" the precipitous decline of journalism into gossip-mongering. Comparing the content of newspapers published in 1881 to those appearing in 1893, he announced, "But in all four of the papers under consideration there were only four and one-half columns of gossip and one column of scandal against one hundred and sixteen and one quarter of gossip this year and seven and a half columns of scandal." In "The Ethics of Modern Journalism" (1896), another critic, describing "the shocks which [modern journalism] gives to our reticences, and the offense which it is to our reserves," voiced the common complaint: "Many of us feel that, since the newspapers constitute by far the greatest factor in the education of countless thousands in our country, the fundamental irreverence of modern journalism, its materialism, its deification of the most facile point of view, is one of the serious ethical dangers of the time."[3]

Denunciations of invasions of privacy, like condemnations of sensational news stories about divorces and crimes, were key components of the controversy over the proper role of the free press in a democracy. Writers for such journals as *Arena, The Atlantic Monthly, The Dial, Forum, Harper's, Lippincott's, The Nation, North American Review,* and *Scribner's* continued to insist that the press in a democratic society was responsible for promoting knowledge, educating the citizenry, molding public opinion, and discussing issues concerning the public good, and they were alarmed by the proliferation and popularity of papers devoted only to boosting their circulation by any available means. In 1886, in an essay entitled "The Pretensions of Journalism," George T. Rider spelled out what had by then become the standing indictment: "There is a deep and growing belief . . . that there are fundamental failures in journalism, that there are portentous and perilous abuses of function and misconception of duty, that there are infringements and intrusions, both insolent and incendiary, together with pretensions that threaten private right and public well-being."[4]

The most pressing worry about the new journalism was its flagrant disregard of privacy. Outraged critics, in order to capture the magnitude of the crimes committed by new-breed journalists, resorted to increasingly extravagant language. The prying newspaperman "passes the bounds set up by personal reserve with the daring and the dash of a swine running at a swill-trough," one critic observed. "Is it good journalism to convert half a reportorial corps into detectives and spies of the baser sort; to teach them the habits of the mole without being able to endow them with the mole's extra protection against dirt?" demanded another. "To reward them with extra pay who can wax their ear closest to a keyhole or climb most noiselessly to a full view of a woman's chamber through the transom at the door?" Invasive journalism had become such a common feature of the modern landscape that Henry James declared, "One sketches one's age imperfectly if one doesn't touch on that particular matter: the invasion, the impudence, the shamelessness of the newspaper and the interviewer, the devouring publicity of life, the extinction of all sense between public and private." He acknowledged that he created the obnoxious reporter, Matthias Pardon, in *The Bostonians* so as "to *bafouer* the vulgarity and hideousness of . . . the impudent invasion of privacy," and in his notebook took pleasure in imagining another prying reporter, George Flack in *The Reverberator*, as "the most vulgar character. . . . He of course hasn't a grain of delicacy in his composition . . . no tradition of reserve or discretion."[5]

The party of reticence marshaled all its rhetorical energy to capture the quality of the world where the sense of difference between public and private was, as James put it, on the verge of "extinction." The favorite metaphor was the actual invasion of the home—revealing not only the connection of privacy to private property in the nineteenth-century liberal imagination but also the sanctity of the home associated with the cult of domesticity. "Instantaneous photographs and newspaper enterprise have invaded the sacred precincts of private and domestic life," Brandeis and Warren began their famous essay. "And numerous mechanical devices threaten to make good the prediction that 'what is whispered in the closet shall be proclaimed from the housetops.' " "The very walls of our houses appear to have been turned into telephones," wrote the critic William Bushnell, "and bells to be furnished with telegraphic connections with newspaper offices." "Journalism," according to yet another critic, "plucks off the roof, and pulls down the walls and sheltering partitions, and wantonly lays bare all defilement and consuming lust of poor human nature." Or, as one observer put it, "No man's house is any longer his castle. . . . Our very thoughts are no longer our own, and we shall be forced 'ere long to distrust the very walls and beams of our bedrooms, and to disburden our secrets only to the buttercups and daisies of the honest earth. The streets are infested with journalistic footpads."[6]

THE PSYCHIC DEVASTATION
OF EXPOSURE

One of the most devastating consequences of prying journalism, critics repeatedly pointed out, was the psychic damage visited upon the subject of the story. (This is the only harm that our contemporary debates continue to acknowledge.) Brandeis and Warren gave voice to what was already a common accusation when they insisted that invasions of privacy subjected a person "to mental pain and distress far greater than could be inflicted by mere bodily injury." Charles Eliot Norton's angry letter of 1888 to his longtime friend John Ruskin paints a more elaborate picture, and shows how thoroughly publicity had penetrated American society. Complaining of the indignity he had been made to suffer on account of Ruskin's indiscreet and inaccurate portrayal of their first meeting in his memoirs, *Praeterita*, the usually retiring Norton exploded:

> I, the one man in America who have kept myself private, who have hated the publicity and advertising and notoriety which in these days even our poets have sought; who have believed it the disgrace and shame of the time that the Gods cannot enjoy their own felicity unless it be "reported,"—I, the lover of seclusion, am suddenly to be brought before the public under the tremendous light thrown by your affectionate imagination![7]

In an essay entitled "Newspaper Espionage," a writer detailed the anguish suffered by a respected merchant and civic leader when newspapers shamelessly exploited his daughter's secret and unwise marriage. A letter the merchant sent to one of the offending newspapers reveals the scope of his injury:

"No newspaper has a right to publish broadcast a matter which belongs to my hearth-stone. I have lived my whole life as a just man, and have tried to do my duty to society and to my country. When a blow is struck at my breast, when I am prostrated with grief, it is an outrage upon me as a citizen to have dragged into print a story which I kept to myself."[8]

The intensity of this grief was brought to life in James's novel *The Reverberator* (1888). It recounts the courtship of Francie Dosson, a young, rich, vivacious American, and Gaston Probert, a cultivated young man whose American family had long been a part of French high society. Probert values Francie's innocence and candor, what he calls her "natural delicacy," and seeks her company as refuge from the artificiality of aristocratic life. But these very qualities bring seeming disaster. While Probert is away on a business mission for her father, Francie spends an afternoon with a family friend, George Flack. Flack, an overzealous reporter for a gossip sheet called *The Reverberator*, convinces Francie to speak freely about her engagement and her fiancé's illustrious though all too human family. From this innocent chat, he publishes an exposé. The Proberts are scandalized by "the flood of impudence on decent, quiet people who only want to be let alone."[9] Flack's piece so violates their family honor that the Proberts can imagine restoring their good name only by challenging the reporter to a duel.

The idea that impudent reporters were best dealt with "by means of duel or single combat, or some sort of corporal chastisement" was also considered by Godkin. In disputes concerning property, he observed, people were generally willing to relegate their claims for justice to the state; but when it came to matters of personal insult, they continued to cling to an older code of honor which held that "there is certain peculiar fitness in protecting reputation or privacy against libel or intrusion by the cudgel or the horsewhip." The German sociologist Georg Simmel, writing at the same time, convincingly explains why this should be the case. Violations of privacy were literal violations of the "ideal sphere [that] lies around every human being." If that sphere is penetrated by another person, "the personality value of the individual is thereby destroyed." "Language," he continued, "very poignantly designates an insult to one's honor as 'coming too close': the radius of this sphere marks, as it were, the distance whose trespassing by another insults one's honor." James's description of the "sense of excruciation—of pollution" which the Proberts experience upon seeing the published account of their personal foibles perfectly expresses Simmel's point. Their mortification stems from what young

Probert refers to as his "father's influence, his very genius, the worship of privacy and good manners, a hatred of all the new familiarities and profanations."[10]

For speakers of the discourse of reticence, with its key words "honor," "reputation," and "privacy," this kind of thinking was second nature, and thus they were mystified and appalled by a class of people who apparently lacked this sense of honor yet still yearned for public recognition, what Godkin characterized as "a passion for notoriety of any kind" on the part of "the obscure." Like James, who linked the mania for publicity with the leveling forces of democracy, Godkin observed that "the eagerness [for notoriety] is inevitably great in a society in which there are no distinctions of rank and no recognized social grades," and where the desire to be distinguished from the crowd "is sufficiently widely diffused not only to diminish popular sympathy with people who love the shade of private life, but to some extent to make this particular state of mind somewhat incomprehensible." As early as 1870 the novelist and critic Richard Grant White had been shocked to learn that some society people were actually furnishing journalists with guest lists and detailed descriptions of their receptions and private parties: "The journalist is the man who holds the key of their paradise, and they will pay him in what coin he likes for his labor, and fawn on him for his favor. I am inclined to believe that some people think that no pleasure is fully enjoyed until an account of it is published." In a letter of 1874, Charles Eliot Norton complained, "I know no worse calamity that can overtake a man than to have a thirst for publicity, and yet it is the common vice of able men in this epoch of the newspaper reporter."[11]

Undeserved, and, in some cases, unwanted publicity tended, in the prophetic words of another critic, to "repel from civic life those who could do most to enlighten, and therefore benefit, the community, and to confine activity to the pushing and brazen, who are generally, though with exception, inferior men." This new concern about "the frenzy of renown" is part of a larger story regarding the decline of eternal fame and the rise of fleeting celebrity or, as the narrator in Edith Wharton's *The House of Mirth* (1905) puts it, "a world where conspicuousness passed for distinction, and the society column had become the roll of fame." Yet, as the once-durable public realm receded before an amorphous wave of society-page gossip and human-interest stories, publicity and advertising, the desire to appear before others did not dissipate. To the contrary, as these examples suggest, the craving not so much for honor and fame as for celebrity accelerated. Surely it is no coincidence that two institutions whose raison d'être is to acclaim those who would be famous—*Who's Who* and the Hall of Fame—were founded in 1898 and in 1900, respectively.[12]

THE TRIVIALIZATION OF INTIMATE LIFE

As an intimate of the most revered men of his time, Charles Eliot Norton was entrusted with editing and publishing the private letters of Carlyle, Emerson, Lowell, and Ruskin. In his introductions to their letters and in his public tributes to these men, Norton's writings exemplify the reticent sensibility at its most discerning and circumspect. He was especially sensitive to the question of which aspects of an author's life were large and significant enough to occupy the common world and which were so small and vulnerable that they required the refuge of privacy to survive. Since this is key to understanding the reticent sensibility and because this way of judging which things belong in public has simply vanished, we must approach this most unfamiliar aspect of Norton's thinking with the greatest care. In his introduction to *Letters of James Russell Lowell* (1894), he made a declaration that has become virtually unintelligible in our post-Freudian world of boundless confession: "Portions of every man's life are essentially private, and knowledge of them belongs by right only to those intimates whom he himself may see fit to trust with his confidence." Addressing the suspicious mental habit that detects an admission of guilt in every protestation against publicity, Norton insisted, "There was nothing in Mr. Lowell's life to be concealed or excused. But he had the reserves of a high and delicate nature, reserves to be no less respected after death than during life." For Norton, the only public expression suited for conveying the glimmerings of the inner life was an artistic one, for the arts have the formal means to transform personal feelings and intimate experiences into a whole that is deserving of public attention: "Mr. Lowell, indeed, made to the public in his poetry such revelations of his inward experiences and emotions as he alone had the right to make, and such as may well suffice to satisfy all legitimate interest in the spiritual development of the poet and in the nature of his most intimate and sacred human relations."[13]

In a description of the editorial practices he followed in preparing *Letters of John Ruskin to Charles Eliot Norton* (1904), Norton once again employed language that today is all too easily and automatically construed as guilty cover-up. Intimate matters, he insisted, because of their smallness and fragility, needed to be tenaciously guarded against curious eyes lest they be deformed:

> The omissions, which are indicated by dots, consist for the most part of passages too personal, too intimate, or of too slight interest for publication. I have not printed all the letters which Ruskin wrote to me. In spite of the poets, in spite of modern usage, in spite of Ruskin's own example, I hold with those who believe that there are sanctities in love and life to be kept in privacy inviolate.[14]

Delivering a eulogy in honor of Lowell in 1893, he elaborated upon the dangers posed to private life when things of a too personal nature are carelessly spoken of. While he acknowledged his intimacy with the poet, he also articulated the limits to what he could say about that friendship, evoking not only the fragility of private life but its sacred quality, too:

> I cannot take my readers, however worthy of confidence they may be, within the inner circle of intimacy, of which the charm would suffer were its sanctity violated and its seclusion disturbed. . . . [n]ot even a friend who sticketh closer than a brother may draw away the veil [of privacy]. And yet so often is this done that we are losing the sense of the sacredness of the private life. We submit to the vulgarizing of its loveliest enclosures, and we give prizes to the betrayers of confidence.[15]

Perhaps the most poignant expression of the reticent temperament can be found in a letter Norton wrote to Ruskin twenty years earlier, in which he apologized for not being able to return a copy of one of his old friend's letters. In his pained description of his "old custom" of burning both "trivial notes" and extremely personal letters—"those that are like intimate talks, when confidences are given to which no third person should be privy"—Norton again invoked the sanctity of privacy and the respectful distance owed to private matters: "I hold these last letters sacred, and often make a holocaust of what it pains me to sacrifice, and of what I would keep among my treasures if I could be sure they would be buried with me."[16]

Norton's confession to Ruskin that he burned "those [letters] in which you told me of sorrowful experience in love, for they were secrets between you and me," underlines a crucial component of the reticent sensibility: personal affairs, because they can only be made intelligible by the tender understanding of a trusted intimate, must be protected from the unsympathetic gaze of strangers lest they become slight or ridiculous:

> No man or woman shall have to reproach me with violating the trust they have given me. And, only yesterday afternoon, I read and re-read

your letter about Connie, and questioned with myself, and wanted to keep it, and thought, *no*, I alone can interpret it perfectly, it is a little *scène de la vie intime* for me, I shall not forget it, I will not leave it to chance, and to cold eyes,—and so I cut the first pages off to keep, and put the rest in the flames and it sparkled and shone for a minute— like a symbol of itself,—and then turned gray and fell to ashes, like a symbol of so much else.[17]

Tenderness, then, protects intimacy by clothing us in the love of another, making personal life possible where our all too obvious short-comings would otherwise make us most vulnerable. Tenderness teaches us to forestall overly searching glances and to neglect harsh observations, ensuring that we never view our loved ones distanced, as in a photograph, but through a sympathetic lens that enables us to situate shortcomings within the unfolding narrative of our shared existence.

For editors who did violate the trust of their famous friends by publishing their intimate letters or writing revealing memoirs or bi-ographies, Norton had the harshest words. "Vulgar curiosity is, in-deed, always alert to spy into these sanctities [of private life]," he complained, "and is too often gratified, as in some memorable and mournful instances in recent years, by the infidelities of untrustworthy friends." Upon reading James Froude's account of Carlyle's life, *Rem-iniscences*, in which he published some of Carlyle's love letters, Norton commented to Mrs. Alexander Carlyle: "It is impossible to forgive him for the gross indelicacy of publishing the most private, sacred, and tender expressions of the love of two such lovers as those whose lovely letters he has ventured to print." To discredit this damaging and faulty picture of Carlyle's courtship and early marriage to Miss Welsh, Norton eventually published a few letters from the original correspondence, though he confessed that he had done so "with ex-treme reluctance, and with reverential respect for the sacredness of their contents." "The letters of lovers are sacred confidences," he declared, "whose sanctity none ought to violate."[18]

This same reserve and respect for the integrity of the most personal and revealing aspects of other people's lives color Norton's answer to Ruskin's rebuke that he had neglected to write "a proper epilogue" to his edition of the Carlyle-Emerson correspondence. Again, in lan-guage so foreign to the modern sensibility of exposure as to be literally stunning, Norton replied, "The sentiment of the book was too inti-mate for a third person to intervene in it."[19] For the reticent sensi-bility, genuine intimacy emerged from the mutual baring of one's innermost self to another person and to no one else; this is quite unlike the modern therapeutic mode of effusive openness and confession to anyone who will listen, and it could be maintained and flourish only in the most guarded relationship.

This injunction to maintain silence, to willfully avert one's gaze, is no doubt the most alien aspect of the reticent sensibility to moderns who have been schooled in habits of relentless scrutiny of motives of both the self and others. So accustomed have we become to detecting repression, cover-up, and hypocrisy that we can see little else when confronted with reticence. Yet it is precisely this way of thinking that we must recover—even if we reject it anew—if we are ever to move beyond our stalemates in contemporary debates about which things belong in public.

James Fitzjames Stephen, in his *Liberty, Equality, and Fraternity* (1873), permits us a further glimpse into this unfamiliar territory. Like Norton, he recognized that just as undesired publicity destroyed private life, an insensitive question or a penetrating glance delivered by a trusted intimate could be equally devastating. "All the more intimate and delicate relations of life," wrote Stephen, "are of such a nature that to submit them to unsympathetic observation, or to observation which is sympathetic in the wrong way, inflicts great pain, and may inflict lasting moral injury." Discretion—the sensitivity that enables us not only to respect another person's secrets but also to gracefully sidestep knowing something that the person does not want us to know or does not expressly reveal to us—is necessary not only with strangers and friends but also, according to Stephen, in one's own internal life: "Privacy may be violated not only by the intrusion of a stranger, but by compelling or persuading a person to direct too much attention to his own feelings and to attach too much importance to their analysis." For Stephen, the overly analyzed life was nothing less than an invitation to indecency: "That any one human creature should ever really strip his soul stark naked for the inspection of any other, and be able to hold up his head afterwards, is not, I suppose, impossible, because so many people profess to do it; but to look on from the outside is inconceivable."[20] Contrary to modern expectations, Stephen believed that confession and mutual exposure do not foster intimacy. Instead, repeated uncoverings of innermost thoughts and feelings brutalize not only loved ones but also the self with truths too devastating to bear, and, at the same time, distort personal matters by focusing too closely upon them. It is discretion that permits us to render truth about our lives sensitively, making a home for ourselves and others who are always only human and therefore not deserving of the brutality of full disclosure.

The party of reticence never tired of making this point, and they characteristically observed that the parade of intimate details of a person's life not only disgraced the victim of the story but trivialized the meaning of those details. Whereas old-fashioned local gossip typically circulated among people who were acquainted, however slightly, with those involved and could thereby judge the significance of the rumor, published gossip took the story away from its local setting and therefore deprived it of sympathetic reception. This removal, according to Godkin, "inflicts what is, to many men, the great pain of believing that everybody he meets in the street is perfectly familiar with some folly, or misfortune, or indiscretion, or weakness, which he had previously supposed had never got beyond his domestic circle." Just as Norton insisted that personal letters be guarded against prying eyes lest their delicate contents be misconstrued and thereby made light or laughable, so it was with published gossip. By depriving a person's "folly," "misfortune," "indiscretion," or "weakness" of the larger narrative of his or her life story, published rumor stripped the experience of its meaning and emotional resonance. What would undoubtedly be significant and important in private—e.g., the personal intrigues of the Proberts, the intimate letters of a famous writer, the honeymoon of President Cleveland, the unfortunate marriage of the merchant's daughter—is inconsequential and banal when paraded before strangers. Surely that is the meaning of the common criticism of newspapers' coverage of weddings: "Even the sanctities of domestic life and marriage suffer violence, profane eyes become as familiar with bridal trousseaux as the ladies maids themselves."[21]

This crucial component of the party of reticence's indictment of invasive journalism hinged on a shared sense of which things were large enough to deserve the attention of strangers and sturdy enough to withstand the glare of publicity, and which things were so small, personal, fragile, or vulnerable that they required the cover of privacy to retain their significance and emotional vibrancy. In the volatile controversy over the realist literary movement, associated with Emile Zola in Europe and William Dean Howells in America during this period, these questions of proportion and scale dominated the discussions. Repeatedly, opponents of Howells complained that his chronicles about the middle classes were "dull," "trivial," "wearisome," "petty." In 1885, the literary critic Hamilton Wright Mabie voiced the typical reproach: the actions of Howells's characters were so ordinary and their inner lives so shallow that they merited the attention of neither the reader, the author, nor the fictional character.

Realism is crowding the world of fiction with commonplace people; people whom one would positively avoid coming in contact with in real life; people without native sweetness or strength, without acquired culture or accomplishment, without that touch of the ideal which makes the commonplace significant and worthy of study. . . . The analysis of motives that were never worth an hour's serious study, the grave portraiture of frivolous, superficial, and often vulgar conceptions of life, the careful scrutiny of characters without force, beauty, aspiration, or any of the elements which touch and teach men, has become wearisome.[22]

In his *American Writers of To-day* (1894), Henry Clay Vedder also attacked Howells for setting his aesthetic sights too low—on characters who led "trivial," "commonplace" lives. Although Vedder allowed for "a place in art for the grotesque, for the painful," he nevertheless insisted that "its chief function is to please and ennoble." So he doubted whether any author could successfully take "the trivial" or "the vile" as "a proper subject matter," for "great artists have always appealed to the moral as well as to the aesthetic faculties." "To the healthy mind," Vedder declared, "they give no pleasure; they inspire only *ennui* or disgust."[23] For detractors of realism, this lack of discrimination in subject matter was the realist's greatest failing.

The reticent sensibility relied on unspoken rules of scale and proportion to determine which things were fit to appear before strangers, before intimates, and even before the self, but in the realms of aesthetics and rhetoric, a formal theory, known as the doctrine of distinct levels of style or the hierarchy of genres, had since antiquity classified different genres of art and oratory. Founded on the classical principle of decorum—each subject matter required a style of representation appropriate to the aesthetic scope and moral weight of the subject— this doctrine held that the undistinguished, everyday life of common people was worthy of treatment only as comedy, satire, or farce, or in explicitly didactic or moralistic terms; and that only the large and extraordinary lives of highborn and powerful people were the stuff of tragedy, deserving of elevated style. When Mabie complained of Howells's novels, "One cannot but regret such a comparative waste of delicate, and often genuine art; it is as if Michael Angelo had given us the meaningless faces of the Roman fops of his time instead of Moses and Hercules," he was restating this classical prescription. The same was true for Vedder when he professed his respect for Howells's project of faithfully depicting everyday life yet faulted his want of propriety, especially in his portrayals of women characters as "silly and flighty." "The plea that [such women] exist is not a valid defense to our accusation . . . that there has been a failure in literary perspective, an artistic blunder of which even a demonstration of realistic truth furnishes no justification."[24]

To proponents of literary reticence, this flouting of the hierarchy of genres revealed a want of tact. For them, tact was indispensable—for the creation of art of the highest order but also for the flourishing of civility and sociability. Like discretion and tenderness in intimate life, tact enabled one gracefully to pass over things that would otherwise be too offensive, insulting, or hurtful if they were subjected to a direct encounter. In this way, tact allowed one to maintain a respectful distance that gingerly acknowledges the unsaid, yet violates neither the intimate sphere of the person nor public standards of taste and morality.

THE DERANGEMENT OF THE PUBLIC SPHERE

The Romantics were the first to self-consciously break the rules of classical decorum by treating ordinary and domestic life in a serious manner. By the mid-nineteenth century, realist novelists and artists —especially in France—began to approach the affairs of common people and of the demimonde as if they had tragic dimensions. Howells's realism was criticized for its blandness and triviality, but Emile Zola's scientific realism—with its credo, "The metaphysical man is dead; our whole domain is transformed with the coming of the physiological man"[25]—was deplored for presenting an "inhuman" picture of life.

Of the many essays about the clash between the aesthetic-moral sensibility underlying the doctrine of classical decorum and the new scientific method of realism, the most penetrating is "The New Story-Tellers and the Doom of Realism" (1894) by a former disciple of Howells, William R. Thayer. Thayer observed that modern science, in contrast to science of the past, had abandoned "the search for the Absolute, and has been scrutinizing every atom, to weigh and name it, and to discover its relation with its neighbors. 'Relativity' has been the watchword." Novelists who adopted these methods in literature, however, were resourceless in faculties vital to the creation of art, especially taste and judgment:

> Arguing from analogy, the Realist persuaded himself that the only means for attaining perfect accuracy in fiction must be experiment and observation, which had brought such rich returns to Science. . . . To him, as to the man of science, there should be, he declared, neither beauty nor ugliness, great nor small, goodness nor evil; he was impartial; he eliminated the personal equation; he would make his mind as unprejudiced as a photographic plate.[26]

This stance of neutrality—a studied remove from both aesthetic and moral judgment—is the hallmark of scientific knowledge, and as we shall see, it was an important aspect of the intellectual mood of "relativity" that emerged at the turn of the century, which assumed facts could be successfully divorced from value judgments. Once realists confounded the hierarchy of genres by declaring that their only responsibility was to portray life truthfully, then all other concerns—aesthetic and moral—were suddenly beside the point. It is with this claim that realists did their greatest damage to the aesthetic-moral continuum at the foundation of classical decorum. And champions of reticence were appalled. Henry James, in an exasperated review of Zola's *Nana*, charged that "decency and indecency, morality and immorality, beauty and ugliness, are conceptions with which 'naturalism' has nothing to do. . . . The only business of naturalism is to be natural, and therefore, instead of saying of *Nana* that it contains a great deal of filth, we should simply say of it that it contains a great deal of nature." He pointed out that "the real has not a single shade more affinity with an unclean vessel than with a clean one," and insisted that Zola's method could "dispense as little with taste and tact as the floweriest mannerism of a less analytic age." To make taste irrelevant to art was to deprive the novel of its rightful subject matter—the human condition. For James, fiction could "never leave taste behind without leaving behind . . . the very grounds on which we appeal, the whole human side of the business." In the end, he declared, "taste, in its intellectual applications, is the most human faculty we possess, and as the novel may be said to be the most human form of art, it is a poor speculation to put the two things out of conceit of each other."[27]

For the party of reticence, the scientific method was inadequate to art because it examined the human condition at too far a remove. According to Thayer, this reduced

> literature, art, and morals to anarchy. The "scientific method," applied in this way, is not the method for portraying human nature. Only the human can understand, and consequently interpret, the human: how, therefore, shall a man who boasts that he has *dehumanized* himself so that his mind is as impartial as a photographic plate, enabling him to look on his fellow-beings without preferring the good to the bad, the beautiful to the ugly—how shall he be qualified to speak for the race which does discriminate, does prefer, does feel? The camera sees only the outside; the Realist sees no more, and so it would be more appropriate to call him "Epidermist," one who investigates only the surface,

the cuticle of life,—usually with a preference for the very dirty skin.[28]

As part of their indictment of exposure, critics also repeatedly warned of the terrible damage inflicted on the character of the common world and the tone of public discussion. Like their dire warnings about the trivialization of private life, these warnings, too, have disappeared from our now-interminable contemporary debates about invasive journalism and obscenity, thereby severely limiting our sense of what is at stake. In fact, most moderns can no longer detect the public harm that was deplored in almost every nineteenth-century attack on exposure. It turns out that liberals at the close of the nineteenth century had a far richer appreciation of the public realm than is usually acknowledged by their modern critics.

When newspapers print "good and bad, instructive and noninstructive, decent and indecent, pure and vile, and spread the strange medley, the dreadful mélange, out on broad sheets for the public to read," one critic complained, "then journalism is only a species of gossiping run mad, of ill-bred rehearsing in public and private circles, before men, women, and children, of what its all-devouring eyes, lensed like a carrion-seeking bird for all distances, beholds in this God's and devil's world of ours." This "dreadful mélange," many thought, wore away people's sense of proportion and their ability to discern the right measure of things; this, in turn, made for an increasingly deranged and insubstantial common domain. As Godkin put it, in the hands of an unscrupulous journalist private affairs become elevated to causes célèbres and "a petty scandal swells to the dimensions of a public calamity." Another critic deplored the way the reporter's "fertile imagination magnifies the most minute and innocent mole-hills into the most lofty and disreputable of mountains." Brandeis and Warren also drew attention to the distortion wrought by the commercial trade in gossip: "When personal gossip attains the dignity of print, and crowds the space available for matters of real interest to the community, what wonder that the ignorant and thoughtless mistake its relative importance. . . . Triviality destroys at once robustness of thought and delicacy of feeling."[29]

Repeatedly, advocates of reticence warned that gossipy journalism warped the community by elevating "unimportant persons to public notice." In an early article, "Opinion-Moulding" (1869), Godkin made this position clear: squandering attention on the unworthy constituted nothing less than "a fraud on the public," giving an obscure person's "opinions and wishes an amount of respect . . . to which they are not entitled." Worse, "by perverting the public judgment, [indiscriminate publicity] deprives men of real value of their proper place in the public estimation." The only defense against these twisted versions of reality, according to yet another critic, was for publishers to print material "in which the quality and proportion of news shall bear some relation to the needs and decencies of human life."[30]

Criticism of Zola's novels closely resembled these denunciations. In "The Relation of Art to Truth" (1890), the critic W. H. Mallock conceded that Zola and writers like him accurately portrayed much that is "prurient and filthy . . . [and] detestable in human nature," yet he believed that "they represent it out of all due proportion; and thus their works are no more true to life than a picture of a man would be . . . in which the stomach was colossal and everything else microscopic." Not that he was advocating the suppression of such writing, but he thought it was "a question of all the many aspects and facts of human nature, and the proportionate prominence and space which art should allot to each."[31]

A related objection concerned the dead seriousness of the party of exposure. In her "Fiction in the Pulpit" (1890), the well-known essayist Agnes Repplier chided Howells for his overwrought warnings about the deleterious effects of adventure stories and romances on children: "Ah, leave to the child at least his clear, intuitive, unbiased enjoyment, his sympathy with things that have been!" Reminding her readers that children are "not so easily hurt as we suppose," Repplier made a plea for playfulness and a sense of humor if life is to have any richness at all: "Mental hygiene, it is said, is apt to lead to mental valetudinarianism; but if we are to turn our nurseries into hotbeds of prigs, we may say once more what was said when Chapelain published his portentous epic, that 'a new horror has been added to the accomplishment of reading.'" James criticized Zola for the same reasons, complaining of his "extraordinary absence of humor, the dryness, the solemnity, the air of tension and effort."[32]

The capacity to discern the proper ordering of things, which these critics prized, was crucial to legal determinations of obscenity, for the very definition of obscenity depended on knowing which things belonged in public and which in private. In trial after trial, judges defined "obscene" as "offensive to chastity and decency, expressing or presenting to the mind or view something which delicacy, purity, and decency forbid to be exposed." "Indecency," too, was a key word, and judges emphasized that decency indicates fitness for appearance in public, citing dictionary definitions of "indecent" as "the wanton and unnecessary expression or exposure, in words or pictures, of that which the common sense of decency requires should be kept private or concealed," or that which is "unfit to be seen or heard."[33]

THE CORRUPTION OF TASTE
AND JUDGMENT

Proponents of reticence worried that the new journalism, along with sentimental and romantic novels, would "debauch" the intellect and make people "passive"—thereby anticipating criticisms of mass culture made a half century later. Whether sensational journalism and mediocre fiction actually would enfeeble people's minds ultimately is not so important as the belief that they were having this effect. Charles Dudley Warner's vigorous condemnation of "the habit of excessive newspaper-reading" was typical of this position. Because newspapers treated too many topics in a superficial manner, "the mind loses the power of discrimination, the taste is lowered, and the appetite becomes diseased." The critic Condé Benoist Pallen put it vividly, and his warning should rewaken us today to the issues at stake in a debate that has become thoroughly exhausted. He saw "the mental powers grown stagnant, the judgment warped, and intellectual freedom an impossibility. . . . The brain degenerates into a pulpy, spongy mass, through which daily percolate the falsehood and immorality of the world's 'news.' "[34]

One of the most popular metaphors used to capture the degradation that comes with mass entertainment was drug addiction; this contrasts sharply with our contemporary talk about individual choice, "lifestyles," and "taste cultures." Thus, one critic observed that to people "addicted" to the "Newspaper Habit," "its greatest fascinations are that it 'kills the time,' satisfies the thirst for scandal, and acts as a preventive to thinking." Howells spoke derisively of the "novel habit": "It may be safely assumed that most of the novel-reading which people fancy an intellectual pastime is the emptiest dissipation, hardly more related to thought or the wholesome exercise of the mental faculties than opium-eating; in either case the brain is drugged, and left weaker and crazier for the debauch."[35]

In these discussions of the pernicious effects of mass entertainment, another founding article of the mass-culture debate was introduced. Godkin raised the specter of American culture being increasingly split into competing realms catering to different audiences. There was a "segregation of the newspaper-reader from the book-reader," a "deep and increasing scorn on the part of the book-reader and book-maker for the man who reads nothing but the newspapers, and gets his facts and opinions from them." Godkin observed that in circles made up of "scientific" and "cultivated" people, "you will have the mental food which the newspapers supply to the bulk of the population treated with ridicule and contempt, the authority of a newspaper as a joke, and journalism used as a synonym for shallowness, ignorance, and blundering."[36]

Howells also pointed to the expanding gulf between audiences, and he insisted that distinctions be drawn and maintained "between the different kinds of things that please the same kind of people; between the things that please them habitually and those that please them occasionally; between the pleasures that edify them and those that amuse them." While Howells noted that the most that could be said for "literary amusements" was that they were "harmless," he instructed the reader that "these amusements have their place, as the circus has, and the burlesque and negro minstrelsy, and the ballet and prestidigitation. No one of these is to be despised in its place; but we had better understand that it is not the highest place, and that it is hardly an intellectual delight."[37]

In sum, from the perspective of the reticent sensibility, journalism and novels geared to the marketplace were undermining individual morality and the public good in a number of distinct yet related ways: they gave undue prominence to matters not large enough to legitimately deserve attention, and thereby demeaned and trivialized the quality of public conversation; they wore down people's sense of proportion and of the right ordering of things, corroded their powers of concentration, and destroyed their capacity to appreciate more demanding, let alone excellent, material; and finally, these developments made for an increasingly polarized society, where distinction would reside with the cultivated few who were capable of recognizing excellence.

As we have seen, the party of reticence characteristically employed moral and aesthetic language interchangeably. An introduction to a symposium on journalism in 1893 is typical: journalists, the editors insisted, "should carefully exclude, or at least minimize to the utmost, those facts . . . of which the knowledge is likely to vulgarize popular taste and lower popular standards of morality." Or, as Godkin put it, the worst offense of the new journalism was "that its pervading spirit is one of vulgarity, indecency, and reckless sensationalism; that it steadily violates the canons alike of good taste and sound morals; that it cultivates false standards of life and demoralizes its readers."[38]

The party of reticence was convinced that overfamiliarity with the literature of exposure could so completely dull people's judgment that they would eventually lose the capacity to recognize improprieties. Francie Dosson in *The Reverberator* worries that she and her family have "become coarse and callous," that they have "lost their delicacy, the sense of certain differences and decencies." And in "Newspapers Gone to Seed" (1886), James Parton furnishes a powerful account of this habituation. While his target was the impudent journalist, his description of the journalist's hardness in the face of suffering can easily be extended to newspaper readers in general. He thought journalists associated "too much with their own class" and became "too familiar with the materials they handle," like "medical students who see daily before their eyes two or three hundred human bodies." He recounted a story of "a medical student's holding a piece of pie in one hand and the dissecting-knife in the other, and giving alternate attention to nourishing his own body and cutting up another." The incapacity to recognize such gross incongruities was part and parcel of the journalist's trade: "The journalist is occupied every hour with events which carry misery and despair to large numbers of his fellow-beings, and he gradually loses all sense of the hideous impropriety which he commits in hot haste at a quarter past one in the morning when he writes at the top of a page of horrors, 'Three Bibulous Suicides.'"[39]

Covering similar terrain, Godkin observed that a "free and unbridled press" deadened public sensitivity "to spoken or printed ridicule, or abuse, or depreciation," and lessened popular sympathy "with the victim of it." In the same spirit, Pallen charged that newspapers "habituated and familiarized" the public with "crime and sin." He gave voice to the popular belief that "a daily and unremitting familiarity with any sin or crime must degrade the moral tone, until from toleration we go to commission of what at first we detested."[40]

In the landmark obscenity trial *United States* v. *Harmon* [sic] (1891), in which Moses Harman, the outspoken editor of the free-love journal *Lucifer, the Light-Bearer*, was convicted for publishing shocking personal histories of sexual perversions, Judge Philips chastised the defendant in almost identical language: "When the defendant and his coadjutors say that such language and subject matter is only impure to the overprudish, it but illustrates how familiarity with obscenity blunts the sensibility, depraves good taste, and perverts the judgment." In another striking passage, where Judge Philips described the habituation that accompanies overfamiliarity with indecency, one can easily substitute invasive journalism for obscenity without doing violence to the judge's remarks:

> No ordinary mind can subject itself to the repeated reading and contemplation of such subjects and language without the risk of becoming indurated to all sense of modesty in speech and chastity in thought. The appetite for such literature increases with the feeding. The more it is pandered to, the more insatiable its craving for something yet more vicious in taste.[41]

The price of too frequently and too regularly crossing the ever-shifting border between desire and taboo, curiosity and injunction, is desensitization: what was once shocking becomes commonplace and trivial, what was once obscene becomes banal and dull; these are two sides of the same coin. This was considered true not only of invasive journalism and of obscenity, but also of the realist novel. Hamilton Wright Mabie thought it significant that the vigor of such fiction was "mainly on the side of moral pathology," and that it denied "the spiritual side of life." He then pointed to two predictable results: "Naturalism inevitably portrays the repellant, and a refined realism the superficial aspects of life."[42]

THE POLLUTION OF PUBLIC SPACE

The problem of recognizing indecency has a quaint ring today, since a belief made popular by the party of exposure is that concern for indecency is nothing more than a foolish Victorian or Puritan throwback. But for the party of reticence a hundred years ago, ideas about indecency were bound to ideas about sanctity and shame. Critics of exposure habitually evoked the sacred quality of privacy when they lashed out against prying biographies, published personal letters, invasive and sensational journalism, clinical descriptions of sexual hygiene, and realist novels. What William Thayer said about the threat that realism posed to civilized life is true of all forms of exposure from the perspective of reticence: "It required no keenness to perceive that decency, modesty, sanctity—conceptions which, after many painful centuries, the more civilized minority of the human race has begun to venerate—could not protect themselves against the brazen presumptions of Realism."[43]

Just as the metaphor of drug addiction was used to suggest the insidious personal harm in mass entertainment, metaphors of "contamination" and "pollution" were ritually invoked to capture the public dimension of the harm. These, too, have vanished from our contemporary discussions of the same issues, and critics have virtually nothing to say about the character of our common domain. The earlier use of contamination and pollution metaphors, however, makes explicit the gravity of the harm of exposure—that its violation was of public space and that it was uncontainable. Condé Benoist Pallen, like so many of his contemporaries, conjured up the striking image of a filthy public sewer:

> It is the *cloaca maxima* of Newspaperism,—the common sewer for public and private immorality. In this department are chronicled the sins, the crimes, the misfortunes, and the weaknesses of our poor humanity; sensationalism is its dominating principle. Here, spiced and fetid with all the filth of a degraded *morale* and an infamous taste, designed to cater to the morbid imagination of the masses, is served up the record of the murders, rapes, hangings, poisoning, incendiarisms, suicides, divorces, thefts, burglaries, incests, lusts, and all other abominations perpetrated by perverted humanity.

Appalled by the "shameless effrontery" of daily journalism, he dared his readers to "see if you can escape contamination." For the party of reticence, indecent, filthy, unnamable, and shameful things went beyond the limits of human understanding and transgressed the boundaries of social order; consequently, speaking of them was to commit a powerful act of pollution and contagion. "Through contagion," the anthropologist Franz Steiner has noted, "there is social participation in danger, and social relations are describable in terms of danger."[44]

Metaphors of disease were also freely employed. As one critic described the prying journalist: "His breathings taint the social atmosphere, and develop in us all a moral disease, the seeds of which are in every heart." William Bushnell was even more adamant in equating the moral harm visited upon society by invasive journalism with the dreaded contagion of disease: "Such journalism is a cancerous ulcer that is eating its way to the very heart of all that is noble, refining, exalting; it is moral leprosy that is fast spreading over the entire body of the press." In perhaps the most telling description of prying newspapers, George Rider equated sensational journalism with obscenity:

> Mr. Comstock and his associates are busily wiping out, here and there, sly, furtive driblets of vicious and obscene literature; but what can their little mops achieve against this perpetual, foul, flood-tide of journalism? The Hayden and Malley trials suffused the whole community with their deadly infestations. Who shall antidote or disinfect after such

contagion—what moral prophylactic resist the virus of such soul-poisoning?[45]

Denunciations of realist fiction typically took this same form, as when William Thayer excoriated Zola's novels as "shameless products," "obscenities," "filth," or when another critic warned that Zola's novels "seem not only to affront the dignity of life, but to endanger it, and to threaten society with a blood-poisoning." Observing that a man who reads French novels will always take precautions to keep such books safely locked away from his family, Henry Clay Vedder noted: "If he runs the risk of moral contagion himself, as he might risk catching small-pox or typhus, he has no idea of exposing his wife and children to contamination."[46]

The pollution metaphor was so much a part of nineteenth-century language that it found its way into the legal discourse about obscenity. Because obscenity comes into existence through the verbal or pictorial representation of private experiences about which social conventions command silence, nineteenth-century judges were confronted by the vexing problem of how to comment on obscenity without producing more of it. Judges sidestepped this trap by flatly refusing to introduce allegedly obscene passages into court records. A number of defendants claimed that this violated their constitutional right to be informed of the nature and the cause of their accusation, but none of the judges found the argument compelling. Instead, they repeatedly denounced obscene language as inappropriate to the records of the public domain and, more tellingly, as possessing the power to "pollute" and "contaminate" them. The same sense of pollution was behind the Comstock Act, passed in 1873, which made it illegal to send in the mails any materials relating to sex.* One judge declared, "The object of the statute [the Comstock Act] was to suppress the traffic in obscene publication, and to protect the community against the contamination and pollution arising from their exhibition and distribution." Another spoke the common wisdom of the day when he declared, "Courts will never allow their records to be polluted by bawdy and obscene matters. To do this would be to require a court of justice to perpetuate and give notoriety to an indecent publication."[47]

---

* The Comstock Postal Act, named after Special Prosecutor Anthony Comstock, banned five types of materials from the mails: (1) "an obscene, lewd, lascivious book, pamphlet, paper, print, or other publication of an indecent character"; (2) information and devices relating to birth control (both contraception and abortion); (3) things "intended or adapted for immoral use or nature"; (4) any information regarding how to obtain or make the materials mentioned above; (5) envelopes and postcards with "indecent or scurrilous epithets." Comstock Act of March 3, 1873, 17 Stat. at L., 598.

From the perspective of modern anthropology, this idiom of pollution and dirt speaks to the magnitude of the danger posed to the late-nineteenth-century social order—notably its cult of domesticity —by the new modes of journalism, fiction, and clinical discussions of sexual intimacy. "Pollution beliefs are cultural phenomena," according to Mary Douglas. "They are institutions that can keep their forms only by bringing pressure to bear on deviant individuals."[48] Above all, these agencies of exposure threatened the sanctity of the household, which had become a refuge from the world of the aggressive marketplace, as well as being the only refuge for activities connected to the life process. In an effort to make the bodily part of existence worthy of its new social importance, the Victorians wrapped intimate matters in elaborate social conventions so as to deepen their moral content and emotional resonance. In the protected sphere of intimacy, the self was to find its fullest expression through intense love relations, family involvement, and close friendships. To portray or discuss this intimacy was to violate morality and, with it, the social structures in which the deepest meanings resided.

Given this sense of the sanctity of privacy, it is not surprising that critics pictured those who violated it as leering voyeurs. Edith Wharton gave unforgettable expression to this sensibility in her novel *The Touchstone* (1900), about the publication of the love letters of a famous deceased author by her unscrupulous ex-lover:

> "I believe it is a vice, almost, to read such a book as the *Letters*," said Mrs. Touchett. "It's the woman's soul, absolutely torn up by the roots—her whole self laid bare; and to a man who evidently didn't care; who couldn't have cared. I don't mean to read another line: it's too much like listening at a keyhole."

In the same vein, James Russell Lowell vividly captured the demeaning effects of reading indiscreet biographies: "There are certain memoirs after reading which one blushes as if he had not only been peeping through a keyhole, but had been caught in the act." Recounting instances of published scandalmongering, Lowell declared, "Somewhere in our inhuman nature there must be an appetite for these unsavory personalities, but they are degrading in a double sense—degrading to him whose secret is betrayed, and to him who consents to share in the illicit knowledge of it."[49]

DEMOCRACY, BRAZEN CURIOSITY,
AND THE URGE TO LOWER

While personal freedom and individuality are among the most cherished values of liberal democracy, they can become problematic when democracy is equated not with self-rule among equals, public deliberation and debate, or open elections, but with equality of social condition, with the imposition of mass standards of taste, or with the display of relaxed, casual manners. This was frequently the case at the close of the nineteenth century, as it is today. Recalling a line of thought that had tormented his forebears such as Alexis de Tocqueville and John Stuart Mill and his friend Charles Eliot Norton, E. L. Godkin observed that democracy was intrinsically at odds with privacy and distinction: "In all democratic societies today, the public is disposed either to resent attempts at privacy, either of mind or body, or to turn them into ridicule." Mill had feared that democracy might wear away distinction and hoped that privacy would guarantee the space needed for individuality to flourish, but Godkin saw the unintended consequences of this desire for privacy. People now suspected it as a breeding ground of privilege: "There is nothing democratic societies dislike so much today as anything which looks like what is called exclusiveness, and all regard for and precautions about privacy are apt to be considered signs of exclusiveness."[50]

Amplifying this point, an editorial in an English journal, *The Spectator* (1891), noted that a person who lives an unusually retired life risks becoming an object of popular suspicion: "The Russell family were recently treated almost as public offenders because some of them wished that details of a relative's suicide should not be made needlessly public." "The horror of reserve and seclusion," the editorialist continued, was further illustrated by the public's annoyance with people who refused to be interviewed. The common view held that such a person was "either ashamed of himself or . . . capable of an insolent disregard of the rights of his fellow men." But the prying spirit was actually "an excessively vulgar form of spite, seclusion being regarded as superiority."[51]

While the party of reticence acknowledged that the tension between legitimate distinction and arbitrary social privilege could fuel resentment, they also believed that resentment of privacy, and, in turn, receptivity to the new agencies of exposure, had deeper roots. Richard Grant White located this other source in "a monstrous and distorted form of the desire of knowledge, a perversion of the humanity supposed to be expressed in Terence's famous line, 'I am a man, and regard nothing human as foreign to me.' " For Godkin, the disposition to intrude on privacy came from an insatiable curiosity about other people's affairs and an incurable love of scandal, especially those of the great. While he acknowledged that curiosity "in its larger and nobler aspect" had been the motor of Western civilization, he denounced curiosity in its modern form, published gossip, as "the chief enemy of privacy in modern life." Reciting Rochefoucauld's popular aphorism—"we take a secret pleasure in the misfortunes of our best friends"—Godkin identified the driving force behind the easy circulation of gossip: "the general desire for superiority, no matter how acquired, with which we are all consciously or unconsciously motivated." Journalism was the great equalizer, lowering the subject of the story to the same level as the journalist and reader. "The dragging down of the mighty," he observed, "has been not unpleasing sport to the natural man in all ages."[52]

In "The Ethics of Journalism" (1889), W. S. Lilly also made much of the envy which drives the journalist "to bring down as many as possible to his own level." "Is a man the object of reverence and admiration for piety, highmindedness, purity?" asked Lilly. Then journalists, avowing their hatred of "hypocrisy," would set the record straight by "strip[ping] off the veneer which imposes on the unsuspicious."

> [They] will show their readers that these pretended virtues are a mere cloak for some base or sordid end; will demonstrate conclusively that "old Cato is as great a rogue as you." . . . One of the main achievements of the newspaper press during the last quarter of a century has been to deidealize [sic] public life.[53]

Aline Gorren, in an essay with almost the identical title, "The Ethics of Modern Journalism" (1896), also thought that modern journalism "works subtly to cheapen the ideal, wherever it is found; to make every delicacy seem a prejudice, a superstition; to rob, by colloquializing them pitilessly, even the common events of existence of that dignity that inheres, to the right vision, in everything human." She invoked, unsurprisingly, the idiom of the sacred: "Against this result, the best in our moral nature, the highest conviction that inheritance and tradition have given us, rebels. Reverence, born of mystery, is the power by the aid of which the greatest spiritual advance has hitherto been got out of the race."[54]

This powerful impulse to efface distinction attracted the notice of Matthew Arnold during his 1883 lecture tour in America. In his famous account of that tour, "Civilization in the United States" (1888), he observed: "Everything is against distinction in America, and against the sense of elevation to be gained through admiring and respecting it." Above all else, he blamed the newspapers: "If one were searching for the best means to efface and kill in a whole nation the discipline of respect, the feeling for what is elevated, one could not do better than take the American newspaper."[55]

Henry James made the connection between contempt for distinction and the urge to violate privacy even clearer in his characterization of the brash reporter, Matthias Pardon, in *The Bostonians*: "For this ingenuous son of his age all distinction between the person and the artist had ceased to exist; the writer was personal, the person food for newsboys, and everything and everyone were everyone's business." For James, the modern newspaper represented "the highest expression of 'familiarity,' the sinking of manners, in so many ways, which the democratization of the world brings with it." In this same vein, Godkin told a story about a traveler's experience at a hotel in a Western mining town who "pinned a shirt across his open window on the piazza while performing his toilet; after a few minutes he saw it drawn aside roughly by a hand from without, and on asking what it meant, a voice answered, 'We want to know what there is so darned private going on in there?' "[56]

The stinging demand—"What is so darned private going on in there?"—signals the propensity of the vulgar to focus exclusively on what everyone has in common—their bodily functions. And the accusatory tone shows a kind of hatred or envy of those people who, because of a highly cultivated sense of modesty, do feel they have something to hide if they are to maintain their dignity. As James once observed: "There are decencies that in the name of the general self-respect we must take for granted, there's a kind of rudimentary intellectual honor to which we must, in the interest of civilization, at least pretend." By drawing attention to the lowest common denominator of the condition of having a body, the vulgar approach to privacy does away with social or hereditary differences, effectively reducing everyone to so much flesh and bones. The prying spirit of journalism—as well as the "impartial" spirit of scientific method, whether expressed in fiction or in sex education—accomplishes much the same thing by transforming the fragile activities of a person's private and intimate life into common property. Georg Simmel's remarks about the leveling potential of sexual intimacy makes the threat to selfhood even clearer: "On the one hand," he wrote, "sexual intercourse is the most intimate and personal process, but on the other hand, it is absolutely general, absorbing the very personality in the service of the species and in the universal organic claim of nature."[57]

The reason, then, that bodily activities must be covered by cultural artifice or carefully secreted away is that they lodge us directly into the realm of necessity—the realm of sexual desire, birth, death, hunger, sickness, pain, exhaustion, excretion—and force us to acknowledge our unexceptional place in nature and, in turn, our all too human limits. Thus, the reticent sensibility pays homage to privacy in its timeless, universal function of sheltering the fragile, bodily aspects of the human condition. Because of the frailty of most people's sense of selfhood and the extreme pressure liberal society puts on individuality, the recognition of the inherent equality of the condition of having a body—of being part of biological time—must be continually suppressed lest it extinguish one's sense of uniqueness. Consequently, if private, bodily experiences are not fully contained in aesthetic or moral language (as in the case of obscenity), or if the public gaze abruptly intrudes upon them (as in the case of invasive journalism), they risk becoming degraded, subhuman, or merely physical processes.

This reverence for privacy should not simply be dismissed, as it always is today, as mere Victorian prudery. Instead it should be understood as a highly elaborated form of the age-old wisdom that joins privacy, shame, and the sacred at the very deepest level of consciousness. The reticent sensibility is at one with the perspective of all societies that recognize limits to knowledge and thus approach the unknowable with awe and wonder. As W. S. Lilly put it:

> The great ethical principles of reserve, shame, reverence, which have their endless applications in civilized life, prescribe limits to imagination as to action. There are moods of thought which do not yield in heinousness to the worst deeds—moods of madness, suicidal and polluting. To leave them in the dark is to help towards suppressing them. And this is a sacred duty. "We are bound to reticence," says George Eliot, "most of all by that reverence for the highest efforts of our common nature, which commands us to bury its lowest fatalities, its invincible remnants of the brute, its most agonizing struggles with temptation, in unbroken silence."[58]

More than anything else, it was the party of exposure's attempt to turn what was distinctive, unique, or individual into common coin that mortified the party of reticence. Giving this sentiment its fullest expression, Hamilton Wade Mabie lamented the way realism had deprived art of its grand scale and life of its profundity, since scientific method not only had no use for revelation, spirituality, or idealism, but actively denied their existence:

> Under the conditions which it imposes, art can see nothing but the isolated physical fact before it; there are no mysterious forces in the soil under it; there is no infinite blue heaven over it. . . . It is, in a word, practical atheism applied to art. It not only empties the world of the Ideal, but, as Zola frankly says, it denies "the good God"; it dismisses the old heaven of aspiration and possible fulfillment as an idle dream; it destroys the significance of life and the interpretative quality of art.[59]

Because so many of us today conduct our lives without the comfort and rigor of religion, it is hard to imagine how atrocious and preposterous this still-novel idea must have seemed to most people only a century ago, how outraged they must have felt as the doctrine of "practical atheism" was extended from religion to art to love. To live in a world without illusions is always daunting, so it is no wonder that feelings of powerlessness and disillusionment are common responses to the disenchanted world of "isolated physical facts." This helps to explain the limited range of tones—from mocking to condescending—that color the discourse of exposure when its speakers make their vaunted claims for the truth they believed science would bring. The shamelessness which the party of reticence repeatedly attributed to marauders of privacy can best be understood as overweening pride—the flip side of impotence—born of a hubristic desire to cross all boundaries, whether between people or between the knowable and the unknowable in nature. Brazenness is emblematic of the sensibility of exposure, as is enmity, envy, resentment of and contempt for all those who have not yet been disillusioned or enlightened—depending on the viewpoint—and thereby continue to hold privacy, reticence, and modesty in the highest esteem.

3

THE DISCOURSE
OF EXPOSURE AND THE
VALUE OF PUBLICITY

In their battles against the new agencies of exposure during the last quarter of the nineteenth century, protectors of reticence were forced to give concrete form to what had previously been more a sensibility than a self-conscious language. Because their struggle against the new publicity was essentially a fight over what should appear in public, they appealed to the authority of faculties that had traditionally determined how the world was to look—taste, judgment, and common sense. Knowing which things were grand enough to withstand public scrutiny and which were so small or vulnerable that they required privacy to retain their meaning also depended on a strong sense of the sacred and the shameful. And because sociability and intimacy were considered the primary settings for the cultivation of moral character, politeness was among their highest aspirations. The practice of good manners was believed to shape every aspect of civilized conduct, and nowhere was it more crucial than in the commercial exchanges that took place daily between strangers.

Just as social relations are by their nature tenuous, intimate ones are at best fragile. If such relations are to anchor individual life and provide existence with its deepest meanings, as the architects of liberal society promised they would, then sensitivity toward the feelings of others would need to be painstakingly cultivated. Sympathy was the keynote here, and reticence, reserve, tact, discretion, propriety, modesty, delicacy, and tenderness would provide an array of finely modulated approaches toward the privacy of others so as to foster the conditions necessary to life under the ever closer range of intimacy and sociability. Where the discourse of reticence had provided intimacy and sociability with a richness never before seen in history, its values and aspirations were coming under attack. In the same way that political economy would have been oxymoronic from the ancient Greek perspective, since it blurred the public (*polis*) and the private household (*oikos*), so, too, the late-nineteenth-century notions of public sex instruction, published gossip, and serious novels about private life confounded the traditional demarcations of public and private.

But a growing chorus of angry dissenters was beginning to make itself heard. For advocates of exposure, this was a debate about the place of democracy, science, and new technologies in modern life. They questioned whether the reticent sensibility had miscarried, and whether its notions of public and private were in keeping with the most progressive tendencies of the time. Their suspicions drove them to demand a more thoroughgoing application of tenets associated with liberalism than could have ever been imagined by classical liberals, or by their progeny, the party of reticence: in the name of truth and liberty, enthusiasts of exposure extended the Enlightenment commitment of flooding light into dark places to matters previously believed to be either private or not worthy of public consideration; in the name of equality, they stretched the prospect of democracy to realms previously understood as being non-political, specifically the home and the arts. And by speaking in the name of progress, they indicted privacy for blocking the light of emancipation and in so doing, successfully discredited the discourse of reticence as a language of cover-up and repression.

THE EXPOSURE OF EVILS

Many in the party of reticence would no doubt have agreed that exposure was a legitimate tool to reveal and correct wrongdoings that took place under cover of darkness. "In our communities nothing essential ought to be concealed," observed the freethinker O. B. Frothingham. "The secret cogitations of leading men should, in so far as they concern the public, be known." What was novel about mass-circulation journalism was the application of this idea to subjects traditionally regarded as of no legitimate concern to the public—invasive accounts of domestic and private life, published gossip and scandal, and sensational stories of divorce trials and crimes. Advocates of exposure, however, justified their probings by claiming that publicity and openness were best suited to a democracy; they tirelessly evoked "the public's right to know" and argued that "the exposition and depiction of vice have the salutary effect of a warning to evildoers and others, by picturing to them the terrible retribution of sin and crime." In each case, they succeeded in associating privacy with a particularly malevolent kind of secrecy or, in the words of one commentator, with "either an ill motive or an insolent motive."[1]

In *The Reverberator*, Henry James captures this suspicious habit of mind in his portrait of Francie Dosson's guileless father. Because the Dossons are "sunk in their innocence, sunk in their irremediable un-awareness almost beyond fishing out," they are incapable of under-standing the Proberts' feelings of disgrace and mortification when they see accounts of their private affairs in print. Naturally Mr. Dos-son suspects the worst: "Well, if folks are immoral you can't keep it out of the papers—and I don't know as you ought to want to." Or, as the narrator put it: "Deep in Mr. Dosson's spirits was a sense that if these people had done bad things they ought to be ashamed of themselves and he couldn't pity them, and if they hadn't done them, there was no need of making such a rumpus about other people knowing."[2]

Social reformers were suspicious of privacy and for similar reasons. Like the new journalists, many free-love proponents, sex reformers, feminists, and sociologists were convinced that if private misconduct was flooded with light, good people would act to correct it. Animated by the highest of purposes, they led the most radical wing of the larger nineteenth-century reform project to reconstruct American public and private life according to positivist, rational, cooperative, and egalitarian principles. In some versions, sex reform was closely linked to spiritualism and free thought. At its most extreme, as artic-ulated by self-avowed sex radicals such as Ezra Heywood, editor of the free-love journal *The Word*, or Moses Harman, editor of *Lucifer, the Light-Bearer*, it shaded into anarchism. But at the root of virtually every version of sex reform was what the historian William Leach has called a "doctrine of no secrets." Elizabeth Cady Stanton expressed its first principle when she cautioned, "Danger lies in darkness and distance." Its highest aspiration was voiced by the feminist doctor Mary Putnam Jacobi in a public lecture before the New York City Positivist Society in 1872 when she exhorted her audience, "Live in the open air!" She was explicit—and fierce—about her deep-seated suspicion of privacy: "A thing that one is not willing the whole world should know is wrong." Employing this same idiom, the sociologist Lester Ward spelled out the dangers inherent in "mysteries, deep hid-den secrets," and warned against modesty and prurience in sexual relations: "Whatever must be done secretly and clandestinely will be done improperly and become an evil, though it possesses no intrin-sically evil elements." He was confident that the new social sciences would "strip all physical realities of their masks" and "drag them before the light."[3]

The crucial problem for early sex reformers was to create a language that would enable them to discuss what had previously been held to be unspeakable without slipping into the illicit region of obscenity, for this would leave them open to legal prosecution under the Comstock Act, which included information about contraception in its definition of obscenity and made its distribution a criminal offense. The need to develop an appropriate language was particularly urgent for advocates of free love, who pressed the promise of happiness offered by the cult of domesticity to its logical conclusion. They sought to bring about equality and freedom in private life and to elevate love to a higher spiritual plane. Thus sex radicals insisted on speaking plainly not only about sexual morality, hygiene, and contraception but about sexual misconduct as well. "Claiming a higher purity than puritanism," the historian Hal Sears has observed, the sex radicals "challenged the Victorian code of secrecy; exposure of evils, regardless of how 'awful,' constituted the first step in healing them." It was this muckraking impulse that brought the wrath of Anthony Comstock in his role as Special Prosecutor upon them, which led to repeated arrests, trials, and prison terms.[4]

These early sex reformers were confident they could invent a vocabulary that would free both sexual intimacy and discussions about it from the corruptions that had entangled it, in the popular imagination and in the law, with obscenity. The wholesomeness of sex could be restored, they insisted, if people learned to think and speak plainly about it. In 1880 the pioneering free-love advocate Stephen Pearl Andrews articulated this position before the Union Reform League Convention:

> Since there is no obscenity in Nature, no obscenity in science, and no obscenity in Art, there seems no place left for obscenity but in the defilement of our imaginations; . . . when our thoughts and imaginations are freshened to the naturalness of nature, used to the clean-cut precision of science, and to the gracious sweetness of Artistic beauty, obscenity will cease to exist among us.[5]

In this description of how obscenity enters the world, the simple optimism and one-dimensionality of the sensibility of exposure are disclosed. Just as Mr. Dosson believed nothing in people's private lives could be threatened by publicity if they were living honestly, so Andrews believed that nothing in nature, science, or art was unfit for public appearance. The long-standing injunction voiced by the party of reticence—experiences that are at once sacred and shameful must not and cannot be spoken about lest they become desacralized, the public sphere polluted, and private life trivialized—was from this perspective simply mistaken. Only people with "defiled imaginations" could object to frank talk about sex, just as, from the standpoint of the new journalists, only people with something to hide could resist publicity. This propensity for cover-up was also suggested by William Dean Howells in his discussion of the great dramas of Henrik Ibsen:

> A great many good, elderly minded people think it dreadful Ibsen should show that the house we have lived in so long is full of vermin, that its drainage is bad, that the roof leaks and the chimney smokes abominably; but if it is true, is it not well for us to know it? It is dreadful because it is so, not because he shows it so; and the house is no better because our fathers got on in it as it is.[6]

The problem for sex reformers and realist authors alike, then, was to learn to speak the truth in a fresh, unadulterated language. In the *Woman's Journal* (1871), the Reverend Dr. Boynton announced, "It is time for women . . . who care for their own sex to call things by their right names." In 1880 the notorious free-lover Ezra Heywood complained of the "utter stupidity, nonsense, and villainy of evasion and cowardice," and, like Andrews, questioned whether obscenity actually resided in words, which he dismissed as "simply letters in line, sociated [sic] in sentences." Again like Andrews, he insisted that obscenity sprang from "dirty thought, unclean habit, dishonest action relative to body forces." The only remedy was plain speech: "The sex organs and their associative uses have fit, proper, explicit, expressive English names; why not have character enough to use them and no longer be ashamed of your own creative use and destiny?" Even people who actively supported Comstock and the Society for the Suppression of Vice took as their motto "Purity Through Knowledge," by which they meant frank and open discussions about sex, venereal diseases, prostitution, and divorce.[7]

For Howells, too, calling things by their proper names was a rallying point for modern literature. In the opening pages of his manifesto *Criticism and Fiction* (1891), a collection of incendiary pieces from his column "The Editor's Study" at *Harper's New Monthly Magazine* written between 1886 and 1891, he argued for a new standard of criticism that would highly prize "simple, natural, and honest" art. The standard of a work's excellence would be "what there is of truth, sincerity, and natural vigor in it." In his attempt to foster realism, Howells repeatedly argued for the accurate representation of reality to replace the "old trade of make-believe." Issuing his dictum, "Let fiction cease to lie about life," he challenged writers to "portray men and women as they are, actuated by the motives and the passions in the measure we all know. Let it leave off painting dolls and working them by springs and wires." For Howells, it was imperative that writers refrain from manipulating characters and employing improbable plot devices and instead let the truth of the fictional situation speak for itself: "Let [fiction] show the different interests in their true proportions; let it forbear to preach pride and revenge, folly and insanity, egotism and prejudice, but frankly own these for what they are, in whatever figures and occasions they appear." He was adamant that fiction speak to everyone, that the author not "put on fine literary airs; let [fiction] speak the dialect, the language, that most Americans know—the unaffected people everywhere—and there can be no doubt of an unlimited future, not only of delightfulness but of usefulness, for it."[8]

THE PERSISTENCE OF THE
RETICENT SENSIBILITY

Howells's efforts to make his novels speak the language of "unaffected people everywhere" were usually dismissed by his contemporaries as dull and trivial at best and, at worst, soulless, but no one thought of them as legally actionable. In contrast, reformers who undertook frank discussions about sex frequently found themselves in the legal pincers of Anthony Comstock. It is important to recall that sexual obscenity as a legal category simply did not exist before this time. Although several states had anti-obscenity laws on their books in the early years of the republic, it was not until 1842 that Congress enacted the first federal law restricting trade in obscenity more narrowly defined as sexual in nature.[9] Aimed at the French picture-postcard trade, the Tariff Act empowered the customs office to confiscate, bring suit against, and destroy "obscene or immoral" prints and pictures within its purview. In 1857 Congress added to the list not only "obscene images," including photographs and daguerreotypes, but "obscene articles" as well. It was at least in part because the issues raised by sex reformers were so at odds with popular ideas of morality and politeness that, in 1873, Congress passed the Comstock Postal Act banishing all sexual literature and devices, including information about contraception, from the mails.

In striking contrast to our contemporary obscenity proceedings, the earliest trials centered not on art, but rather on sex-education publications. In *United States* v. *Bennett* (1879)—a leading precedent in obscenity law through the 1930s—D. M. Bennett, the outspoken editor of the free-thought journal *Truth Seekers*, was tried and convicted for mailing an obscene pamphlet, *Cupid's Yokes, or The Binding Forces of Conjugal Love* by Ezra Heywood. First and foremost *Cupid's Yokes* is a polemic against "scandal-begetting clergymen and bribe-taking statesmen" as authorities in sexual matters. In calling for independent thought and "sexual self-government," Heywood bolstered his argument with quotations from an eclectic range of writers—Tocqueville, Darwin, Newton, Plato, Aristotle, Montesquieu, John Stuart Mill, Henry James, Victor Hugo, Shakespeare, "A German Proverb," to name a few. The pamphlet was not an exercise in sexual muckraking, but in the footnotes Heywood cited reports of sexual misconduct and detailed various methods of birth control—and these resulted in Bennett's indictment. Like so many nineteenth-century reformers, Heywood's high moral purpose was unimpeachable and his faith in progress boundless: "My object in writing 'Cupid's Yoke' [sic] was to promote discretion and purity in love by bringing sexuality within the domain of reason and moral obligation."[10]

What is most remarkable about Heywood's pamphlet is its commingling of vocabularies from a number of distinct linguistic paradigms. The classical liberal language of natural rights and self-government, which originally articulated the relation of the individual to the state, was used to describe the individual's relation to his private passions and, furthermore, the proper relation of husband and wife within a region previously believed to be beyond the scope of such political notions as rights. While Heywood's continued insistence on "discretion," "purity," and "moral obligation" in sexual matters shows how deeply his thinking was rooted in the familiar grounds of the reticent sensibility, he moved into uncharted territory when he introduced ideas of "knowledge" and "reason" in this context. Whereas classical liberals and the party of reticence held the highest hopes for the emancipatory promise of reason, Heywood and his circle pushed the parameters of reform in directions unforeseen by their predecessors. They applied reason not only to politics and institutional life, which had always been a significant component of liberal thinking, but also—and here lies their innovation—to the most intimate regions of private life in the hope of freeing love from irrational taboos.

This momentary holding together of conflicting vocabularies shows the persistence of established paradigms even in the minds of those most committed to overthrowing the old regime. For Howells, the tenuous balance between customary reticence and the emerging values of exposure was especially difficult to maintain. In an essay accounting for the dearth of American novels depicting adultery and the demi-monde, he simultaneously and without apparent contradiction used both modes of discourse. With deference to politeness and good taste, he argued that the subject and tone of American novels was in harmony with social progress: "The manners of the novel have been improving with those of its readers." Because Americans lived in a democracy, they did not suffer from Old World vices: "Gentlemen no longer swear or fall drunk under the table, or abduct young ladies and shut them up in lonely countryhouses, or so habitually set about the ruin of their neighbors' wives as they once did." He was proud of this humanitarian sensibility, which, he thought, had reached its apex during his lifetime. Reflecting a cardinal faith of the party of reticence, he observed that the widespread practice of good manners and morals had also brought with it a civilized dread of the unspeakable: "Generally, people now call a spade an agricultural instrument; they have not grown decent without having grown a little squeamish; but that they have grown comparatively decent; there is no doubt of that." Yet Howells insisted that the novelist who "proposes to deal with certain phases of life" needed to exercise "a sort of scientific decorum"—a phrase that neatly combined his sympathy for reticence with his devotion to scientific method. (The phrase also echoes the language of sex reformers.) Howells maintained that the novelist "can no longer expect to be received on the ground of entertainment only; he assumes a higher function, something like that of a physician or a priest, and [readers] expect him to be bound by laws as sacred as those of such professions."[11]

"THE POETICAL LANGUAGE OF SCIENCE" AND UTOPIAN REFORM

The sex-reform project depended, above all, on the use of a particular sort of reason associated with science. By the last quarter of the nineteenth century, the prestige of science had given rise to what the historian D. H. Meyer has called "a disposition to restrict the range of rational inquiry, to limit, in other words, what we rationally 'know.' " Reason informed by critical observation, experiment, and empirical evidence promised to unlock not only the mysteries of nature but also, as Darwin had shown, the mysteries of all living things, including man. Just as agnostics challenged Christianity with the skeptical language introduced by scientific inquiry, so, too, would reformers employ this language to undermine common beliefs about intimate life. In an article in the *Woman's Journal* (1874), an early feminist complained that there had been "much false modesty—rising from religious creeds and from ancestral ignorance of physiology and anatomy." She believed that "when we know more of the body and mind we shall use the poetical language of science." ("The poetical language of science" is another example of the strange mingling of the vocabularies of reticence and exposure.) This faith in science sometimes verged on utopian fervor as when Parker Pillsbury, an advocate of free religion, declared, "No miracles, no mystery, nothing supernatural, nothing *unscientific* will exist, when Science her whole lesson we shall have studied and learned."[12]

For these reformers, unhappiness existed not because of limitations inherent in the human condition but because of social conventions that had rigidified over time. Consequently, many reformers rejected custom and religious injunctions, and appealed to nature as the only guide in sexual matters. Lester Ward's position in his pioneering study *Dynamic Sociology* (1883) exemplifies this approach: "It will be seen that all love is pure, since it is natural; for nature, not convention, is the true standard of purity." The natural workings of the body as revealed by science would not be the esoteric property of the few; they would be accessible to anyone who employed rational inquiry, which promised release both from the dictates of traditional morality and from the patriarchal rule of fathers, husbands, and priests. The party of exposure lauded not only the impartiality of experimental method but also the authority of the empirical fact. What Emile Zola said about the role of science in his manifesto "The Experimental Novel" (1880), could just as easily be proclaimed about sex reform. Zola quoted a doctor, Claude Bernard:

> "The revolution that the experimental method has brought to the sciences consists in having substituted a scientific criterion for personal authority. The strength of the experimental method is that it depends only on itself, because it contains in itself its criterion, which is experiment. It recognizes no other authority than that of facts; it has freed itself of personal authority."[13]

Scientific inquiry took center stage in Howells's controversial volume of essays, too. The very first sentence of *Criticism and Fiction* introduces the question that is at the heart of aesthetic judgment: whether there is "a final criterion for the appreciation of art." Taking John Addington Symonds's work on the Italian Renaissance as his guide, he rejected "sentimental or academical seekings after the ideal," as well as "momentary theories founded upon idiosyncratic or temporary partialities." Following Symonds and most progressive thinkers of his time, Howells posited what he hoped would be a lasting basis of aesthetic judgment on "the scientific spirit" of the "enlightened man," who can discern and apply "the laws of evolution in art and in society."[14]

As Joseph Wood Krutch pointed out in his penetrating study *The Modern Temper* (1929), this first generation of social reformers and novelists were hoping for "a society which placed no unnecessary restrictions upon emotional fulfillment . . . for an age in which men should love more freely, more fully, and more perfectly."[15] This, in short, was the promise that liberal society offered when it made the cult of domesticity, with its emphasis on emotional fulfillment through love and marriage, the primary source of meaning. While optimism and a refusal to face up to the facts of reality are charges twentieth-century critics have characteristically lodged against the party of reticence, there can be no doubt as to the highly optimistic and utopian tenor of the late-nineteenth-century party of exposure. Obviously, these writers did not believe that nature harbored mysteries that were very deep or dark, nor did they believe that the worst about existence or human nature could be very bad. Those who urged a doctrine of no secrets believed that the universe was made for human happiness and pictured the psyche as innocent and good or, at the very least, neutral and malleable. It is precisely this cheery optimism that distinguishes this earliest group from later advocates of exposure.

In detaching love and lust from their traditional religious and moral moorings, advocates of the scientific approach toward sex invented a realist language of their own. In the name of a purer and freer love, they demoted sex from the realm of mystery to the level of any bodily function, no different from eating or sleeping. In an essay entitled "The Shame of Nudity" (1878), the purpose of education in reacquainting the self with the wholesomeness of the naked body is celebrated: "Naturally no one organ of the body is more obscene than another . . . the exposure of no portion of the human body, *if one were properly educated*, would be considered obscene." Nowhere is this boundless faith in the moral law of nature more apparent than in Ward's *Dynamic Sociology*:

All desires are alike before Nature—equally pure, equally respectable. All are performed with the same freedom, the same publicity, the same disregard for appearances. Nature knows no shame. She affects no modesty. The acts which are necessary to the perpetuation of a species possess no quality which distinguishes them from those necessary to its preservation.

In an essay entitled "The Ethics of Touch—Sex-Unity," which appeared in the Heywoods' publication *The Word* (1889), Angela Heywood gave full expression to this notion of public address that takes nature as its model, of speech that affects no shame or modesty:

> Such graceful terms as hearing, seeing, smelling, tasting, fucking, throbbing, kissing, and kin words, are telephone expressions, lighthouses of intercourse centrally immutable to the situation; their aptness, euphony, and serviceable persistence make it as impossible and undesirable to put them out of pure use as it would be to take oxygen out of air.[16]

This ecstatic vision of a world in which all distinctions between nature and culture, inner and outer, private and public, shameful and sacred, obscene and prosaic, dissolve is most familiar to us as the pastoral. In the pastoral world, there is no shame, no modesty, no obscenity, because there is a willful disregard for the boundaries that limit not only what can be known about nature but also what can be known about other people and the self as well. The pastoral is a close relative to the vulgar approach to privacy: whereas the Dossons of the world are cultural outlaws by default—their sense of propriety and decency is so poorly developed that they lack the wherewithal to knowingly transgress conventions but are nevertheless self-satisfied in their ignorance—sex reformers are all too well acquainted with and overburdened by these conventions; they strive to forget and thereby undermine them in what amounts to a quest to found a new Eden. "The sentiment of shame in general," Ward insisted, "had no existence until there had been established fixed customs. Shame itself, a wider term than modesty, is simply regret at having violated a custom."[17] And the spirit that animates the sex radicals is distinct from that of purveyors of published gossip and their hungry audience, who want to demolish privacy the better to proclaim that everyone is the same under the skin. Yet the sensibilities of all three share much: a lack of awareness that intimate affairs, because of their frailty, cannot withstand the pressures of publicity; incomprehension that compromising anecdotes can only make sense in the larger context of a person's life story; and the naïve, misguided conclusion that all concerns for privacy signal efforts to cover up wrongdoing. And it is precisely the one-dimensionality of their approach to privacy, their lack of imagination about the tangled motives that complicate life and provide it with tragic potential, that lend these types their unflappable sense of confidence and moral superiority.

While Howells was always reticent about sexual intimacy and no doubt would have been stunned by Angela Heywood's plain speech and Ward's iconoclasm, he nevertheless shared their desire to dethrone love from its overly exalted position and put it in a more ordinary place. His target was the sentimental, romantic, and melodramatic novelists who were crowding the world with books spiced with improbable and sensational love stories.[18] In a favorable review of Frank Norris's controversial *McTeague* (1899), however, Howells's dual allegiance to reticence and exposure was once again put to the test. While he praised "the great original power" of Norris's portrait of the "squalid and cruel and vile and hateful" aspects of life, he also faulted its want of "spiritual light and air." He questioned whether there might be limits to the literary exposure he had been championing: *McTeague* raised the issue of "whether we shall keep to the bounds of the provincial proprieties, or shall include within the imperial territory of our fiction the passions and the motives of the savage world which underlies as well as environs civilization." Norris's strength as a novelist, Howells insisted, was that he forced the reader to face up to "the hypocrisies which the old-fashioned ideal of the novel involved." Yet Howells also spoke of the need to preserve some hypocrisies—which he equated with propriety, decency, and morals —in the name of civilized society. Pondering how much artifice a society required before it would degenerate into "a tissue of hypocrisies"—and at the same time never losing sight of the necessity of *not* drawing too much attention to the frailer aspects of life—he tried to keep an open mind:

> But society, as we have it, is a tissue of hypocrisies, beginning with the clothes in which we hide our nakedness, and we have to ask ourselves how far we shall part with them at [Norris's] demand. The hypocrisies are the proprieties, the decencies, the morals; they are by no means altogether bad; they are, perhaps, the beginning of civilization; but whether they should be the end of it is another affair.[19]

As we have seen, the more extreme advocates of exposure like Lester Ward, Moses Harman, and the Heywoods believed that social conventions were only and always hypocrisies and that the road to freedom lay in exposing them through plain speech. Still, reformers who dared to speak openly about sex nevertheless felt compelled to justify their seeming brazenness. They calculated a new equation, assuring their audiences that the truth gained from scientific discoveries would more than compensate for any loss of delicacy or embarrassment. Even the bold Lester Ward was cautious in introducing the subject of "the science of reproduction": "Before proceeding further with this part of the discussion, deference to established customs constrains me to offer to the reader all the apology in my power for its introduction." Describing the innovation of his task, Ward insisted on the exceptionality of scientific language: "Science has never found it possible to defer to the prevalent sentiments of delicacy which are properly recognized in all the departments of literature proper. . . . All truth is proper and dignified. *Quicquid essentia dignum est, id etiam scientia dignum.*"[20]

Employing this same strategy, the defense in *United States* v. *Bennett* (1879) did not deny the shocking style or controversial subject matter of Heywood's *Cupid's Yokes*. Instead, they argued that consideration of the author's intention as a social reformer and of the larger context in the work would demonstrate that his language could not properly be construed as obscene:

> [Although] some of the words and sentences used may be from certain points of view, and generally, immodest, indelicate, impolite, unbecoming, blasphemous, irreligious, immoral, and bad in their influence upon society, . . . the whole scope of the essay and the purpose and the intent of the author must be considered, before it is found that the words and sentences claimed to be objectionable bring it within the meaning and purpose of the law.

The language and style of *Cupid's Yokes* were part of a well-established reform genre, the defense insisted, which exempted it from conventional standards of obscenity: "Where words might otherwise be obscene or indecent are used in good faith, in social polemics, philosophical writings, serious arguments, or for any scientific purposes, and are not thrust forward wantonly, or for the purpose of exciting lust or disgust, they are justified by the object of their use."[21]

Undergirding this position was the belief that intimate subjects, which are liable to evoke shame when exposed in public, shed their obscene associations when put forward in the name of intellectual, social, or moral progress. This was the largely unspoken presupposition of the new mass-circulation newspapers, though profit was more often the motive force behind them. And this belief was also offered, as we shall see, as the basis of artistic progress. The willingness to distinguish between material deemed educational and material deemed obscene—that is, to make distinctions between subject matter and value judgment—is one of the most reliable markers of the great divide separating Victorians and moderns. While this capacity is such a commonplace in modern thought as to seem completely unremarkable, only a few renegades possessed it a century ago. And when they used the public mails to distribute material they sincerely believed to be educational, they were invariably found guilty of distributing obscenity. It did not matter that the language was scientific or clinical or that the author's intent was educational and uplifting. For the party of reticence, sex-reform literature was obscene because it exposed experiences that could have meaning only in private, and in so doing, not only coarsened the tone of public conversation but polluted the public atmosphere.

The reticent sensibility was inscribed into American law both in the Comstock Act and in the legal test for obscenity imported from the English landmark decision *Regina* v. *Hicklin* (1868). The trial in the English case had centered on whether a pamphlet entitled *The Confessional Unmasked: Showing the Depravity of the Roman Priesthood, the Iniquity of the Confessional, and the Questions Put to Females in Confession* should be censored. The pamphlet detailed actual seductions of women during confession and the court found it obscene for this reason. The determination, which in the United States came to be known as the Hicklin Test, hinged upon "whether the tendency of the matter charged as obscenity is to deprave and corrupt the morals of those whose minds are open to such influences, and into whose hands a publication of the sort may fall."[22] Even though American obscenity law was deeply concerned with public pollution and threats to public standards of taste and morality—in short, the public good—the Hicklin Test gave priority to individual morality in making determinations of obscenity.

In the trial of Heywood's *Cupid's Yokes*, Judge Blatchford found against the defendant, and insisted that neither the intent of the author nor the context of the passage was relevant: "The question is, whether this man mailed an obscene book; not why he mailed it." Following the Hicklin Test, the only point of determination was the consequences of obscenity:

> An argument has been made here to show you that Mr. Heywood was a moral man, a well-behaved man, and that his design in publishing this work was a good one, that he really believed the doctrines which he taught. But the Court say to you, that, such an argument cannot be received and considered by you, and cannot make any difference in the question of guilt or innocence.[23]

In 1891, in another important case, Moses Harman was found guilty of obscenity for publishing shocking personal histories and confessions of sexual misconduct in his journal. Harman had published a letter from a New York doctor explicitly detailing sexual perversions which he had seen and treated during his career. The letter, according to the court transcript, related the "practice of abuses of women by their husbands in coercive cohabitation; of family habits of men, boys, and girls, gratifying an unnameable propensity of the father; and the unnatural intercourse between a man and beasts."[24] The reader of Dr. O'Neill's actual letter is confronted by a vivid depiction of marital rape in the first case, incestuous homosexual practices in the second, and bestiality in the third—each described with an aura of scientific detachment though replete with sensational details.

During the trial, the defense, as in *Bennett*, raised the question of Harman's intentions and the context of the alleged obscenity, but the court flatly rejected motive as having any bearing on the case, though the judge did not deny the legitimacy of public discussions about sexual relations. He made the distinction between instruction and seduction paramount: "The problem of population, and other questions of social ethics and the sexual relations, may be publicly discussed on such a high plane of philosophy, thought, and fitness of language as to make it legally unexceptional. They may be discussed so as to be plain, yet chaste, so as to be instructive and corrective, without being coarse, vulgar, or seductive." Where Harman went wrong, according to the judge, was in publishing a piece in which the "low plane of indecent illustrations and grossness of expression" as well as its "bluntness of speech and baldness of immodesty" had plunged it into the baseness of obscenity. Annie L. Diggs, editorialist for one of the leading papers of the Populist Party, the *Topeka Advocate*, and former co-editor with Harman of the *Kansas Liberal*, also condemned Harman's publication and for the same reasons. She charged that *Lucifer*'s "constant parade of obscenity in a publication designed for miscellaneous distribution among the people, in our opinion oversteps the bounds of educational necessity and propriety, and panders to the passions of the vulgar instead of improving the morals of the masses."[25]

As these trials show, the distinction between moral uplift and pandering, scientific truth and obscenity, was not clear-cut. Four decades later, with the judicial vindication of *The Sex Side of Life* by the birth-control leader Mary Ware Dennett (*United States* v. *Dennett*, 1930), the belief that scientific truth in the service of education, social reform, or progress justified and compensated for any breach in propriety became the common wisdom. But in the intervening years, saying shocking things in public became a badge of courage, not only for birth-control advocates like Margaret Sanger and Emma Goldman but also for successive generations of avant-garde writers, artists, and their champions. Howells's confidence in the infallibility of "the scientific spirit" in fiction is an early and tamer example of this argument. For Howells, the only measure of excellence was fidelity to truth: "Is it true?—true to the motives, the impulses, the principles that shape the life of actual men and women?" Out of this criterion —for which he provided no further argument—sprang his definition of realism: "Realism is nothing more and nothing less than the truthful treatment of material."[26]

This appreciation of fiction that portrayed the truth about "men and women as they are" was to have radical implications not only for the future of the novel, but also for the future of American culture and public conversation. While Howells's quest for truth was tempered by his lingering attachment to reticence and his staunch faith in a democratic metaphysics (which I will presently discuss), his doctrines were later overextended to justify increasingly explicit and extreme representations of sex and violence—from Henry Miller's novels in the 1950s to Robert Mapplethorpe's photographs in our own time. In his essay "Novel-Writing and Novel-Reading, an Impersonal Explanation" (1899), Howells initiated a line of reasoning that would later prove uncontainable: "The truth may be indecent, but it cannot be vicious, it can never corrupt or deprave, and I should say this in defense of the grossest material honestly treated in modern novels as against the painted and perfumed meretriciousness of the novels that went before them." Howells pressed candor in the name of truth even further: "Let us know with [the novel's] help what we are and where we are. Let all the hidden things be brought into the sun, and let every day be the day of judgment. If the sermon cannot any longer serve this end, let the novel do it."[27]

The urgent task for realist fiction to tell the truth about life was, for Howells, above all related to the moral and political imperatives of exposing the truth about the "victims" of society—not only the poor, "the hungry, the houseless, the ragged" but also the rich, "cursed with the aimlessness, the satiety, the despair of wealth, wasting their lives in a fool's paradise of shows and semblances, with nothing real but the misery that comes of insincerity and selfishness."[28] The truth thus exposed would move good people to act in the name of justice. Writing realistically and changing the world were part of the same imperative, as the commitment to political action on the part of dedicated realists like Howells, Tolstoy, and Zola shows. In its tutelary role, realist fiction was no different from muckraking journalism that exposed corruption and hypocrisy, or from sex-education pamphlets that guided people through the mysteries of sex. Here we see that the strongest suit of the party of exposure was its claim that, by speaking in public about matters that had previously been unarticulated, they were improving the quality of both individual and social life.

THE MARKETPLACE AS THE DEMOCRATIC STANDARD

Sex reformers and champions of realist fiction had far more in common with one another than they did with prying journalists, though they shared enough common ground so that the party of reticence responded to each in precisely the same way. All three linked their respective endeavors with the extension of democracy. The promoters of the new journalism, for instance, argued that because a democracy was made up of common people, traditional news stories about the upper echelons of society were out of step with the times. O. B. Frothingham made it a difference between the old world and the new: "Foreigners are shocked at our system of interviewing, as they would naturally be, not being democratic." And he assumed a balance-sheet approach to exposure, chalking it up as one of the inconveniences of life in a democracy:

> The Englishman's house is his castle, the American's is the place where he permanently stays. We have no castles. The latch-string hangs out. The American lives out of doors. If he does not like it, he must learn to, for it is his privilege, and he should endeavor to give it welcome, bearing its burden while grateful for its advantages.

Another defender of the new journalism made the point—repeated endlessly into our own day—that journalistic excesses were the price that must be paid for democracy:

> We are aware that entire liberty of the press, especially in a democracy like ours, must run into license. But, if we restrict it, a greater evil results; and, rather than it should be shackled in the least, we are willing that its freedom should be carried to extremes.[29]

Another related claim was that mass-circulation papers were inherently more democratic than genteel ones, since they satisfied the demand for all kinds of news captured by the phrase "the public wants to know." In *The Reverberator*, James painted an unforgettable portrait of the journalist's enthusiastic embrace of this position when George Flack expresses his ambitions to Francie Dosson:

> "I'm going for the inside view, the choice bits, the *chronique intime,* as they say here; what the people want's just what ain't told, and I'm going to tell it. . . . That's about played out, anyway, the idea of sticking up a sign of 'private' and 'hands off' and 'no thoroughfare' and thinking you can keep the place to yourself. You ain't going to be able any longer to monopolize any fact of general interest, and it ain't going to be right you should; it ain't going to be possible to keep out anywhere the light of the Press. Now what I'm going to do is set up the biggest lamp yet made and make it shine all over the place. We'll see who's private then, and whose hands are off, and who'll frustrate the People, *the People that wants to know.* That's a sign of the American people that they *do* want to know."

For Flack, privacy is an impenetrable wall hiding privilege, exclusivity, and advantage. Journalists of his ilk believe that "the inside view," by willfully overstepping the bounds of propriety previously accorded to superiors, helped to equalize conditions in a democracy. But democracy in this perspective has little political resonance; it is understood primarily as adherence to standards of mass taste. The question, What can legitimately occupy public space? is automatically met with the response, Anything the people want to know. This gave rise to the constant refrain of newspapermen and publishers of sentimental and romantic novels that they were simply giving the people what they wanted and that it was condescending to imagine that people wanted something else.[30]

This position was a commonplace by the time Howells dramatized it in his novel *A Modern Instance* (1882). In a conversation between the young, aggressive newspaperman Bartley Hubbard and the established, genteel publisher Ricker, Howells vividly sets out the two competing positions. Ricker insists that a newspaper is

> "a public enterprise with certain distinct duties to the public. It's sacredly bound not to do anything to deprave or debauch its readers; and it's sacredly bound not to mislead or betray them, not merely as to questions of morals and politics, but as to questions of what we lump together as 'advertising.' "

Hubbard responds "with a scornful laugh" that Ricker "ought to be on a religious newspaper." He boasts to Ricker that his ideal newspaper would include accounts of gossip, suicide, elopements, murder, and accidents:

"I don't believe that a newspaper is obliged to be superior in tone to the community," he said.

"I quite agree with you."

"And if the community is full of vice and crime, the newspaper can't do better than reflect its condition."

"Ah! There I should distinguish, esteemed contemporary. There are several tones in every community, and it will keep any newspaper scratching to rise above the highest. But if it keeps out of the mud at all, it can't help but rising above the lowest. And no community is full of vice and crime any more than it is full of virtue and good works. Why not let your model newspaper mirror these?"

"They're not snappy."

"No, that's true."

"You must give the people what they want."[31]

Giving the people what they want was also an article of faith with promoters of mass entertainment. Howells brings this view to life when Hubbard, drinking alone in a restaurant to forget his troubles, overhears a conversation about the theater:

"What's that new piece of yours, Colonel?" . . .

"Legs, principally," sighed the manager. "That's what the public wants. I give the public what it wants. I don't pretend to be any better than the public. Nor any worse," he added, stroking his dog.

Hubbard, uninvited, joins the conversation:

"It's just so with the newspapers, too," said Bartley. "Some newspapers used to stand out against publishing murders, and personal gossip, and divorce trials. There ain't a newspaper that pretends to keep anyways up with the times, now, that don't do it! The public wants spice, and they will have it!"[32]

The trouble with this allegedly democratic standard—which continues to be offered today as a justification not only for the most violent and sexually explicit mass entertainment but also for the most vapid—is that it is never clear by what authority producers of such material know what the public wants, and furthermore, why popularity should be *the* determining factor. More often than not, producers and distributors of mass entertainment—then and now—turn to the marketplace as the only arbiter of value. Just as the new journalist's envious spirit to lower everyone to the common denominator of the body was worlds apart from the more utopian spirit of both sex reformers and champions of realism, so in this instance, too, the link of sensational journalism with commerce places the journalist in the self-interested realm of profit rather than in the reformist realm of the sex radicals and realists.

In his scathing attack entitled "Journalistic Barbarism" (1886), William Bushnell demanded, "All the sanctities of life are ruthlessly violated by the 'satanic press,' and for what?" He knew the disingenuous answer always offered by journalists: "The people like news of this kind and it pays to publish it, it being the newspapers' business to give the people what they want." And he dismissed it as cynical, spelling out the dire consequences of journalism fueled solely by the profit motive: "The theory is unsound; the premises false. They are based upon the most sordid of motives and wanton disregard of all the amenities that make life pleasant and worth the living. . . . It is the 'put money in thy purse' doctrine without the slightest regard to the feelings or rights of others to truth, manhood, honor, or common decency."[33]

Critics were appalled by the swiftness with which the new journalists abandoned their obligation to keep the public well informed. Time after time they deplored the way journalists habitually excused their worst abuses by boasting of "their prodigious circulation and large pecuniary receipts, and their close contact with the practical business of life." The profit motive, because it had no attachment to principles, should have no role in determining what should appear in public. One critic angrily observed: "Money has no conscience, no honor, no patriotism, no sympathy with truth, right, and decency, and never had. It loves and seeks but one thing—profits. Whatever will make the paper sell, goes into it, right or wrong, true or untrue, slanderous or just, clean or unclean, it is all the same to money." Incensed by the implications of such mercenary thinking, another critic pointed out that if journalism were merely a "profession in which it is allowable to do anything that pays," then it was "lower than brothel-keeping or liquor-selling, for these make no pretense to respectability, while the journalist pretends to be a public guide and teacher; and the spectacle which he presents, peddling out moral precepts with one hand and scandal, vulgar gossip, and family secrets with the other, is most revolting." He made the familiar point that in this respect the new journalism was no different from obscenity: "The argument that it pays, because people want it, covers equally well the printing and selling of obscene books and pictures. That sort of trade pays so well that it is necessary to prohibit it by strict penal laws."[34]

Much to the dismay of serious novelists like Howells and James, the standard of the marketplace determined not just the news that was printed but the books, too. In a penetrating analysis of the author's uneasy relation to the marketplace, "The Man of Letters as a Man of Business" (1893), Howells recounted the changed condition of the writer since the Civil War, when literature first became "a business with us." Once a market developed in magazines for the serial publication of fiction, authors of the postwar generation were free to spend all their time writing rather than making a living as editors or professors, as they had once been forced to do. Yet, with this newly won independence, the author found himself compromised anew by the demands of the marketplace: the nontangible value of his art was standardized and thereby degraded by a commercial system that set payment per individual word.[35] In addition—and this is where the commercial spirit of the new journalism coincides with that of the new book publishing—the merit of a novel was now to be measured by market considerations of salability and popularity.

THE DEMOCRATIC METAPHYSICS OF REALISM

In both sex reform and realism, advocates of exposure had something more elevated in mind than "giving the people what they want" when they linked their projects with democracy. Sex reformers, as we have already seen, sincerely tried to extend the Enlightenment ideal of reason to the private domain in hopes of making the love relation freer and healthier so that intimate life might better fulfill the high expectations placed on it by the cult of domesticity. They demanded public exposure of closely guarded secrets about sex as an integral part of their attempt to reorganize marriage along more democratic and egalitarian lines. Whereas the democratic impetus of the new journalism to expand the scope of newsworthy subjects was compromised not only by its decisively pecuniary cast but also by a vindictive spirit of leveling, the sex-reform project to make love and marriage more democratic by reconceiving sex in hygienic terms introduced unforeseen dangers to intimate life the more it succeeded: hygienic conceptions of the body tend toward homogeneity, and all too often the project of making sex healthy and clean risked making it commonplace and weightless.

As we have seen, Howells's critics often dismissed his novels as commonplace, finding the "ordinary lives" depicted in them too small and insignificant to merit serious literary treatment. But for Howells a love of the commonplace was the prerequisite for both the creation and the appreciation of a new kind of fiction that would embody and enlarge the democratic ethos of America. His insistence that it was the high value of the commonplace that made America not only democratic but distinctive—qualities usually understood to be in tension if not in outright opposition—left him with two related problems. The first was essentially aesthetic: how to create a new style that would capture the never-before-seen vitality and significance of the lives of common people. The second was more political: how to reconcile a high valuation of the commonplace with the long-standing charge against democracy that it leveled distinctions and tended toward conformity. We have already seen Howells's answer to the aesthetic problem in his tenets of realism. His answer to the second problem, formulated in a number of essays in which he directly addressed the enduring tension between democracy and distinction, is especially important: it stands as the most principled case for the claim that exposure is inherently democratic.[36]

Howells was perhaps the last American thinker to make the democratic metaphysics of Emerson and Whitman—which celebrated the presence of the whole in the part—the foundation of a vision of a democratic national literature. For Emerson, the commonplace swelled to cosmic proportions: "The near explains the far. The drop is a small ocean. A man is related to all nature." The majesty of the commonplace endowed democracy with the potential for grandeur, since democracy was the political and cultural expression of the common people. Extending this idea to the realm of art, Emerson and Whitman held that literature dedicated to the commonplace could not help being democratic *and* elevated. Howells heartily approved of the genteel critic Barrett Wendell's assessment of Whitman: "The saving grace of American democracy has been a tacit recognition that excellence is admirable. . . . The glories and beauties of the universe are really perceptible everywhere, and into what seemed utterly sordid Whitman breathed ennobling imaginative fervor." Giving these sentiments a more scientific cast in keeping with the realist method, Howells believed that the realist "cannot look upon human life and declare this thing or that thing unworthy of notice, any more than the scientist can declare a fact of the material world beneath the dignity of his inquiry. He feels in every nerve the equality of things and the unity of men."[37]

In a key section in *Criticism and Fiction,* where he bemoaned the popularity of "the ordinary English novel, with its hackneyed plot, scenes, and figures," which are "easy things to understand," Howells appealed to Emerson to ratify the American realist novel. Tongue in cheek, he allowed that enjoying them "costs an intellectual effort, and an intellectual effort is what no ordinary person likes to make," but he counseled the reader to become "extraordinary" like Emerson. The following quotation from Emerson immediately appears:

> "I ask not for the great, the remote, the romantic. . . . I embrace the common; I sit at the feet of the familiar and the low. . . . Man is surprised to find that things near are not less beautiful and wondrous than things remote. . . . The perception of the worth of the vulgar is fruitful in discoveries. . . . The foolish man wonders at the unusual, but the wise man at the usual."[38]

Readers who preferred an "English novel full of titles and rank" over an American novel full of ordinary people and everyday life, Howells chastised as complacent, dulled by a "weak and childish imagination." On the questionable premise that realist fiction could faithfully represent life, Howells wrongly inferred that people who rejected this type of fiction were actually rejecting the reality it depicted rather than the realist genre or his practice of it. Here he smuggled a problematic assumption about the nature of fiction and readers' receptivity to it into the less pliable world of politics: at bottom, he charged, readers who refused to embrace the common "in the good company of Emerson" had not fully embraced democracy.

It was in this context, then, that Howells introduced an antidemocratic idiom—which converts any objection to exposure into an attack on democracy—into the debate about realism. In its most vulgar form, this idiom was exploited by apologists for journalistic exposure, who professed that their gossipy articles were democratic because they were giving the people what they wanted and had the receipts to prove it. It became the native tongue of Americans who were suspicious of distinction in a society founded on principles of democracy and equality. As for Howells, he used it in the final section of his study as part of his fierce censure of novelists and critics who continued to worship at the shrine of romanticism:

> The art which in the meantime disdains the office of teacher is one of the last refuges of the aristocratic spirit which is disappearing from politics and society, and is now seeking to shelter itself in aesthetics. The pride of caste is becoming the pride of taste; but as before, it is averse to the mass of men; it consents to know them only in some conventionalized and artificial guise. It seeks to withdraw itself, to stand aloof; to be distinguished, and not to be identified. Democracy in literature is the reverse of all this. It wishes to know and to tell the truth, confident that consolation and delight are there; it does not care

to paint the marvelous and impossible for the vulgar many, or to sentimentalize and falsify the actual for the vulgar few.[39]

In this passage, Howells left no doubt as to the political implications of his literary doctrine. In later years, this argument was used, in more and more explicit ways, in defenses offered not only of Theodore Dreiser's novels in the 1910s and 1920s, "proletarian" fiction in the 1930s, and "political art" in our own time, but also of mass culture in general: to reject the common in culture was not only to be a snob and an elitist but, more menacingly, to be an enemy of democracy.

Another defense of the commonplace that Howells offered turned on his socialist vision, which valued equality, solidarity, and fraternity over the liberal principles of liberty, individuality, and distinction. Responding to Matthew Arnold's famous criticism in "Civilization in the United States" that "he found no 'distinction' in our life," Howells tried to convert this perceived deficiency into a democratic virtue. He proudly described the history of American democracy as one in which the people had been "building up a state on the affirmation of the essential equality of men in their rights and duties." The success of this project had been achieved, Howells coyly pointed out, with "a civilization in which there is no 'distinction' perceptible to the eye that loves and values it." This was not to say that political equality had so leveled experience that beauty and grandeur had disappeared, as critics of the United States from Tocqueville to Arnold to Norton had worried. Rather, Howells observed, "such beauty and such grandeur as we have is common beauty, common grandeur, or the beauty and grandeur in which the quality of solidarity so prevails that neither distinguishes itself to the disadvantage of anything else." No doubt Howells's commitment to Christian Socialism and populism allowed him to perform this sleight of hand innocently. Without further ado, he simply made the enduring tension between distinction and democracy disappear by declaring all distinctions subservient to "the quality of solidarity."[40]

Howells urged writers and artists not to dwell on differences that put distance between people but, rather, to learn to appreciate and portray what everyone has in common: "Men are more like than unlike one another: let us make them know one another better, that they may all be humbled and strengthened with a sense of their fraternity." If American writers succeeded in making the everyday world their subject matter, then, by Howells's lights, they would succeed in creating a democratic art, which, in turn, would distinguish the United States from all other nations: "The arts must become democratic, and then we shall have the expression of America in art; and the reproach which Mr. Arnold was half right in making us shall have no justice in it any longer; we shall be 'distinguished.'" This rather insubstantial solution gains solidity when read in tandem with the final section of *Criticism and Fiction*, where Howells grounded his vision of democratic arts in a society of non-degraded labor. Believing as he did that the average American led a relatively good life, he now turned his attention to the "vast masses of men [who] are sunk in misery that must grow every day more hopeless, or embroiled in a struggle for mere life that must end in enslaving and imbruting them."[41] In his concern for the dignity of the worker, Howells's vision of democracy reached further than that of his contemporary genteel reformers, who hoped to vanquish the ill effects of rapacious materialism and improve the chances for democracy by offering everyone access to a vast array of cultural institutions.

While Howells, too, put stock in the regenerative powers of culture—he has Bromfield Corey remark in *The Rise of Silas Lapham*, "All civilization comes through literature now, especially in our country. . . . We must read or we must barbarise"—his commitment to democracy, like his courageous condemnation of the executions of the Haymarket anarchists, set him apart from most of his contemporaries. He hoped to spread the teachings of John Ruskin and William Morris—that art could not be separated from work without doing terrible harm to work, leisure, and art itself, that art "perceives that to take itself from the many and leave them no joy in their work, and to give itself to the few whom it can bring no joy in their idleness, is an error that kills." Developing the political significance of this argument, Howells declared, "And the men and the women who do the hard work of the world have learned from [Ruskin] and from Morris that they have a right to pleasure in their toil, and that when justice is done them they will have it." From this call for justice, he made explicit the role of realist art in the fight for the dignity of labor: "In all ages poetry has affirmed something of this sort, but it remained for ours to perceive it and express it somehow in every form of literature."[42]

THE DISPLACEMENT OF CRITICISM
BY "PERSONAL ABUSE"

The best argument made on behalf of the emerging discourse of exposure, then, was that it advanced progressive causes. The pursuits of truth, higher morality, and democracy were so tightly entwined with the clearly worthy ideals of democracy and progress that they demanded immediate allegiance of all right-thinking people. From the perspective of those who valued reticence, however, exposure was almost always violating and shameful, no matter whether the language was scientific or aesthetic or the aim reformist and progressive. The gulf dividing these competing worldviews stretched so wide that partisans of each often abandoned reasoned argument altogether; sometimes fueled by frustration and sometimes by sheer iconoclasm, enthusiasts of exposure diverted their argument away from concern about the common world and resorted to personal attacks, ridicule, name-calling, and debunking. A number of distinct yet related rhetorical strategies emerged, one of the most powerful being the antidemocratic idiom which, as we have seen, construed any objection to exposure as proof of haughty disdain toward ordinary people. In addition, journalists, sex reformers, and realists insinuated to good effect that love of privacy signaled guilty cover-up—thus the accusing question "What have you got to hide?" They also increasingly stooped to caricature and outright dismissal of their opponents: not only did they theatrically unmask advocates of reticence as snobs and hypocrites, but, more sweepingly and damningly, they charged them with opposing that most hallowed of liberal values, progress.

Junius Henri Browne's impassioned rebuttal to criticism of invasive journalism, "Newspaperism Reviewed" (1886), exemplifies the style of the most dogmatic wing of the party of exposure. Instead of directly addressing the critic Condé Benoist Pallen's specific charges that the new journalism corrupted individual and social standards of taste and morality, trivialized private life, and polluted the public domain, Browne baited his opponent and dismissed his article as "more flatulent and convulsive than usual." Sarcastically granting that "a good deal is prodigally said by Mr. Pallen, in the old well-worn vein, concerning the invasion of private life of person and family," Browne maintained that he had taken "everything too seriously" and "exaggerated" both the harms and the influence of journalism. Pallen's worst failing was that he underestimated American readers: they "read more and more between the lines" and were not so easily "duped by editorial charlatanry" as Pallen foolishly supposed.[43]

Godkin's early analysis of the iconoclastic spirit of mass-circulation newspapers draws further attention to the way "personal abuse" was replacing reasoned argument and principled debate about the world: "Everything grave or thorough [the newspaper] stamped as 'old fogy' and 'fossil,' and treated religion and wisdom and morality and knowledge and discretion, and everything that makes individuals or states in the slightest degree respectable, as funny but transparent humbugs." Ridicule, scorn, and contempt were among the most effective weapons used to batter the long-standing authority of the party of reticence; and the repeated charges of hypocrisy and evasion raised questions about their motives and integrity. "A large class of persons," declared Browne, "babble and rail about the printing of gossip, murders, suicides, divorces, and the rest, though they are deeply interested in such things, and would shun any journal that should exclude them." Showing just how fully he equated disdain for the new-style newspapers with snobbery and with a hypocritical play for distinction, he complained:

> They appear to imagine that their pseudo-protests will yield them a reputation for refinement, sensibility, and superior virtue. There is an extraordinary amount of sham among newspaper-readers, notably among those accustomed to complain loudly and pharisaically about what they really relish and would on no account relinquish. Readers who actually dislike the sensational method quietly stop the papers that adopt it, and take such as are free from it.[44]

In the decades to come, these attacks would be charged with a kind of giddy energy that multiplied in the process of unmasking the alleged twisted psychology of advocates of reticence. Proponents of exposure took great pleasure in turning their opponents' own arguments about prurience and immorality against them. An early example of this powerful tactic is B. O. Flower's article attacking the officials who tried (and failed) to block the importation of Tolstoy's *Kreutzer Sonata*. Flower's slurs were of the type that would eventually prove irresistible to moderns committed to sexual emancipation:

> No greater enemy to society can be found than the man who would strike down those who are conscientiously seeking to tear aside the mask which is hiding the corrupting evils that are now eating into the vitals of society, and threatening the true progress of the race by producing a set of moral dwarfs, who see in almost everything, from a piano leg up to an exquisite statue of Venus, something *dangerously obscene*.[45]

These tactics and others like them have for almost a century effectively diverted attention away from discussions about the quality and character of our common world and they continue to hold sway even today when the mere mention of Puritans is enough to demolish an enemy. When, in addition, reformers and moderns insisted that to be against exposure was to be against progress itself, the argument had taken on virtually every contour of its contemporary shape.

Flower skillfully combined all the rhetorical strategies available in the discourse of exposure, resulting in a damning portrait of the reticent sensibility as enemy to all the values that inhabitants of modern, democratic society cherish:

> The time has come when it should be clearly understood that those who raise the cry against every book written with a view to elevate morals by a merciless unmasking of the great wrongs, the corruption and immoralities which are festering under the surface of society, are the real enemies of true morality, as well as freedom, progress, and equal justice.[46]

Howells, in his defense of realism, employed these same strategies. While his own portraits of the vacillations of middle-class family life by no means qualify as avant-garde, his insistence that an author be judged by his fidelity to the reality of his own time and "not in his proportion to any other author or artist" who came before him securely places him in the modernist camp. In his assault on his critics, Howells took the high ground of modernism, asserting not only that aesthetic freedom was at stake but also that progress was on his side —a strategy still favored today by "advanced" artists and their promoters. And he invoked the earlier heroic struggle of romanticism against classicism to elevate his own cause: "The romantic of that day and the realist of this are in certain degree the same." Aligning realism with "aesthetic freedom," Howells attempted to discredit any resistance to it as resistance to progress: "Romanticism then sought, as realism seeks now, to widen the bounds of sympathy, to level every barrier against aesthetic freedom, to escape from the paralysis of tradition." By these lights, to question the value of the new in art was to profess allegiance to the old order: "Criticism has . . . always fought the new good thing in behalf of the good old thing; it has invariably fostered and encouraged the tame, the trite, the negative." So deeply had this myth of the avant-garde taken root—even in provincial America—that Howells could turn hostility to realism into proof not only of his movement's importance but of its eventual assured victory: "Every literary movement has been violently opposed at the start, and yet never stayed in the least, or arrested, by criticism; every author has been condemned for his virtues, but in no wise changed by it."[47] In view of these anything but genteel sentiments, Howells's later reputation as the incarnation of gentility is indeed ironic.

THE BATTLE AGAINST RETICENCE WAGED FROM WITHIN

By the close of the nineteenth century, the battle lines had been clearly drawn between proponents of reticence and exposure over the pressing question of what should appear in public. The sex radicals had been legally censured, even jailed, and realist novelists had received only cool receptions, which suggests that the party of reticence, at least in matters associated with social reform and art, still maintained its authority. Yet that authority was being undermined not only from without but from within. The hypocrisy, snobbery, and artificiality of high society, as well as the nastiness and shallowness of its overrefined denizens, did not escape the attention of the most refined novelists of the time. Howells's *The Rise of Silas Lapham*, Henry James's *Portrait of a Lady*, and Edith Wharton's *The House of Mirth* and *The Age of Innocence*, to name a few, all reveal polite society as a minutely choreographed dance of shadows and phantoms. Those people who live within its beautiful confines, whose leisure has presented them with the burden of free time, are often depicted as selfish manipulators and rapacious consumers of people and things.[48] The others, whose fate it is to be manipulated and consumed, play their allotted roles gracefully, knowing that appearances and proper form will carry them through even the most compromising situations and put them in good standing with their wealthy benefactors. In these unsentimental portraits, politeness and refined manners are but desiccated forms, and reticence a tactic for evading unhappy truths about oneself as well as others. These characters know that their individual yearnings and desires must, for the sake of appearances, be sacrificed to the strict conventions of the clan or they will face ostracism, even while an unwritten code hypocritically allows their fulfillment in secrecy. For people not fortunate enough to be born and bred in this refined atmosphere yet harboring ambitions to rise to its Olympian heights, humiliation awaits them at every pass. No quantity of etiquette books, as the wealthy businessman Silas Lapham ruefully discovers, or number of business connections, as the Jewish millionaire Sim Rosedale quickly learns, can prepare them adequately for the intricacies and subtleties of polite conversation, elaborate table manners, elegant bearing, and proper attire that are the very substance of this version of refined living. Not that Howells, James, or Wharton were counseling the abandonment of this life. Rather, their wonderfully crafted novels reveal the many tensions inherent in that highly stylized society and remind readers that only the most disciplined character could save the exacting practice of reticence from being marred by conduct that was also rooted in reticence but had lost its bearing in principle, such as duplicity and hypocrisy.

The relatively easy victory of the new journalism, on the other hand, suggests the declining influence of the party of reticence in matters of so-called popular taste, especially when purveyors to "popular" taste could claim the authority of the marketplace. As we shall see, during the period 1900–30, the party of exposure would intensify its campaign and eventually succeed in discrediting reticence not only in the name of the social goods of progress and democracy but also in the name of private goods, notably individuality and personal freedom.

4

THE DEFEAT OF THE "CONSPIRACY OF SILENCE"

One of the foremost concerns of this study is to understand how the idea of exposure, which once had been equated with shamelessness, impudence, and impropriety, came to be celebrated as the premier agency of enlightenment and emancipation. How is it that the qualities associated with the reticent sensibility, once regarded as the very foundation of civilized life, came to be blamed as the root cause of personal misery, social evil, and impoverished national culture?

During the first quarter of the twentieth century, a new generation completed the project begun by sex radicals, realists, and prying journalists. A younger group of sex reformers, headed by Margaret Sanger and defended by outspoken legal advocates, joined forces with a new, "Progressive" breed of social reformer. Together they managed to turn the once-respectable social practice of reticence into a malevolent "conspiracy of silence," indicting it for deforming the marital relation and giving rise to a double standard of conduct, which, in turn, deformed society at large. At the same time, cultural critics associated at one end with Randolph Bourne and at the other with H. L. Mencken and a new group of novelists best represented by Theodore Dreiser went far beyond their predecessors in opening the public sphere to matters that had previously been thought to be unrepresentable. Just as the term "comstockery" had been instrumental in discrediting Comstock's priggish brand of moral reform, the label "the genteel tradition," and ruthless caricatures of William Dean Howells as its representative figure, would accomplish much the same task in the realm of arts and letters, making New England's literary culture synonymous with prudery, evasion, and hypocrisy.

This unrelenting attack on the authority of the party of reticence would result, by the beginning of World War I, in the invention of new cultural types representing an important consolidation of the influence of this new class of intellectuals and reformers: the polite, refined Brahmin man of letters was outflanked by rebellious Greenwich Village bohemians and Wobbly hoboes; the delicate, protected young lady bred for domesticity was replaced by the smoking, drinking, plain-speaking flapper who blushed at nothing and also haunted Greenwich Village. (The importance of Greenwich Village cannot be overestimated: it was both the actual home of many vocal proponents of exposure and the intellectual and spiritual home of political radicalism, experimental art, and bohemian ways of life.) The all-encompassing nature of this revolt can been seen in the extraordinary coming together of people with apparently little in common save their rebelliousness in Mabel Dodge's now-famous salon on lower Fifth Avenue. In 1913 and 1914, her meticulously staged evenings sparked fights between, as she described her guests, "Socialists, Trade-Unionists, Anarchists, Suffragists, Poets, Relations, Lawyers, Murderers, 'Old Friends,' Psycho-analysists [sic], I.W.W.'s, Single Taxers, Birth Controlists, Artists, Modern Artists . . ." Margaret Sanger, Emma Goldman, Alexander Berkman, Bill Haywood, Jessie Ashley, Elizabeth Gurley Flynn, Max Eastman, John Reed, Theodore Schroeder, Lincoln Steffens, Walter Lippmann, William English Walling, Norman Hapgood, Hutchins Hapgood, Marsden Hartley, Max Weber, John Marin, and Francis Picabia were but a few of the famous writers, artists, and radicals who visited Dodge's salon. "The radical IWWs, Emma Goldman, the anarchists connected with the Ferrer School, and many cognoscenti of the Salon Dodge," according to the historian David Kennedy, "demanded not only political but also aesthetic and especially psychological revolution. And the cutting psychological theories the anarchists constantly invoked aimed at one central fact of life: sex."[1]

THE RISE TO PROMINENCE
OF "THE NEW CLASS"

Nineteenth-century sex reformers had celebrated publicity for exposing evils that festered in the dark. This new generation of reformers went a step further: they now held society responsible for spreading the darkness. Whereas earlier reformers had used the metaphor of darkness to conjure a murky realm of superstition and ignorance that came with reticence, these younger rebels invented a new metaphor better suited to indicting an entire social practice and era—the "conspiracy of silence." By the second decade of the twentieth century, the assault on the reticent sensibility had cut so deeply that a number of writers sympathetic to it were forced to admit defeat. In "The Repeal of Reticence" (1914), Agnes Repplier acknowledged that "the 'Conspiracy of Silence' is broken. Of that no one can doubt. In its day it was a menace and few of us would now advocate the deliberate ignoring of things not to be denied. Few of us would care to see the rising generations as uninstructed in natural laws as we were, as adrift amid the unintelligible, or partly intelligible things of life." "A clearer understanding of sexual relations and hygienic rules" was, she thought, in order. In the same year, William Trufant Forster, vice president of the Social Hygiene Association, president of the Pacific Coast Federation, and president of Reed College, declared in a letter to the editor at *The Nation*, "The silence is now broken. Whatever may be the wisdom or folly of this change of attitude, it is a fact, and it constitutes a social emergency."[2]

Repplier and Forster each sketched a picture of a world inundated by discussions, displays, and representations of sex that earlier generations would have found shameful and kept hidden from public view. By 1914 such discussions were routinely taken up, in Repplier's words, by "teachers, lecturers, novelists, story-writers, militants, dramatists, social workers, and magazine editors," who spread their message to adults and children alike "from the platform, the stage, the moving-picture gallery, the novel, [and] the ubiquitous monthly magazine." She pointed to the proliferation of sensational news stories minutely detailing "houses of ill-fame," "novels purporting to be candid and valuable studies of degeneracy and nymphomania," plays and pamphlets urging eugenics, papers on venereal diseases, and open comment upon homosexual relations. Forster compiled a similar catalogue, and singled out the same group of social reformers, writers, and producers of commercial entertainment who promoted sex talk —"the plain-spoken publications of social hygiene societies," "public exhibits setting forth the horrors of venereal diseases," "motion-picture films portray[ing] white-slavers, prostitutes, and restricted districts," "problem plays concerned with illicit love, with prostitution, even with the results of venereal contagion," mass-circulation newspapers "with detailed accounts of divorce trials, traffic in women, earnings of prostitutes, and raids on houses," "novels that might have been condemned and suppressed a few decades ago," "lectures on sex hygiene and morals," and "fraudulent doctors" who take advantage of the alarm generated by the theater "as a means of snaring new victims."[3]

What is most remarkable about these catalogues is what they tell us about the dramatic change in both the kinds of things appearing in public and their means of appearance. The only items on these lists that earlier opponents of exposure also commonly cited are sensational reports of divorce trials and public lectures about sexual hygiene and morals. In less than twenty years the debate had narrowed considerably: criticisms of invasions of privacy and complaints against the banality of realist fiction—both of which had figured prominently in earlier indictments of exposure—had almost completely disappeared. Moreover, new experts and reformers, writers and intellectuals, and producers of mass entertainment had emerged, whom historians and social theorists have called "the new class" or the "professional-managerial class."[4]

The rise to prominence of the new class in these matters, however, did not go unchallenged. Repplier insisted that it was not "the nature of the information showered upon us to which we reasonably object, but the fact that a great deal of it is given in the wrong way by the wrong people." She took umbrage at busybody reformers—"ardent but uninstructed missionaries who have lightly undertaken the rebuilding of the social world," "self-appointed instructors [who] assume that because we do not chatter about a thing, we have never heard of it." Describing the spectacle of the "engaging Mrs. Pankhurst," who, during a performance of *The Lure* in New York, "arose in Mrs. Belmont's box, and unsolicited, informed the audience that it was the truth which was being nakedly presented to them, and that as truth it should be taken to heart," she asked, reasonably enough, "Who made the Pankhursts our nursery governesses and put us in their hands for schooling?" Exasperated by prominent women endorsing film exposés with "lurid titles about 'White Slaves' and 'Traffic in Souls,' " she demanded, "Why should these ladies assume an intimate knowledge of such alien matters, and why should they play the part of mentors to such an experienced Telemachus as the public?"[5] The story of how the public came to rely on these new authorities rather than trust common sense is, as we shall see, an important chapter in the defeat of the reticent sensibility.

Even though Repplier welcomed the end of the conspiracy of silence, she also maintained, "Surely the breaking of silence need not imply the opening of the floodgates of speech." She decried "the lack of restraint, the lack of balance, the lack of soberness and common sense" in the "babbling about matters once excluded from the amenities of conversation" and reminded her readers that "the well-ordered mind knows the value, no less than the charm, of reticence." In the same way, an unsigned editorial in *The Dial* entitled "Raw Material"

(1912) criticized the cynicism and naïveté promoted by H. G. Wells's brand of realism, while at the same time acknowledging that "English writers of the Victorian period" were "hemmed in somewhat too closely." Modern authors should not "let down the bars of reticence on all sides. . . . Reticence may possibly go too far, but no sane person can deny that there are ugly things in life that had better be kept in the dark corners of consciousness." In another article hostile to Wells in *The Dial* four years later, H. W. Boynton declared, "Heaven defend us from a return to the prudery of the Victorian regime! The nineteenth century was deplorably fond of playing ostrich." Yet, he confessed, "I for one believe that reticence, in life and in art, is a less corrupting influence than loose babbling. By all means let us tell our children all we can, as simply as we can, about the essential facts of sex. But it does not follow that we need introduce them into brothels, or even into our own bed chambers."[6]

"CIVILIZED" SEXUAL MORALITY
AND ITS DISCONTENTS

Writers who were unambivalent about exposure, who were certain that the conspiracy of silence was destroying intimate life and culture, in the end carried the day. In her spirited essay "The Hypocrisy of Puritanism" (1910), Emma Goldman castigated puritanism for warping intimate life: "It repudiates, as something vile and sinful, our deepest feelings; but being absolutely ignorant as to the real functions of human emotions, Puritanism is itself the creator of the most unspeakable vices." Similarly, in his volume of essays, *"Obscene" Literature and Constitutional Law* (1911), the free-speech advocate Theodore Schroeder also chronicled the devastating toll that "the infamous and ignorant conspiracy of silence" exacted. Following the example of Ezra Heywood's "awful letters," which exposed the dirty secrets of marriage in muckraking fashion, Schroeder detailed how "compulsory ignorance" could result in rape on wedding nights. In some cases, he claimed, this experience led horrified brides to demand immediate divorce; it drove others insane; and, at the most extreme, there were those "not infrequent accounts one reads in the newspapers of young women who commit suicide during their 'honeymoon.'" In 1916, Maurice Bigelow deplored "the time honored policy" of "silence and mystery concerning all things sexual" in his textbook *Sex-Education*, and repeated the standing indictment: the conspiracy of silence was a "gigantic failure because it has not preserved purity and innocence and because it has allowed grave evils, both hygienic and moral, to develop under the cloak of secrecy."[7]

Not only did the injunction to silence have the power to make intimate life beastly, extinguishing forever the promise of marital happiness offered by the cult of domesticity and, at worst, actually destroying lives; it also made the outcome of intimate relations burdensome and sometimes ruinous. The Comstock Act had made mention and distribution of contraceptive methods illegal, and champions of birth control such as Emma Goldman and Margaret Sanger repeatedly blamed it for large, poverty-stricken families and for the wretched health of countless women forced into a life of perpetual childbearing. Women made desperate by an imposed state of ignorance all too often resorted to unsound folk remedies or illegal and dangerous abortion procedures. Sanger decried "the hundreds of thousands of abortions being performed in America each year . . . [as] a disgrace to civilization. I lay the blame for them and the illness, suffering, and death resulting from them at the door of a government which in its puritanical blindness insists upon suffering and death from ignorance rather than life and happiness through knowledge and prevention."[8]

In this fervent indictment of the conspiracy of silence, one can immediately see changes in the language of exposure. Earlier sex reformers—who were, largely, on the defensive—felt obliged to apologize for using language ordinarily considered obscene but, they claimed, necessary and proper in the service of truth, freedom, and higher morality. In contrast, Sanger was on the attack. Not only did she feel no obligation to justify her boldness, she simply dismissed her opponents as exhibiting "puritanical blindness." Given the urgency of saving women's lives, private interests such as life and happiness began to take center stage as the most compelling reasons for exposure.

Individual suffering and death were also raised by another unspeakable phantom—prostitution, which Goldman characterized as puritanism's "most cherished child, all hypocritical sanctimoniousness notwithstanding." "Out of the unchallenged policies of continence, abstinence, 'chastity,' and 'purity,'" Sanger angrily observed, "we have reaped the harvests of prostitution, venereal scourges, and innumerable other evils." It was not only prostitutes and their patrons who were vulnerable to venereal scourges; unsuspecting wives contracted disease from their unfaithful husbands. Schroeder quoted the "awful words from a specialist of high authority" that " 'there is more venereal infection among virtuous wives than among professional prostitutes in this country.' " This was because prostitutes use "personal prophylaxis, and secure treatment after infection, while the ignorant virtuous wife continues to suffer in silence." This powerful new line of argument presented reticence as a social conspiracy bent on destroying the lives of innocent women, and a key role was played in it by the family doctor, who, as Schroeder put it, "continues to lie to the wronged wife, in order to protect her husband, and maintain the 'sanctity' of such a home." He set dramatic terms for the battle between reticence and exposure: "Will you by education help protect the innocent sufferers or will you through moral cowardice give silent support to the infamous taboo upon sexual education?"[9]

Abraham Jacobi, the venerated father of pediatrics, made a similarly impassioned appeal in his presidential address to the American Medical Association in 1912. In a frontal assault on the Comstock Act and associated legislation, Jacobi spoke not only of the important question of family size but also of the terrible consequences of habitual evasion:

> There is only one country in which that question is regarded with hypocritical sneers, and that country is ours; there is only one country in which a man and a woman must not think of framing their own future, and constructing their fate and that of their born or unborn children—that is the "land of the free."

Calling for an immediate repeal of federal and state laws that took the Comstock line, Jacobi made explicit what was at stake in slaying the conspiracy of silence: "personal freedom," the "independence of married couples," the "health and comfort" of families, and the "health" of the nation in that "the future children of the nation be prepared for competent citizenship."[10]

In addition to enumerating these grave hygienic, moral, and social ills, proponents of exposure described another very compelling kind of harm—psychological damage. Sigmund Freud was already a towering influence on this generation, and Freudian thought personally touched a number of figures central to this story: Emma Goldman heard Freud lecture in Vienna in 1895 and attended his famous lectures at Clark University in 1909; Walter Lippmann, when he was writing *A Preface to Politics*, shared a cabin in the Maine woods with his friend Alfred Booth Kuttner, who was translating Freud's *Interpretation of Dreams* at the time and who had been a patient of A. A. Brill; Brill, Freud's leading disciple in the United States, spoke at Mabel Dodge's salon at Lippmann's suggestion, and was both her analyst and Max Eastman's, as well as a close friend of Theodore Dreiser; Theodore Schroeder became a disciple of Freud after becoming acquainted with his work through G. Stanley Hall in 1914.

And it was Freud, himself a Victorian *and* a rebel against Victorian mores, who did more than any single person to elevate that most private of matters—sex—to the most visible and central place in his new science of psychoanalysis. His essay " 'Civilized' Sexual Morality and Modern Nervousness" (1908) is not only an important contribution to his theoretical work on repression, sublimation, neuroses, and perversions, but also an indictment of the actual conditions of "the code of sexual morality at present prevailing in our Western society." Contesting the reigning psychological wisdom that attributed nervousness to the unrelenting pace of modern city life, Freud offered the shocking thesis that nervousness was caused by " 'civilized' sexual morality"—"the undue suppression of the sexual life in civilized peoples." Absolute abstinence before marriage, lifelong abstinence for all who did not marry, and sexual relations exclusively in the service of procreation within marriage were the defining features of this strict moral code. And it was precisely the impossibility of adhering to these stringent standards, according to Freud, that was responsible not only for an ever-growing class of miserable people plagued by neuroses and perversions, but also for a hypocritical society that forces "its members to concealment of the truth, to euphemism, to self-deception, and to the deception of others." "The 'double' code of morality conceded to the male in our society," Freud observed, "is the plainest possible admission that society itself does not believe in the possibility of adherence to those precepts which it has enjoined on its members."[11]

Freud paints a dismal picture of a society whose severe injunctions cause its members terrible suffering at every pass. In trying to subordinate the sexual impulse of young men, society robs them of their energy. "Suppression very often goes too far, with the unwished-for result that when the sexual instinct is set free it shows itself permanently impaired." For the young woman, chastity and purity are so overemphasized as to cause irrevocable harm. Kept under constant surveillance, which retards her intellectual and emotional capacities, she is also kept "in ignorance of all the facts concerning the part she is ordained to play." This artificial state of innocence leaves the young woman completely resourceless at the time of marriage: "Psychically she is still attached to her parents, whose authority has brought about the suppression of the sexual feeling; and physically she shows herself frigid, which prevents her husband finding any great enjoyment in relations with her." From which Freud drew the ines-capable conclusion: "The anaesthetic type of woman is directly cul-tivated by education."[12]

For young people who strive for the ideal of purity, the long-sought prize of marriage turns out to be a kind of cultural swindle. Just as "civilized" sexual morality "tabooed" sexual intimacy before marriage, it also severely restricted it within marriage. These restraints, com-pounded by the fear of pregnancy, in Freud's words, "dissipates the physical tenderness of the married couple for each other, and usually, as a more remote result, also the mental affection between them which was destined to succeed the originally tempestuous passion." The ar-duous preparation for marriage ends, tragically, by destroying it: "A marriage begun with impaired capacity to love on both sides suc-cumbs to the process of dissolution even more quickly than other-wise." "Spiritual disappointment" and bitter disillusionment ensue, prompting men to seek guilty pleasures with mistresses and prosti-tutes, and women to displace their frustrated desires onto their chil-dren, making the mother "over-tender and over-anxious in regard to the child." Both kinds of compensation inevitably backfire: perver-sions in men and neuroses in women find new grounds in which to multiply. In turn, strained relations between parents poison the family atmosphere, overstimulating the child's emotional life and setting the stage for "lifelong neurosis."[13]

Freud's description of "civilized" sexual morality—with its excess of sensibility, fastidious attention to the most minute details, acrobatic display of interpretation, appreciation of delicious ironies, and exqui-sitely overwrought tone—marks him as a writer of the late Victorian era in the company of Henry James and Edith Wharton, though they were concerned more with surfaces and appearances, he with deep structures. Where Freud broke with them and his era was in his unblinking candor about sex. Philip Rieff has made explicit Freud's central role in transforming the previously respectable code of reti-cence into the sinister conspiracy of silence:

> Freud reversed . . . the usual conception: man's chief moral deficiency
> appears to be not his indiscretions but his reticence. . . . What is for
> Freud "repression," psychologically understood, is "secrecy," morally
> understood. Secrecy is the category of moral illness, for it provides a
> hiding place for false motives.[14]

While Freud was an astute critic of the repressiveness of Victorian sexual morality, he nonetheless defended it as necessary: "Civilization is, generally speaking, founded on the suppression of instincts." As a man of his time, he gave credence to the popular notion that the arduous taming of the sexual instinct steeled one's character by "strengthening . . . all ethical and aesthetic tendencies," and led to "a differentiation of individual character." Moving beyond his contemporaries, he made what must have seemed an extraordinary claim at the time: that the highest achievements of culture are actually the fruits of sublimation—"diverting the sexual energy away from its sexual goal to higher cultural aims."[15] With this breathtaking assertion, Freud succeeded in combining in a previously unimaginable way the two great preoccupations of late-nineteenth-century liberal society— sexual intimacy and culture. Whereas genteel reformers envisioned culture as an antidote to anarchy and vulgarity, in Freud's hands it became the fortunate by-product of the unconscious displacement of intense libidinal energy. In the extreme subjectivity of this psychological perspective, culture—traditionally regarded as a storehouse of the most excellent achievements and, for the party of reticence, a kind of substitute for politics—was on the verge of losing its public dimension.

But American enthusiasts of exposure frequently misinterpreted Freud as they embraced him. Lippmann, for example, whose *Preface to Politics* (1913) was filled with Freudian language, turned sublimation into a conscious rechanneling of antisocial energies, calling on reformers to transform boys' gangs into Boy Scouts. Cultural critics, too, often missed Freud's point, and went on blaming "puritanical repression" for enfeebling American arts and letters. American reformers were more loyal to Freud's ideas in their catalogue of nervous conditions stemming from "civilized" sexual morality. Sanger was taking directly from Freud, for example, when she argued that impossibly stringent moral codes gave rise to "neurosis and hysteria on the one hand; or concealed gratification of suppressed desires on the other, with a resultant hypocrisy and cant," when she criticized the way earlier generations had tried "to control, civilize, and sublimate the great primordial natural force of sex, mainly by futile efforts at prohibition, suppression, restraint, extirpation. Its revenge, as the psychoanalysts are showing us every day, has been great. Insanity, hysteria, neuroses, morbid fears and compulsions."[16]

This emphasis on the gruesome consequences of reticence—which dovetailed with the Hicklin Test's focus on the moral corruption of the most susceptible person in ways that would have surprised and appalled its supporters—marks the beginning of a new and powerful argument against reticence. These catalogues of hygienic and psychological injuries—along with the promise of their remedy through the "talking cure"—swiftly eclipsed the party of reticence's larger concern for injuries to sensibility, taste, and the tone of public discussion, harms that came to seem puny when compared with psychological suffering, but also harms that eluded objective measurement and therefore were easy to ignore or dismiss.

THE RELATIVISM OF MANNERS
AND MORALS

Theodore Schroeder's collected essays, *"Obscene" Literature and Constitutional Law* (1911), anticipated much that is still distinctive about the modern infatuation with exposure, down to the ever-present quotation marks around such suspect concepts as obscenity, morality, and purity. Schroeder was closely associated with leading Progressives and radicals at the turn of the century: not only did he found the Free Speech League in Albany in 1911, but he was also legal adviser to both Emma Goldman and Margaret Sanger in their advocacy of birth control. His book was considered so dangerous at the time of its publication that it was "sold only to libraries and persons known to belong to one of the learned professions." By the late 1920s, however, influential legal writers regularly cited and praised him for having presciently laid the foundations of the modern approach toward obscenity.[17]

As a social reformer and champion of free speech, Schroeder employed his considerable energies to discredit obscenity laws which he believed not only were unconstitutional but also stood in the way of individual freedom and social progress. But the furthest-reaching component of his work was his effort to wrench obscenity from its traditional position within morality and lodge it instead in the domain of psychology (though he wrote these articles before he heard of Freud in 1914)—a strategy that continues to be effectively employed today. His most potent weapon was to raise doubts about the very existence of obscenity. "All obscenity," Schroeder declared, "is in the viewing mind, not the book or the picture." Repeatedly he made the provocative claim that obscenity was merely the stuff of personal and social pathologies; belief in it was as irrational, superstitious, and tyrannical as the old belief in witchcraft. Standing on its head the conventional wisdom that obscenity corrupted morality, he asserted, "The 'immorality' resulting from reading a book depends not upon its 'obscenity,' but upon the abnormality of the reading mind, which the book does not create, but simply reveals."[18]

Whereas earlier sex reformers like Stephen Pearl Andrews and Ezra

Heywood had debunked obscenity by characterizing it as the fruit of "defiled imaginations," Schroeder displayed a nastier streak. Time after time he sneered that reticence was nothing more than morbid sensuality run riot. Sensitivity to obscenity—the capacity to experience shock and revulsion, which had once been considered the distinguishing mark of cultivation and delicacy—became, in Schroeder's hands, the very sign of pathology. Anticipating the later psychoanalytic theory of projective identification, he converted modesty and shame, which for the party of reticence were vigilant sentinels at the border between private and public, into evidence of morbidity:

> The emotional state underlying modesty and shame arises simply from a fear-induced application to ourselves of judgments primarily passed upon others. . . . It is this emotional aversion and fear, with the blurred vision coming from psychologic [sic] ignorance, which has produced such tremendous success for the vehemence of our moralists-from-diseased-nerves.[19]

Schroeder did his best to discredit "modern modesty" by comparing it to "milder forms of monomania, arising due to a lost perspective, imposed by perverse education." Instead of distinguishing between modesty, which protects the fragile aspects of bodily experience, and prudery, which so exaggerates modesty that it swells to prurience, Schroeder equated the two, triumphantly declaring that they both betrayed "excessive sensuality." Having linked them, he proceeded to demolish prudery, claiming that it usually comes "with a proportionately extravagant, fear-created, desire to conceal" the sensuality at its base, "all inducing violent emotion of aversion, either simulated or real." Anticipating Freud's ideas about denial, he gloated that if his own "theory is correct, we should expect that the most vehement denial of it must come from the very persons who feel that by our analysis we have uncovered the very thing in themselves which they are most anxious to conceal." Schroeder went far in stripping conventional morality of its authority, and in his caricature of "hyperaesthesia"—an oversensitivity to anything remotely relating to sex, such as the shock men allegedly felt on seeing a women's shoe displayed in a shopwindow—he put the finishing touches on what became a defining portrait of pathological Victorian prudery. With obvious relish, Schroeder mocked those people who "have their modesty shocked by seeing in the store windows a dummy wearing a corset; some are shocked by seeing underwear, or hearing it spoken of otherwise than as 'unmentionables'; still others cannot bear the mention of 'legs,' and even speak of the 'limbs' of a piano."[20]

Because obscenity was merely the stuff of sick minds in Schroeder's account, any law designed to suppress it was automatically suspect, based on "superstitious" and "moralistic" foundations. Time after time, Schroeder belittled obscenity laws as the expression of a "public conscience [which] feels the same passionate 'moral' necessity which once impelled judges to exercise their wits and their might in a crusade against witchcraft and verbal treason." And he objected vigorously to the overly emotional quality of obscenity trials: "The avalanche of righteous vituperation creates such a mist of emotional disapproval that the juror forgets or loses what little capacity he may have had for looking behind the question-begging epithets."[21] He urged a strict application of reason and logic, as well as a thorough scientific education in sexual psychology. A "scientifically exact yardstick" was needed to measure the effects of obscenity—a yardstick still called for today, though science has yet to develop one. Like all Progressives, Schroeder had boundless faith in science and little patience with those blind to its promise. It was this conviction that science could shed light on every question, no matter how private or intimate, that led him to formulate the dispute about obscenity as a battle between enlightened, scientific analysis and old-fashioned, irrational moralism—terms that soon dominated all discussions and were irresistible to forward-looking moderns in pursuit of sexual emancipation.

Enthusiasts of exposure quickly discovered that they could ruin their opponents simply by casting disagreements in these terms. By presenting himself as an advocate of the party of logic and reason, Schroeder could stack the deck against reticence as the party of out-of-control emotion:

> If the emotional predisposition of the judge is but properly enlisted on the side of the "moralists" of hysteria, we may expect to find that mere figures of speech will be mistaken for analogies, question-begging epithets will take the place of fact and argument, and mere empty verbalisms, born of self-righteous emotions, will have the probative force of a mathematical demonstration in the mind of the average judge, though he has been warned against this dangerous source of error.

Here Schroeder had his way with proponents of reticence because they were literally tongue-tied when it came to discussing sex in public. His characterization of their reticence as "mere figures of speech," "question-begging epithets," and "mere empty verbalisms" reveals his mystification in the face of tact, discretion, and decorum. Like all those who embraced candor and frankness, Schroeder interpreted reticence not as politeness, prudence, or restraint but as something malevolent deserving suspicion. The corrective, he insisted, lay in speaking the clear language of science and logic.[22]

Once Schroeder formulated the controversy in this way, it was a small step to pose the question that would eventually shake obscenity proceedings and all disputes about the public realm to their foundations. In an attempt to demonstrate the vagueness and unreliability of the Hicklin Test, Schroeder demanded, "Does this particular book really tend to deprave, and how, why, and by what code of morality is depravity to be determined?" This question shows how easily obscenity could be made relativistic and even trivial if its presence or absence was established by considering only the effect of words or images on individual morality. But, as early critics of this subject had made clear, and as the courts themselves noted when they refused to reprint obscene passages lest they pollute the public record, the question of obscenity also required assessment of the effect of words and images on the entire community. In addition, the ease with which Schroeder put this question reveals how deeply relativism had penetrated American intellectual life by the beginning of the twentieth century. New ethnographic studies—especially those of Havelock Ellis, whom Schroeder, Margaret Sanger, and Emma Goldman liberally quoted—detailed the sexual practices of civilized and primitive peoples all over the world and throughout history, and reported on the sexual behavior of animals as well. These findings delivered a devastating blow to the old moral certitudes: "Our best scientific thinkers," boasted Schroeder, "concur in the belief that morality is relative and progressive."[23]

By pitting the scientific claims of ethnography—that modesty varied according to "geography and evolution," for example—against the "intuitive" assertions of American judges—that determinations of obscenity were based on "common knowledge"—Schroeder dramatized the unscientific and therefore arbitrary nature of the legal consensus. The lesson he drew—that modesty and obscenity were bound by time and place—led him to conclude that obscenity was beyond the range of adjudication. This embrace of relativism launched what was to become a classic indictment of the vagueness and arbitrariness of obscenity law:

> Is "obscenity" a matter of sense-cognition, discoverable by unerring and uniform standards, existing in the nature of things, or does it exist wholly within the contemplating mind, so that every verdict or judgment is therefore dependent, not upon the letter of any general law,

but in each person according to his personal whim, caprice, prejudice, "moral" idiosyncrasies, varying personal experiences, and different degrees of sexual hyperaestheticism or of intelligence about sexual psychology? If the latter, then the statute is clearly void for uncertainty.[24]

In his eagerness to undermine the repressive moral code of his own time, Schroeder failed to accept the logic of his own relativistic argument: *all* law is rooted in the customs of a particular place and time, as it is codified in common law and in legislation, and it can never adhere to "unerring and uniform standards." This discovery of contingency was used by rebels as a call to arms against their hated Victorian forebears, but they might have reached a different conclusion: the very contingency and therefore fragility of customs, which preserve the best common wisdom of a people thus far and give life its distinctive moral shape, make it imperative to be discerning and sympathetic even as one is critical. Nothing less than an entire people's all too human way of life and its memory through history hang in the balance. But the crimes that could be laid at the feet of the perpetrators of the conspiracy of silence dictated a merciless policy of take no prisoners and an expunging of the enemy from history as anything but prurient prudes.

The Rebel Spirit and the Drama
of Social Progress

The relativistic frame of mind, which has made people then and since leery of calling anything obscene for fear of "imposing" their culturally bound values on others, along with the long-standing belief that free speech is the vehicle of progressive enlightenment and censorship the weapon of the tyrant, committed liberals to the side of exposure in controversies about obscenity. Even though the First Amendment's protection of free speech was, surprisingly, seldom invoked as a defense in obscenity trials prior to the 1950s, it was central to Schroeder's concerns, as the title of his volume *"Obscene" Literature and Constitutional Law* suggests. His dramatic story of progress was repeated with astonishing regularity by later advocates of exposure both in social reform and in the arts. Following John Stuart Mill in the argument that free speech was essential to the advancement of knowledge, that open inquiry had freed individuals from the tyranny of the church and the absolute state—"One by one advocates of mystery and blind force have surrendered to the angels of enlightenment, and every enlargement of opportunity for knowledge has been followed by the moral elevation of humanity"—Schroeder extended this argument into the private realm. He complained, "Only in one field of thought do we still habitually assume that ignorance is a virtue, and enlightenment a crime. Only upon the subject of sex do we by statute declare that artificial fear is a safer guide than intelligent self-reliance, that purity can thrive only in concealment and ignorance, and that to know all of one's self is dangerous and immoral."[25]

Schroeder self-consciously pictured himself and his comrades as actors in this magnificent drama and chided his opponents for being on the wrong side of history. Just as history had vindicated earlier radicals, so would it vindicate his crusade. He attempted to shame his contemporaries with the specter of future generations regarding their time with "mingled feelings of pity and scorn, even as we are so moved when looking back upon the 'Dark Ages.' " (When Sanger's sister, Ethel Byrne, went on a hunger strike to protest her imprisonment for distributing birth-control pamphlets at Sanger's Brownsville clinic, the *New York Tribune* observed: "It will be hard to make the youth of 1967 believe that in 1917 a woman was imprisoned for doing what Mrs. Byrne did.") And just as earlier proponents of exposure construed resistance to publicity as a sign of anti-democratic sentiment, so, too, Schroeder chastised his adversaries for condescendingly believing that ordinary people could not be trusted to think for themselves: "Formerly it was thought extremely dangerous to allow common people to read the Bible because of the awful consequences of erroneous private judgment, just as now sexual discussion and sciences must be withheld on account of the same stupid fear."[26]

Schroeder's position was characteristic of enthusiasts of exposure: they always regarded mystery as a temporary state of ignorance to be overcome, a roadblock to be removed from the path of progress. For the party of reticence, in starkest contrast, this desire to be conversant with unspeakable things was brazen. The sphere of intimacy simply could not sustain the kind of scrutiny Schroeder and his associates were advocating. To them, Schroeder's "angels of enlightenment," far from bringing about a "moral elevation of humanity," were spreading an unbearable condition of weightlessness throughout society.

Nevertheless, because every rebel believed that progress was possible only if courageous individuals faced the forces of repression head-on, every rebel knew in advance the role to play in this pre-scripted drama. At the end of the last century, D. M. Bennett, Ezra Heywood, and Moses Harman paid the price of imprisonment for flouting the Comstock laws. And it is at this point in my story that exposure in the name of reform coincides with journalistic exposure in the name of boosting circulation. These early rebels quickly mastered the secret of modern publicity: the more outrageous they dared to be in speech, print, or action, the more attention they attracted to their cause and to themselves. When Harman considered publishing the "awful letters" that led to his imprisonment, he was savvy enough, according to Hal Sears, to expect that their shock value might turn *Lucifer, the Light-Bearer* "into a paying enterprise and assure Harman a hero's niche in history." Harman believed that his fellow radical Ezra Heywood would compare him "to William Lloyd Garrison and John Brown, as well as to D. M. Bennett, whose trial and imprisonment 'boomed his books, made his paper a paying, world-wide power, and himself immortal in history!' "27

Victor Robinson's *Pioneers of Birth Control* (1919) and Margaret Sanger's *An Autobiography* (1937) each detail the travails that reformers bent on teaching women about birth control were forced to endure. It is clear from both accounts that a rebellious spirit, a desire to shock the bourgeoisie, and a willingness to challenge the laws, even or especially when such action could land one in jail, were animating motives of these "pioneers." Robinson used Jessie Ashley's provocative words as the epigraph to his chapter "Woman's Share": "Let us insist upon Birth Control now—even in the face of statutes, magistrates, courts, and jails. The rebel spirit is of great social value; it keeps the race from becoming craven." Sanger described the stance of her short-lived journal *The Woman Rebel* as "To look the world in the face with a go-to-hell look in the eyes; to have an idea; to speak and act in defiance of convention." Recalling her early Greenwich Village days, she remarked, "It was a marvelous time to say what we wished. All America was a Hyde Park corner as far as criticism and challenging thought were concerned."28

Sanger was an adept, if ambivalent, maneuverer of publicity. In her autobiography she relates harrowing tales of persecution—self-imposed exile; numerous scuffles with the law, sometimes leading to short stays in prison; and repeated attempts by the authorities to prevent her from giving public lectures. Not only does she present each event as a hair-raising drama, she also provides a detailed account of the publicity generated by her calamities. Here we begin to see the way the newspapers' commercial imperative to manufacture news— the more sensational, the better—could have the unintended consequence of endowing controversial causes with legitimacy. Whereas publicity surrounding Emma Goldman's espousal of free love and anarchism in the 1890s made it impossible for her to find a room in

New York except among prostitutes, Sanger's meticulous staging of "scandals"—along with her connections in high places—aroused public interest in birth control and made her a celebrity.[29] By the 1920s, publishing houses had also learned to exploit the "bad publicity" generated by obscenity prosecutions; they proudly affixed to books the label BANNED IN BOSTON, the better to boost their sales. What had once sounded a death knell for an author was converted into a lucrative marketing strategy. And this tried-and-true strategy has become a mainstay in our own time, not only of commercial mass entertainment but also of avant-garde art, which indeed has come more and more to resemble mass entertainment in its effort to titillate jaded sensibilities.

As Sanger reveals in her memoirs, she was well aware of both how she could use publicity and how it could use her. In some instances, her tone is triumphant. Describing the arrests at the Brownsville clinic and the commotion caused by her sister's hunger strike, she noted proudly that this competed with war reports for headlines: "Ethel and her hunger strike had been front-page news for ten days; in the subway, on street corners, everywhere people gathered, she was being discussed." Sanger came to appreciate that her opponents' repressive methods could be used to draw attention to herself and to the movement: "As a propagandist, I see immense advantages in being gagged. It silences me, but it makes millions of others talk about me, and the cause in which I live." And she attributed her unexpectedly large audiences to curiosity fanned by the press. In 1921, when she was forced from the stage of Town Hall in New York and arrested (on the recommendation of the Catholic archbishop) for holding a meeting "contrary to public morals," the newspapers reported the furor that ensued. The following day, when she was rescheduled to speak, more than 2,000 people were turned away. Her highly publicized arrest and immediate release forced newspapers to take a stand on her constitutional right to free speech, and this, in turn, lent support to her cause: "Even the most conservative [newspapers] were placed in the trying situation of defending birth control advocates or endorsing a violation of the principle of free speech, which 'must always find defenders if democracy is to survive.' "[30]

In other instances, however, Sanger's feelings about publicity were hostile. She understood its potential corrupting effects: "Now, I believe the three chief tests to character are sudden power, sudden wealth, and sudden publicity. Few can stand this latter; nothing goes to the head with more violence." Describing the police raid on the Brownsville clinic and her proud march to the police station surrounded by her terrified supporters, she took umbrage at a reporter who tried to engineer a dramatic escape for her: "It was fantastic for anyone so to misconstrue what I was doing as to imagine I would run around the block for a publicity stunt." And she was quick to observe that the press was a poor forum for conducting meaningful public debate. Controversy might give her cause "free publicity," but it was "of the negative kind." "The truths falsified and motives aspersed had to be debated, corrected, and argued away, and this took time from constructive work." She understood that modern publicity trivialized important matters, and concluded, "The press wanted to keep up the excitement and manufacture news, but I did not."[31]

THE NEW RESPECTABILITY
OF THE BIRTH-CONTROL MOVEMENT

In 1930, the battle over sex education landed in court yet again. This time it concerned Mary Ware Dennett's pamphlet *The Sex Side of Life: An Explanation for Young People.* Dennett, an artist by training, was active in organizing the first arts-and-crafts society in America. She was also active in the suffrage and single-tax movements, and was a founder of both the National Birth Control League and the Voluntary Parenthood League, the sole aim of the latter being the repeal of federal obscenity statutes. In 1918, she had written a description of basic sexual matters for her two adolescent sons. The *Medical Review of Reviews*, an organ of the birth-control movement, subsequently published it. The piece was so popular that the editor persuaded her to have it reprinted as a pamphlet for general distribution. The pamphlet included detailed illustrations of male and female sexual anatomy and employed clinical language to describe the development of the body, especially puberty, as well as masturbation, sexual intimacy, pregnancy, labor, childbirth, and venereal diseases.[32] It was widely and continuously circulated until 1922, when the postal authorities suddenly ruled it unmailable. Although Dennett asked the Postmaster General several times to specify which portions were in conflict with the Comstock Act, she received no explanation. In 1928, trapped by a decoy letter requesting a copy of the pamphlet, Dennett was indicted for sending obscene material through the mails, and her trial took place the following year.

Represented by the rising legal star Morris L. Ernst, Dennett was found guilty by a Brooklyn jury and fined $300. The trial, widely covered by the newspapers, raised a storm of protest. The *Detroit Free Press*, for example, called the conviction "atrocious," bemoaning "the fact that an intelligent and earnest mother can be exposed to such a sentence for no greater crime than attempting to give boys and girls the benefit of mature experience on the most important subject in life." That the newspaper could describe sex as "the most important subject in life" suggests the overheated atmosphere of the time. While the American Civil Liberties Union had not participated in the battles over literary censorship during the 1920s, since its focus was the protection of political dissenters, by 1929 this had begun to change. With the conviction of Dennett, the ACLU established a National Mary Ware Dennett Defense Committee to publicize the trial and raise money, and began to work in collaboration with Ernst's appeal on her behalf.[33]

In 1930 Judges Augustus Hand, Swan, and Chase heard the appeal in the Second Circuit Court of Appeals; in unanimously reversing the conviction, they forever changed the course of American obscenity law. From that time on, sex-education material was no longer considered illicit, and obscenity law focused, rather, on representations of sex in fiction and in the theater. In the decision, written by Judge Hand, the account of the facts of the case emphasized that Dennett had not been motivated by profit: she had published the pamphlet on her own for 25 cents per copy, which barely covered its cost. 25,000 copies had been distributed to many respectable agencies, including the Union Theological Seminary, the Child Study Association, the YMCA, the public-health departments of various states, and no fewer than four hundred welfare and religious organizations as well as clergymen, college professors, and doctors.[34] That Dennett could count among her supporters public-health departments, professors, and doctors is to be expected: more surprising was the support her pamphlet garnered from some of the staunchest opponents of exposure—the YMCA and clergymen. This new backing, along with the court's departure from the well-established tradition of refusing to print the contested passages for fear of polluting the public record, testifies to the emergence of a new social consensus about Dennett's brand of sex instruction.

In her "Introduction for Elders"—which the court admitted into the record—Dennett described the organization of the pamphlet around the four "sides" of sex—physiological, natural scientific, moral, and emotional. In the opening paragraphs she evoked the party of exposure's cardinal belief in the efficacy and power of plain speech in sexual matters: "I believe we owe it to children to be specific if we talk about the subject at all." "The proper terminology for the sex organs and functions" was necessary so that children accustomed to hearing them spoken of in "poetic or colloquial terms" will not be "needlessly mystified when they hear things called by their real names." Dennett was devoted to candor, but at the same time she was sensitive to the potentially frightening and alien picture of the body that such descriptions might conjure for children. She acknowledged that writers had once been reticent

> from a most commendable instinct to protect the child from the natural shock of the revelation of so much that is unaesthetic and revolting in human sex life. The nearness of the sex organs to the excretory organs, the pain and messiness of childbirth are elements which certainly need some compensatory antidote to prevent their making too disagreeable or disproportionate an impress on the child's mind.[35]

For Dennett, the "compensatory antidote" was not only enlightenment; the "unaesthetic" facts, she hoped, could also be redeemed by familiarity with the "emotional side" of sex. Drawing direct attention to the radicality of her project, she called for an open celebration of the "emotional side" of sex, a subject she thought other writers "persistently neglected": "In not a single one of all the books for young people that I have thus far read has there been the frank unashamed declaration that the climax of sex emotion is an unsurpassed joy, something which rightly belongs to every normal human being, a joy to be proudly and serenely experienced."[36] This "frank unashamed declaration" signaled a dramatic shift in modern attitudes toward sex, and many of her contemporaries undoubtedly found it shocking. "Love" or "lust," with their implicit moral connotations, were the terms most widely used to discuss intimate life. Nineteenth-century reformers, in their attempt to separate sexual intimacy from conventional moral values, had preferred the more neutral term "sex." With Dennett's mention of "joy," our modern-day obsession with pleasure and its techniques—i.e., self-help books with titles like *The Joy of Sex*—entered the discussion.

Dennett wanted to discredit popular notions of sexual desire as something to be ashamed of, to be curbed as much as possible, or to be rigorously postponed until marriage. By speaking candidly to children about these matters, she wanted to end the "civilized" sexual morality that made sex a duty and produced anesthetic wives and unfaithful husbands. Her unorthodox view that children should have foreknowledge of the joy of sex required her to marshal all her resources, resulting in a mélange of conceptual fragments from psychology, from religion, and, surprisingly, from the reticent sensibility with its emphasis on taste, restraint, and high ideals: "Give them some conception of sex life as a vivifying joy, as a vital art, as a thing to be studied and developed with reverence for its big meaning, with understanding of its far-reaching reactions, psychologically and spiritually, with temperament restrained, good taste, and the highest idealism." At her most innovative, Dennett argued in highly aestheticized language that sex was crucial to a good marriage, thereby placing extraordinary weight on the ever-vulnerable experience of sexual intimacy: "We have contented ourselves by assuming that marriage makes sex relations respectable. We have not yet said that it is only beautiful sex relations that can make marriage lovely."[37]

Just as adults guide children in developing "their taste and ideals in literature and ethics," Dennett insisted the same kind of preparation was needed in "the marvelous place which sex emotion has in life." Once again she drew from competing conceptual frameworks, from both the nineteenth-century language of refinement and character building and from the new language of therapeutic self-help: "Only such an understanding can be counted on to give [young people] the self control that is born of knowledge, not fear, the reverence that will prevent premature or trivial connections, the good taste and finesse that will make their sex life when they reach maturity a vitalizing success."[38]

This eclectic approach to sex instruction contained the seeds of many future unintended developments. In the years to come, the more sex was treated as a matter of "taste," as a private "lifestyle" choice, the more it was trivialized and flattened. Dennett's notion that one's intimate life may be regarded as a success or failure eventually led to endless public discussion and analyses, overburdening this most fragile and private of experiences with expectations that are difficult if not impossible to satisfy. The more people became obsessed with achieving "successful sex" *and* talking openly and endlessly about it, the more intimacy was to be stripped of privacy and meaning. As the party of reticence had always feared, the tone of public conversation was cheapened by free-and-easy talk of subjects that had once been approached with reverence. And, in our own time, we have learned that public sex education does not guarantee effective birth control, happier marriages, and public health: American society knows well the soaring rates of teenage pregnancy, divorce, and venereal disease, not to mention the contemporary scourge of AIDS.

After admitting Dennett's complete introduction into the court record, Judge Hand praised her pamphlet for warning "against perversion, venereal disease, and prostitution," and lauded its high moral purpose of arguing for "continence and healthy mindedness and against promiscuous sex relations." Nonetheless, citing precedents, he found her motives immaterial in determining whether she had violated the law. Like his predecessors, he used the Hicklin Test to determine whether the pamphlet was obscene, but, breaking with prior decisions, he declared:

> But it can hardly be said that, because of the risk of arousing sex impulses, there should be no instruction of the young in sex matters, and that the risk of imparting instruction outweighs the disadvantage of leaving them to grope about in mystery and morbid curiosity and of requiring them to secure such information as they may be able to obtain from ill-informed and often foul-minded companions, rather than from intelligent and high-minded sources.[39]

He concluded that the style of the pamphlet "tends to rationalize and dignify such emotions rather than to arouse lust." That he narrowed the test of obscenity to encompass only "arousal of lust" without addressing the public dimensions of the harm testifies to the distance the court had moved away from the earlier, broader understanding of obscenity. Even more telling, Judge Hand advanced the very argument that previous courts had refused to accept: "We hold that an accurate exposition of the relevant facts of the sex side of life in decent language and in manifestly serious and disinterested spirit cannot ordinarily be regarded as obscene."[40]

In the Dennett case, ideas, events, and experiences outside of the law appeared to supersede precedent. As a legal commentator in 1928 observed about the enforcement of obscenity laws:

> Nowhere are the courts more influenced by contra-legal currents of opinion which begin to flow at once, and with considerable vehemence, as soon as any question arises before the public. Nowhere, except in the closely related conflicts over free speech, do parties align themselves with such bitterness and such irreconcilable attitudes.

The Second Circuit's decision in *Dennett* registered this conflict in opinion, but also made clear that the authority of the party of reticence had been undermined once and for all: "The old theory that information about sex matters should be left to chance has greatly changed, and while there is a difference of opinion as to just the kind of instruction which ought to be given, it is commonly thought in these days that much was lacking in the old mystery and reticence."[41]

The vindication of Dennett's pamphlet, allowing "an accurate exposition of the relevant facts of the sex side of life," then, reflected a dramatic change in public perception. Shaped in part by the controversy over birth control, the new social consensus held that information about sexual hygiene was essential to the well-being of young people. It also held that the benefits of such knowledge outweighed what earlier generations had understood as the corruption of morals. As Judge Hand put it: "It also may reasonably be thought that accurate information, rather than mystery and curiosity, is better in the long view and is less likely to occasion lascivious thoughts than ignorance and anxiety."[42] But ignorance and anxiety had been only one component of the earlier situation; equally important were considerations of the inherent fragility of intimate life, the tone of public conversation, standards of taste and morality, and reverence owed to mysteries. These defining characteristics of the reticent sensibility had been lost.

In the struggle to destroy the conspiracy of silence, the party of exposure had compiled an abundant collection of winning modern values that left no place for such concerns. Since their argument against reticence came down to a simple choice between progress and tradition, enlightenment and superstition, reason and emotion, expert opinion and common sense, honesty and hypocrisy, sexual emancipation and prudery, urbanity and provinciality—in short, a choice between the modern and the old-fashioned—it is no wonder that many people sided with the party of exposure. In their pathbreaking book *To the Pure . . . A Study of Obscenity and the Censor* (1928), Morris L. Ernst and William Seagle employed precisely this balance-sheet approach. They had weighed, they wrote, "the advantages and disadvantages of censorship. The scales weigh heavily in favor of freedom and liberty. On the other side are deep-rooted desires for conformity, the censor's conviction of his own infallibility, and the obscene idea that sex is filthy and passion immoral."[43]

One of the key claims advanced by proponents of reticence—that repeated exposure to unseemly things blunts people's sensibilities—seems to have been lent credence by this turnaround in opinion. After fifty years of open controversy about sex education, birth control, eugenics, and population, many people apparently were so accustomed to clinical descriptions of sexual intimacy and its consequences that they lost their capacity for shock—which for the party of reticence had been the very sign of cultivation. This loss of sensitivity was precisely what enthusiasts of exposure like Schroeder had been hoping for all along. He had bragged that his "sex-sensibilities" had become "considerably blunted . . . partly as a result of my study of sexual psychology," and questioned whether " 'blunted sensibilities' are not a good kind to be encouraged in the matter of sex." "Who would be harmed," demanded Schroeder, "if all men ceased to believe in the 'obscene,' and acquired such 'blunted sensibilities' that they could discuss matters of sex—as we now discuss matters of liver or digestion—with an absolute freedom from lascivious feelings?"[44]

By the early 1930s, the defeat of the party of reticence was virtually complete. In her autobiography, Sanger confessed that she "could sympathize with an indignant old radical who left a birth control congress sniffing, 'This thing has got too darned safe for me.' "[45] The birth-control movement, against all odds, had become respectable. After the Dennett case, discussions of sexual hygiene and morality were raised from the illicit realm of the unspeakable. From this time on, obscenity prosecutions would be aimed at representations of sex in novels, plays, paintings, and, in our own time, photographs and popular music.

5

THE DEFEAT OF GENTILITY

The year 1930 marks not only the legal repeal of reticence in sex education but an important turning point in the history of American fiction. On December 12, 1930, Sinclair Lewis was awarded the Nobel Prize for Literature. The Nobel committee's choice of Lewis— the first American ever to receive the honor—announced that American literature had finally come of age. Like Judge Hand's decision vindicating Mary Ware Dennett, Lewis's Nobel lecture detailed the shortcomings of the social practice of reticence and gave authority to the new candor. Yet, where Judge Hand confidently spoke of the new openness about sex education, Lewis complained that American literary culture was still dominated by academic pedants who "like their literature clear and cold and pure and very dead," and by writers and readers who are "still afraid of any literature which is not a glorification of everything American, a glorification of our faults as well as our virtues."[1]

Lewis situated himself in the generation of writers that included Eugene O'Neill, James Branch Cabell, Willa Cather, H. L. Mencken, Sherwood Anderson, Upton Sinclair, Joseph Hergesheimer, and Ernest Hemingway. He declared that this entire generation owed its greatest debt to Theodore Dreiser, who was most deserving of the Nobel Prize. Theatrically invoking the myth of the long-suffering, neglected genius whom history would vindicate—Dreiser "march[ed] alone, usually unappreciated, often hated"—he offered Dreiser's outsider status as proof of his worthiness. Just as the social avant-garde canonized the rebels who risked jail in the name of their cause, the literary avant-garde also held the outlaw in the highest esteem. "Without [Dreiser's] pioneering," Lewis mused, "I doubt if any of us could, unless we liked to be sent to jail, seek to express life and beauty and terror."[2]

Dreiser's signal accomplishment, declared Lewis, was "clear[ing] the trail from Victorian and Howellsian timidity and gentility in American fiction to honesty and boldness and passion of life." This formulation is a variant of the position which pits the forces of reason and enlightenment against superstition and repression. For Lewis's generation, the revolt against gentility meant a revolt against Victorian manners and morals, puritanism, shallow optimism, "the happy ending," and England and New England as centers of culture. It is surprising, then, that Lewis used Howells's name as a derisive adjective since, as we have seen, Howells had been a fierce champion of realism in the 1880s and 1890s, and had been criticized for his boldness in representing everyday life. By 1930, however, a new generation of critics had amazingly turned Howells into the literary counterpart of Comstock, and Lewis could discredit the entire body of American literature that preceded his own time by ridiculing and misrepresenting Howells: "Mr. Howells was one of the gentlest, sweetest, and most honest of men, but he had the code of a pious old maid whose greatest delight was to have tea at the vicarage. He abhorred not only profanity and obscenity but all of what H. G. Wells has called 'the jolly coarseness' of life."[3]

The history of the victory of exposure over reticence, then, has at its heart the repudiation of one of its founding fathers, William Dean Howells. Even though birth-control advocates like Margaret Sanger and Emma Goldman had differed from their nineteenth-century counterparts, they nevertheless claimed the old tradition of anarchism and radicalism as their own. In *Living My Life*, Goldman paid tribute to her predecessors: "Neither my birth-control discussion nor Margaret Sanger's efforts were pioneer work. The trail was blazed in the United States by the grand old fighter Moses Harman, his daughter Lillian, Ezra Heywood, Dr. Foote and his son, E. C. Walker, and their collaborators of a previous generation."[4] A new generation of American writers, in contrast, renounced their literary predecessors. Where Howells was too provocative for his own generation, he was too tame for the next. This extraordinary shift in Howells's reputation introduces a recurring theme into this narrative: the logic of the artistic avant-garde demands not only an escalating series of provocation against the status quo but also an automatic rejection of predecessors.

THE NEW REALISM

Where the new generation regarded the polite and cultivated Howells as their enemy, Dreiser, the working-class immigrant, was their hero.

It is surprising, then, that Dreiser's earliest pronouncements on realism sound identical to Howells's. The realist novel as an active force of social reform was an article of belief for both of them. Justifying the candor of his controversial first novel, *Sister Carrie* (1901), Dreiser made a predictable argument: "If life is to be made better or more interesting, its conditions must be understood. No situation can be solved, no improvement can be effected, no evil remedied, unless the conditions which surround it are appreciated."[5] In "True Art Speaks Plainly" (1903), he reaffirmed his view of the cardinal virtue of art: "The sum and substance of literary as well as social morality may be expressed in three words—tell the truth." Honesty in fiction was related to moral and aesthetic excellence, for Dreiser as for Howells: "To express what we see honestly and without subterfuge: this is morality as well as art. . . . The extent of all reality is the realm of the author's pen, and a true picture of life, honestly and reverentially set down, is both moral and artistic whether it offends the conventions or not."[6]

Howells's contemporaries had differed with him not so much over the nature of reality as over his methods of impartial observation, but the younger generation took issue with his very notion of reality. They scoffed, above all, at his belief that American life was filled with hope and promise, that the average American enjoyed greater freedom, wealth, and well-being than his European counterpart. With this sanguine picture of American life in mind, Howells wrote the fateful phrase in *Criticism and Fiction* that his detractors would lift from its context and mercilessly use against him: American novelists were rightly concerned with "the more smiling aspects of life, which are the more American." The entire passage, however, is essential to understand the meaning of this much-abused phrase:

> Whatever their deserts, very few American novelists have been led out to be shot, or finally exiled to the rigors of a winter at Duluth; and in a land where journeymen carpenters and plumbers strike for four dollars a day the sum of hunger and cold is comparatively small, and the wrong from class to class has been almost inappreciable, though all this is changing for the worse. Our novelists, therefore, concern themselves with the more smiling aspects of life, which are the more American, and seek the universal in the individual rather than the social interests.[7]

Contrary to charges made by his detractors, Howells did not deny that America had its share of "purely mortal troubles"—"sin and suffering and shame" as well as disease and death—rather, he insisted that "this is tragedy that comes in the very nature of things, and is not peculiarly American, as the large, cheerful average of health and success and happy life is." In this same vein, Howells accounted for the relative "purity" and "innocence" of the American novel by invoking American exceptionalism, but it was a claim that sounded preposterous to the next generation of liberationists. Howells insisted that in America, "the guilty intrigue, the betrayal, the extreme flirtation even, was the exceptional thing in life, and unless the scheme of the story necessarily involved it . . . it would be bad art to lug it in, and as bad taste as to introduce such topics in a mixed company." The American "tradition of decency," when measured against the French "tradition of indecency," was "not only more tolerable, but on the whole was truer to life, not only to its complexion, but also to its texture."[8] But Dreiser's generation was mesmerized by the dark underside of the American dream, and obsessed with exposing the miserable conditions of what they claimed was the true American reality.

Insisting that any realism worth its salt would not shy away from representing the unlovely and tragic aspects of life, Dreiser opposed his detractors'

> quiet acceptance of things as they are without any regard to the well-being of the future. Life for them is made up of a variety of interesting but immutable forms and any attempt either to picture any of the wretched results of modern social conditions or to assail the critical defenders of the same is naturally looked upon with contempt or aversion.[9]

The charge of evasion, which Dreiser and the young rebels used to vanquish not only Howells but any enemy of Dreiser, is, ironically, a variant of the anti-democratic idiom that Howells himself had developed to discredit those who objected to his picture of reality.

THE AESTHETICIZATION OF REALISM

In the hands of some enthusiasts, exposure became a type of guerrilla action, and the modern artist a type of revolutionist. In an essay entitled "The Drama and Morality" (1914), Reginald Wright Kauffman exclaimed, "If it is right to tell the truth, every place is the right place to tell it." Infatuated with the power of realist representations to shake up middle-class complacency, he gleefully announced, "One of the first justifications of the great drama of modern times is the fact that it does disturb; that it does uncover sorrow, sin, poverty, diseases, and dirt; that it does show us the evils to which our eyes have been too long closed." For him, like many cultural rebels during the 1910s, the need to fight against "life as it is" was so pressing that nothing less than a wholesale redefinition of art and the artist was necessary: "If [drama] interprets life truthfully and dramatically, it is art; and if its interpretation enlists us in the fight against life as it is, it is moral. For the modern artist, the two things are one, because the modern artist is a revolutionist."[10]

The aim of literary exposure—social change—was becoming increasingly obscured by this kind of bravado. H. G. Wells—whose ardent embrace of "the jolly coarseness of life" had earned him high marks in Lewis's Nobel Prize speech—gave more attention to the literary act of unveiling than to its social consequences, demonstrating how effortlessly muckraking could sink into an aesthetic of debunking for its own sake:

> We are going to write about it all. We are going to write about business and finance and politics and precedence and pretentiousness and decorum and indecorum, until a thousand pretenses and ten thousand impostures shrivel in the cold air of elucidations. . . . Before we have done, we shall have all life within the scope of the novel.[11]

Leading literary figures began to praise realism for representing life as a self-contained aesthetic experience, and they no longer seemed so concerned with marshaling people's energies to change the world, instructing readers in the ways of morality, or rehabilitating fallen characters in contrived happy endings. These new critics and writers hoped to create a realm of aesthetic experience independent of moral values so as to enlarge the scope of art. Instead of appealing to taste, judgment, and sensibility, as nineteenth-century critics had done, or summoning good people to action, as social reformers had done, these writers called for a new kind of fiction that would be aesthetically coherent, truthful, sincere, and interesting.

Randolph Bourne, for example, insisted that "any real literature is . . . impossible without a democratic attitude towards experience." By this he meant that writers and readers must approach all the things ordinary people think and feel on the grounds that they are interesting in themselves, instead of consigning them "to a moral heaven, purgatory, or hell." He bristled at the influence of the nineteenth-century literary tradition, which he believed inhibited representations of complex, tragic, or unseemly aspects of life. "Our literary poverty is due to a sort of fear of the dark," he complained, "a dread of grappling with the stuff of life, which men and women actually experience—

their half-understood motives and feelings, the groping ache of their desires, their unrecognized bestialities." He dared writers to create a literature that would candidly portray people "living an interior life of struggle and feeling, caught perhaps in coils of desire and personal issues," a literature that would not shun "the irrevocable, the insoluble" or be afraid "of feeling deeply, or looking boldly at the obscure and sinister forces at the background of human life."[12]

This challenge to confront reality apart from moral values appears in almost all of the "advanced" criticism of the time, and it received its classic expression in H. L. Mencken's study of Joseph Conrad which appeared in his hugely influential collection of essays *A Book of Prefaces* (1917). (It is significant that while Mencken crowned Conrad the most accomplished practitioner of the new novel, he claimed Dreiser was his American equal.[13]) Quoting Arthur Symons on Conrad, Mencken set out the virtues of art disentangled from moral values. First, the necessary distancing from the material at hand: "At the centre of his web sits an elemental sarcasm discussing human affairs with a calm and cynical ferocity." Next, the requisite toughness: author and reader must display not only their hard-won capacity to witness human vices without recoiling, but also their world-weariness. They scoff at those who in naïveté or out of cowardice have not yet opened their eyes. This studied indifference to moral distinctions, finally, gives rise to the characteristic stance of the modern enthusiast of exposure—ironic detachment: "And in all this there is no judgment, only an implacable comprehension, as of one outside nature, to whom joy and sorrow, right and wrong, savagery and civilization, are equal and indifferent."[14]

The party of exposure had so successfully made this case that by 1915 Stuart P. Sherman, a prominent apostle of the New Humanism and critic of realism, could caricature it in a withering review of Dreiser that appeared in *The Nation*. It was precisely the author's presumed duty to represent reality, no matter how brutal or criminal, and the reader's duty to face up to it squarely that Sherman ridiculed. He laughed at the world-weary sophisticates' naïveté, especially their inflated sense of the riskiness of their enterprise and their high estimation of their own courage:

> Now, for the first time in history, men are facing unabashed the facts of life. "Death or life," we cry, "give us only reality!" . . . The critic who keeps pace with the movement no longer asks whether the artist has created beauty or glorified goodness, but merely whether he has told the truth. . . . If you do not like what is in the picture, you are to be crushed by the retort that perhaps you do not like what is in life. Perhaps you have not the courage to confront reality.[15]

Sherman's arguments echo the cosmopolitanism and learning that was at the heart of the reticent sensibility, but his theatrical style was more in keeping with the new brashness of exposure. That he felt obliged to employ the debunking style of his opponents shows how successful the party of exposure had been in discrediting the vocabulary of reticence.

THE RESOURCELESSNESS OF THE
AMERICAN LITERARY TRADITION

Once the new generation had redefined the realist project as impartially exposing the dark underside of American life, questions of literary style immediately came to the fore. Along with writers and critics, lawyers who defended controversial works from Dreiser's *An American Tragedy* to James Joyce's *Ulysses* to Henry Miller's *Tropic of Cancer* would debate which style and language were most appropriate for truthfully representing the reality of the lower classes and the demimonde. Where Howells's critics had taken him to task for using slang and idiomatic expressions, Dreiser's critics—and his champions, too—repeatedly noted the glaring inadequacies of his prose style. Yet because Dreiser's admirers found in him the promise of an authentic American voice, they forgave him his literary flaws. In fact, they went further. Randolph Bourne, for instance, not only forthrightly enumerated "his slovenliness of style, his lack of nuances, his apathy to the finer shades of beauty, his weakness for the mystical and vague," but drafted them into a defense of Dreiser's "sincerity." Repeatedly, he applauded this "sincere groper after beauty," excusing his sentimentality on the grounds that it "captivates you with its candor," and attributing the strength of his novels to their "authentic attempt to make something artistic out of the chaotic materials that lie around us in American life."[16]

Champions of realism identified this new style of writing with an aesthetic of unmediated experience. Whereas proponents of realism beginning with Howells had insinuated that any objection to realism was in fact an objection to the thing being represented rather than a distaste for a literary style, Dreiser's champions pressed this logic further: they argued that to accurately represent life beyond the narrow confines of middle-class reality, not only the content but the style of the novel would have to break with existing literary conventions, the implication being that the conventions themselves conspire to keep working-class and immigrant experiences out of the realm of the representable. This suspicion of literary convention led critics like Bourne to argue that Dreiser's artistic flaws not only reflected but actually illuminated the non-genteel world the author inhabited and struggled to depict, and that despite or rather because of their aesthetic failings, his novels deserved special dispensation. His many shortcomings, Bourne extravagantly claimed, constituted nothing less than the living embodiment of "the American soul": "Mr. Dreiser is complicated, but he is complicated in a very understandable American way, the product of the uncouth forces of small-town life and the vast disorganization of the wider American world. As he reveals himself, it is a revelation of a certain broad level of the American soul."[17] With this move, we see the return, albeit repressed, of the classical hierarchy of genres: if the subject is uncouth and disorganized, then the style, too, should be uncouth and disorganized.

Dreiser's autobiographical novels detailing his impoverished childhood gave Bourne the opportunity to censure American society for its inhospitality to artists "outside of the ruling class." "His hopelessly unorientated, half-educated boyhood is so typical of the uncritical and careless society in which wistful American talent has had to grope." For Bourne, Dreiser's poor, immigrant ancestry was an antidote to Americans' "tenacious cultural allegiance to the mother country." It was precisely this slavish imitation and devotion to all things English that Bourne blamed for the sterility and provincialism of American culture. In consequence, he enthusiastically embraced Dreiser's "conglomerate Americanism," embodied in both his flawed style and his unorthodox "themes of crude power and sex and the American common life." Both were an affront and an alternative to the English tradition: "His emphases are those of a new America which is latently expressive and which must develop its art before we shall really have become articulate. For Dreiser is a true hyphenate, a product of that conglomerate Americanism that springs from other roots than the English tradition."[18] Dreiser's deficient artistry was, then, more real, more authentic, more sincere than a highly finished style—finish meaning the lifeless conformism associated with the English tradition, and deficient artistry meaning the rawness and energy of those outside it.

Bourne also spoke for his entire generation when he charged, "Certainly the older generation is rarely interested in the profounder issues of life. It never speaks of death—the suggestion makes it uncomfortable. It shies in panic at hints of sex-issues." In his "Pageantry and Social Art" (1918), he ridiculed the prudery of the old culture: "A bare-legged dancer jumping into America of 1900 would have caused a moral panic," and complained bitterly of "growing up . . . in an atmosphere that was afraid of personal and aesthetic expressiveness unless it was carefully justified and decently clothed." He praised "Pagan expressiveness," claiming that it was "far more revolutionary than any other social change we have been making." For Bourne, Dreiser was an exemplar of "Pagan expressiveness," and thus he vigorously defended his candor about sex, which continually got his work into trouble not only with societies for the suppression of vice but also with his publishers and with the law.[19]

Dreiser deserved the younger generation's gratitude, according to Bourne, for "slay[ing] the American literary superstition that men and women are not sensual beings." His novels rose above the "sniggering" treatments of sex offered by popular magazines, and escaped the reductive psychological understanding of sex that "saturated the sexual imagination of the younger American intelligentsia." Bourne was sensitive to the difficulties of speaking candidly about intimate life, and believed that only one kind of expression could begin to capture the mysteries of love: "Sex has little significance unless it is treated in personally artistic, novelistic terms." But because "the American tradition had tabooed the treatment of those infinite gradations and complexities of love that fill the literary imagination of a sensitive people," he observed that writers who wanted to approach such matters found themselves resourceless. The only language available was the reformers' "pseudo-scientific jargon," but it was disastrously inadequate to the task and ultimately impoverished the imagination: "When curiosity became too strong and reticence was repealed in America, we had no means of articulating ourselves except in a deplorable pseudo-scientific jargon that has no more to do with the relevance of sex than the chemical composition of orange paint has to do with the artist's vision."[20]

Here Bourne managed to move the debate beyond the terms formulated by the competing parties of reticence and exposure. He argued that because Dreiser had pictured "sex as it is lived in the personal relations of bungling, wistful, or masterful men and women," he had "made sex human, and American tradition had never made it human . . . only . . . either sacred or vulgar, and when these categories no longer worked, we fell under the dubious and perverting magic of the psychoanalysts."[21] In this context, Bourne pointed to the promise of art to imbue fragile, private experiences with a distinctive shape and thereby make them fit for public appearance and thus he put to rest one worry constantly plaguing the party of reticence: that casual talk about intimate life deprived it of emotional resonance, trivializing and demeaning it. But his formulation did not take full account of the other part of their criticism, rooted in the classical hierarchy of genres: that to introduce subjects not large enough to command widespread attention or sturdy enough to withstand extended scrutiny degrades the character and tone of public discussion.

Moreover, Bourne's defense of Dreiser was marred by his overly sanguine opinion of the aims and motives of most American novelists of the realist school. While his ideal of a finely balanced artistic treatment of sex points the way toward a non-obscene expression of intimate life, it could succeed only so long as a novelist was animated by a humanist love of the world and not by a cynical debunking spirit. But in later decades successive generations of rebels and their promoters—from Henry Miller to Robert Mapplethorpe—claimed, employing the same idiom, that their representations of sex were realist expressions of life as they found it.[22]

Comstockery as Epithet

All students of this historical juncture have remarked on the vehemence with which the younger generation denounced their elders.[23] Proponents of exposure in the 1880s and 1890s had many words of derision for their opponents—old fogy, snob, hypocrite, dude, fossil —but it is striking that puritanism, comstockery, and genteel had no place in this string of invectives. This is largely because their battle had not yet taken on the character of generational warfare. Late-nineteenth-century critics were themselves Victorians, and it was not their aim to discredit and relegate to the trash heap of history the century of which they were a part. The epithets Puritan, comstockery, genteel, and Victorian made a sudden, explosive appearance in the opening decades of the twentieth century when a younger generation of feminists, birth-control champions, anarchists, free-speech lawyers, cultural critics, realist novelists, and Greenwich Village bohemians attacked their forebears for their refusal to engage life in all its complexity. By tracing the creation of these new cultural villains, I hope to recover what is arguably the most important chapter in the story of how reticence got a bad name.

Even though the man Anthony Comstock and the jeer "comstockery" have largely fallen from contemporary memory, in his own time Comstock was both powerful and famous. By 1915, the year of his death, *Harper's Weekly* declared that the name of Comstock "is known all over the country and over most of the civilized world." In 1917,

Mencken announced that "Comstock became a national celebrity. . . . His doings were as copiously reported by the newspapers as those of P. T. Barnum or John L. Sullivan." When Morris Ernst and William Seagle wrote *To the Pure . . . A Study of Obscenity and the Censor* (1928), they were confident they could dispense with a detailed account of his role because "the main outlines of his career are so familiar to the average American of mid-years." By 1955, however, when the journal *Law and Contemporary Problems* devoted an entire issue to "Obscenity and the Arts," only one contributor, Edward De Grazia, mentioned Comstock, and then as an adjective: he equated the " 'comstockian mind' " with "neurotic minds" that "project their collective neurosis and their sexual mores on to all of American literature and art." Perhaps the last serious invocation of comstockery was Robert W. Haney's *Comstockery in America* (1960), which was dedicated to debunking the censor as "sick," "repressed," "afraid of the real world."[24]

Although Comstock is notorious for hounding those who distributed contraceptive information and devices, he was also a kind of consumer advocate, mounting numerous campaigns against gambling, lotteries, quacks, medical hoaxes, fraudulent advertising, and swindles. His labors brought about the arraignment of 3,697 people in state and federal courts, of whom 2,740 either were convicted or pleaded guilty. Comstock's boast about his conviction rate to an interviewer in the New York *Evening World* in 1913 is characteristic of his theatrical style: "In the forty-one years I have been here I have convicted persons enough to fill a passenger train of sixty-one coaches, sixty coaches containing sixty passengers each and the sixty-first almost full. I have destroyed 160 tons of obscene literature."[25]

While nineteenth-century sex radicals like D. M. Bennett, Ezra Heywood, and Moses Harman personally battled Comstock and publicly attacked him as a religious zealot, grand inquisitor, hypocrite, and sneak, his name and cause received little abuse from established journals of opinion or from the newspapers. Then, during the first decade of the twentieth century, Comstock's reputation began to suffer: not only did cultural radicals present him as an object of ridicule but the popular press joined in the fun. Because Comstock publicized his vice-hunting adventures in bold, detective-style books with sensational titles like *Traps for the Young* and in muckraking reports for the New York Society for the Suppression of Vice—both included lists of obscene publications as well as descriptions of obscene public lectures, plays, and the lure of brothels and saloons—his opponents were able to use his own words against him to good effect. Theodore Schroeder, for example, noted:

Mr. Comstock is . . . an unconscious witness to the harmlessness of obscenities. In a recent report he informs us that for thirty years he has "stood at the mouth of a sewer," searching for and devouring "obscenity" for a salary; and yet he claims that this lucrative delving in "filth" has left him, or made him, so much purer than all the rest of humanity that they cannot be trusted to choose their own literature and art until it has been expurgated by him. . . . If it is true that his morality is still unimpaired, then it would follow that "obscenity" cannot injure the ordinary normal human.

In Schroeder's view—and this view was widespread—Comstock was a "prurient prude" who suffered from "diseased nerves" and "nasty mindedness." Comstockery was nothing less than "prudery legalized and unlegalized"; it promoted ignorance, which in turn promoted vice.[26]

In 1905, Comstock's name was transformed into an epithet in its own right by George Bernard Shaw in response to threats that Comstock would have his play *Mrs. Warren's Profession* banned from the American stage: "Comstockery is the world's standing joke at the expense of the United States," Shaw observed. "Europe likes to hear of such things. It confirms the deep-seated conviction of the Old World that America is a provincial place, a second-rate country-town civilization after all." While Shaw's caustic remarks confirmed the worst fears plaguing young American intellectuals of the time, Comstock, in his sanctimonious fashion, turned the expression to his own purposes. To the New York Society for the Suppression of Vice, he opined:

Mr. Shaw, in expressing his contempt for the work of this Society, has coined a new word, "Comstockery." We gladly contribute its meaning to this country, to wit: "Comstockery"—the applying of the noblest principles of law, as defined by the Higher Courts of Great Britain and the United States of America, in the interest of Public Morals, especially those of the young.[27]

It was not only the ridicule by sophisticated moderns like Shaw that made Comstock's name synonymous with prudery, provincialism, and moral idiocy. Comstock's devotion to exposing and prosecuting vice the better to display his own high moral tone and the purity of his cause in the end destroyed his and its legitimacy. As Mencken laughingly pointed out:

Old Anthony . . . did more than any other man to ruin Puritanism in the United States. When he began his long and brilliant career of unwitting sabotage, the essential principles of comstockery were believed in by practically every reputable American. Half a century later, when he went upon the shelf, comstockery enjoyed a degree of public esteem . . . half way between that enjoyed by phrenology and that enjoyed by homosexuality. It was, at best, laughable. It was, at worst, revolting.[28]

In the summer of 1906, for instance, Comstock tried to prevent the New York Art Students' League from mailing a student pamphlet containing reproductions of studio nudes. When the perpetrator of the mailings turned out to be a nineteen-year-old female student, the case provoked not only angry public protest, with newspapers denouncing Comstock as the "prosecutor of innocent womanhood," but also public ridicule with cartoonists lampooning him. This event signaled the beginning of the end of Comstock's reign. Rumors (which turned out to be false) flew that he would be dismissed due to a visit to Washington by a member of the Art Students' League who complained that the veteran inspector was abusing his privileges.[29]

These antics gave Comstock's detractors easy opportunities to sneer at his fanaticism and philistinism, and even the National Purity Federation, an organization that had supported Comstock for decades, began to desert him when they started to favor open, clinical discussions of sexual hygiene and eugenics. In 1906, members at its annual meeting listened to Comstock's avowed enemy, Theodore Schroeder, argue against the Comstock Act on grounds of its uncertainty. Comstock, who was scheduled to respond, did not appear. The *New York Sun*, commenting on the conference, not only expressed the shift in the popular assessment of Comstock's ideas and tactics but used invective over substantive argument to discredit him: "The truth is that a new school of purity has sprung into the world, and for the present, Mr. Comstock must be content to pass as an old fogy, out-of-date, mid-Victorian, unfashionable, or whatever the stronger party chooses."[30]

The power and proliferation of such invective soon overwhelmed any necessity to mount reasoned arguments against Comstock and his Society for the Suppression of Vice. In public discussions of his career, it became customary merely to recite the litanies, and this further bolstered their authority. Even in an interview sympathetic to him published in *Harper's Weekly* (1915), the interviewer felt obliged to mention that "it has been the policy of those who oppose his work to speak flippantly of it and to minimize its results." Speaking flippantly of Comstock's work reached its most extravagant expression in Mencken's "Puritanism as a Literary Force" (1917). In this devastating satire, Mencken put his legendary wit in the service of exposing the shallowness, timidity, and conformism in American literature and criticism rooted in Puritan moralism and also of warning of the dangers posed to American culture by puritanism in its modern guise, comstockery.[31]

THE CIVILIZED MINORITY VS. PURITANISM

Mencken took as his starting point that comstockery was responsible for a "dread of free inquiry," "childish skittishness in both writers and public," and a "dearth of courage and even of curiosity" in American cultural life. Because Mencken was not so much an intellectual in pursuit of truth as a polemicist dedicated to vanquishing his enemy and demonstrating his own credentials as a sophisticated modern, he recounted a Whig history of American reform, in which all previous reform movements (characterized as Puritan) anticipated and led up to Comstock and his "career of terror."[32] In his fervor to discredit comstockery, he created a ridiculous character type that still continues to hold power over the modern imagination: the Puritan reformer as a smug, rude, provincial busybody who will stop at nothing, not even censorship and imprisonment, to impose his self-righteous morality upon others.

Mencken began his account with a list of reform projects of Puritans a century before, giving pride of place to abolitionism and temperance. After the Civil War, he continued, Puritans organized new associations—the Salvation Army, temperance leagues, and Sunday schools. The new Puritan had become an "entrepreneur," Mencken scoffed, and offered the flourishing of the YMCA and the American Bible Society as proof that religion had become "big business." With this new basis in business enterprise, comstockery made its appearance. While Mencken apparently cared little about the theology of the original Puritans, he took special pleasure in using the common wisdom about them to make comstockery appear even more laughable by comparison. There was a difference, as he put it, between "*re*nunciation and *de*nunciation, asceticism and Mohammedanism, the hair shirt and the flaming sword."

> The new Puritanism is not ascetic, but militant. Its aim is not to lift up saints but to knock down sinners. Its supreme manifestation is the vice crusade, an armed pursuit of helpless outcasts by the whole military and naval forces of the Republic. Its supreme hero is Comstock Himself.[33]

Comstockery consisted of organized efforts to police what Mencken believed was essentially private conduct—drinking, gambling, prostitution, and obscenity. Sex reformers belonged in this meddlesome company, he thought, for only a Puritan would become involved with the "general ploughing up and emotional discussion of sexual matters, with compulsory instruction in 'sex hygiene' as its mildest manifestation and the medieval fury of the vice crusade as its worst." To fill the void left by the church, private reform agencies and, later, state-sponsored vice commissions had tried to enforce standards of moral conduct. These various "Puritan enterprises" shared one characteristic: "They were all efforts to combat immorality with the weapons designed for crime. In each of them there was a visible effort to erect the individual's offence against himself into an offence against society." In his screed on the professionalization of reform, Mencken put the finishing touches on his caricature of the puritanical reformer: the "essential fact" was his "recognition of the moral expert, the professional sinhound, the virtuoso of virtue." Comstock, he scoffed, was "more than the greatest Puritan gladiator of his time; he was the Copernicus of a quite new art and science, and he devised a technique and handed down a professional ethic that no rival has been able to better."[34]

Without a doubt, Mencken's greatest and most enduring contribution to the discourse of exposure was his "smart-set" style of debunking. Barbed witticisms, dazzling put-downs, extravagant sarcasm, acrobatic displays of contempt—Mencken singlehandedly invented a new style of criticism. Yet, as Louis Kronenberger has noted, Mencken's "wholesale muckraking" led not to political or social reform but self-satisfied withdrawal. "It fostered the cult of the civilized minority."[35] And in his merciless caricature of the Puritan as a social type, Mencken created a number of occasions to theatrically display his own aesthetic and moral superiority as cultivated sophisticate. Since his style is one and the same with the content of his criticism, we need to see in detail how he painted his devastating portraits of the Puritan as prude, censor, and philistine.

Christening the last quarter of the nineteenth century "the Golden Age of euphemism," Mencken compiled a list of evasions that rivaled Schroeder's "hyperaesthesia" in making the Victorians laughable:

The word "woman" became a term of opprobrium, verging close upon downright libel; legs became the inimitable "limbs"; the stomach began to run from the "bosom" to the pelvic arch; pantaloons faded into "unmentionables"; the newspapers spun their parts of speech into such gossamer webs as "a statutory offence," "a house of questionable repute," and "an interesting condition."[36]

He also skewered the Puritan as censor, giving his dogmatism and self-righteousness mythic proportions:

> The Puritan's utter lack of aesthetic sense, his distrust of all romantic emotion, his unmatchable intolerance of opposition, his unbreakable belief in his own bleak and narrow views, his savage cruelty of attack, his lust for relentless and barbarous persecution—these things have put an almost unbearable burden upon the exchange of ideas in the United States.

And for Mencken, puritanism and philistinism were synonymous:

> [Puritanism] is, indeed, but a single manifestation of one of the deepest prejudices of a religious and half-cultured people—the prejudice against beauty as a form of debauchery and corruption—the distrust of all ideas that do not fit readily into certain accepted axioms—the belief in the eternal validity of moral concepts—in brief, the whole mental sluggishness of the lower orders of men.[37]

With these dazzling verbal pyrotechnics, Mencken impressed his audience that he and they belonged to a superior sort of society—the cultivated and civilized few. In the same way that birth-control champions succeeded in joining their cause with the cherished liberal values of progress and freedom, Mencken joined his with the winning modern values of sophistication and urbanity. And the distinguishing mark of the modern sophisticate was the hard-won ability to detach aesthetic from moral judgment—the capacity to regard *all* aspects of the human condition without blanching or passing moral judgment. This aestheticized position repudiated the nineteenth-century moral stance of the Hicklin Test and the Comstock Act, but it also challenged the reticent sensibility, indeed, willfully conflated the reticent sensibility with comstockery and puritanism. Puritanism as a literary force, Mencken repeatedly charged, had led to the "wholesale and ecstatic sacrifice of aesthetic ideas, of all the fine gusto of passion and beauty, to notions of what is meet, proper, and nice."[38]

Again and again, Mencken tore into American literary critics for their alleged failure to "estimate a piece of writing as a piece of writing, a work of art as a work of art." Winking to the cognoscenti, he wrote: "The American, try as he will, can never imagine any work of the imagination as wholly devoid of moral content. It must either tend toward the promotion of virtue, or be suspect and abominable." Mencken stacked the deck against old-fashioned criticism by portraying it as an agency of conformism: "Books are still judged among us, not by their form and organization as works of art, their accuracy and vividness as representations of life, their validity and perspicacity as interpretations of it, but by their conformity to the national preju- dices, their accordance with set standards of niceness and propriety."[39]

For Mencken, the self-avowed disciple of Nietzsche, it was precisely this distinction between those who can appreciate aesthetic qualities independent of moral content and those who cannot which sets the aesthete off from the common herd. This way of using culture as a sign of personal distinction radically breaks with earlier understand- ings of culture. For the party of reticence, the acquisition of culture was never intended as a sign of distinction; rather, following Matthew Arnold, culture was an antidote to political and moral anarchy, the "pursuit of our total perfection by means of getting to know, on all the matters which most concern us, the best which has been thought and said in the world." Mencken's use of a strictly aesthetic appre- ciation of the arts to distinguish between the "civilized minority" and the "philistine," the "smart set" and the "booboisie," expressly re- jected this Arnoldian understanding of culture. Instead, it bolstered the power of a new generation of critics by attributing authority to their allegedly advanced taste and superior understanding.

With these standards in place, Mencken was then able to position reticent critics who had judged literature according to the classical hierarchy of genres on the same side as comstockery and puritanism. In retrospect, we can see this was a grievous mistake, and we have yet to recover from its consequences. The reticent sensibility intersects with puritanism and comstockery at two points: in their belief in the continuity of moral and aesthetic judgment and in their concern that private matters not be spoken of casually in public. Comstock's in- tolerance and self-righteousness, along with his obsessive desire to unmask his opponents' misdeeds the better to reveal his own superior morality, shares a good deal with Mencken's theatrical style; it has nothing to do with the party of reticence's solicitude for the feelings of others and their concern about which things belong in public.

Mencken also reserved a special place of opprobrium for "the dean of American letters"—"the virtuous, kittenish Howells."[40] Mencken's caricature of Howells, in its savagery and mean spirit, rivals his cari- cature of Comstock. Whereas Comstock became the symbol of evan- gelical zeal, fanatical moralism, and prurient prudery, Howells became the symbol of overfastidiousness, evasiveness, and cloying gentility. The ease with which he demolished Howells's reputation (and Com- stock's, too) suggests that an enormous amount of damaging material must have already been in wide circulation by the teens. Yet it was Mencken's special talent for inverting conventional prejudices that gave his caricatures their particular force.

Howells's most egregious failing, according to Mencken, was his naïve insistence on the continuity of the true, the beautiful, and the good, and his patently silly belief that realist fiction had an important function in the life of democratic society. In Mencken's hands, Howells's moralism swelled to Comstockian proportions. In a merciless assault on popular book reviewers—"pious old maids, male and female"—Mencken invited his readers to laugh at their "heavy pretension to culture," "campus cocksureness," and "laborious righteousness."

> The normal American book reviewer, indeed, is an elderly virgin, a superstitious blue-stocking, an apostle of Vassar *Kultur;* and her customary attitude of mind is one of fascinated horror. . . . William Dean Howells, despite a certain jauntiness and even kittenishness of manner, was spiritually of that company. For all his phosphorescent heresies, he was what the uplifters call a right-thinker at heart, and soaked in the national tradition. He was easiest intrigued, not by force and originality, but by a sickly, *Ladies' Home Journal* sort of piquancy.

Mencken sneered that Howells's realism was neither true nor profound, showing "an almost equal vacuity and lack of veracity."

> The action of all the novels of the Howells school goes on within four walls of painted canvas; they begin to shock once they describe an attack of asthma or a steak burning below stairs; they never penetrate beneath the flow of social concealments and urbanities to the passions that actually move men and women to their acts, and the great forces that circumscribe and condition personality.[41]

Mencken was the undisputed master of the smart-set style of debunking and Puritan-baiting, but it was also performed by his accomplished followers. Heywood Broun and Margaret Leech's *Anthony Comstock, Roundsman of the Lord* (1927) added a smattering of psychology, producing the definitive portrait of the Puritan as censor, and the censor as "neurotic" and "fool." With an air of haughty amusement, they noted that Comstock had become a popular target of ridicule by the turn of the century and, by the time of his death in 1915, "a great tradition, a joke, a scapegoat." They had a good deal of fun with his private life, mocking his "Puritanism," sneering at his close relationship with his "beloved," "pious" mother, and drawing simpleminded Freudian conclusions about his marriage to a woman ten years his senior. In an afterword on censorship, Broun repeated what by the 1920s was a stock indictment: "It is not lustful thoughts which mar human personality, but only the sense of shame," and, he asserted, "Comstock spread shame about very widely and it was a force much more debilitating than any exotic notions which might have come from the books he seized." Sharp-witted debunking swiftly sank into nasty name-calling: "As things are constituted," Brown triumphantly concluded, "it is pretty safe to assume that any given censor is a fool. The very fact that he is a censor indicates that."[42]

ALIENATION, GENERATIONAL CONFLICT, AND THE DEBUNKING STYLE

Although an entire generation marched proudly under Mencken's banner of the civilized minority, there were outspoken skeptics who warned that he had overstated the case. Responding to Mencken's "Puritanism as a Literary Force," Bourne cautioned, "It is an exposure that should stir our blood but it is so heavily documented and so stern in its conviction of the brooding curtain of bigotry that hangs over our land, that its effect must be to throw paralyzing terror into every American mind that henceforth dares to think of not being a prude." Contrary to Mencken's assertions about the "cultural terrorism" of puritanism, Bourne observed that younger writers seemed wholly oblivious to it. Pointing to the large number of publishers and magazines willing to circulate "vigorous and candid work," he concluded, "comstockery in art must be seen as an annoying but not dominating force." Bourne also faulted Mencken's "self-conscious bluster" on the grounds that it "plays into the hands of the philistine, demoralizes the artist, and demoralizes his own critical power." For Bourne, it was, ironically, Mencken who exhibited traits of "the moralist contra moralism," and was himself "a product of the genteel tradition . . . for he represents a moralism imperfectly transcended."[43]

Self-consciously drawing attention to the popularity of debunking quickly became a staple of the party of exposure. As Walter Lippmann announced in the opening pages of his acclaimed book *A Preface to Politics* (1913), for example: "If tradition were a reverent record of those crucial moments when men burst through their habits, a love of the past would not be the butt on which every sophomore radical can practice his wit." When H. W. Boynton raised reservations about the new novel in *The Dial* in 1916, he observed that "the ridicule of ancestors is now as obligatory among Western people as their worship is in China. The unpardonable sin is regard for convention." Some enthusiasts of exposure even began to express surprise at the ease with which the reticent sensibility had been demolished.

In a celebratory review of Lytton Strachey's *Eminent Victorians*, Bourne noted that "the fashion became gradually for us to roll our resentments into a blanket indictment of the Victorian Age. This happy way of taking the offensive-defensive . . . has been almost too successful." Bourne thought that the all-out assault on Victorians was itself a cliché, and he thanked Strachey for reinvigorating the debate, writing his book "just at the time when the fun of hitting the Victorian Age over the head, the delight of referring all our spiritual disorders, bonds, and tensions back to the innocent maleficence of what was after all a varied and vivid time, is becoming a little stale."[44]

By 1918, critics of Puritan-baiting had made the debunking strategy an object of satire in its own right. In a book review in *The New Republic*, well-known writers such as Lippmann, Mencken, Dreiser, Van Wyck Brooks, Floyd Dell, and the magazine *Seven Arts* were singled out for censure:

> In fact, the whole younger set, including Mr. Dreiser, never see the word "Puritan," without getting out their axes, refreshing their memories of Freud and Forel, remembering bitterly the small towns they were brought up in, thanking god they can find the way to Greenwich Village, even if they do not live there—and then taking another whirl at the long-suffering men whose manners and customs, distorted and unillumined by that unearthly light in which they lived, have yet been the mold in which our country's laws, literature, education, religions, economics, morals, and points of view have become purified.

By the beginning of this century, the parties of both exposure and reticence had largely jettisoned serious public debate with the object of persuading opponents of the rational superiority of one's argument. Stridency of tone and interminability of outcome became the distinguishing characteristics of their ever-escalating exchanges over the public sphere, characteristics that are emblematic of the larger story of modern moral and aesthetic rebellions.[45]

In the most literal way, the modern rebellion against Victorianism was a conflict between generations. The leading sex radicals, Ezra Heywood and Moses Harman, were born in 1829 and 1830, respectively, and died in 1892 and 1910. Their nemesis, Anthony Comstock, lived from 1844 to 1915. Charles Eliot Norton lived from 1827 to 1910; Henry James, from 1842 to 1916; and William Dean Howells lived long enough to see his reputation tarnished, from 1837 to 1920. All of them came to maturity before the Civil War and died by the close of World War I. Among the cultural rebels of the 1910s, all but Theodore Schroeder (1864–1953), Emma Goldman (1869–

1940), and Theodore Dreiser (1871–1945) came of age during the final decades of the Victorian era, and many of them lived well into our own time: H. L. Mencken from 1880 to 1956, Margaret Sanger from 1883 to 1966, Van Wyck Brooks from 1886 to 1963, Morris L. Ernst from 1888 to 1976, and Walter Lippmann from 1889 to 1974. (Randolph Bourne's life, from 1886 to 1918, was cut miserably short by the influenza epidemic.)

Lippmann's *Drift and Mastery* (1914), which he wrote when he was twenty-five years old, announced the deep estrangement of his generation from the past:

> We are unsettled to the very roots of our being. There isn't a human relation, whether of parent and child, husband and wife, worker and employer, that doesn't move in a strange situation. We are not used to a complicated civilization, we don't know how to behave when personal contact and eternal authority have disappeared. There are no precedents to guide us, no wisdom that wasn't made for a simpler age.

With even more vehemence, Bourne introduced the idea of generational conflict into the rhetorical arsenal of the party of exposure:

> For making a younger generation of rebels and malcontents, the Victorian Age gets and deserves a good deal of reproach. . . . A budding young middle class in England and America found itself too tightly encased in tastes and values that did not at all accord with the pushings within or the faint but tantalizing interests without.

Bourne informed his readers that his generation was provoked by "the mournful inadequacies of religion, the urgency of socialism, sex-expression, and worthy work." This rift between the aims of energetic youth and the complacency of their elders caused "contempt, disdain, irreverence, flightiness, bumptiousness, and rebellion [to] raise their horrid heads."[46]

To these young intellectuals, the reticent sensibility and its associated values were a set of unintelligible and arbitrary prohibitions that needed to be cast off in the name of individual freedom and happiness. They had lost hold of the lived experience of Victorian manners and morals and could only find in them, at best, empty rituals associated with moribund traditions and, at worst, self-serving justifications for power illegitimately acquired. Repeatedly, they insisted that these manners and morals were nothing more than "irrational taboos"—one of their favorite expressions. For Lippmann, this concept held so much explanatory power that he titled the second chapter of his *A Preface to Politics* "The Taboo." It was the absoluteness and arbitrariness of the prohibitions it demanded that irked him: "The routineer in a panic turns to the taboo. Whatever does not fit into his rigid little scheme of things must have its head chopped off."[47]

Bourne struck a more anthropological note. In his essay "Old Tyrannies" (1919), he denounced all customs as "conformist," and using a favorite technique of the party of exposure, he sought to undermine their authority by calling them "almost wholly irrational." Like all of the most radical thinkers of his time, Bourne had absorbed the new ethnography and used its findings to throw the old verities off balance. "The customs . . . of primitive tribes seem to practically everybody in a modern Western society outlandish and foolish," but, he insisted, the same skepticism could be applied to Western customs: "What evidence is there that our codes and conformities which perform exactly the same role, and are mostly traditional survivals, are any the less outlandish and irrational? May they not be tainted with the same purposelessness? Is not the inference irresistible that they are?"[48]

This relativist position, which so many young moderns found exhilarating, derived not only from ethnography but also from Nietzsche, whose work was a touchstone for both Bourne and Mencken. Alasdair MacIntyre's penetrating account of our reigning contemporary moral perspective, which he calls "emotivism," is suggestive in this context. Emotivism, "the doctrine that all evaluative judgments and more specifically all moral judgments are *nothing but* expressions of preference, expressions of attitude or feeling, insofar as they are moral or evaluative in character," was, MacIntyre has convincingly argued, the brainchild of Nietzsche, best expressed in the proposition that "if there is nothing to morality but expressions of will, my morality can only be what my will creates."[49]

In essay after essay, Bourne sharpened this Nietzschean insight, demonstrating that he had acquired the hardheadedness and irony needed for facing up to unpleasant truths. He had seen through the morals of his parents' generation, and he set out to expose them for what they really were:

> Morals are always the product of a situation; they reflect a certain organization of human relations which some class or group wishes to preserve. A moral code or set of ideals is always the invisible spiritual sign of a visible social grace. . . . These old virtues upon which, however, the younger generation is already making guerilla warfare are simply the moral support with which the older generation buttresses its social situation.[50]

In his most self-consciously Nietzschean essay, "The Puritan's Will to Power" (1917), Bourne engaged in that characteristically modern enterprise: unmasking the morals of an opponent by exposing his ulterior motives. In his opening salvo, he characterized Puritans as those people who "give up the primitive satisfactions of sex and food and drink and gregariousness and act the ascetic and the glumly censorious." But they were not content to rest there. They felt superior in their acts of renunciation and were proud of their humility. Because Bourne was personally so remote from the kind of life that would have given meaning to such values, and he correctly saw that those who continued to esteem them were equally remote, he dismissed such values as arbitrary. Then he revealed the unexpected source of the Puritan's power: "In the compelling of others to abstain, you have the final glut of puritanical power." Puritan morality, like all morality, was nothing more than an expression of arbitrary individual will: "To the true Puritan, the beauty of unselfishness lies in his being able to enforce it on others. He loves virtue not so much for its own sake as for its being an instrument of his terrorism." With this Nietzschean emphasis, Bourne wrenched the Puritan out of his historical and theological contexts and successfully redefined him as a nasty, manipulative character type thinly disguised as social reformer. This figure he then disposed of with one cutting remark: "The Puritan is a case of arrested development."[51]

By the first decades of the twentieth century, then, the party of exposure could never win their argument through rational persuasion because their opponents, whose convictions were based on incommensurable premises rooted in competing moral and aesthetic frameworks, were necessarily deaf to such persuasion. And vice versa. With these irreconcilable differences at bottom, no matter how arduously the younger generation tried to convince the older of the rational superiority of their positions, they were bound to fail. In consequence, they were reduced to making insinuations about their opponents' psychological state and resorting to name-calling and Puritan-baiting.

For the rebels who came of age during the final decades of the nineteenth century, the unctuous Comstock and his flamboyant purity crusades represented the forces of reactionary politics, evangelical zeal, prurient prudery, philistinism, provincialism, and censorship that were destroying not only American culture but private happiness as well. In their urgency to defeat him and everything he stood for, they discredited nineteenth-century manners and morals wholesale, thereby giving an entire century a bad name based solely on their opposition to its most obnoxious representatives. At the same time, their battle revealed how swiftly smart-set debunking could degenerate into a politics of the self, theatricalizing the speaker's own sophistication and sexual liberation instead of addressing substantive issues about the world. Most important, their all too easy victory deflected attention away from the important insights contained within the reticent sensibility regarding the fragility of intimate life and the susceptibility of the public sphere to pollution.

The Invention of
the Genteel Tradition

A number of thoughtful writers sought explanations for the gross deficiencies of American intellectual life—in particular, the lack of a vital high culture—in history. The most famous and influential of these endeavors are George Santayana's "The Genteel Tradition in American Philosophy" (1911) and Van Wyck Brooks's *America's Coming-of-Age* (1915). Together, they exerted tremendous influence upon an entire generation, articulating the categories of thought that defined the limits of their rebellion against the past, and creating many new rhetorical weapons.[52] The history of literary missteps and failures they uncovered represented a legacy to be overcome if America were to finally come of age, as Brooks's title suggested.

The most original insight of this criticism was Santayana's description of America as "a country with two mentalities." He traced this double-mindedness back to the earliest days of the republic when "the country was new, but the race was tried, chastened, and full of solemn memories." From the very beginning, America was divided between hereditary, traditional habits of mind that had become "perfunctory," "conventional," and "stale" and modern ways of acting associated with "invention and industry and social organization." He gave this dichotomy its classic expression: "The American Will inhabits the skyscraper; the American Intellect inhabits the colonial mansion. The one is the sphere of the American man; the other, at least predominantly, of the American woman. The one is all aggressive enterprise; the other is all genteel tradition." Brooks, similarly, attributed the poverty of American culture to the division between intellect inherited from England and duties growing out of the American experience. The result, in his famous words, was "desiccated culture at one end and stark utility at the other."

> On the one hand, a quite unclouded, quite unhypocritical assumption of transcendent theory ("high ideals"), on the other a simultaneous acceptance of catchpenny realities. Between university ethics and business ethics, between American culture and American humor, between

Good Government and Tammany, between academic pedantry and pavement slang, there is no community, no genial middle ground.[53]

They traced the origins of this dual American consciousness to the "high ideals" of the genteel tradition in puritanism and to the "catch-penny reality" of aggressive enterprise. The vitality of Calvinism in early American life, Santayana argued, was manifest in the Puritan's "agonized conscience," which issued forth feelings of abasement and elation, distress and ecstasy, and thereby provided a foundation for a rich cultural life. But this culture was doomed from the start, since America was founded in a society of aggressive enterprise peopled with "practical sages, like Franklin and Washington." These apostles of pragmatism, however, recommended many of the same virtues as the Calvinists—vigilance over conduct and personal integrity—"because they were virtues that justified themselves visibly by their fruits."[54]

Santayana found this early marriage of convenience ironic: while devotion to practicality insured that the fledgling republic would flourish, it also changed the mood of the young country from tragedy to sugary optimism. In consequence, "the sense of sin totally evaporated," and Calvinism lost its original basis in American life. In its place, a new theology emerged, stressing tenderness over hellfire and infant damnation. Watered-down nineteenth-century Calvinism deprived anybody "with a special sensibility or a technical genius" of a foundation to build high culture on, which is why the writing of Emerson, Poe, and Hawthorne "had all a certain starved and abstract quality." Their work, Santayana observed, "was a refined labor, but it was in danger of being morbid, or tinkling, or self-indulgent. . . . Their manner, in a word, was subjective." The genteel tradition was, above all, unable to confront complexity and tragedy:

> Serious poetry, profound religion . . . are the joys of an unhappiness that confesses itself; but when a genteel tradition forbids people to confess that they are unhappy, serious poetry and profound religion are closed to them by that; and since human life, in its depths, cannot then express itself openly, imagination is driven into abstract arts, where human circumstances are lost sight of, and human problems dissolve in a purer medium.[55]

Following Santayana's lead, though without his appreciation for the subtleties of Calvinism, Brooks provided a light and airy version of the same story, poking fun at Jonathan Edwards as the representative Puritan and Emerson as his latter-day incarnation as transcendental-istic. Locating the source of the "highbrow" in both these systems of thought, Brooks blamed them for producing "the fastidious refinements and aloofness of the chief American writers, and resulting in the final unreality of most contemporary American culture." The trouble with American literature was that it stood too "remote from life," thereby "achiev[ing] its own salvation (after the Puritan fashion) by avoiding contact with reality."[56]

By articulating these flaws in American cultural life, Santayana and Brooks bequeathed an entire generation a new grammar and vocabulary with which to dissect that culture. Sometimes rebellious critics used the phrase "the genteel tradition" to deprecate the complacency, conformism, and evasiveness of American life in general. In other instances, they employed it to capture the barrenness of high culture, which they attributed to the divide separating the life of the mind from the life of everyday affairs. Santayana and Brooks repeatedly identified both these senses of the genteel—remoteness and passivity—with a feminine sensibility, thereby revealing the popular assessment of women and culture as little more than useless refinements. In his essay "The Academic Environment," Santayana singled out the influence of women teachers in promoting the aloofness of things of the mind, which "helps to establish that separation which is so characteristic of America between things intellectual, which remain wrapped in a feminine veil, and as it were, under glass, and the rough passions of life." With Brooks, the attack on the feminine was directed at refined sensibility more than at flesh-and-blood women: "We have in America two publics, the cultivated public and the business public, the public of theory and the public of action, the public that reads Maeterlinck and the public that accumulates money: the one largely feminine, the other largely masculine."[57]

It is striking that the two critics cast the trouble with American culture in this anti-feminine form; it is an old form, the beginnings of which can be traced to antiquity, when male citizens were urged to assert their *virtu* (from the Latin, *vir*, meaning man) both to counter and to invigorate an increasingly effeminate culture that threatened the republic. In late-nineteenth-century America, this idiom appeared in politics, when "mugwump" reformers were ridiculed by their adversaries as "gelded men" and "political hermaphrodites."[58] Theodore Roosevelt's "cult of the strenuous life" was another manifestation of the American enthusiasm for virility, and the concomitant association of gentility and culture with effeminacy and impotence.

But, in part, the unflattering connection of culture with the feminine was also a consequence of the cult of domesticity having soured. This cult of the private sphere, in which proper wives and mothers taught morality and imparted refinement to their families and to society at large, depended on women actually staying at home and selflessly performing their duties. By the turn of the century, however, women were leaving the home to enter the workforce in record numbers, and feminists were angrily denouncing the customs of genteel society, in which the sole purpose of a young woman's training in social refinements was to make her attractive in the marriage market. Leading figures including Charlotte Perkins Gilman, Margaret Sanger, Emma Goldman, and Jane Addams vigorously criticized this training in feminine wiles, arguing that the more women's lives were divorced from the outside world of useful endeavor, the more enfeebled, foolish, and parasitic they became. Christopher Lasch's observation regarding the conventional role of women as "moral custodians of society" and the simultaneous rethinking of that role by feminists sheds light on this common conflation of culture and femininity: "Under those circumstances the rebellion against culture necessarily became a rebellion also against the definition of woman's 'place' with which the nineteenth-century concept of culture was so closely bound up."[59]

Yet, as we have seen, the nineteenth-century concept of culture was also closely bound up with the appreciation of arts and letters and the belief that culture could counterbalance anarchy, both political and spiritual. Many enthusiasts of this formulation, however, were blind to an irony inherent in it. Both the appreciation and the creation of culture always entail a certain distance from everyday life in order to provide the space necessary for contemplation. This distancing, which is at the heart of the act of creativity, in turn introduces the possibility that the arts may become arid, mannered, detached. For the educated classes of the late nineteenth and early twentieth centuries, this remoteness was particularly acute—thus their common complaint that they were plagued by "weightlessness," "overrefinement," and "overcivilization."[60]

Advocates of literary exposure had taken the high ground from defenders of reticence by portraying them as too sweet and genteel—that is, effeminate and ineffectual. But even more crucial to their victory was their successful redefinition of the very nature of reality. Lionel Trilling, in a famous essay, "Reality in America" (1946), was one of the first to notice that "in the American metaphysic, reality is always material reality, hard, resistant, unformed, impenetrable, and unpleasant." Richard Hofstadter expanded upon this definition in his work on American politics: the muckraker's key article of faith—that appearances were deceiving—had completely infiltrated the Progressives' picture of reality. For them, reality was "rough and sordid. It was hidden, neglected, and offstage. It was conceived essentially as the stream of external and material events which was most likely to be unpleasant." Howells, too, had criticized some of his contemporaries for the inordinate attention they paid to the shadier aspects of life, insisting that pictures based exclusively on them were both incomplete and misleading.[61]

Early-twentieth-century critics who invented this particular understanding of reality had done so in the context of their own caricature of the genteel tradition. It is important to recall that Santayana had maintained that American culture was crippled by a deep split between the life of the mind and the life of mundane affairs, that Brooks also argued that the historic rift between the overly intellectual "highbrow" and the excessively practical "lowbrow" had made American culture barren. These early analyses criticized the spirit of puritanism *and* aggressive enterprise with equal vehemence, culminating in Brooks's call for the creation of "a genial middle ground" as antidote.

The younger generation's disgust with their elders' avoidance of reality in the end defined the limits of their own rebellion. Advocates of literary exposure became increasingly absorbed with exposing the repressiveness and sterility of the genteel tradition, deploring its smug complacency and morbid self-absorption, its timidity, evasiveness, sentimentality, and shallow moralism. But, above all else, they scorned its abstract, detached quality, its remoteness from everyday reality. In consequence, they collapsed all activities of the mind with what they found contemptible about the genteel tradition, giving rise to an indiscriminate celebration of life in the "back streets" and the "rawness" of reality and to insinuations that writers and critics who cared about refinement were elitists. Malcolm Cowley's disdain for the "refined and bloodless" tone of genteel literature is typical of this position. He objected that such writing had "nothing to do with the back streets where people quarreled and made love and died without benefit of Coleridge or Pater."[62] Leaving aside the argument that the "stark utility" and "catchpenny reality" of daily life was equally to blame for the dearth of world-class literature in America, these critics commanded writers to represent reality as they found it, the better to liberate fiction from the shackles of gentility. Thus, what had originally been an integral part of the indictment against American culture came to be offered as the cure.

It was Trilling's insight that American intellectuals' devotion to crude experience and to exposing its most sordid aspects showed they were "still haunted by a political fear of the intellect which Tocqueville observed in us more than a century ago." Pointing to the way liberal critics had consistently treated Henry James with severity and Theodore Dreiser "with the most sympathetic indulgence," Trilling drew attention to the "cultural assumptions that make politics." He argued that Dreiser's apologists not only pleaded that his literary faults were "essentially social and political virtues" but also excused his poor style by attributing it to Dreiser's impatience with "the sterile literary gentility of the bourgeoisie." (Similarly, today's rebels in the universities charge that the voices of excluded minorities cannot be heard or properly evaluated because of the hegemony of dead white European male standards.) Trilling pungently observed: "It is as if wit, and flexibility of the mind, and perception, and knowledge were to be equated with aristocracy and political reaction, while dullness and stupidity must naturally suggest a virtuous democracy, as in the old plays." He pointed to the way Dreiser's defenders had succeeded in making objections to his work appear politically retrograde as well: "It has been taken for granted that the ungainliness of Dreiser's style is the only possible objection to be made to it, and that whoever finds in it any fault at all wants a prettified genteel style (and is objecting to the ungainliness of reality itself)."[63]

Trilling's penetrating analysis of the "political fear of the intellect" should focus our attention on an especially insidious strain of anti-intellectualism on the part of some intellectuals. The source of this uncritical celebration of crude reality was the political conviction popular among young rebels that cultural radicals must side with the dispossessed. This, in turn, was rooted in their unexamined premise that the experience of such people, because it lacked the comforts that come with middle-class solvency, was the most authentic. It is not surprising, then, that for many bohemian-inclined intellectuals of the 1910s, the bum, the hobo, the tramp, and the vagabond were heroes, just as during the 1920s and 1930s Marxist intellectuals idealized the virile worker.[64] Thus writing unflinchingly about blighted lives, degraded labor, or love in back alleys came to be seen as proof of one's ability to confront reality, to be "hard-boiled," which further demonstrated one's allegiance to political radicalism. Writing and reading realism became a substitute for actually living a strenuous life or engaging in political action. A dedication to facing up to the hard facts in fiction became a way of testing one's mettle without any real risk.

Critics of this kind recognized that people most confined to the realm of necessity have the least opportunity for refinement, cultivation, or self-reflection—which, for them, are truly luxuries—but then they wrongly went on to conclude that concern for and appreciation of such enterprises was not only idealistic, escapist, and romantic, but also, and more damningly, elitist and antidemocratic. This mania for naked reality marks the beginning of the attitude so popular in our own time that gives priority to the experience of the downtrodden simply on account of the prejudiced view that the very status of being downtrodden qualifies as more deserving of attention. It is as if the few people who manage to escape the pull of necessity and exercise their freedom—in short, who achieve distinction—are inevitably suspect, or that their experience and accomplishments amount to nothing other than evidence of domination and privilege.

This obsessive interest in the most mundane aspects of life, which almost always involves private bodily activities, is a key feature of the discourse of exposure, which its speakers employ when they want to extinguish differences by drawing attention to the inherent equality of the condition of having a body. The scientific version of this discourse tries to speak the truth about "the facts of life" by unmasking moral language and demystifying cultural conventions. The vulgar version, by invading privacy, obliterates distinctions and demands, "What have you got to hide?" And so it is with realist fiction that focuses on crude experience and makes a cult of "life on the edge." In each of these renditions of exposure, enthusiasts not only display a passion for bringing everyone down to the same low level, they also successfully insinuate that any concern for reticence, privacy, modesty, or decency signals prurient prudery, morbid sensitivity, a romantic or sentimental disposition, or downright elitism.

6

THE LEGAL DEBATE
ABOUT THE RIGHT TO
PRIVACY

While the party of exposure discredited the reticent sensibility by recasting its values of tact, discretion, good taste, and politeness as signs of guilty cover-up or elitism, and mercilessly caricatured its respect for modesty and shame as prurient prudery, in the end, it would be the legal profession that would acquire the final authority to resolve disputes about which things may appear in public. It is important, then, to ask why those who sought to safeguard privacy so quickly conceived of it as a legal right, and why it was the courts rather than local or more informal agencies of control that were considered the best means of keeping private matters private. When nineteenth-century critics suggested means of punishing impudent journalists, avenging insult to honor emerged as their most pressing concern. The Proberts in Henry James's *The Reverberator*, for instance, consider a duel with the journalist who has printed the details of their personal lives in a gossip sheet. E. L. Godkin pointed to the popular belief that the most fitting retribution for invasive journalism was "by means of duel or single combat, or some sort of corporal chastisement."

> The idea that this class of injury is most appropriately punished by personal violence has in fact survived down to our own day. There still lingers in the minds of the public . . . the notion that, though one ought to rely on the police and the courts for the protection of one's goods and chattels, yet there is certain peculiar fitness in protecting reputation or privacy against libel or intrusion by the cudgel or the horsewhip.[1]

EFFORTS TO CONTAIN PRYING JOURNALISTS

That such exemplars of civility as James and Godkin continued to relish the prospect of personal violence in retaliation for violations of privacy reveals the magnitude of the harm. The menace posed by invasive journalism, however, could not be adequately met by personal violence, not only because such violence was against the law but also because the would-be duelist would have a difficult time locating his defamer in the modern, anonymous world of large-scale publishing. Thus instead of thrashing impudent reporters, editors, and publishers, Godkin and others counseled the public to chastise members of this ignominious group. One writer demanded that the offending journalist be treated as "a moral outcast": "There is no more important work to be done for our civilization today than that of shaming such newspapers either out of existence or into amended lines, and the responsibility for that work is shared by all alike." Another suggested that "every man who desires something better [should] put the pressure of his opinion upon editor and management" by writing "letters of protest," and then by requesting "ten neighbors" to follow suit. Others urged people to shun sensational newspapers altogether. "If readers are self-indulgent and willing to gratify curiosity by patronizing and helping support a trashy publication," declared Richard Watson Gilder, "the moral responsibility rests on them as well as on the owners. Publishers will furnish better papers if readers refuse to buy poor ones."[2]

Still others pleaded with publishers to renounce their self-serving, moneymaking strategies and reclaim their true mission: to educate the public about matters that legitimately concerned citizens. Journalists needed to regard themselves as part of "a profession, with inherent, peculiar, and far-reaching responsibilities," who could reform themselves with a code of ethics regulating journalistic conduct by ostracizing those who offended such standards. Other critics floated the idea of an endowed press along the lines of the endowed college. They called for a philanthropist to counteract the economic pressures which publishers faced by the competition of the market. An endowed paper, in the words of the editors of *The Dial* (1893), "could not fail in time to react upon the journalists of the country at large, and would offer a standing protest against the methods now current."[3]

Whether journalism was a profession dedicated to furthering the public good by educating citizens or whether it was a business enterprise that would stop at nothing to increase its owners' private wealth underlay all other issues in the controversy over invasive journalism —thus the oft-repeated justification that the newspapers were "giving the people what they want" and had the receipts to prove it. Because the discussion was formulated in these terms, traditional reliance on informal, local means of control—ostracism, boycotts, letters of protest, codes of professional ethics, endowments—no doubt appeared to be reasonable ways to contend with the excesses of the new journalism. Yet public debate and moral suasion seemed inadequate to the daunting task of reining in impudent journalists; some critics called for the law to intervene. As one commentator put it, "The liberty of the Press is and should be held sacred in every free community, but the license of the Press should be put under ban and without a day's delay."[4]

With this controversy raging, two young lawyers, Louis Brandeis and Samuel Warren—the latter having personally suffered the sting of published gossip—turned to the law in their pathbreaking essay "The Right to Privacy" (1890), which became the cornerstone of American legal discourse about the right to privacy. According to the jurist Roscoe Pound, it "did nothing less than add a chapter to our law." The essay was immediately declared authoritative by judges presiding over right-to-privacy litigation, and it also articulated (and continues to articulate) the very terms in which people think, speak, and argue about the subject. Fluent speakers of the discourse of reticence, Brandeis and Warren indicted the instant photograph, the proliferation of mass-circulation newspapers, and the growing use of mechanical recording devices for invading, in their words, "the sacred precincts of private and domestic life." They detailed the dangers posed by the thriving commercial trade in "idle gossip" that pandered to "a prurient taste [for] the details of sexual relations." Invasive journalism not only subjected its victim "to mental pain and distress, far greater than could be inflicted by mere bodily injury," but also "results in a lowering of social standards and of morality . . . it belittles by inverting the relative importance of things, thus dwarfing the thoughts and aspirations of a people," and its "triviality destroys at once robustness of thought and delicacy of feeling."[5]

To strengthen the enfeebled boundary separating private and public, Brandeis and Warren called for the immediate recognition of a legal right to privacy. This resort to the law, however, led them to attempt to translate the concerns of the party of reticence into legal language. It now appears that this project was ill-fated from the start, because of the untranslatability of the one language into the other. The defining category of liberal jurisprudence is "rights"—the relation between people, and the relation between people and things rooted in the possession, distribution, and administration of property. Since the law is bound to understand all disputes as disputes about rights, the defense of privacy was quickly assimilated to this mode of thought. That the judiciary became the final arbiter in disagreements about what might appear in public follows from the liberal assumption that the state exists to safeguard rights and thereby ensure peace so that individuals are free to pursue their private interests. The legal paradigm, however, constricted the scope of considerations central to the party of reticence by obliging advocates to think and speak in terms of rights. This narrowed focus made it virtually impossible to take account of the sweeping damages to taste and judgment or address the coarsening tone of public discussion, matters that were central to the debate about privacy.

The law's inability to safeguard the world of gentility and manners is an ironic turn in the narrative, related by J. G. A. Pocock, about the emergence in the eighteenth century of a psychology of politeness, sociability, and sentiment that accompanied the birth of commercial society, "largely in consequence of the jurists' fascination with the universe of *res*." "The concept of 'manners,' " according to Pocock, "though it does not belong to the operational vocabulary of jurisprudence, was in fact enormously advanced by and through the study of natural and civil law."[6] The jurists' preoccupation with manners, which had launched the discourse of reticence and the culture of politeness a century earlier, could not in the end generate a conceptual framework large enough to encompass the culture it had summoned forth.

PRIVACY, PROPERTY, AND INVIOLATE PERSONALITY

The legal framework of Brandeis and Warren's right to privacy was the new "sociological jurisprudence," which held that laws must periodically be reassessed and adapted in accordance with changing political, social, and economic conditions. The common law, by these lights, not only would safeguard "material" interests, as it had traditionally done, but keeping in step with progress and the movement toward more individuality and emotional depth, it would also protect evolving "spiritual" interests, such as those threatened by invasions of privacy. "Thoughts, emotions, and sensations," wrote Brandeis and Warren, "demanded legal recognition, and the beautiful capacity for growth which characterizes the common law enabled the judges to afford the requisite protection, without the interposition of the legislature."[7]

Brandeis and Warren's most crucial transformation of the party of reticence's understanding of privacy was their famous definition of privacy as "the right to be let alone," which effectively, if inadvertently, displaced the public dimension of the harm. In what follows, it will become evident that Godkin's essay "The Rights of the Citizen: To His Own Reputation" largely determined the contours of the lawyers' understanding of privacy and reputation. First, they acknowledged that the right to privacy superficially resembles the right to reputation—both are violated by the publication of information about a person's life and character—but insisted that laws protecting reputation (i.e., slander and libel) cover "a radically different class of effect." Defamation law deals exclusively with damage "done to the individual in his external relations to the community by lowering him in the estimation of his fellows." In contrast, invasions of privacy affect a person's "estimate of himself and his own feelings." "In short," they observed, "the wrongs and correlative rights recognized by the law of slander and libel are in their nature material rather than spiritual."[8]

To address the harm experienced by the individual, Brandeis and Warren needed to distinguish between material and spiritual interests, but this distinction left them in a trying predicament. The right to privacy, by their lights, protects spiritual interests, the damages of which are manifested as mental anguish. While American law takes mental suffering into account in ascertaining the damages related to a legal injury, it "does not afford a remedy even for mental suffering which results from mere contumely and insult, from an intentional and unwarranted violation of the 'honor' of another."[9] Consequently, they needed to find a cause of action other than mental anguish in order to assert a general right to privacy.

To meet this challenge, they applied common-law reasoning to decisions about analogous issues such as disputes concerning "intellectual and artistic property." In these cases, the common law secures a person's right to determine "to what extent his thoughts, sentiments, and emotions shall be communicated to others." The key concept here—"intellectual and artistic *property*"—propelled Warren and Brandeis to their most innovative piece of legal reasoning. They made a distinction between two kinds of property: one as expressed in profits arising from publication; and the other as expressed "in the peace of mind or the relief afforded by the ability to prevent any publication at all." The latter, they granted, is difficult to regard as a right of property "in the common acceptation of that term," which, in turn, led them to reconceive the locus of privacy. After reviewing English right-to-privacy precedents, they concluded that courts thought of private property as a kind of fiction to rationalize a form of relief that was actually rooted in what they called "inviolate personality":

> [The general right to privacy] is merely an instance of the enforcement of the more general right of the individual to be let alone. It is like the right not to be assaulted or beaten, the right not to be imprisoned, the right not to be maliciously prosecuted, the right not to be defamed. In each of these rights . . . there inheres the quality of being owned or possessed—and (as that is the distinguishing attribute of property) there may be some propriety in speaking of these rights as property. But obviously they bear little resemblance to what is ordinarily comprehended under that term. The principle which protects personal writings and all other personal productions, not against theft and physical appropriation, but against publication in any form, is in reality not the principle of private property, but that of inviolate personality.[10]

Brandeis and Warren insisted that their formulation of the right to privacy was new only in instance, not in principle, "when it extends this protection to the personal appearance, sayings, acts, and to personal relation, domestic or otherwise."[11] Their equation of the right to be let alone with the right to privacy—the right to determine what will be published about one's self—simply adapted and extended the traditional liberal understanding of negative liberty to a society soon to be dubbed "the information society." The right to privacy, then, would continue to safeguard the essential conditions necessary so that freedom and individuality might flourish, a liberal project which, as we have seen, had its beginnings with John Stuart Mill.

The novelty in their argument springs from their insistence that the right to privacy is rooted *not* in property but in inviolate personality. As I have already suggested, they were forced to make this claim because, in order to justify the recognition of a right to privacy, they needed to demonstrate the inadequacies of the traditional safeguards of reputation. Whereas laws of slander and libel protect against inaccurate portrayal, the right to privacy, in their words, "not merely prevents inaccurate portrayal of private life, but prevents its being depicted at all."[12] This crucial point led them to create their slippery distinction between the material interest of reputation rooted in property (the community's estimate of a person) and the spiritual interest of privacy rooted in personality (the individual's estimate of himself or herself). As we shall see, this formulation plagued right-to-privacy litigation from the start, largely because judges and lawyers were accustomed to thinking in terms of the rights of property—that is, in terms of a system of legally defined relations between persons and tangible things.

Brandeis and Warren's article also signaled a major reconceptualization of liberal principles. From the time of Locke, liberals had traditionally regarded property as the material embodiment of liberty and personality that resulted once man mixed his labor with nature. Within this context, it is surprising to see Brandeis and Warren trying to separate and then recombine what had long been held to be the unity of property, liberty, and personality. In addition, by linking the right to privacy to the "spiritual precincts of inviolate personality," they unwittingly drew attention to fundamental changes taking shape in the culture at the time they wrote. The 1890s mark the beginning of large-scale organization and administration in government and business alike. Although Brandeis and Warren did not explicitly address issues related to the consolidation of monopoly capitalism and the gradual disappearance of independent landholders, their attempt to ground privacy (and negative liberty by their definition) in personality unintentionally acknowledged and bolstered the emerging social reality: twentieth-century America was to be a society inhabited primarily by people defined in reference to their personality rather than their property. A person would be able to exercise his (and, by 1920, her) privilege to vote based on a conception of "human rights" alone. The quality of being human, of having a personality, would replace the older liberal position that had defined a citizen as a man who had "a stake in society," that is, a property owner.

In the concluding section of their essay, Brandeis and Warren specified limitations to the right to privacy and the legal remedies for its enforcement. The first limitation concerned the publication of matters of legitimate public interest, thereby raising two questions that would repeatedly appear in the actual litigation: Who is properly a public figure? And to what guarantees of privacy is he or she entitled? For Brandeis and Warren, public figures include candidates for public and "quasi-public" office as well as elected and appointed officeholders. And they acknowledged that the rules of privacy as applied to a strictly private individual were different from those applied to people who "have renounced their right to live their lives screened from public observation." They argued that since "the propriety of publishing the very same facts may depend wholly upon the person concerning whom they are published, no fixed formula can be used to prohibit obnoxious publications." Thus, the two lawyers cautioned that any right-to-privacy law must be elastic enough to account for subtle distinctions. As for safeguarding the private affairs of public figures, they were adamant that "some things all men alike are entitled to keep from popular curiosity, whether in public life or not."[13]

The other important limitation they mentioned was that neither the truth of the matter published nor the absence of malice in the publisher would afford a defense against invasions of privacy. The question of truth or falsehood, according to Brandeis and Warren, was irrelevant to right-to-privacy proceedings, since the laws of slander and libel already provided adequate protection for injury to character. The right to privacy reached further: it prevented *any* depiction, true or false, of private life. It is striking that they did not even mention the potential conflict between the right to free speech and the individual's right to privacy. As we shall see, this tension between competing rights would have profound consequences for the legal debate during the very earliest phase of litigation.

As for actual legal remedies, Brandeis and Warren suggested "an action of tort for damages in all cases" as well as "an injunction, perhaps for a very limited class of cases." By envisioning invasion of privacy as a tort—a civil wrong which entitles the injured party to compensation—the scope of protection was immediately limited: tort law is always remedial and particular rather than preventive and general. While they also urged the added protection of criminal law, they acknowledged that such protection would require the legislature to act. And finally, as if offering an apology for the limitations of their formulations, Brandeis and Warren reiterated the conviction of the party of reticence "that the community has an interest in preventing such invasions of privacy." But as advocates of the law—which, because of its adversarial role as defender of individuals' rights, is forced to hunt for victims whose rights have been violated and whose consequent injuries demand state intervention—they added, "Still, the protection of society must come mainly through a recognition of the rights of the individual."[14] Their willingness to use the law as an agency of social reform, however, distinguishes the two legal writers from other critics of invasive journalism who argued that public opinion would be the most effective regulator of the press.

THE STRUGGLE TO ESTABLISH LEGAL PROTECTION
OF PRIVACY

The records of the trials from 1890–1919[15] reveal that legal discourse slipped effortlessly away from Brandeis and Warren's innovative attempt to protect inviolate personality and instead became riveted to considerations of reputation, private property, and First Amendment rights, which were more in keeping with long-standing principles of liberal jurisprudence. The vast majority of these early trials centered on unauthorized use of a person's name, likeness, or photograph for advertising or trade purposes. (Other cases included a women's reform group's attempt to erect a statue honoring the memory of a prominent reformer against the wishes of her family,[16] the police use of photographs of criminals for display in the rogues' gallery,[17] and disputes over rightful ownership of photographs.[18]) It is puzzling indeed that Brandeis and Warren's most urgent concern—that victims of unwanted publicity be protected—almost never resulted in legal action.

For in truth, invasions of privacy were multiplying. Specific intrusions included the publication of names of people involved in a supposed scandal, the nature of an anticipated lawsuit, the name of an author of an originally unsigned article, the name of a private guest of a public man, and the details of a marriage proposal by a distinguished politician. One critic bemoaned the way "the President is photographed and described in all possible and impossible places and positions, dignified and otherwise, and his family are pictured in detail, mostly from imagination." The *New York Times* (1902) complained about the regular abuse public men such as President Roosevelt and the millionaire J. Pierpont Morgan suffered at the hands of the press: "When they revolt from the continuous ordeal of the camera, it is shown that there is something very irritating to normal nerves in chronic 'exposure.'" Particularly offensive to the editors was the press's "wanton invasion of privacy and grief" when it printed the picture and tale of a young woman whose fiancé had committed suicide.[19]

Since the absence of litigation cannot be attributed to any newfound respect for privacy in the newspapers, why did these violations of privacy never result in legal action? What accounts for the divergence between the kinds of intrusion that early commentators deplored and the actual offenses that came to trial? Godkin's largely skeptical response to Brandeis and Warren provides some important clues. Godkin believed that there was a pervasive American antipathy toward privacy, and as a consequence "there would be no effective public support or countenance" for its legal protection. He noted that the greatest obstacle was rooted in the very nature of the injury: the people who would most benefit from litigation would also be the most wary about subjecting themselves to the further publicity that would inevitably arise if they took their grievance to court. As Condé Benoist

Pallen put it, a lawsuit "only makes matters worse by the publication of everything sacred to your privacy, conjoined with a detestable notoriety and the expense of a wearisome litigation with a soulless, conscienceless corporation." An article in *The Arena* (1890) spelled out the dilemma: "If a public man dare defend himself, his very defense is turned against him. If, maddened at the outrage, he shows his anger, he is jeered at, and misrepresented the more. If the attack drives him from public life, he finds no protection in privacy."[20]

The right to privacy, then, was plagued from the beginning by both a general cultural attitude that was highly ambivalent about its protection and the perplexing task of preserving reticence through aggressive legal speech. In addition, it was confounded by conflicts of opinions within the legal profession. As early as 1912, a judge reviewing right-to-privacy precedents commented upon "the irreconcilable conflict of opinions" surrounding the cases. Brandeis and Warren had anticipated such difficulties when they called for an "elastic law," which they knew "unfortunately renders such a doctrine not only more difficult of application, but also to a certain extent, uncertain in its operation and easily rendered abortive."[21] They did not, however, anticipate that it was their own key distinction—between the protection afforded reputation founded in private property and that afforded privacy founded in inviolate personality—that would hopelessly confuse legal proceedings.

The most important decision in the early litigation was *Roberson v. Rochester Folding Box Co.* (1902), in which the court refused to recognize a legal right to privacy. This case is pivotal because it strained the dispute about privacy to a breaking point: it excited public outrage, which in turn provoked one of the judges to take the unprecedented step of responding to public criticism in a law journal; the decision also forced the New York legislature to pass a law protecting privacy in 1903.

In this trial, a young woman named Abigail Roberson brought suit against a mercantile company for obtaining and using without her permission 25,000 lithographs of her likeness to promote their product, flour, with the caption above it: "Flour of the Family." These advertisements were conspicuously posted and displayed in stores, warehouses, saloons, and other public places. Formulating the harm as an insult to her honor, Roberson described how her "good name" had been attacked and how she had been "greatly humiliated" by the "scoffs and jeers" of persons who recognized her. The incident caused "her great distress and suffering both in body and mind"; she "suffered a severe nervous shock" which confined her to bed under a physician's care. The specific and remedial nature of the tort (and its incapacity to address the public dimension of the harm) was immediately apparent when Roberson claimed she had suffered $15,000 in damages and asked for an injunction against further display of her likeness.[22]

In the court's 4–3 decision against Roberson, the limitations of the legal vocabulary to provide a coherent definition of privacy, address the public aspects of the harm, and formulate an adequate remedy came to the fore. In addition, the irritation that colors Chief Justice Parker's opinion introduced what became the distinctive tone of the party of exposure when confronted by the reticent sensibility. Observing that the plaintiff made no complaint of libel—"indeed, her grievance is that a good portrait of her, and, therefore, one easily recognized, has been used to attract attention"—Judge Parker characterized Roberson's complaint in such a way as to make her appear overly sensitive and her suffering trivial:

> Such publicity, which some find agreeable, is to plaintiff very distasteful, and thus, because of defendants' impertinence in using her picture without her consent for their own business purposes, she has been caused to suffer mental distress where others would have appreciated the compliment to their beauty implied in the selection of the picture for such purposes.[23]

At the outset, Judge Parker declared there were no precedents for recovery in such cases and denied the existence of the right to privacy. He argued that the common-law decisions Brandeis and Warren had cited "rested either upon the ground of breach of trust or that plaintiff had a property right in the subject of litigation which the court could protect." Further undercutting and reshaping their original formulation, he made a number of important claims, including some that Brandeis and Warren had already addressed, such as the "purely mental" cause of the complaint not being sufficient grounds for recovery, and that it was the task of the legislature, not the judiciary, to pass a law to protect privacy. Judge Parker feared that if the protection of privacy became law, a flood of litigation, much of it "bordering on the absurd," would ensue, and he cautioned that it would lead to suits about "a comment upon one's looks, conduct, domestic relations or habits"—all trivial offenses in his opinion. A court of equity was inappropriate, he went on, because equity "deals only with matters of contract and property, and does not exercise jurisdiction in matters of morals or conduct." And finally, introducing claims that would have far-reaching consequences for later litigation, the judge asserted that drawing a distinct boundary between public and private characters was highly problematic, and that recognition of the right to privacy might threaten freedom of the press.[24]

Judge Gray's dissent took exception to three specific features of this opinion. First, he disputed the condescending characterization of Roberson's injury—"In the present case, we may not say that the plaintiff's complaint is fanciful, or that her alleged injury is, purely, a sentimental one"—and was emphatic that her claim was not merely a matter of "caprice" or "taste." Reiterating even as he modified Brandeis and Warren's definition of the right of privacy as the right to be let alone, he emphasized the liberal principles underlying the defense of privacy and blurred Brandeis and Warren's distinction between personal rights and property rights: "The principle is fundamental and essential in organized society that every one, in exercising a personal right and in the use of his property, shall respect the rights and properties of others."[25] The distinction between the protection accorded to privacy rooted in inviolate personality and the protection accorded reputation rooted in private property was elusive at best, even when it was meant to protect a person from the indignity of published gossip, and in trials concerning the unauthorized use of a person's likeness for advertising purposes, it was virtually impossible to maintain.

Next, Judge Gray praised the flexibility of courts of equity which enabled them to remedy "a wrong, which, in the progress of civilization, has been made possible as the result of new social or commercial conditions."[26] Sharing Brandeis and Warren's sociological perspective, he argued that the invention of instantaneous photography exposed people to unprecedented threats to their privacy; he had nothing to say about the equally important harm suffered by society at large, however. Constrained by the legal paradigm, he could formulate the issue only in terms of the harm suffered by an individual whose rights had been violated and thereby deserved state protection; he argued that the state must ensure the security of person which, in his words, "is as necessary as the security of property." And he appealed to an older definition of property that equated property with the rights of the owner: "Property is not, necessarily, the thing itself, which is owned; it is the right of the owner in relation to it."[27]

While Judge Gray's definition of property shows how constricting legal categories of thought are, he further impoverished the meaning of privacy and gave it a pecuniary cast when he added:

> This plaintiff has the same property in her right to be protected against the use of her face for defendant's commercial purposes, as she would have, if they were publishing her literary compositions. The right

would be conceded, if she had sat for her photograph; but if her face, or her portraiture, has a value, the value is hers exclusively.

This proprietary vision of the self has gained tremendous influence in our own time, largely through C. B. Macpherson's *The Political Theory of Possessive Individualism* (1962). The ideology of possessive individualism, the beginnings of which Macpherson traced to Locke, expresses the right of the individual to proprietorship of his or her own person, capacities, or attributes. Society, in this perspective, consists of relations of exchange between proprietors, "a calculated device for the protection of this property and for the maintenance of an orderly relation of exchange."[28] Though this proprietary understanding of the self does not exhaust the richer senses of the self as envisioned by the party of reticence, it does succinctly capture a key aspect of liberalism bequeathed by jurisprudence. Anglo-American jurisprudence, beginning in the seventeenth century, was a fundamental expression of possessive individualism, in which the individual and his social and moral world were defined in terms of the property transactions that he engaged in.

The Roberson decision, declared an editorial in the *American Law Review*, "shocks and wounds the ordinary sense of justice of mankind." The *New York Times* (1902) reported that the "decision excited as much amazement among lawyers and jurists as among the promiscuous lay public." After detailing the relentless pursuit by "Kodakers" of public figures and private individuals alike, the editors observed that "these things appeal to the decent and unsophisticated human mind as outrages." A community which permits such outrages could not be considered "civilized," and they demanded in the name of "decent people" that the New York legislature protect the public from "these savage and horrible practices." The editors of the *Yale Law Journal* (1902) also articulated the public dimension of the harm, deploring the Roberson decision for lending support to the claims of "the sensational press . . . of a right to pry into and grossly display before the public matters of the most private and personal concerns." They feared it set "a precedent whose undeniable effect must be to cheapen the standards of a press already none too high and thereby of the ever-increasing public which reads that press."[29]

Public outrage was so great that Judge O'Brien took the unprecedented step of defending the court's ruling in the *Columbia Law Review* (1902). His article began with the *New York Times* editorial, which he tried to discredit by pointing to the obvious irony of a newspaper championing a right to privacy. Then, reiterating the basis for the decision, he made two points: the plaintiff's injury concerned questions of libel, not privacy; and "courts do not make laws, but enforce those that exist." "The right of privacy, so-called," he continued, "represents an attractive idea to the moralist and the social reformer, but to the lawmaker, who seeks to embody the right in a statute, the subject is surrounded with serious difficulties." The primary difficulty was to define and determine the remedy. Although Judge O'Brien was more sympathetic to the reticent sensibility than was his associate Judge Parker, he still held that it was preferable to endure minor affronts than to employ the law as an agency for social change:

> The commercial and money-making spirit of the age in every department of human exertion may have adopted methods that offend the sensitive and shock the general sense of propriety, but when courts or legislators attempt to meddle with such things it often happens that they do more harm than good.[30]

(Throughout the legal debate on privacy, the question whether law should be adapted to changing social conditions appears time and again. The "progressive" sociological view of adaptive law was marshaled to protect the traditional idea of the right to be let alone, whereas the "conservative" view of law, steeped in precedent, ended up siding with the voices of modernity, refusing to protect privacy because there were no precedents.)

Responding to public pressure, the New York legislature passed a law in 1903 protecting the right to privacy:

> A person, firm, or corporation that uses for advertising purposes or for the purposes of trade, the name, portrait, or picture of any living person without having first obtained the written consent of such person, or if a minor of his or her parent or guardian, is guilty of a misdemeanor.[31]

Obviously the law had been framed in these narrow terms because it was formulated to placate public anger over the brazen exploitation of Roberson's likeness. For this reason, the law addressed only what Judge O'Brien had called "the commercial and money-making spirit of the age" and had nothing to say about broader and more far-reaching concerns expressed by the party of reticence.

It is clear that early right-to-privacy litigation had already radically departed from what Brandeis and Warren originally had in mind, because the people most jealous of their privacy were also the ones who would be most reluctant to take their complaint to court. The people most likely to press their grievances turned out to be those whose names or likenesses had been blatantly exploited for economic gain. Whereas advertising abuses could actually be stopped by a court injunction, injunctions against published gossip would come only after the fact and thus too late. And while commercial exploitation of private individuals was no doubt disturbing to its victims for the reasons advanced by Brandeis and Warren, the law, as it entered the books, displaced their formulation of the right to privacy as the protection of the spiritual interest of inviolate personality, which would provide a remedy for the "mental suffering" that results from "an intentional and unwarranted violation of the 'honor' of another."[32] Instead, it made official a line of thought more in keeping not only with the spirit of the aggressive, material age but also with the proprietary sense of self implicit in liberal jurisprudence: the real interest of the right to privacy was the proprietary control over a person's name or likeness.

The Right to Privacy
Vindicated but Misconstrued

A decision more in keeping with Brandeis and Warren's original formulation was *Pavesich* v. *New England Mutual Life Insurance Co.* (1904). Because this opinion rejected the Roberson decision point by point, it became the leading case establishing a right to privacy. Like *Roberson*, it involved the unauthorized use of a person's likeness in advertising. A likeness of the plaintiff, well-groomed and robust, had been placed in the Atlanta *Constitution* next to the likeness of an ill-dressed, sickly-looking man. Above Pavesich's picture were the words: "Do it now. The man who did." Above the other man's picture were the words: "Do it while you can. The man who didn't." Beneath both images was the caption: "These two pictures tell their story." More advertising copy stated that Pavesich had bought insurance from New England Mutual Life, his family was protected, and he was drawing a dividend; under the other man's picture it said he had not taken insurance and now realized his mistake. Invoking his legal right to privacy, Paolo Pavesich sued for damages of $25,000.[33]

In his judgment in favor of Pavesich, Judge Cobb disposed of many of the objections raised in the Roberson trial. The charge that equity deals only with matters of contract or property was dismissed as hopelessly inadequate and "conservative." He compared Judge Parker's refusal to recognize the right to privacy to the decisions of ignorant judges of the past who sentenced witches to death. Whereas the majority opinion in Roberson feared that a "vast amount of litigation" would ensue if the right to privacy were recognized, Judge Cobb was confident this would not happen, just as he was confident that "honest and fearless" judges and competent juries could be trusted to distinguish between private and public figures. He also was unperturbed by the prospect of balancing the right of free speech with that of privacy.[34]

To counter Judge Parker's assertion that there were no legal precedents for the right to privacy, Judge Cobb marshaled an impressive array of evidence. Like Brandeis and Warren, he argued that the right to privacy was new in instance, not in principle, and he referred to the common-law basis of privacy—"every man's house is his castle" —as well as the common-law protection from nuisances such as bad odors and eavesdropping. In addition, he argued that the right to privacy was derived from natural law: "It is recognized intuitively, consciousness being the witness that can be called to establish its existence." He also anticipated the landmark decision *Roe v. Wade* (1973) when he found precedents for a constitutional right of privacy in the Fourth and Fourteenth amendments, and inferred its existence from the constitutional guarantees of the protection of life, liberty, and happiness. "The right of privacy," wrote Judge Cobb, "is embraced within the absolute rights of personal security and personal liberty."[35]

Judge Cobb also gave greater scope to Brandeis and Warren's definition of the right to be let alone. In so doing, the debt to John Stuart Mill's famous discussion of liberty—that the sole end for state interference with an individual's right of action is to prevent harm to others—was made explicit:

> Liberty includes the right to live as one will, so long as that will does not interfere with the rights of another or of the public. One may desire to live a life of seclusion; another may desire to live a life of publicity; still another may wish to live a life of privacy as to certain matters and of publicity to others. The right of one to exhibit himself to the public, and in a proper manner is embraced within the right of personal liberty. . . . Each is entitled to liberty of choice as to his manner of life, and neither an individual nor the public has a right to arbitrarily take away his liberty.[36]

Although the judge acknowledged that publicity was "absolutely essential to the welfare of the public," he also reiterated the party of reticence's understanding of privacy, that it "is not only essential to the welfare of the individual but also to the well-being of society," though he made no use of the idiom of desecration that usually accompanied such pronouncements:

> The law stamping the unbreakable seal of privacy upon communications between husband and wife, attorney and client, and similar provisions of the law, is a recognition, not only of the right of privacy, but that for the public good, some matters of private concern are not to be made public even with the consent of those involved.[37]

Finally, Judge Cobb rebuked the court for refusing to take seriously Roberson's complaint and the gravity of her suffering. Knowing one's features and form are being exploited for purposes of advertising, he argued,

> brings not only the person of an extremely sensitive nature, but even the individual of ordinary sensibility, to a realization that his liberty has been taken away from him, and, as long as the advertiser uses him for these purposes, he cannot be otherwise than conscious of the fact that he is, for the time being, under the control of another, that he is no longer free, and that he is in reality a slave without hope of freedom, held to service by a merciless master.[38]

Significantly, Judge Cobb said nothing about property or about privacy rooted in proprietary claims to one's features. His rendering of the damages caused by commercial exploitation, although heavy in rhetorical flourish, is closer in spirit to Brandeis and Warren's as well as to the liberal tradition that values privacy as essential to the flourishing of individuality and personal freedom.

Although plaintiffs frequently complained about "wounded feelings" and "mental distress," judges routinely dismissed the claim of mental anguish—if it was the only claim—as insufficient grounds for action. More often than not, mental anguish was subsumed within a larger barrage of complaints of "humiliation," "public scandal," "ridicule," "contempt," "disgrace," "infamy," and "odium." Instead of recognizing such suffering as evidence of invasions of privacy, the courts interpreted them as injury to reputation, a wrong traditionally protected by libel and slander laws. Unaccustomed to thinking about new menaces to privacy occasioned by technological innovations, speakers of the legal discourse effectively reshaped the right to privacy into an expanded version of the protection of reputation. Consequently, the danger posed to privacy by the instant photograph was met by an enlarged understanding of libel, which would protect a person from appearing in a false light. The danger posed to privacy by published gossip was not met, however, because, as we have already noticed, libel and slander laws could prevent only the depiction of an *inaccurate* portrayal of private life, whereas what was needed was the prevention of *any* depiction of private life whatsoever. As we shall see, it was legal conventions pertaining to the defense of reputation that inhibited the protection of privacy as a defense of inviolate personality—that is, in the manner in which Brandeis and Warren had originally envisioned.

Early advertisers were quick to exploit the possibilities of imbuing a product with the aura of authenticity by associating it with the name of an expert. In *Mackenzie* v. *Soden Mineral Springs Co.* (1891), the defendants used a facsimile of the plaintiff's signature under a supposed endorsement of their product, Soden Mineral Pastilles. Although Mackenzie, a well-known throat specialist living in England, asserted that his right to privacy had been violated, the larger part of his complaint stated that he had lost prestige, trust, and money as a result of the unauthorized advertisement, since commercialization ran "contrary to the ethics of the profession." The court found in his favor, arguing that the defendant had "trad[ed] upon his professional reputation" and that the ad was "a fraud upon the public and upon this plaintiff's professional standing and reputation, and offensive to his feelings."[39]

Similar circumstances surrounded *Foster-Milburn Co.* v. *Chinn* (1909). Here it was the easy recognition of the plaintiff's name as a public figure that was exploited. Chinn, a senator from Kentucky, sued Foster-Milburn Co. for a forged recommendation of its kidney pills along with a picture of him. The senator complained that he had been "ridiculed and laughed at by his friends," that the publication subjected him to "disgrace, ridicule, odium, contempt in the estimation of his friends and acquaintances." The court found not only that the senator's right of privacy had been violated but also that he had been libeled, the gist of the action being injury to character.[40]

Not only did advertisers attempt to exploit the names of experts and public figures, they also used private persons, as we have seen in the Roberson and Pavesich trials.[41] As all these examples make clear, even though the plaintiffs complained of invasion of privacy and mental anguish, the claims succeeded *only* when they were coupled with libel or fraud, thereby testifying to the tenacity of the judiciary to understand the injury as defamation. Such cases were certainly not right-to-privacy suits in the form proposed by Brandeis and Warren. But they bring to light the largely forgotten sensibility that despises publicity for its implied suggestion that the person allowed his or her name to be used for commercial gain. The plaintiffs' repeated claims of mental anguish suggest that even though liberal jurisprudence had no trouble imagining people as proprietors of their attributes, the plaintiffs themselves, steeped in the social practice of reticence, found this vision repugnant.

The distaste for commercializing one's personality constantly appears in court records but nowhere is it more vivid than in *Binns* v. *Vitagraph Co.* (1913). John R. Binns, a wireless telegrapher, had acted heroically when he remained at his post during a collision between steamships at sea. Although Binns had refused "to allow himself to be publicly exploited as a hero," Vitagraph hired an actor to play him in "scenes representing the disaster, and exhibited photographs so obtained as moving pictures, showing the person representing the plaintiff in ludicrous attitudes." Finding in Binns's favor, the court concluded: "The plaintiff claims that he was greatly disturbed in mind and that his feelings were injured by the acts of the defendant and the inference which would be drawn therefrom that he had commercialized his fame thus accidentally received."[42] The last sentence discloses a great deal about the kind of injury many of these people sustained: Binns was mortified by the wrongful implication that he had used his accidental fame as a source of income.

Many plaintiffs made a similar complaint: they were scandalized by the possibility that people would assume they actually endorsed commercial products, or worse, that people would know they did not and suspect them of duplicity for the sake of profit. In *Kunz* v. *Allen and Bayne* (1918), the court found the exhibition in a moving-picture theater of a photograph of a woman taken without her consent and "for the purpose of exploiting the publisher's business" was a violation of her right of privacy. Kunz had been in a dry-goods store when a film was surreptitiously taken of her. Afterward, the defendants showed the film in a movie theater in her neighborhood. Kunz "became the common talk of the people in the community, it being understood, and believed among the people generally that she had for hire permitted her photo to be taken and used as a public advertisement."[43] That the victims of unwanted publicity couched their complaint in terms of invasion of privacy demonstrates how ill at ease many people felt in this new atmosphere of exposure and commercial exploitation. That the cases were usually interpreted by the judiciary as defamation, however, shows how persistent and unresponsive traditional categories of legal thought were to these new technological threats. It was only with the advent of the movie star and the proliferation of advertising and public relations in the 1920s that this long-standing ambivalence to publicity began to disappear.

THE COMMERCIAL EXPLOITATION OF "NEWSWORTHY" FIGURES

While the law failed to encompass the public dimension of the harm because of its fixation on proprietary rights of individuals, the recurring question whether the right to privacy threatened freedom of the press was an indirect acknowledgment that the public did indeed have an interest in determining what is said or shown in public. Yet, because the issue was formulated as a conflict between competing rights and interests, crucial concerns of the reticent sensibility, largely alien to the language of law—maintaining public standards of taste and morality, and protecting the sense of the sacred—never entered the legal debate.

By 1904, the conflict between the right to privacy and the constitutionally protected free press had already flared so often that one judge remarked, "The stumbling block which many have encountered in the way of a recognition of a right of privacy has been that the recognition of such right would inevitably tend to curtail the liberty of speech and of press." Because this "stumbling block" is ritualistically invoked by commentators today, it is essential to understand how it came to dominate the debate in the first place.[44] Its beginnings can be traced to the effort legal thinkers made to distinguish between public and private figures. This undertaking gave them a new way of thinking about and formulating the issue of newsworthiness and, with it, the language to express the conflict between freedom of the press and the right to privacy.

For Brandeis and Warren, an "obvious and fundamental distinction" existed between public and private persons. The former were candidates for public office and public or "quasi-public" officials (e.g., railroad bosses) whose activities were open to public scrutiny. Frequently, judges expanded this list to include not only people in politics but also artists, authors, inventors, the "learned professions," and people who either transgress the law or evoke its aid.[45]

Entangled in the question of who was to be recognized as a public figure was the problem of how much privacy should be forfeited as a consequence of appearing in public. As we have seen, Brandeis and Warren were adamant that "some things all men alike are entitled to keep from public curiosity, whether in public life or not." These things "concern the private life, habits, acts, and relations of an individual, and have no legitimate connection with his fitness for a public office." But their position was open to dispute. In an early decision, *Corliss* v. *E. W. Walker* (1894), the judge declared that a public person was like a published manuscript—he could be read by everyone—and therefore he had forfeited his right of privacy. At a South Carolina Press Association meeting in 1905, a participant named Paul M. Brice insisted that it is "the duty of the public serving newspaper" to provide material about the private life of public figures, especially candidates for public office. If a candidate "is found wanting, lacking in that character and those high attributes which would make him the proper custodian of the people's moral and industrial welfare," he insisted, "it is not unethical for a newspaper to publish proved, unquestioned facts as to his private life which will inform the people of the manner of man he is and what they may logically expect should they confer their suffrages upon him."[46]

Judges presiding over right-to-privacy trials frequently took exception to these formulations. They often appealed to the civic principle that linked public appearance with duty and responsibility, and feared that undesired publicity would discourage the best people from entering politics. In *Atkinson* v. *Doherty* (1899), the widow of a well-known lawyer and politician wanted to restrain the use of her husband's name and likeness on a label of a brand of cigars named after him. The judge declared, "We are loath to believe that the man who makes himself useful to mankind surrenders any right of privacy thereby." In the Roberson decision, the court elaborated upon this position: "Is the right of privacy the possession of mediocrity alone, which a person forfeits by giving rein to his ability, spurs to his industry, or grandeur to his character?"[47]

Some judges also raised the question when, if ever, a private person—one who did not fit any of the "public" categories—could be safely exposed to the glare of publicity. The judge presiding over *Munden* v. *Harris* (1911), where a child's picture was used in an advertisement to sell jewelry, gave the issue a distinctly modern cast: "Though one has the right of privacy in his picture as a right of property, he may waive the right by becoming a public character or by conduct exciting public interest." A legal journal of the time gave substance to this formulation: "It is . . . right to publish an account of an act of heroism by a formerly obscure person or even of his calamity in a street accident." In *Hillman* v. *Star Publishing Co.* (1911), a newspaper published an article stating that the plaintiff's father, a millionaire real-estate operator, had been charged with using the mails to defraud potential buyers. The article announced he would be arrested and published a photograph of his family, including the plaintiff. Even though the judge recognized that a wrong had been committed, he found against Hillman on the grounds that the article and the photograph, taken together, were not libelous. Again revealing the way adversarial legal proceedings always involve a hunt for victims, the judge declared that the article and photograph did not tend "to expose the plaintiff to ridicule or contempt or deprive her of social enjoyment, but rather excit[ed] pity for her."[48]

It is at this point that the story of whom the world treats as a public figure coincides with the story of the conflict between a free press and the right to privacy. This vague, broad formulation of a public person as one who excites public interest gave credence to the press's claim that the alleged "newsworthiness" of an article or the "public's right to know" should take precedence over, or at least be balanced against, the individual's right to privacy. The claim that the public had an interest in newsworthy events was also used to permit the very kinds of material—invasive and sensational journalism—which the party of reticence was most concerned to control. In *Commonwealth* v. *Herald Publishing Co.* (1908), a number of newspapers were indicted for printing parts of testimony from the notorious Thaw trial, in progress in New York at the time. Instead of claiming that the articles violated Mrs. Thaw's right to privacy—which would have been preposterous, given that the papers were reprinting her testimony in open court—the papers were indicted for printing obscenity when they published "a part of Mrs. Thaw's evidence . . . describing the manner in which Stanford White drugged and seduced her." Judge Carroll focused attention on the public dimension of the harm—obscene materials "have a tendency to corrupt the morals and deprave the taste of the people"—yet he all too easily slipped into the circular reasoning which holds that people who excite public interest become legitimate public characters: "The Thaw trial was a notable criminal case—the public everywhere were interested in all of its details—and the newspapers of the country, to gratify this desire, however depraved it might have been, published full accounts of it."[49]

Judge Carroll went on to enumerate precisely which material the court could not prevent daily newspapers from publishing, providing a good description not only of trials commonly being conducted at the time but also of stories newspapers regularly reported—"accounts of crimes or the proceedings of criminal courts," "matters relating to divorce suits, or breach of promise cases, or actions for alienation of affections," "prosecutions for rape or unlawful detention," "scandals that appear in private life," even when there are "suggestions or facts that are immodest and immoral, if not indecent." Although he maintained that a newspaper is not "privileged to publish all the filthy and disgusting details that are developed by the evidence in court proceedings," the judge hoped to distinguish between the application of obscenity law to daily newspapers as opposed to books and pamphlets. Employing the justification developed by realist novelists and their champions who claimed they were simply portraying life as they found it, Judge Carroll insisted that the newspaper was an impartial purveyor of "the news of the day, made up as it is of a multitude of incidents gathered from all quarters of the globe, embracing every phase of human life, and dealing with every feature of human endeavor." Thus, he found that the publication of "a truthful record of a court proceeding" did not fall within the precincts of obscenity law.[50] In such an instance, the claim that it was the newspaper's duty and right to truthfully report what happens in society took precedence over the threat of public pollution.

The reticent sensibility, however, had not been completely silenced. In a *Dial* editorial entitled "What the Public Wants" (1909), the writer once again rejected not only the giving-the-people-what-they-want alibi but also the pose of the impartial reporter: "Democracy becomes an exquisite absurdity if it be taken to mean that in these matters there is to be no guidance, no attempt to uplift the general taste, no function higher than that of supplying an untrained demand." Despite the persistence of public sentiment against invasive and sensational newspapers, in *United States* v. *Journal Co.* (1912), the court found that mailing copies of a reputable newspaper containing accurate, though sensational, reports of testimony in open court during the trial could not be held a criminal offense. In this case, District Judge Waddill directly addressed the First Amendment question: "The guaranty of freedom of the press was granted, not alone because of the necessity therefore for its protection, but that thereby many of the dearest and most essential rights and privileges of the citizen might be assured and protected."[51]

In right-to-privacy trials, too, the First Amendment quickly became the primary point of contention. The courts in *Corliss* v. *E. W. Walker* (1894) and *Atkinson* v. *Doherty* (1899) asserted freedom of the press over the individual's right to privacy, though the judge in Corliss included a proviso: "Under our laws one can speak and publish what he desires, provided he commits no offense against public morals or private reputation." In contrast, the judge presiding over *Marks* v.

Jaffa (1893) maintained the opposite position: "No newspaper or institution, no matter how worthy, has the right to use the name or picture of anyone for such a purpose [photographs of two actors in a popularity contest] without his consent." In *Pavesich* v. *New England Mutual Life Insurance Co.*, the judge was more prudent: since both were "natural rights," they must exercise mutual respect for each other and their particular interests be balanced. In hindsight, it seems strange that the free press ever became an issue in the right-to-privacy cases because, as we have seen, practically all the early litigation concerned the unauthorized use of a person's likeness or name for advertising or trade purposes. Yet the only judge to make this point was the one who presided over *Pavesich*: "There is in the publication of one's picture for advertising purposes not the slightest semblance of an expression of an idea, a thought, or an opinion within the meaning of the constitutional provision which guarantees to a person the right to publish his sentiments on any subject."[52]

The tension between these competing rights was further heightened by the 1903 New York law making it illegal to use without written consent a living person's name or likeness for advertising or trade purposes. What is implicit here is the assumption that a precise distinction can be drawn between unauthorized use of a person's likeness or name for legitimate purposes—when the person is a public figure whose actions affect the public, for example—and exploitation of a person's likeness or name for the sole purpose of turning a profit. Most certainly the law was devised in this way to put an end to the kind of advertising abuses which had given rise to the Roberson trial. The addition of the phrase "trade purposes," however, opened up to litigation a new and ambiguous area between commercial exploitation of personality and the legitimate reporting of news.

In *Jeffries* v. *New York Evening Journal Publishing Co.* (1910), Jeffries had written an autobiography and against his wishes, a newspaper wanted to print his picture in connection with the publication of the book; a motion for injunction was denied. The judge asserted, "A picture is not used 'for advertising purposes' within its meaning, unless the picture is part of an advertisement, while 'trade' refers to 'commerce or traffic,' not to the dissemination of information." What the judge had failed to observe here is that "information," too, can be exploited to sell newspapers, as critics of the new journalism tirelessly pointed out.[53]

While the Jeffries decision showed how so-called information could be manipulated to increase newspaper circulation, *Colyer* v. *Richard K. Fox Publishing Co.* (1914) introduced into the legal proceedings what had long been a staple in sensational reporting: the unauthorized use of a person's picture in a publication that makes no claim to the picture's "newsworthiness" but instead exploits its sensational qualities to promote sales. May Colyer was a young actress and professional high-diving entertainer. A photograph of her clad in her high-diving costume was published without her consent in the *National Police Gazette* (1913). Below the picture, a caption read: "May Collier [sic], a Great Trick Diver." On the same page appeared pictures of four women vaudeville performers in their stage costumes. At the bottom of the page were the words: "Five of a Kind on this Page. Most of Them Adorn the Burlesque Stage, All of Them Are Favorites With the Bald Headed Boys." Colyer did not claim damage to her reputation or mental anguish or invasion of privacy. Instead, she relied strictly on the New York law. She complained that the magazine carried "a very considerable amount of reading matter that scarcely appeals to a refined mind, and likewise a great number of advertisements of quack nostrums and trivial things." The court responded,

> From these circumstances, the appellant asks this court to hold from a mere inspection of the paper that it is but a mere advertising sheet sold as a matter of trade, and that, therefore, every one of its photographic illustrations must be deemed to be used "for advertising purposes or for the purposes of trade" within the meaning of the statute.[54]

The judge, however, was unconvinced. He maintained that since Colyer's photograph was not used in an actual advertisement, it was beside the point that the *Gazette* consisted primarily of advertisements. In addition, he rejected her claims on the grounds that as an entertainer she was a public figure and had thereby forfeited her right to privacy. The court's decision permitting the undisguised exploitation of Colyer's picture gave legitimacy to a kind of journalism that surpassed in sensationalism what Brandeis and Warren's original formulation had been designed to outlaw.

In the end, the controversy over the competing interests of privacy and the press was a pseudo-controversy. The issue was not the real tension that might occasionally pull between an individual's right to privacy and the exposure of matters of legitimate public interest. Rather, what needs to be emphasized is that the press's self-imposed task of constantly discovering news drives it to invade people's privacy in order to promote and then satisfy a voracious appetite for sensationalism which the press itself has manufactured. That the debate about privacy has ossified in this intractable form points to a fundamental shift in the metaphors that shape our way of thinking about public and private. Whereas the party of reticence had once spoken of "separate spheres," clearly demarcated, to prevent the trivialization of private life, the coarsening of the tone of public conversation, and the lowering of standards of judgment, legal writers employed the image of a balancing act of discrete interests—the individual's right to privacy, the press's right to free speech, and the public's right to know. These interests, however, are by definition incommensurable and therefore impossible to balance with any precision or justice. Nevertheless, the incommensurability of these interests has continued to fuel the controversy over invasive and sensational news into our own time.

The Failure of the Legal Remedy and the Triumph of Invasive Journalism

Because flagrant advertising abuses provided the specific occasions for legislative action, the scope of the legal protection of privacy was severely constricted from the start. In 1913, for example, twenty states considered newspaper regulation aimed at controlling unscrupulous advertisers, and Congress, too, entertained several bills designed to the same end. At the same time, the commercial imperative of advertising pushed issues about ownership into the fore, which, in turn, dovetailed with the liberal juristic definition of selfhood in terms of proprietary interests and the law's propensity to hunt for individual victims. Taken together, these circumstances made for a privacy law very different from the one originally envisioned by Brandeis and Warren. Instead of safeguarding "the spiritual precincts of inviolate personality" or protecting the public atmosphere from "pollution," the law was inclined to address only the injury inflicted upon an individual's reputation, and only when that injury closely resembled defamation. Merle Thorpe, editor of a symposium on journalism published under the title *The Coming Newspaper* (1915), made clear the legislators' failure to imagine invasions of privacy as something different from libel when he observed that "most states in the past five years have in one way or another made their libel laws more drastic" as a response to intrusive journalism.[55]

In an essay tracking the dismal legal career of the right to privacy, "Paul Pry and Privacy" (1932), a critic named Mitchell Dawson complained of both the ineffectiveness of right-to-privacy trials and the narrowness of the New York law. He noted that the right-to-privacy disputes which actually landed in court almost never dealt with the "outrageous disregard of personal rights and feelings as shown a dozen times a day in almost any newspaper." On the rare occasion when impudent reporting actually resulted in a trial, the judge, according to Dawson, consistently found against the plaintiff. Attempting to make sense of this, he speculated that "even those judges who might otherwise accept Justice Brandeis's doctrine [concerning "the right to be let alone"] will not apply it to newspapers for fear of interfering with the freedom of the press, even though it was precisely the misconduct of the newspapers which first inspired his defense of privacy."[56]

While legislation eventually succeeded in controlling the unauthorized use of a person's likeness for advertising or commercial purposes, intrusive and sensational reporting continued to multiply, even though scores of states passed laws to quell it. Frederick S. Siebert, in *The Rights and Privileges of the Press* (1934), noted that to "combat the flood of pernicious publications devoted to stories of lust and crime, a number of states have passed statutes providing for the prosecution of publishers who pander to the baser instincts of the reading public." The target of these statutes were newspapers and other printed matter " 'devoted to the publication, or principally made up of criminal news, police reports, or pictures and stories of bloodshed, lust, or crime.' " Just as Dawson had expressed surprise at the virtual impossibility of getting a conviction in right-to-privacy trials, Siebert noted with some perplexity that "a large newspaper of general news content seems never to have been prosecuted under these statutes."[57]

Since fear of infringing First Amendment rights gave even the most egregious violators of privacy immunity, intrusive journalism as such was never subject to government regulation. Instead, the newspaper industry periodically indulged in an orgy of self-accusation and breast-beating, which typically produced anguished pleas for self-policing. Beginning in the 1890s and continuing into our own time, the favored solution has been "professionalism." Using as their model the licensing requirements and review boards of doctors and lawyers, journalists have repeatedly attempted to transform the brash, prying reporter into a disciplined, responsible professional. To that end, universities and colleges founded schools of journalism and reporters formed professional organizations—establishing codes of professional ethics, standardizing academic requirements, and licensing nonacademically trained reporters.[58] Yet, because of the wide protection afforded journalism by the First Amendment, coupled with the gradual reorientation of the press as a form of mass entertainment rather than an agency of civic education, the profession, so called, was loath to enforce its professional ethics with any rigor. More often than not, journalists preferred to rely on the standard of the marketplace and the ready excuse that they were giving the people what they want.

With the rise of ever more brazen and outrageous tabloids in the 1920s—culminating in the frenzied feedings on the Lindberghs' privacy when their infant was kidnapped and murdered—the attack on invasive journalism gathered new force. Just as it was popularly believed in the nineteenth century that invasions of privacy were most fittingly countered by personal violence, the American Society of Newspaper Editors, a watchdog organization established in 1923, reported that it had received numerous complaints from its members about not only contempt citations but also physical assaults upon reporters and photographers.[59] In a deluge of attacks in journals of opinion, magazines, and even full-length books, critics repeatedly deplored the depths to which the tabloids had sunk, making the abuses of earlier times pale in comparison. In his "Tabloid Offenses" (1927), Oswald Garrison Villard, the well-respected editor first of the *New York Post* and then of *The Nation*, exclaimed, "No journalism of the nineties ever went so far in the portrayal of the nude, or in the faking of pictures, and frank description of crime and degeneracy, as do the tabloids in New York today." Villard no doubt had in mind such outrages as the fake photograph of a woman standing nude in front of the jury in the scandalous Browning marriage annulment trial, published by the *New York Graphic* in 1924, and the lurid exhibition in newspapers of photographic close-ups of the body of the murdered man in the notorious Collings murder case.[60]

In broad outline, the new indictment of these scurrilous reporters remained the same as the nineteenth-century one, except for one important difference: critics of tabloid journalism hailed not from the party of reticence but either from the remnant of responsible journalists or from the smart-set wing of the party of exposure. The old question of the proper role of the press in a democracy continued to occupy center stage. Repeatedly, these critics made the traditional claim that "the press is burdened with responsibility for general well-being, public morality, and the harmonious operation of democratic government." They also continued to alert their readers to the regrettable fact that the press no longer considered "theirs a public trust, or that they have any civic or social duty to the community which supports them." And following in the footsteps of their nineteenth-century counterparts, they always made the point that "the newspaper is a manufacturing concern producing goods to sell at profit" and that profit was more likely to accrue the more the newspaper resembled "the department store," "the variety show," and "the brothel." They typically deplored the way newspapers and especially tabloids had become single-mindedly focused on exploiting gossip, human-interest stories, scandal, sex, and crime. Their catalogues of press misconduct rivaled earlier ones in both their scope and their triviality. According to Silas Bent, a former newspaperman who became a professor of journalism at the New School for Social Research and author of *Ballyhoo: The Voice of the Press* (1927): "The newspaper reader perceives in the freedom of the press the privilege to invade his personal privacy, print his picture without his consent, dump onto his doorstep filth collected from the courts, and ballyhoo, for the aggrandisement of its own treasure, prize-fighters, channel swimmers, football players, chorus girls, and aviators."[61]

What is most immediately apparent from this catalogue is that by the 1920s the press had become a form of mass entertainment in its own right. In addition, Bent's slangy book title, *Ballyhoo*, as well as the debunking tone and absence of moral language reveal a critic educated in the hard-boiled, modern school of journalism. His disdain for the commercialization and vulgarization of the press, however, recalls the nineteenth-century reticent sensibility. The same features can be seen in Mitchell Dawson's "Paul Pry and Privacy," in which he claimed that the modern prying reporter was the most recent incarnation of the nineteenth-century stock character of the insufferable busybody, a traditional object of common "ridicule and contempt." By 1934, the list of modern-day "Paul Prys" had swelled to include many denizens of mass entertainment—"tabloid reporters, radio gossips, Sunday-supplement writers, camera-men, wire-tapping dry agents, black-mailing shysters, and back-fence biographers." In his "Tabloid Offenses" Villard alone continued to make the old point that what was at stake in the controversy over sensational journalism was "good taste and decency." Because Villard was a staunch supporter of free speech in both journalism and modern literature, he had nothing but contempt for those who appropriated hard-won libertarian arguments in the name of the tabloids:

> Stripped of all humbug and hypocrisy, these papers are synonymous with bad taste, vulgarity, a degenerate sensationalism, a devotion to the drab and seamy sides of life which cannot be successfully championed on the ground that they are modern and therefore good and inspiring; but simply on the ground that they sell.[62]

It is significant that by the mid-1920s, only Villard (who had been educated at Harvard at the close of Charles Eliot Norton's career there) continued to use the vocabulary of the reticent sensibility. Yet key components of the earlier indictment of invasive journalism— such as public pollution, the waning of the sense of the sacred and the shameful, the damage inflicted upon people's sense of proportion, and their incapacity to make the right ordering of things—had either been made irrelevant by modern developments or, worse yet, simply faded from common memory. "The pendulum has swung far since the hyper-reticent days of our grandmothers," concluded Dawson. "We have achieved a healthy freedom of mind, body, and limb, but in that process the majority have lost all desire for privacy, either for themselves or anyone else."[63]

Along with this debunking style went a contempt for the taste of ordinary people, both of which had been pioneered by Mencken and were eminently popular among intellectuals and cultural critics during the 1920s. Speaking in the name of the civilized minority, John Macy, in *Civilization in the United States* (1922), dismissed both the commercial press and its rapacious audience. He noted that "an intelligent populace would buy [periodicals like the *New Republic* or the *Freeman*] by the million. So we leave the responsibility where, after all, it belongs. The American press is an accurate gauge of the American mind." Villard, too, implicated the reading public when he pointed to "the obvious fact that [the tabloids'] conductors are pandering to a certain popular liking for sensationalism and the prurient." E. L. Godkin had singled out the desire for notoriety on the part of the obscure as the motor of invasive journalism, and Dawson, forty years later, offered a similar, though more jaundiced, view: editors were "occupied solely with giving the public what it wants," he observed, and they were "unfortunately abetted by the willing exhibitionism of a large part of the public they serve. The average newspaper reader would give what passes for his soul to strut just once across the headlines in any role, no matter how ignominious." People resorted to such foolish stunts as marathon dancing and flagpole sitting because of their hunger for any kind of public notice. Anticipating Andy Warhol's prediction that everyone would be famous for fifteen minutes, Dawson announced, "Every undistinguished ego may escape anonymity for at least a few brief ecstatic moments." Public opinion could never effectively rein in sensational journalism, he thought, since it was the public that demanded it: "It is precisely against the curiosity and pruriency of that ravening monster—the public—that protection is needed."[64]

In 1927, *The Forum* published an exchange entitled "Are Tabloids a Menace?" Villard set out the indictment against tabloids that I have described above and Martin Weyrich, an editor for the *New York Graphic*, which had gained notoriety for its lurid reporting of the Browning trial, responded. Like earlier apologists for invasive journalism, Weyrich employed the anti-progress idiom, calling Villard's attack "just one more symptom of the present powerful conservative undertow." For Weyrich, to speak disparagingly of tabloids was to declare allegiance to "traditionalism" in all things: "It is a skirmish in the war traditionalism is waging to block liberalization of education, music, art, dress, literature. It is the protest of the static against the movie; the drab expressing distaste at the dramatic; the ghostly dead moaning at the ways of the quick." Tabloids, he insisted, were "just as inevitable as jazz." They epitomized modern America and criticism of them bordered on being anti-American: "They are as truly expressive of modern America as World Series baseball, skyscrapers, radio, the movies, Trudy Ederle, Billy Sunday, taxicabs, and beauty contests. They are feared because they are jolting the pillars of conservatism."[65] This list makes clear not only the kind of things filling public space but also that promoters of tabloid journalism proudly regarded their product as one of the new species of commercial entertainment.

Rather than addressing his opponents' criticisms head-on, which would have moved the debate to the issue of the character of the common world, Weyrich reduced them to personal, base motives, insisting that old-style newspapermen objected so strenuously to tabloids because they were threatened by their higher circulations which attracted more advertisers. He also smuggled in hard-won literary arguments from the controversy over realism: tabloids were superior to the traditional press because "they introduced a style of journalism that concerns itself primarily with the drama of life. . . . Old press journalism," he sniggered, "is based as of yore upon academics, politics, and polemics," all of which was "eminently proper and unquestionably dull." Saving for last what he obviously believed would be the most devastating blow, he giddily announced that psychoanalysts would classify his opponents as "personalities that veer so certainly to nasty thoughts."[66]

That Weyrich was able to caricature the school of thought represented by Villard in this fashion testifies to the way debunking had deteriorated into sheer cant. Throughout his long career, Villard had distinguished himself as a vigorous opponent of the forces of censorship. During the 1920s, according to the historian Paul S. Boyer,

"Villard's *Nation* . . . was unremitting in its blasts at the depredations of the 'smut-hunting society' and the 'illiterate constable.' " Villard was so prominent a defender of the First Amendment that he was a featured speaker at an anti-censorship rally in Boston in 1927 on behalf of Dreiser's *An American Tragedy* that included such luminaries as Morris Ernst, Clarence Darrow, Arthur Garfield Hays, Arthur Schlesinger, Sr., and Margaret Sanger.[67]

In an essay entitled "Good Manners in Literature" that appeared in the same issue of *The Forum*, the question as to what should appear in public was broached again, this time in relation to modern literature. A critic named Richard Burton condemned popular novels like *An American Tragedy* and *Gentlemen Prefer Blondes* in language that resonates with Brandeis and Warren's original formulation of the right to privacy almost forty years earlier. Such writing, he claimed, had made "violent inroads into what used to be regarded as the private domains of personal life." Burton observed, "It is now quite in the literary mode to speak in print of almost anything that has happened in the personal experience, to air the rankest thoughts—I suppose upon the Freudian principle of cure by public ventilation."[68]

To illuminate what was wrong with this growing "incontinence" in talk, Burton summoned the testimony of two nineteenth-century cultural arbiters. (The prestige of the reticent sensibility was so faded that its loyal remnant needed past authorities to attest to it.) Thus he conjured James Russell Lowell, who, "complaining of the encroachment upon legitimate privacy, declared we flattened our noses against the window panes of the living and rifled the tombs of the dead, in our insatiate curiosity." And this, he reminded his readers, in a generation before the "present license" to write or print anything "that may come into a human head." He also conjured Henry Holt—"that charming example of the gentleman-publisher uniting old-style manners with an intellectual equipment that kept him apace with every shade of modern thought." He quoted Holt's standard for the proper subject matter of literature: "There ought to be no difficulty, though some is alleged, in deciding what is proper for literature. Obviously, the functions of the body, which even savages consign to privacy, are not fit subjects for literature, nor is any allusion to them which is avoided in polite society."[69]

Burton apparently felt so beleaguered by the attack against reticence that he was obliged not only to point out that Holt had "kept . . . apace with every shade of modern thought," but also to observe, "One can hear the scornful shriek of denial that assaults the welkin, after such a statement." His display of self-consciousness reveals how effective the party of exposure's strategy had been of portraying any and all criticisms as desperate rearguard actions. Burton was equally on the defensive when he knowingly remarked that to object to the new novels' "vulgarity, coarseness, slovenly disregard of inherited decencies and fitnesses" was "to announce oneself as hopelessly out of the movement." So powerful were the charges of outdatedness and elitism that he felt the need to declare himself just as opposed to the "obnoxious" quality of the "namby-pamby . . . extreme of lady-like avoidance" as he was to the extreme to "which the present tendency is a reaction and, in its initial purity, a legitimate one."[70]

In the end, he lamented the general deterioration of modern literature, and he pointed an accusing finger at the commercial press: "In this unsavory spectacle of tasteless, ill-mannered, forced, and vulgar writing, the influence of the newspaper is unhappily in evidence. Journalism, which has to appeal to the jaded, must deliver 'punch' or 'wallop.' "[71] And with this indictment he made apparent that, with the failure of the legal right of privacy to regulate invasive and sensational journalism, the floodgates for all manner of writing had been flung wide open.

7

THE LEGAL DEBATE
ABOUT OBSCENITY

A legal defense of privacy that proved surprisingly more resistant to the paradigm of rights and interests emerged in the debate about obscenity. Where early right-to-privacy disputes had shown what people had in mind when they claimed their privacy had been violated, the legal debate about obscenity, in roughly the same time period, 1873–1934, revealed what was at stake when people insisted that a given publication was obscene and therefore unfit for public display. (The time is framed by passage of the Comstock Act, which set the parameters of what legally qualified as obscene and the trial *United States* v. *One Book Called "Ulysses,"* which effectively reformulated these boundaries.) During this early period, juries almost always found the contested material—and the greatest number of cases concerned sex-education—to be obscene. Only two kinds of material consistently escaped regulation: sealed, private, personal letters, even if they contained obscene materials,[1] and "classics" such as *The Arabian Nights, Tom Jones, The Decameron*, and Ovid's *Art of Love*.[2]

Obscenity was successfully regulated because there was a broad consensus about indecency, rooted in the old standards of the reticent sensibility. Thus, disputes about obscenity were initially resistant to adversarial legal proceedings, and judges continued to speak the well-established language of reticence when assessing the consequences for private and public life when fragile personal matters were indiscriminately paraded in public. As we saw in Chapter 2, early decisions drew attention to the way obscenity corrupted private morality and "polluted" the public atmosphere. By making people overfamiliar with indecency, so the argument went, obscenity inured them to its impropriety and ultimately weakened their judgment, paving the way for an ugly, vulgar world devoid of legitimate standards of taste and judgment.

OBSCENITY DEFINED

From our contemporary perspective, where obscenity is often held to be purely subjective or best left to experts to define, the nearly universal agreement as to its meaning in the early trials is indeed remarkable. Judges were so confident about this consensus that they dispensed with definitions altogether, one declaring them "entirely unnecessary, for these words are in common use, and their meaning is readily comprehended by men of ordinary intelligence." Even though this was an era in which experts were establishing their authority in a number of arenas that had previously been trusted to common sense, judges typically insisted that recognizing obscenity was by no means an esoteric exercise:

> [Obscene words] are in common use, and every person of ordinary intelligence understands their meaning, and readily in most cases, accurately applies them to any object or thing brought to his attention which involves a judgment as to the quality indicated. It does not require an expert in art or literature to determine whether a picture is obscene or whether printed words are offensive to decency and good morals.

Another judge thought that since the words " 'obscene,' etc." had not "acquired any technical significance" but were "terms of popular use, . . . the court might perhaps with propriety leave their import to the presumed intelligence of the jury." Summing up the qualities required to determine whether a publication was obscene, another judge declared, "The case is one that addresses itself largely to your good judgment, common sense, and knowledge of human nature and the weaknesses of human nature."[3]

When defendants challenged the court to specify the meaning of obscenity, some judges made an unparalleled move outside the law, appealing to the dictionary for definitions of three key words— "obscene," "indecent," and "lewd." "Obscene," according to the dictionary that one judge read in court, meant "offensive to chastity and decency, expressing or presenting to the mind or view something which delicacy, purity, and decency forbid to be exposed." Obscenity was also that which is "offensive to decency or chastity, which is immodest, which is indelicate, causing lewd thoughts of an immoral tendency." In the same vein, another judge defined the obscene as "something that is offensive to chastity, something that is foul or filthy, and for that reason is offensive to pure-minded persons," while still another described it as that which "offend[s] decency and outrage[s] modesty."[4]

Judges also tried to clarify the meaning of another crucial term, "indecent." Here one sees a sensibility that so takes for granted the importance of common sense, judgment, and a sense of proportion that it is blind to the circularity of its definitions. "Indecent," according to one judge, meant "the wanton and unnecessary expression or exposure, in words or pictures, of that which the common sense of decency requires should be kept private or concealed," that which is "unbecoming, immodest, unfit to be seen." Another judge consulted the dictionary: "*Worcester* defines [indecent] as something 'unbecoming, unfit for eyes or ears.' The *Century Dictionary* defines it as that which is 'obscene or grossly vulgar; unbecoming, unseemly, violating propriety of language, behavior, etc.' " Sometimes this line of thought verged on tautology: the indecent "tend[s] to obscenity—having that form of indecency which is calculated to promote the general corruption of morals." "Lewd," the third term in question, the judges defined as "given to the unlawful indulgence of lust, eager for sexual indulgence," or "incited by lust, or incites lustful thoughts, leading to irregular indulgence of animal desires; lustful, lecherous, libidinous."[5]

The discourse of reticence, then, furnished the courts with the vocabulary and grammar to develop two distinct lines of definition: one characterized obscenity in terms of indecency, a quality that inheres in things and not in individual judgment; the other fused obscenity with subjective response—the excitement of lust. These two lines of definition would lend themselves to quite different interpretations of the harm stemming from obscenity. The first—obscenity as that which was unfit to be seen or heard—could be construed broadly as threatening the quality of public life by placing things in common view that are not large or sturdy enough to withstand the attention; it represented those aspects of the reticent sensibility that share in the sanctification of the private sphere as the protective cover for fragile, vulnerable experiences. The second—obscenity as that which excites lewdness—narrowed the scope of the harm to a particular individual's morality; this accommodated the law in its hunt for individual victims—a hunt which had so marred right-to-privacy proceedings. This emphasis, when it was not tempered by taste and judgment, also produced the warped offshoot of the reticent sensibility, comstockery.

While key components of the reticent sensibility were never incorporated into laws protecting privacy, some were successfully incorporated into obscenity law in 1873 when Congress passed the Comstock Postal Act. That law, as we have seen, banned five kinds of materials from the public mails: (1) "an obscene, lewd, lascivious book, pamphlet, paper, print, or other publication of an indecent character"; (2) information and devices relating to birth control; (3) things "intended or adapted for immoral use or nature"; (4) any information regarding how to obtain or make the materials mentioned above; and (5) envelopes and postcards with "indecent or scurrilous epithets." Once a defendant was charged with breaking this law and brought to trial, a jury was instructed to determine whether the material was obscene according to the standard derived from the English case *Regina* v. *Hicklin* (1868), which came to be known as the Hicklin Test. The judgment of obscenity hinged upon "whether the tendency of the matter charged as obscenity is to deprave and corrupt those whose minds are open to such immoral influences, and into whose hands a publication of this sort may fall."[6]

As the early trials make clear, however, to understand the Hicklin Test exclusively in terms of individual morality is to misunderstand both its premises and its breadth. Implicit in its formulation was the widely held conviction that public and private were inextricably joined, that things which appear in public exert "influence"—an exceedingly popular word in nineteenth-century vocabularies—over the reader or viewer.[7] This belief was part of a tradition which held that literature and art play a crucial role in character building. Just as stories about great people and virtuous deeds offer examples to emulate, the depiction of dissolute activities could presumably corrupt a person's character, especially that of youth.[8] In *Dunlop* v. *United States* (1897), where the court found advertisements in which women solicited "massage treatments" to be obscene, the judge's instructions to the jury make this position clear:

> It is your duty to ascertain, in the first place, if [the advertisements] are calculated to deprave the morals; if they are calculated to lower that standard which we regard as essential to civilization; if they are calculated to excite those feelings which, in their proper field, are all right; but which, transcending the limits of that proper field, play most of the mischief in the world.[9]

Until the 1930s, the public dimension of the harm was a central concern of the law. "It is the legal premise," according to a writer in the *Columbia Law Review* (1928), "that public morals and health are directly affected and deteriorated by obscenity and its vicious brethren." The regulation of obscenity, in the words of the judge presiding over the Harman trial, "rests upon the universal consensus that such things are impure, indecent, and harmful to the public morals and common welfare." "Laws of this character," he explained, "are made for society in the aggregate and not in particular." Leaving no doubt where the primary harm occurred, another judge used the popular image of pollution: "The object of the statute was to suppress the traffic in obscene publication, and to protect the community against the contamination and pollution arising from their exhibition and distribution."[10]

EARLY CHALLENGES TO
OBSCENITY LAW

In starkest contrast to the routine invocation of the First Amendment in right-to-privacy and obscenity cases today, this strategy was mounted in only two early trials—*United States* v. *Bennett* (1879) and *United States* v. *Harmon* (1891), each involving publications by free-love advocates, and then only as an outgrowth of the larger issue of the author's intention. Citing the Supreme Court decision *Ex parte Jackson* (1879) as definitively settling the question of the constitutionality of the Comstock Act, judges in both trials categorically rejected free speech as a defense and thereby banished the issue from actual obscenity decisions, though not from debates outside the courts, until the 1950s.[11]

In *United States* v. *Bennett*, Judge Blatchford concurred with the lower court's ruling on free speech. In the instructions to the jury, the lower court had detailed the scope of the Comstock Act, distinguishing between material that can be mailed and material that can be published. The law, explained the judge, "does not undertake to regulate the dissemination of obscene matter. . . . But, what the United States Government says is, that the mails of the United States shall not be devoted to this purpose." Reiterating that it was not a question of free speech, but rather one of the improper use of the public mails, he declared, "Freelovers and freethinkers may have a right to their views, and they may express them and they may publish them; but they cannot publish them in connection with obscene matter, and then send that matter through the mails."[12]

In *United States* v. *Harmon*, Judge Philips spoke directly to the issue of the limitation of the First Amendment:

> It is a radical misconception of the scope of the constitutional protection to indulge the belief that a person may print and publish, *ad libitum*, any matter, whatever the substance or language, without accountability to law. Liberty in all its forms and assertions in this

country is regulated by law. It is not an unbridled license. Where vituperation or licentiousness begins, the liberty of press ends.

Even though he acknowledged that "the genius" of American institutions resides in according "the largest liberality in the utterance of private opinion, and widest latitude in polemics, touching questions of social ethics, political and domestic economy, and the like," he nevertheless insisted that "this invaluable privilege is not paramount to the golden rule of every civilized society . . . 'so exercise your own freedom as not to infringe the rights of others or the public peace and safety.' "[13]

In contrast to our disputes today about obscenity, where the right of free speech takes precedence over practically every other concern, in the nineteenth century the law did not give priority to the individual's freedom over "public peace and safety." In addition—and this, too, dramatically distinguishes nineteenth-century jurisprudence from that of our own time—Judge Philips explicitly connected the public good to the common sense of decency: "Responsibility yet attaches to him when he transcends the boundary line where he outrages the common sense of decency, or endangers the public safety." He quoted at length from the "eminent jurist" Judge Story, who argued that liberty of the press was not more valuable than other rights and to treat it as such would threaten to turn that liberty into a "despotism," which, in Judge Story's words, would be " 'utterly incompatible with the principles of a free government.' "[14]

The categorical rejection of the First Amendment in the early obscenity trials contrasts sharply with its easy acceptance in the invasion-of-privacy trials. As we have seen, those accused of violating privacy successfully claimed it was not only their right but their duty to provide the public with all kinds of information. In the obscenity trials, even though defendants typically argued that they, too, were trying to enlighten the public, they were invariably found guilty. This dramatic difference in outcomes stems at least in part from the way in which the injury was construed. In privacy disputes, a victim's interest in protecting his or her peace of mind was usually outweighed by the public's right to know and by the constitutional protection of free speech. In obscenity disputes, the right to free speech was not actually denied; rather, the individual's right to use the public mails to distribute questionable material was outweighed by society's interest in maintaining a common sense of decency. Support for a legal right to privacy was further hindered, as we have seen, by society's highly ambivalent attitude toward it. In contrast, widespread condemnation of sexual obscenity was virtually guaranteed—notwithstanding the attack on puritanism, comstockery, and the genteel tradition by intellectuals—because of popular reverence for the cult of domesticity. To speak openly of intimate experiences—activities that had been infused with a moral depth and emotional vibrancy in keeping with the liberal glorification of privacy as the locus of individuality and personal freedom—was to threaten the social order and, with it, the possibility of meaning.

Although the Hicklin Test became the official American standard for determining obscenity when it was first applied in *United States* v. *Bennett* in 1879, and was employed unchanged until the early 1930s, from the very start two of its components—the isolated passage and the most susceptible person—attracted scrutiny and, in consequence, distracted attention from the companion definition of obscenity as the indecent—that which is not fit to be seen or heard. In *People* v. *Muller* (1884), where the defendant was charged with selling prints of nude women, the judge tried to make the test more elastic by including a consideration of context: it was, he declared, "a false delicacy and mere prudery which condemn and banish from sight all such objects as obscene, simply on account of their nudity." Implicit in this statement is the notion that nudity was permissible in some circumstances. As in the defenses mounted on behalf of the sex radicals, which distinguished between blunt language in the name of reform and actual obscene language, the judge in this trial wanted to distinguish between art featuring nudity on the one hand and blatant obscenity on the other. He proposed a test of the "motive" of the painting or statue to determine "whether it is naturally calculated to excite in a spectator impure imaginations, and whether the other incidents and qualities, however attractive, were merely accessory to this as the primary or main purpose of the representation."[15] But, in giving exclusive emphasis to the excitation of "impure imaginations," he neglected the component of obscenity encompassed by the idea of indecency—the quality and character of the common world—as well as the sanctification of the private sphere as a protective cover for intimate experiences.

Another early case, *United States* v. *Clarke* (1889), also raised questions about the Hicklin Test. The jury was charged with deciding whether "Dr. Clarke's Treatise on Venereal, Sexual, Nervous, and Special Diseases" and two circulars that described the symptoms of venereal disease and also answered common questions about it were obscene. Judge Thayer restated the Hicklin Test word for word so as to clarify which kinds of material posed a threat to morality. Again, the judge paid attention only to those threats "calculated to excite lustful or sensual desires in those whose minds are open to such influences," and he had little to say about the tone of public conversation or the fragility of intimate life. Judge Thayer did, however, attempt to refine the Hicklin Test by specifying exactly whose morals needed protection. To that end, he distinguished between "two classes of people": the "intelligent and mature," who were not affected by obscenity; and "the young and immature, the ignorant, and those who are sensually inclined—who are liable to be influenced to their harm by reading indecent and obscene publications." It was this second class alone, he argued, that the statute was designed to protect.[16]

The only early trial to challenge the Hicklin Test directly was *United States* v. *Kennerley* (1913), where Mitchell Kennerley was tried for publishing *Hagar Revelly*, a novel portraying the life of a prostitute as a direct outgrowth of unjust social and economic conditions. Goodman, a thirty-year-old doctor and reformer, claimed he had written the novel to teach "the innocent youth of the land . . . the wiles of vice."[17] In this decision, Judge Learned Hand went further than any of his predecessors in trying to distinguish among different classes of potential victims. For Judge Hand, to accept the potential victim specified by the Hicklin Test—the most susceptible person—meant effectively reducing the "treatment of sex to the standard of a child's library in the supposed interest of a salacious few." With this new gloss on the Hicklin Test, he initiated what would become an extremely effective line of attack: he questioned whether "our society is prepared to accept for its own limitations those which may perhaps be necessary to the weakest of its members." To pose the question in this way was to raise the specter that obscenity laws, instead of helping to maintain high moral and aesthetic standards, actually impoverished the general quality of culture—a claim that was in keeping with the younger generation's assault on puritanism, comstockery, and the genteel tradition.

While Judge Hand continued to employ the Hicklin Test—"that test has been accepted by the lower federal courts until it would be no longer proper for me to disregard it"—he also successfully introduced a relativist tone into the discussion, noting that "however consonant it may be with mid-Victorian morals, [it] does not seem to me to answer to the understanding and morality of the present time, as conveyed by the words, 'obscene, lewd or lascivious.' " Taking as his starting point the progressive belief that morality and obscenity were ever changing, Judge Hand offered a more flexible definition of obscenity: "the present critical point in the compromise between candor and shame at which the community may have arrived here and now."[18]

In later stages of obscenity disputes, judges and legal writers hailed Judge Hand's definition as the only "sane" words on the subject. But at first commentators were distressed. One, writing in the *Illinois Law Review* (1914–15), pointed to the havoc it wreaked. "What is the meaning of obscenity?" he demanded. "The answer to this question, so far as the law is concerned, is somewhat in doubt, for the courts have given at least two different meanings to the word." Another legal writer, James F. Morton, raised two further objections to the Hicklin Test. First, invoking the authority of Havelock Ellis and Theodore Schroeder, he repeated what was becoming the common wisdom concerning the relativity of modesty, propriety, and pruriency; because these notions were not timeless and universal, Morton, like Schroeder before him, declared obscenity laws "void for uncertainty." By these lights, the Hicklin Test only made matters worse. And second, revealing how deeply psychological categories had infiltrated legal thinking, Morton argued that "under this criterion, the abnormal mind is made the standard, and the normal tendency completely ignored."[19]

From this time on, the potential victim indicated in the Hicklin Test could no longer safely be assumed to be the most susceptible person—namely, youth—as it had been during the nineteenth century. More than anything else, the attempt to specify a particular class of victims reveals the coerciveness of liberal habits of mind which demand that an actual injured person be produced if the law is to intervene. It is also part of that strain in modern liberal thinking that envisions the self as essentially "unencumbered"—that core entity which is supposed to emerge once the "accidents" of birth—class, race, sex—are removed.[20] Given that obscenity was always prosecuted in the name of the people, this hunt for specific individual victims should have been difficult to sustain. That it could take place at all, let alone come to dominate obscenity proceedings, once again demonstrates the extreme difficulties liberal jurisprudence has in imagining equally pressing harms, such as the coarsening of the tone of public conversation, the waning of the sense of shame, and public pollution—harms that are more amorphous yet no less devastating than the more concrete ones suffered by individual victims.

THE UNRAVELING OF CONSENSUS
AND THE SUBJECTIVIZATION OF OBSCENITY

In 1928, an anonymous writer in the *Columbia Law Review* set out to analyze the "immediate legal aspects of the problem of enforcement" of obscenity law in New York. He posed two "ethical" questions: "Who are to be protected?" and "From what is the public to be protected?" In 1930, two legal commentators, Sidney Grant and S. E. Angoff, wrote that the enforcement of obscenity law in Massachusetts was in a state of utter disarray. They also demanded, "Who shall be the censor? What shall we censor?" That it was possible to question not only the potential victim but also the judge and the consequences of obscenity signals the dissolution of the old consensus. In 1928, Morris Ernst, who was soon to become the leading attorney for defendants in all of the major obscenity trials during the 1930s, and his associate William Seagle wrestled with these same questions in their influential study *To the Pure . . . A Study of Obscenity and the Censor.* As the title makes clear, they were trying to demolish the very notions of obscenity and censorship in the smart-set style of debunking. In the theatrical fashion of the modern sophisticate, they ridiculed the Hicklin Test as the "Victorian" standard of "the very lowest common denominator." Unintentionally revealing how muddled the argument over the hypothetical victim had become, they complained that "the normally intelligent minor" was no longer the standard; instead, and feeling no need to justify their position, they announced, "If there were one feeble-minded adult in the community, he set the pace for all the rest." Grant and Angoff further confused matters when they complained, "Cockburn's rule makes not the ordinary man the test, but the lewd and the corrupt."[21]

A parallel debate about the potential victim of obscenity raged in Congress in 1930 over the Smoot-Hawley Tariff Act, which would ban the importation of obscene material. In one of Senator Smoot's final proposals before Congress, he indicated that material which corrupted "the moral sense of the average person" would be subject to regulation. This all-important specification of a class of victims led one senator to question, "Who is this average person? An average layman, easily offended, perhaps, . . . or a normal scientist, or man of average culture in polite literature?" So difficult had it become to reach agreement on this crucial point that Senator Smoot simply dropped the phrase from his proposal and, after a few days of agitated argument, the Smoot-Hawley Tariff Act was enacted.[22]

It was not only the victim of obscenity that had come into dispute by the close of the twenties. Ernst and Seagle crossed into the precarious territory pioneered by Theodore Schroeder when they challenged whether obscenity caused any actual harm. Breaking with the long-standing didactic tradition which had assumed the enormous influence of literature in character building, the two iconoclasts demanded, "Is it possible to measure the quantity, quality, and effects of literary influence?" Making clear their disagreement was rooted not so much in aesthetic claims as in scientific ones, they also demanded, "Can science collect the data for judging the consequences of the printed word?" Ernst and Seagle construed the issue in language as indebted to science as to their nemesis, Comstock: "Can analytic method answer the basic questions: In what ways do books stimulate you sexually? If so, what books?"[23] With this line of interrogation, two strands of nineteenth-century thought that had never been securely woven together in obscenity law unraveled: the party of reticence's concern about indecency—how the world will look, which things may appear in it—was completely lost, while the fears of comstockery—the excitement of lewd thoughts—began to dominate the discussion.

The determination of the crucial, if narrow, question as to whether a book can "stimulate you sexually" was best left, in Ernst and Seagle's judgment, to a "trained psychiatrist who is not interested in definitions at all but only in pathological mental states."[24] With the entry of the trained psychiatrist onto the legal stage—and they laud his authority not only over that of common sense but also over the literary expert—the debate about obscenity lost much of its earlier coherence, depth, and meaning. Less and less would disputants evoke things sacred and the awe and reverence due them; rather, the debate became fixed on obscenity as a demon of individual psychology, which effectively denied its public nature as an actual thing that appears in the common domain.

Ernst and Seagle also called for a recognition of "case and questionnaire methods" in "sexual psychology." Acknowledging that science was only in its infancy in matters of sex, the two lawyers were nonetheless hopeful that studies like the one commissioned by the Bureau of Social Hygiene of New York City would eventually set the record straight about whether reading sexual material leads to "libidinous thoughts" or "sexual desires." The Bureau had sent out 10,000 questionnaires to unmarried women who were also college graduates; 2,515 agreed to participate, and 1,200 sets of answers were finally tabulated. Ernst and Seagle dutifully reported that among college women responding to the question, "What things are most sexually stimulating?" 218 answered "a man" while only 95 replied "books." When queried about the source of their earliest knowledge about sex, only 6 percent of the women said they had obtained information from books; gossip from other children ranked first and information provided by parents or guardians second. From these "scientific" findings, Ernst and Seagle concluded that "the whole business of suppression is futile and absurd; no one can know which books to suppress."[25]

Having assumed psychological and sociological positions with great flexibility, Ernst and Seagle were also adept at juggling two additional claims having to do with the nature of sex itself. The first drew from the sex-reform movement, which, as we have seen, did its best to divorce sex from moral values and reconceptualize it as a matter of health and happiness; they questioned whether activities stimulated by so-called obscenity actually did harm. "Medical science, of late, has tended to the view that [masturbation's] evil effects have been exaggerated. At any rate," they laughed, "it is not yet a crime to fall into this indulgence. . . . In most civilized states fornication is not a crime." Flaunting their own worldliness in such matters, they observed, "It is our prurience which makes us assume that unlawful pleasures will be the consequence." Their second claim, reflecting the most "advanced" thinking of their time, anticipated the later formulation of obscenity as a "safety valve" for "anti-social behavior": "One suspects that obscenity may accomplish as much good as evil. Havelock Ellis has asserted that adults need 'obscene' literature as much as children need fairy tales as relief from the oppressive force of convention."[26]

Ernst and Seagle were not alone in their skepticism regarding the alleged evils of obscenity. By 1930, a number of critics argued that repression, not obscenity, was the root cause of evil, that the free circulation of alleged obscenity would accomplish positive good by undermining "taboos" that gave rise to illicit desires. In an article entitled "Who's Obscene?" in *The Nation* in 1930, the longings for a return to pastoral innocence—a state of being that knows no distinctions between private and public, shameful and sacred, obscene and prosaic—reappeared with new force: "The effect of abolishing censorship completely . . . would ultimately be to demolish the notion . . . that the natural processes of the human body . . . are essentially shameful and degrading." The free-speech lawyer Arthur Garfield Hays insisted that if the "mysteries" surrounding sex were eliminated, "society would become so clean-minded that there would be no such thing as 'obscenity'—in the present sense." And at a 1930 booksellers' convention, Mary Ware Dennett showed real fluency in using this idiom of "no secrets" when she asked, "Why not put all the lids in the trash barrel and give what has been under the lid a good sunning and airing and see to it that every one possible is spared from acquiring the dirty feelings that are the foundation of indecency?"[27]

Although a number of critics explicitly challenged the worth of the Hicklin Test and the preconceptions about sex embodied in it, judges presiding over obscenity trials before 1934 continued to employ the Hicklin Test, even while the doubts raised by these critics began seeping into the proceedings. With the exception of a few early trials (discussed above), judges had always found the material in question obscene in accordance with the Hicklin Test—that is, capable of corrupting the morality of the most susceptible person—while they *also* found that obscenity lowered standards of public morality, polluted public space, coarsened taste, and vitiated judgment.

In *People* v. *Friede* (1929), concerning Radclyffe Hall's *The Well of Loneliness*, a novel about "the childhood and early womanhood of a female invert," the defendant's lawyers, Morris Ernst, Alexander Lindey, and Norman Levy, argued that the Hicklin Test "seeks to gauge the mental and moral capacity of the community by that of its dullest-witted and most fallible members." City Magistrate Bushel rejected this definition. The law, he insisted, is "not limited to the young and immature, the moron, the mentally weak, or the intellectually impoverished." Expanding the range of hypothetical victims, he observed they could also be "found among those of mature age and of high intellectual development and professional attainment." (The lower court's decision, however, was reversed on April 19, 1929, by a special sessions court. After launching a massive advertising campaign exploiting its legal battles, the publisher, Covici-Friede, issued and sold more than 100,000 copies of the book within a year.[28])

In *United States* v. *Dennett* (1930), the scope of obscenity law was considerably narrowed. As we have already seen, only one issue concerned the court: the strict application of the Hicklin Test in which morality was equated with sexual morality. On appeal, Judge Hand found Dennett's pamphlet not obscene on the grounds that its "high-minded" style "tends to rationalize and dignify such emotions rather than to arouse lust." Two other decisions relating to sexual hygiene —*United States* v. *One Obscene Book Entitled "Married Love"* (1931) and *United States* v. *One Book Entitled "Contraception"* (1931)—further constricted the compass of the law by directing even more attention to the hunt for an actual injured party, which, in turn, deflected attention from the public dimensions of the harm. Comparing *Married Love*, by the English doctor Marie C. Stopes, to Dennett's pamphlet, Judge John Woolsey maintained that "the present book may fairly be said to do for adults what Mrs. Dennett's book does for adolescents": it pleads with husbands "for a better understanding . . . of the physical and emotional side of the sex life of their wives." Having established that the book had no lascivious intent, Judge Woolsey made an unprecedented move: he incorporated claims advanced by those attacking obscenity laws on psychological grounds into a modified test, replacing the person most liable to be corrupted with "any person with a normal mind." Under this new standard, he determined that Stopes's book would in fact be helpful to married couples.[29]

The other case heard by Judge Woolsey's court, *United States* v. *One Book Entitled "Contraception,"* concerned another work by Dr. Stopes, intended for the medical profession and dealing with the theory, history, and practice of birth control. Judge Woolsey reiterated his modified version of the Hicklin Test, and both the extreme narrowness of this new formulation and the extent of the party of exposure's victory in dissociating clinical treatments of sex from obscene ones become apparent:

> Such a book, although it may run counter to the views of many persons who disagree entirely with the theory underlying birth control, certainly does not fall within the test of obscenity or immorality laid down by me in the case of *U.S.* v. *One Obscene Book Entitled "Married Love"*—for the reading of it would not stir the sex impulses of any person with a normal mind. . . . Actually the emotions aroused by the book are merely feelings of sympathy and pity, evoked by the many cases instanced in it of the sufferings of married women due to ignorance of its teachings.

In his concluding remarks, Judge Woolsey sounded a note in favor of frank discussion of sex, revealing the long distance the judiciary had traveled in only a few decades: sympathy and pity "will be the inevitable effect of reading it on all persons of sensibility unless by their prejudices the information it contains is tabooed." By making freedom from the incitement of "sex impulses" the only interest of the law, and by insinuating that only "prejudiced" and sexually repressed people would object to his interpretation, Judge Woolsey demonstrated that he had lost hold of the vital concerns of the party of reticence that had been safeguarded in earlier obscenity decisions.[30]

This understanding of the Hicklin Test, cut off from the larger reticent sensibility of which it originally had been a part, was shared by all the judges who heard obscenity cases during the early 1930s. Even in the two cases where the courts found the books in question obscene, the manner in which the judgments were rendered speaks volumes about the diminished scope of the law. Reading Judge Pierce's decision (1930) against Theodore Dreiser's *An American Tragedy* is to read a point-by-point reaffirmation of the Hicklin Test *minus* the accompanying sensibility that used to insist on protecting the public good and the faculties of judgment and taste. In this opinion, the standard of "most susceptible person" went unchallenged. Dreiser's book, according to the judge, contained "certain obscene, indecent, and impure language manifestly tending to corrupt the morals of youth," and, following precedent, he declared these offending passages "too lewd and obscene to be more particularly set forth in this complaint" (though he did not use the metaphor of pollution that had always accompanied and justified such exclusions in the past). Like his predecessors, he continued to hold that the author's intent was irrelevant and that the jury was charged only with ascertaining "whether certain passages" were obscene, maintaining that even if the larger story provided a meaningful context for depictions of sex, it was beside the point, since children were apt to read the sex scenes in isolation, which left them open to corruption. In his opinion, the obscene passages could be removed altogether from the novel and "nothing would be lost."[31]

In *People* v. *Pesky* (1930), Arthur Schnitzler's *Hands Around*, a series of vignettes about prostitutes and their lovers, in which "all stratagems of sex are uncovered . . . through the finer eyes of a connoisseur of things human," was found obscene according to the Hicklin Test. The tone of the judgment, however, was clearly defensive. Even though the judge begrudgingly acknowledged the lack of agreement about what might legitimately occupy public space, he still maintained that the Hicklin Test was sound:

> While we appreciate the fact that different people have different standards with reference to such writings and that these standards are often peculiar to understand, nevertheless people generally and the courts have arrived at what they consider a fair standard by which to judge such books and protect those who need protection.

Obscenity, in this judge's account, "must be judged by normal people and not by the abnormal"—and he had in mind a specific notion of "abnormal." He suggested that it was the "literati"—Schnitzler and his champions—who were "abnormal," and took the unusual tack of ridiculing his opponents to justify this ostensibly outdated position:

> As usual [the book] is prefaced by the remark that it will not be appreciated by the Puritan fanatic with his jaundiced inhibitions or the moral idealogist [sic] with his heart of leather. This is the usual cry of the libertine who is attempting to justify his own life or writings. Anyone who differs with his method of living or writing is Puritanical. With such people clean thinking or living is Puritanical.[32]

Even though a dissenting judge defended the book on the grounds of its literary reputation and high style, he, too, appealed to the Hicklin Test as the final authority. *Hands Around* could not be construed as obscene since "the appeal to passion or lechery is wholly lacking."[33] Not only did this opinion disclose how amorphous the Hicklin Test had become once it was divorced from the weightier issues related to the public good, it also demonstrated that this emptied-out version could be used just as effectively to clear a work of obscenity charges as to convict it. Once concern about the quality of public life slipped from legal memory, judgments of obscenity revolved exclusively around the possibility of exciting lust, which made the problem of obscenity increasingly trivial or nonsensical.

The Double Standard of Obscenity Law

While the courts found the work of Dreiser and Schnitzler obscene, there were a number of other trials during the 1920s and early 1930s where the defendants were vindicated. Opponents of the law used these inconsistencies to put the entire enterprise of regulating obscenity into question. Their favorite ploy, which they learned from Theodore Schroeder, was to attack the law on grounds of vagueness and uncertainty. The trouble with obscenity law, according to this view, was that it required universal and timeless standards of decency if it was to be consistent. Yet because manners and morals change over time and vary from place to place, notions of obscenity were inherently unstable. To make this point concrete, critics typically compiled lists of books that had been either suppressed because of pressure from local groups like the Clean Books League and the National Organization for Decent Literature, excluded and destroyed by officials working in customs offices and the postal service, or banned at court. Whitman, Shaw, Ibsen, Flaubert, Balzac, Voltaire, Zola, Joyce,

Lawrence, and Radclyffe Hall were the writers whose works headed these lists. Ernst and Seagle made much of the commonplace that what was considered obscene by one generation was often considered a classic by the next: "Many of them [banned books], indeed, are now required high-school reading." Critics also had fun with the inconsistency in their opponents' logic that allowed for "literary classics" treating sex. Vice societies, sneered Ernst and Seagle, "excuse their leniency upon the ground that Shakespeare, Rabelais, and Boccaccio would not offend against the law today, but, living in a less refined time, they could not but reflect the grossness of their age. What age, then, did Theodore Dreiser, for instance, reflect? At any rate, is obscenity less lewd and lascivious per se if dated?"[34]

Not only did judgments of obscenity change over time, but the vagueness of the law led to an intolerable situation in which the very same book could be found innocent and guilty by different customs officers or courts within the same state. Ernst and Seagle, decrying this "absolutely unpredictable" situation, let the capers of the censors speak for themselves. They invited their fellow sophisticates to laugh at the effort to "bar the official Field Museum importations of Chinese pictures and manuscripts in 1909 as obscene, and the even greater classic of the exclusion from the mails in 1911 of the Chicago Vice Report prepared by an official Vice Commission of the City of Chicago for circulation among clergymen, editors, and social workers." In 1929, when customs officers seized a number of well-known books that were already widely available—Voltaire's *Candide* sent for use in a Harvard classroom and Rabelais's *Pantagruel* imported by an eminent New York book collector—the press joined in denunciations of these antics. In response to these highly publicized gaffes, Congress amended the tariff laws in 1930, so that there would be a jury trial in federal court whenever a seizure was contested and requiring the government, not the addressee, to press the proceedings; the Secretary of the Treasury was permitted, in his discretion, to admit "classics" or books of "recognized literary or scientific merit" even if obscene.[35]

At the same time, legal commentators never tired of pointing to the copious amounts of sexual material countenanced in advertisements and stage shows, not to mention the new tabloids specializing in lurid reports of scandalous trials and gruesome crimes. In a great ironic turn of legal history, the failure to control invasive journalism gave the party of exposure one of its most powerful justifications for ending obscenity regulation. Critics gleefully set forth examples of commercial entertainment—the original target of right-to-privacy law but which the law had failed to regulate—to demonstrate the incongruity of censoring literature in a society that tolerated such salacious material. Ernst and Seagle, for example, took great pleasure in exposing the hypocrisy of "papers [that] spread forth columns of near-smut under the rule of privilege, while the editorial pages inveigh against the corrupting influence of books, entirely overlooking the similar effects which newspapers may produce."[36]

In another section of their book, Ernst and Seagle went a step further in their attack on this unequal application of obscenity laws. Given the saturation of the market for children's entertainment by lurid comic books, "sadistic" fairy tales, and "true confession" magazines—which they dismissed as "dishonest trash"—they opined, "Possibly the reader will agree that in comparison to all such legalized and prevailing environment of degradation, obscenity is a negligible item." In 1938, another legal writer, Leo M. Alpert, took the same tack, exposing the glaring inconsistency of a society that deemed certain novels obscene, but allowed "half-nude women and bathing beauties to bedeck advertisements, and which permits burlesques, leg shows, and frankly erotic motion pictures" as well as "newspapers with their deluge of sensational scandal."[37]

These critics did not chronicle such excesses to draw attention to the general deterioration of the public sphere, even though a few lone voices, like Oswald Garrison Villard, continued to do so. Instead, they had one aim and one aim alone: to unmask the opposition to literature treating sex as nothing more than a hypocritical double standard. As Grant and Angoff put it: "If it is obscene to depict realism in the pages of a novel, it is equally indecent to depict the identical in a newspaper." Not that they were advocating press censorship; rather, they were lambasting what they saw as the arbitrariness and irrationality of obscenity law: "Logic, however, seldom has anything to do with censorship. . . . After all, an immoral press is better than an enslaved one."[38]

The charges of hypocrisy and double standards could cut both ways, however. In Silas Bent's attack on the new journalism, Ballyhoo, he drew attention to the controversy over tabloid coverage of the "Daddy" Browning and fifteen-year-old "Peaches" sex-scandal trial, in which the court had reported on " 'pathological pedophilia,' a sexual aberration causing the 'sufferer to have unnatural love for young girls.' " Outraged by the tabloids' brazenness, an editorial in the World declared, "It would be the sheerest hypocrisy and it would be downright cowardice if the legislature were to put the theatre or the book trade under a censor while it left the press free to exploit the legalized filth of the courts." John Sumner, secretary of the New York Society for the Suppression of Vice, brought action against the publisher of the *New York Graphic* for its sensational accounts of the Browning trial. The judges of General Sessions dismissed the charge, however, stating that "judgment upon a newspaper should be passed only by the public." Nevertheless, public opinion was so inflamed that the New York State Crime Commission issued a forty-page report concluding that censorship might "not be the worst of all evils." Yet, just as the threat to free speech had made it impossible to control invasive journalism in right-to-privacy proceedings, this same threat was successfully used to defeat any such regulation in this instance.[39]

While Ernst and Seagle, as members of the civilized minority, were no enthusiasts of the vulgar tabloid, they still professed admiration for its shrewd managers who knew how to exploit "the phrase 'the freedom of the press,'" causing "the worst reactionary [to] feel a shiver of dread." "They trade in the sacred name of political liberty, which insures the passage of their wares. The freedom of the press has become converted into the freedom of the tabloids." That the lurid tabloids were given such privileges made the censorship of high culture even more intolerable. Drawing attention to how few people regarded the banning of alleged obscene literature as a threat to free speech—which, from our contemporary perspective, is indeed surprising—the two lawyers observed, "The Anglo-Saxon who regards an assault upon free speech with horror views with equanimity its suppression as obscenity."[40]

Because the subtitle of their book promised a study not only of obscenity but also of the censor, Ernst and Seagle devoted enormous energy to unmasking the censor, in smart-set fashion, as prurient prude and hypocrite. In accomplishing this task, they offered a further explanation of the double standard which banned serious literature but indulged lascivious journalism. In their view, obscenity trials were an occasion for jurors, regardless of how lax their sexual morals were in private, to display their moral rectitude in public. "The jurors enjoy taking a stand for the ascetic ideal no matter how inconsistent that may be with their routine swapping of excrementary jokes in Pullman smokers." Although their point here was the hypocrisy of would-be censors, their analysis also drew attention to a growing cultural divide between ordinary people, whose values were rooted in the nineteenth-century reticent sensibility and who used the obscenity issue to parade their own standards of propriety and righteousness, and the cultural vanguard, who were fighting for free expression and sexual emancipation and used the same issue to flaunt their sophistication. In their zeal to discredit their opponents, Ernst and Seagle drew a picture of the dirty-minded censor that rivaled Schroeder's withering caricature of Victorian "hyperaesthesia" but lacked the wit of Mencken's portrait of comstockery:

> Suppressors are found in all classes and places. Look at the men who stood at the Flatiron Building corner in New York City frankly waiting to see girls' thighs on a gusty day. Watch the men who read the details of adultery divorce trials. Keep in mind the men who sit in the front rows of bare-legged revues. Recall those men who belong to vice societies but enjoy showing, of course in a scientific manner, postal cards of homosexual acts. Examples of public hypocrisy are too multitudinous to permit a detailed inventory. This has ever been the case where men have set themselves up as judges of morality, taste, or knowledge.

Ten years later, another legal writer employed a variant of this debunking mode to the same end. Using the psychological idiom that turns all moral questions into matters of mental health, he claimed that the "curious dissociative process within our national mentality" that accepts lubricity in commercial entertainment but condemns literary depictions of sex "demonstrate[s] symptoms a psychiatrist would quickly group as a sex neurosis or psychosis in an individual but which, because of their national extent, are not treated or considered."[41]

THE DECLINE OF COMMON SENSE AND THE RISE OF LITERARY EXPERTS

That this double standard existed at all testifies to the continued strength of the Arnoldian tradition, with its emphasis upon culture as the storehouse of lasting values. This position was restated in an essay, "Good Manners in Literature," that appeared in *The Forum* in 1927: "Culture, in fine, means knowing through training, instinct, taste, the best inherited virtues of English expression and English thought," wrote the author, in the tradition of the nineteenth-century genteel reformer. He hoped that education could further "the preparation of the Catholic-minded, balanced and appreciative reader of good books for the reception of the Best, so that he shall become as sensitive to values as an Amati violin to the right vibrations in the seasoned wood."[42] This concern for the quality of culture went with the well-established belief that a society's greatness could be judged according to its artistic achievements. With so much at stake, it becomes clearer why literature was held to higher standards than mass entertainment.

Yet, at the same time, this consensus about the importance of art and culture was beginning to dissolve, as different literary factions found themselves embroiled in an inconclusive debate about the nature, meaning, aim, and place of literature in modern society. By the 1930s, a new battle about literature was raging between Marxist partisans of "proletarian literature," who self-consciously portrayed the lives of the working class to create a literature for the masses; the New Humanists, who continued to argue in favor of the values of the genteel tradition but with a heavy Protestant inflection; and modernists, who hoped to expand the range of aesthetic experience chiefly through experimentation in form and style.[43]

While the champions of proletarian literature and the New Humanists were avowed opponents, they nonetheless both believed that aesthetics and morality were intertwined, that literature and art shaped character and influenced society as a whole, and, as leftist writers hoped, forged class consciousness and ultimately revolution. In sharpest contrast, modernists, in their desire to push the boundaries of art and social conventions to their outermost limits, split aesthetics apart from morality and in the most extreme version adopted the highly aestheticized spirit of "art for art's sake." Given the number of conflicting positions, it is not surprising that legal discourse became increasingly preoccupied with questions once thought extrinsic to it —the proper subject matter of literature, how such subjects should be represented, whether literature had any influence on people's lives. Ill equipped to deal with these issues, the judiciary came to rely on experts whom they called on to testify to the literary status of a given work. This new dependence on experts suggests that modern literature was becoming so esoteric that the ordinary person could no longer be trusted to grasp its significance—a sharp divergence from the nineteenth-century consensus that judgments of obscenity could be safely left to a jury's common sense.

In *People* v. *The Viking Press* (1933), regarding Erskine Caldwell's *God's Little Acre*, a proletarian-inspired novel about the hard lives of poor, illiterate farmers and mill workers in the South, a number of these questions came to the fore. Just as sex radicals and birth-control advocates had pleaded that the scientific, educational nature of their writings differentiated them from obscenity, the publisher of *God's Little Acre* insisted that "the high literary merit" of the book distinguished it from obscenity. To substantiate this claim, the defense submitted the opinions of forty leading writers and critics who supported the book, including Horace M. Kallen, Carl Van Doren, Raymond Weaver, Malcolm Cowley, Henry S. Canby, Elmer Rice, and Sinclair Lewis. Comstock's successor at the New York Society for the Suppression of Vice, John Sumner, disputed the legitimacy of these writers' opinion, pointedly reminding the court that obscenity laws "represent the whole people and not only the literati." He repeated the opinion from the Schnitzler case—that it was the literati who were the "abnormal people." City Magistrate Greenspan, however, declared that he was impressed by the "large and representative group of people" who endorsed the book, and praised them for having "a better capacity to judge of the value of a literary production than one who is more apt to search for obscene passages in a book than to regard the book as a whole." With this declaration, he broke with the precedent of not allowing expert opinion, which had prevailed as recently as 1929 in the trial of *The Well of Loneliness*, where the judge had rejected the defendant's brief presenting "eminent men of letters, critics, artists, and publishers who have praised [the book]."[44]

In addition, City Magistrate Greenspan added confusion to the already muddled question about the supposed victim by evoking the specter of obscene works appealing to "diseased or disordered minds," and called up the equally disturbing worry that had already been voiced in the Kennerley decision: the potential impoverishment of literary culture if books were judged by standards beneath adult ones. He observed that

> there is no way of anticipating [a book's] effect upon a disordered or diseased mind, and if the courts were to exclude books from sale merely because they might incite lust in disordered minds, our entire literature would very likely be reduced to a relatively small number of uninteresting and barren books. The greater part of the classics would certainly be excluded.

This was a direct rebuttal of the position that public morals and decency took precedence over literary culture. (The judge in the *Well of Loneliness* trial had argued that the court should not make conjectures "as to the loss that its condemnation may entail to our general literature, when it is plainly subversive of public morals and public decency, which the statute is designed to safeguard," but this had been overturned on appeal.) City Magistrate Greenspan raised these considerations, but in the end he used the Hicklin Test most narrowly construed: he exonerated Caldwell's book on the grounds that it "had no tendency to inspire readers to behave like characters and therefore no tendency to incite lustful desire" even though, as he admitted, the novel dealt "frankly" with the sex lives of "primitive people" and consequently was "coarse and vulgar."[45]

With this sharp distinction between obscenity and vulgarity, the judge radically broke with the discourse of reticence, which had always employed moral and aesthetic language interchangeably. This was due at least in part to the growing pressure exerted by the party of exposure to be modern and sophisticated, which meant accepting that realism spread the truth widely even as it also introduced vulgarity into the world; this is what Judge Hand had suggested in the Dennett case, where he argued that accurate information about sex education for the young outweighed any potential corruption. These trials, then, raised new questions outside of the law regarding the relation between the proper subject matter of literature and the appropriate style with which to represent it. Yet, once the legal discourse could speak about aesthetic considerations apart from moral ones, it would have less and less to say about how the world should look, what kind of things should appear in it. And the less it had to say about the quality of the public realm, the more it became mired in a largely fruitless search for individual victims and bogged down with the increasingly absurd project of determining whether anyone was actually corrupted—that is, sexually stimulated—by the material in question.

DISTINGUISHING OBSCENITY FROM VULGARITY: THE SPLIT BETWEEN MORAL AND AESTHETIC JUDGMENT

In the trial of *God's Little Acre*, City Magistrate Greenspan explicitly referred to the problematic link between realism and obscenity: he feared that if the obscenity statute was applied too broadly "its effect would be to prevent altogether the realistic portrayal in literature of a large and important field of life." This confusion about realist literature was made worse when he declared that because he lacked firsthand experience of the world of poor Southern farmers and mill workers, he could not fairly judge whether Caldwell's "book is an accurate piece of reporting." In his summary of the novel, it becomes clear that the vexing problem of realistically depicting the lives of "primitive and impoverished" people closely resembled that of sex reformers who wanted to speak about sex in non-euphemistic yet non-obscene language. At the same time, in the judge's acknowledgment that Caldwell's project of "paint[ing] a realistic picture" of poor workers entailed the use of vulgarity, we see remnants of the classical hierarchy of genres:

> Such pictures necessarily contain certain details. Because these details relate to what is popularly called the sex side of life, portrayed with brutal frankness, the court may not say that the picture should not have been created at all. The language, too, is undoubtedly coarse and vulgar. The court may not require the author to put refined language into the mouths of primitive people.[46]

This key distinction between obscenity—that which corrupts morality—and vulgarity—the unavoidable side effect of realistic portrayals of "primitive people"—was also crucial to the exoneration of the play *Frankie and Johnnie*, a dramatization of the popular song about a country boy's drinking, gambling, and exploits with prostitutes. In *People* v. *Wendling* (1932), Judge Pound found that the play was not obscene since it did not tend to "corrupt morals and excite lustful and lecherous desire" even though its tone was low: the plot was "cheap and tawdry," the scene "laid in a low dive," and the language "coarse, vulgar, and profane." The issue, according to the court, was not whether it might "coarsen or vulgarize the youth who might witness it," but whether the play "tend[s] to corrupt the morals of youth . . . whether it would tend to lower their standards of right and wrong, specifically as to the sexual relation."[47]

This formulation obviously stands in starkest contrast to the nineteenth-century one that considered the coarsening and vulgarizing of young people as part of the same continuum as the corruption of individual morality and the pollution of public space. From the reticent perspective, which habitually linked together decency, propriety, judgment, taste, manners, and morals, it had been literally unthinkable to split morality apart from aesthetics; they were part and parcel of the same mental category. But with the growing prominence of realism, Judge Pound was able to deliver opinions that would have been inconceivable just a decade earlier: "One may call a spade a spade without offending decency, although modesty may be shocked thereby." In the same spirit, he criticized the play for "lacking in taste and refinement," concluding that "a coarse realism is its dramatic effect." But coarseness and vulgarity must not be confused with obscenity: "Unless we say that it is obscene to use the language of the street rather than that of the scholar, the play is not obscene under the Penal Law, although it might be so styled by the censorious."[48]

The question of whether one could write about sexual experience without descending into the realm of obscenity was also broached in earlier trials concerning highly aestheticized European imports, although in these cases the issue was the inappropriate use of high style to depict the low world of the demimonde. In a dissenting opinion in *Halsey* v. *New York Society for the Suppression of Vice* (1922), Judge Crane disputed the majority opinion's claim that Théophile Gautier's *Mademoiselle de Maupin* should be considered a classic. To the contrary, he pointed out that Gautier's work had been condemned during his own lifetime, "and because of its lasciviousness and bad taste, he was forever barred from the French Academy." Where the coarse though honest tone of realist proletarian literature had presented problems of propriety, the high tone of art for art's sake presented problems of duplicity:

> If the things said by Gautier in this book of *Mademoiselle de Maupin* were stated openly and frankly in the language of the street, there would be no doubt in the minds of anybody . . . that the work would be lewd, vicious, and indecent. The fact that the disgusting details are served up in a polished style, with exquisite settings and perfumed words, makes it all the more dangerous and insidious, and nonetheless obscene and lascivious.

Judge Crane evoked the name of Oscar Wilde, the popular symbol of decadence that came from the unholy separation of art and morals: "Gautier may have a reputation as a writer, but his reputation does not create a license for the American market. Oscar Wilde had a great reputation for style, but went to jail just the same. Literary ability is no excuse for degeneracy."[49]

In *People* v. *Seltzer* (1924), where Thomas Seltzer was indicted for publishing Arthur Schnitzler's *Casanova's Homecoming*, these same issues emerged in Judge Wagner's discussion of the inadmissibility of expert testimony. His description of criticism as that which "look[s] with a single eye to purity of construction, vividness of phrase, and skill in implanting ideas in luminous expression" testifies to Mencken's success in defining criticism as an enterprise that cared only for style. But Judge Wagner, a loyal adherent to the waning genteel tradition, saw this split between style and content as an invitation to corruption:

> Charm of language, subtilty [sic] of thought, faultless style, even distinction of authorship, may all have their lure for the literary critic, yet these qualities may all be present and the book be unfit for dissemination to the reading public. Frequently these attractive literary qualities are the very vehicles by which the destination of illegality is reached.

Then, offering the same evaluation of Schnitzler's refined style as Judge Crane had about Gautier's, he concluded, "Neither literary artistry nor charm and grace of exquisite composition may cloak protectively those obnoxious impulses . . . which on patent appearance would be abhorred."[50]

In his dissenting opinion on Schnitzler's *Hands Around*, Judge McEnroy used the novel's high literary style to accomplish exactly the opposite purpose, claiming that its polished manner actually saved it from sinking into obscenity: "The episodes related by the characters less deftly touched would be of a vulgar tone because of the subject, and could be, if written in bawdy phrases, classed as too realistic for common reading."[51] It is a sign of the growing derangement of the obscenity discourse and the decline of consensus about art that one judge exonerated a book by appealing to its high tone, which supposedly made the low subject matter fit for public display, while two others convicted writers for their inappropriate use of high style, which supposedly disguised the baseness of their subjects. Matters were further complicated when the courts cleared *Frankie and Johnnie* and *God's Little Acre*, as we have seen, on the grounds that while undeniably coarse and vulgar, they did not incite lust; rather, their style was appropriate to their characters' low station in life.

This utter confusion about which style—high or low, refined or vulgar—was most appropriate to representations of prostitutes and their patrons, wayward young men, or poor people and, furthermore, whether any of them were obscene, shows that once agreement about the unity of aesthetics and morality fell apart, the law became incoherent about obscenity. Obscenity law, if it is fixed on art, can be coherent only to the extent that aesthetic theory itself is coherent. In the United States, the disjunction between obscenity law and modern literary practice came to a head in 1933 when James Joyce's *Ulysses* was tried and exonerated.

THE SPECIAL RIGHTS OF ARTISTS

A protracted battle concerning whether *Ulysses* would be made available to American readers began in 1918 when *The Little Review* published early installments of it, which the U.S. Post Office immediately seized and burned. In 1920, when *The Little Review* published Leopold Bloom's erotic musings about Gertie McDowell, Sumner filed a complaint, and Margaret Anderson and Jane Heap, editors of the journal, were promptly arrested. The following year they were found guilty and fined fifty dollars. In 1922, five hundred imported copies of the completed book were again confiscated and burned. In 1928, the book was intercepted and a Customs Court found it was "filled with obscenity of the rottenest and vilest character." Finally, in 1933, a copy that Random House imported with the intention to publish was barred at customs. Having consulted with Morris Ernst, by then the leading attorney in obscenity defenses, Random House brought suit to test the provision in the 1930 Tariff Act that allowed the Secretary of the Treasury to "admit the so-called classics or books of recognized and established literary or scientific merit." This resulted in two landmark trials. *United States* v. *One Book Called "Ulysses"* (1933) was presided over by Judge Woolsey who had earlier vindicated Stopes's birth-control writings and reformulated the victim of the Hicklin Test as "any person with a normal mind." Judge Woolsey had the reputation of being "the literary jurist," and was known to be a discerning collector of paintings and rare books.[52] When the government appealed against Woolsey's decision, Judge Augustus Hand, who had exonerated Dennett's sex-education pamphlet four years earlier, and Judge Learned Hand, who had raised serious doubts about the Hicklin Test in the Kennerley decision, affirmed the lower court's decision (with Judge Manton dissenting).

The *Ulysses* case addressed all the issues that had been contested during the previous decade of litigation. First, Judge Woolsey implicitly denied the jury's capacity to judge obscenity when he expressed his approval that both sides had waived their right to a jury trial. He also rejected practically all the key components of the Hicklin Test. Pointing to the novel's tremendous reputation in the literary world, Judge Woolsey insisted that the author's intent, as well as the effect of the book "read in its entirety," be considered; the crux of the matter was whether the intent was "pornographic." This term, new to legal discourse, Judge Woolsey defined as "written for the purpose of exploiting obscenity." Answering in the negative, he explained, "In spite of its unusual frankness, I do not detect anywhere the leer of the sensualist."[53]

Even though Joyce's novel is typically regarded as a modernist masterpiece, Judge Woolsey's defense of it relies more on arguments developed by champions of realism than those offered for modernism. Just as Howells had lauded Zola's sincere depiction of socially marginal characters for their truth and accuracy, and Bourne had defended Dreiser's novels in precisely the same terms, Judge Woolsey made much of the fact that Joyce was writing about "persons of the lower middle class living in Dublin" and doing so "sincerely and honestly." He justified the "dirty words" Joyce had used on the familiar grounds that they "would be naturally and habitually used . . . by the types of folk whose life, physical and mental, Joyce is seeking to describe." After pointing out that one need not associate with such people in real life (thereby confusing mimesis with reality), nor read such a novel, he asked whether the American public should be deprived of "a true portrait of the lower middle class" drawn by "such a real artist in words" simply on account of its intensely realist style.[54]

Judge Woolsey, a man of modern sensibility, did not rest with the realist argument. He also tried to account for Joyce's exceptional candor by way of a fledgling modernist analysis. The brilliance and dullness as well as intelligibility and obscurity of this "amazing tour de force" were the fruits of a pathbreaking technique, he argued, that tried to capture the inner world of characters—what Judge Woolsey called "the stream of consciousness with its ever-shifting kaleidoscopic impressions." Joyce's grand experiment soared beyond the realm of ordinary fiction and, therefore, could not be assessed by conventional standards: "Whether or not one enjoys such a technique as Joyce uses is a matter of taste on which disagreement or argument is futile, but to subject that technique to the standards of some other technique seems to me to be little short of absurd." Judge Woolsey, like so many thoughtful people of the time, was struggling with the question of how to leave open a realm for the really new in art. This move, however, introduced into the legal discourse a way of thinking that eventually came to dominate it and almost immediately became cant within the artistic vanguard itself. As Ernst and Seagle put it: "The dogma is now generally maintained as a canon of aesthetics that the writer cannot shackle himself to current morality in such a way as to make it impossible for him to make art."[55] Modern literature thus deserved special dispensation from the law.

After considering these extenuating circumstances, Judge Woolsey still insisted on applying "a more objective standard" to determine whether the book was obscene. "The meaning of the word 'obscene,' " he wrote, "as legally defined by the courts is: 'tending to stir the sex impulses or lead to sexually impure and lustful thoughts.' " This definition of obscenity was loyal to the Hicklin Test most narrowly construed, but Judge Woolsey made an important modification when he replaced the most susceptible person with "a person with average sex instincts—what the French would call *l'homme moyen sensuel*—who plays, in this branch of inquiry, the same role of hypothetical reagent as does 'the reasonable man' in the law of torts and 'the man learned in the art' on questions of invention in patent law."[56]

It is ironic that Judge Woolsey should land upon this hypothetical victim, *l'homme moyen sensuel,* at the very moment when modern literature had moved so beyond the range of the average reader that disputants waived their right to trial by jury.

Using this standard, which was a more fully articulated version of the one he had offered in the Stopes trials, Judge Woolsey exonerated *Ulysses* on the grounds that "it does not excite sexual impulses or lustful thoughts" in "the normal person." After reaching this conclusion, he had asked two additional "literary assessors"—"men whose opinion on literature and on life I value most highly"—to read the book and decide whether it was obscene according to this definition. While these unusual consultations testify to Judge Woolsey's scrupulousness, they also point to the need for juries in order to consider different perspectives. The "net effect" of the book on himself and his two friends was "that of a somewhat tragic and very powerful commentary on the inner lives of men and women."[57]

As soon as Judge Woolsey rendered his verdict, Random House, under Bennett Cerf's direction, published *Ulysses;* 33,000 copies were sold within a few weeks. Both the legal establishment and the popular press praised Judge Woolsey as "a fine essayist." The Random House edition included an enthusiastic foreword by Ernst, the entire text of the judgment, and "a letter from Mr. Joyce to the Publisher." In his glowing foreword to the Modern Library edition of *Ulysses* (1934), Ernst spoke for an entire generation when he described the publication as a crushing defeat for the forces of puritanism. "The first week of December 1933 will go down in history for two repeals, that of Prohibition and that of legal compulsion for squeamishness in literature." Ernst praised Judge Woolsey's "lucid, rational, and practical" decision in favor of Joyce's book for "rescu[ing] the mental pabulum of the public from the censors who have striven to convert it into treacle, and will help to make it the strong, provocative fare it ought to be." He also spoke out against those judges who had faithfully employed the Hicklin Test, chastising "the censors" who for decades "have fought to emasculate literature." The American Civil Liberties Union also distributed Judge Woolsey's decision, declaring it "a masterpiece" and praising the verdict as "thoroughly wholesome." Sumner and the New York Society for the Suppression of Vice predictably branded the opinion "a literary review trying to explain away the appearance of admitted obscenity and filth," setting the stage for the appeal.[58]

A year later, Judge Augustus Hand affirmed that *Ulysses* was not obscene and upheld the lower court's modifications of the Hicklin

Test. Once and for all, the Hicklin Test's emphasis on the effects of the isolated passage on the most susceptible person was overturned. He ruled that the "dominant effect" of the book as a whole and the intent of the author be considered. Of equal importance, he announced that the "established reputation of the book in estimation of approved critics, if book is modern, and the verdict of the past, if book is ancient, are persuasive evidence," which shifted the authority of obscenity determinations away from the common sense of the jury and toward expert opinion. As for the consequences of obscenity, Judge Hand continued to hold that the crucial point was whether "the book taken as a whole has a libidinous effect." But acceptance of expert testimony virtually guaranteed that literary merit would nullify any libidinous effect, since if it could be proved that the material was art, by definition it could not be obscene. We have already seen this line of thinking applied to sex education. As Judge Hand put it: "The same immunity should apply to literature as to science where the presentation, when viewed objectively, is sincere and the erotic matter is not introduced to promote lust and does not furnish the dominant note of the publication." With these considerations in mind, the court found that "the book as a whole is not pornographic, and while in not a few spots it is coarse, blasphemous, and obscene, it does not, in our opinion, promote lust."[59]

To justify what he acknowledged as the "extreme vulgarity" and "obscenity" of certain passages, Judge Hand resorted to a familiar argument: "The book as a whole has a realism characteristic of the present age." And as for the actual effects of reading *Ulysses*: "The book depicts the souls of men and women that are by turns bewildered and keenly apprehensive, sordid and aspiring, ugly and beautiful, hateful and loving. In the end, one feels more than anything else, pity and sorrow for the confusion, misery, and degradation of humanity." Finally, reiterating Judge Woolsey's plea for special legal dispensation for art, he declared, "Art cannot advance under compulsion to traditional forms, and nothing in such a field is more stifling to progress than limitations of the right to experiment with a new technique." Like Judge Woolsey, Judge Hand dissociated moral from aesthetic judgment to reserve a safe haven for experimental literature. Four years later, in an article, "Judicial Censorship of Obscene Literature," Leo M. Alpert made explicit the underlying assumptions of this special legal treatment of literature: "Literature should disseminate ideas, not moralities. If the author's ideas jar the prevailing mores, it is not the ideas which must be suppressed." Linking advanced art and social progress, he insisted that "both can exist cotaneously [sic], and both must so exist if society is not to stagnate, decay, and die." In what had become an article of progressive faith, Alpert assigned the modern novelist a leading role in the ever-forward march of progress: "Moralities change; ideas develop; and the change in morals springs from the development of ideas. In this sense, to limn with a broad brush, poets *are* the unacknowledged legislators of the world."[60]

It is striking that even though Judge Woolsey and Judge Hand were clearly making a case for atistic freedom, neither of them raised the First Amendment, which by the 1950s was routinely evoked in disputes about obscene literature and which had been an insurmountable obstacle in the legal recognition of the right to privacy from the very start.[61] Throughout the 1920s, even the ACLU, which in our own time has become the bulwark of the rights of pornographers, showed little interest in controversies surrounding book suppression. In a letter to a Springfield librarian who was active in anti-censorship drives in Massachusetts in 1927, Forrest Bailey, co-director of the Union, said he believed that disputes about obscenity were "spasms of morbid conscience" that "die down quickly." "The issue of free speech, in its larger aspects—those affecting criticism of the status quo—appears to us to be so much more important, that it would be inexpedient for us to involve ourselves in controversies where questions of morals are present." By 1929, Arthur Garfield Hays and Morris Ernst became co-counsel of the ACLU, at which time the Union became increasingly involved with the campaign to liberalize obscenity laws in Massachusetts. Yet by that time, according to Paul Boyer, "literary censorship was decidedly on the wane all over America."[62]

The Demise of Reticence

In his dissenting opinion to the *Ulysses* decision, Judge Manton revealed himself as one of the last members of the bench sympathetic to the nineteenth-century understanding of obscenity. After making the familiar observation that the contested passages were "too indecent to add as a footnote to this opinion," he affirmed his support for the Hicklin Test, and restated the ironclad relation between things that appear in public and their effect on both individuals and society at large: "Thus the court sustained a charge having a test as to whether or no [sic] the publications depraved the morals of the ordinary reader or tended to lower the standards of civilization."[63]

Judge Manton held fast to the old notion of protecting "the morals of the susceptible." Echoing earlier critics of the literary vanguard, he insisted that the proper obscenity test could not be keyed merely to "those who pose as the more highly developed and intelligent." "To do so," he insisted, "would show an utter disregard for the standards of decency of the community as a whole." But Judge Manton did not focus on contamination of public space, or the waning of the sense of shame, or the general coarsening of taste and morality, as earlier proponents of reticence had always done in this context; instead he adopted a balance-sheet approach toward the potential corruption of individuals. After weighing the "benefits and pleasures derived from letters" by the cultivated few against "the effect of a book upon the average less sophisticated member of society, not to mention the ad-olescent," he concluded, "The statute is designed to protect society at large . . . notwithstanding the deprivation of benefits to a few, a work must be condemned if it has a depraving influence."[64] The balance-sheet approach deprived the judge of the most compelling aspects of the original reticent position and also disclosed that even someone still sympathetic to it could no longer remember that ob-scenity had important public dimensions.

In 1935, Francis Bertram Elgas, president of Comstock's own cre-ation, the New York Society for the Suppression of Vice, conceded that dramatic shifts in popular standards of morality and taste had made traditional legal prosecutions of obscenity untenable:

> Tastes necessarily differ, and with books that simply offend good taste and are hopelessly vulgar (and not flagrantly pornographic, obscene, or immoral), we cannot in this age, when former notions of propriety and decency have so radically changed, attempt to take restraining steps which might not meet with broader views now taken by our courts. . . . Times have changed and we must change with them.[65]

Even when the memory of reticence was still alive, its most dedicated defenders were so embattled that even they had to make do with a stripped-down version of their own position. This development ob-viously signals the demise of the party of reticence. Whereas earlier proponents of reticence had uttered aesthetic and moral judgments in the same breath when speculating about which things rightly belonged in public, Elgas's air of resignation registered that advocates of literary exposure had been victorious in dividing artistry from morality.

Elgas's tacit acceptance of the new standards for obscenity serves as a notice of surrender of the official protectors of reticence. Ironi-cally, a letter H. L. Mencken wrote to James Branch Cabell in 1934 has a similar tone of resignation; he sounded like that "indignant old radical" mentioned by Margaret Sanger in her autobiography who left a birth-control congress in the early 1930s "sniffing, 'This thing has got too darned safe for me.' " Recalling the pitched battle over Cabell's novel *Jurgen* in 1922, Mencken wistfully observed, "How much water has gone under the bridges since those insane days! The Comstocks are now down and out."[66]

For some advocates of exposure, however, Judge Woolsey's decision did not go far enough. Writing in *Scribner's Magazine* in 1934, the critic Ben Ray Redman acknowledged the enthusiasm that greeted the decision, but he insisted that people needed to reconsider "how much we have really won by our victory over Comstockism." To him, it seemed a rather hollow victory, consisting mainly in the freedom to use four-letter words: "The fight that we have been waging against censorship has, in large measure, been a battle to admit coarseness to the printed page." Redman urged that "nothing less than a radical revision of certain widely held ideas can ensure a continuance of the present state of literary freedom," specifically the need to rethink the legal formula that determined obscenity based on whether the book in question tended to "stir the sex impulses or to lead to impure and lustful thoughts." He denounced that definition as "plain tommyrot because it hypocritically ignores the facts of life and the realities of literature." He pointed out that lust could be stirred by many things, including great literature, and furthermore, there was nothing wrong with that:

> There is great and beautiful literature which owes much of its beauty and greatness, and even more of its reputation, to sexual appeal and its powers of sexual stimulation. Its effects may be sublimated, idealized, romanticized, or purified, of course—and in the case of the greatest literature, these transformations are accomplished; but the nature of the cause is evident.[67]

Even though Redman undoubtedly imagined himself as liberated from the outdated genteel tradition, he uncritically continued to adhere to one of its fundamental tenets: that literature "influences" people. But he reversed the commonly held view that representations of sex, by inciting lust, corrupt morals. Like other advocates of exposure, he split sex apart from traditional ideas about morality, consolidating the now-venerable project to make sex clean. In any case, Redman was right about one thing: "The rule proves asinine the moment we attempt to apply it."[68] The same assessment can just as easily be applied to his position, however. Once discussions about obscenity become fixed exclusively on the incitement of private sexual responses and have nothing to say about the deterioration of the public sphere, the coarsening of standards of taste and judgment, or the waning of the sense of shame, the entire matter becomes weightless.

8

RETICENCE RESTATED

In the conclusion of his excellent study of the vice-society movement and book censorship in America, *Purity in Print* (1968), Paul Boyer describes the way vice societies as agencies of reform and spokesmen for purity were in retreat by the late 1920s. They had been an integral part of the larger reform projects flourishing during the late nineteenth century, and were closely aligned with the Progressive movement in the first decade of the twentieth, but by the close of the 1920s they had lost much of their respectability. This is largely because the movement came more and more under the influence of the Catholic Church and, with this new patron, became increasingly parochial, xenophobic, anti-Semitic, and anti-intellectual. Their attacks upon their opponents were so excessive and shrill that they eventually came to resemble the picture of bigots and prudes which the party of exposure had always drawn of them.[1]

And it is this degenerate form of reticence—a kind of latter-day comstockery—that has come to represent nineteenth-century morals and manners to twentieth-century moderns. Thus, the original reticent sensibility is almost completely lost to us. Yet, by the 1920s, certain aspects of it resurfaced, interestingly enough in the writings of those who had been leaders in discrediting it, including H. L. Mencken, Walter Lippmann, and the drama critic of *The Nation*, Joseph Wood Krutch. When confronted with the fruits of their endeavors, these debunkers of the conspiracy of silence began to wonder aloud about the sorry condition of love in the modern world which they had helped to bring about.

THE RESILIENCE OF MYSTERY

In his swashbuckling attack "The Unblushful Mystery" (1919), Mencken lambasted "the literature of sex hygiene, once so scanty and so timorous, [which] now piles mountain high," for trying "to explain a romantic mystery in terms of an exact science." Like Randolph Bourne, who had taken exception to the "pseudo-scientific" approach to sex because it "has no more to do with the relevance of sex than the chemical composition of orange paint has to do with the artist's vision," Mencken dismissed the entire sex-hygiene movement as absurd: "As well attempt to interpret Beethoven in terms of mathematical physics—as many a fatuous contrapuntist, indeed has tried to do. . . . The only result of the current endeavor to explain its phenomena by seeking parallels in botany is to make botany obscene."[2]

Where sex reformers proudly marched under the banner of progress and partook in Puritan-baiting with as much gusto as cultural radicals and smart-set sophisticates, Mencken, in a move calculated to infuriate, grouped them together with their avowed enemy, the Puritan. "The Puritan, for all his pretensions, is the worst of materialists," sneered Mencken. "Passed through his sordid and unimaginative mind, even the stupendous romance of sex is reduced to a disgusting transaction in physiology." Mencken was so irritated by these reformers that he momentarily made peace with one of his favorite genteel targets, Agnes Repplier. Without the slightest hint of irony, he praised her essay "The Repeal of Reticence" for showing how "innocence has been killed, and romance has been sadly wounded by the same discharge of smutty artillery." He bemoaned the fate of the flapper who "is no longer naïve and charming; she goes to the altar of God with a learned and even cynical glitter in her eye." She knows too much too soon: "The veriest schoolgirl of today, fed upon Forel, Sylvanus Stall, Reginald Wright Kauffman, and the Freud books, knows as much as the midwife of 1885, and spends a good deal more time discharging and disseminating her information."[3]

The debunking style that Mencken himself had perfected left anyone who dared to question frank speech about sex in the indefensible position of being a prurient prude. Thus, Mencken was quick to demonstrate his credentials as world-weary sophisticate. Outdoing the reformers in their vaunted capacity to divorce the biological fact of sex from its moral associations, he declared, "I do not object to this New Freedom on moral grounds, but aesthetic grounds." The trouble with the scientific framework was that it stripped intimate life of its beauty. Surprisingly, Mencken adopted a position rather like that of the old-fashioned reticent sensibility with its awe of mysteries: "In the relations between the sexes all beauty is founded upon romance, all romance is founded upon mystery, and all mystery is founded upon ignorance, or, failing that, upon the deliberate denial of the known truth." But the blasé sophisticate could not be awed for very long, so he immediately twisted this insight into a more amusing, if less complicated, shape: "To be in love is merely to be in a state of perceptual anaesthesia—to mistake an ordinary young man for a Greek god or an ordinary young woman for a goddess."[4]

What Mencken detested most about the new scientific way of talking about sex was its "deadly matter-of-factness," which he thought absurd. "How can a woman continue to believe in the honor, courage, and loving tenderness of a man after she has learned, perhaps by affidavit, that his hemoglobin count is 117%, that he is free from sugar and albumen, that his blood pressure is 112/79 and that his Wassermann reaction is negative?" Not only did scientific descriptions of the body tend to dissolve erotic love to the point of laughter, but "this new-fangled 'frankness' tends to dam up, at least for civilized adults, one of the principal well-springs of art, to wit, impropriety." Pointing to the need for injunctions in these domains, Mencken spelled out the uninspiring future that lay ahead for art once the body had been thoroughly demystified: "What is neither hidden nor forbidden is seldom very charming. If women, continuing their present tendency to its logical goal, end by going stark naked, there will be no more poets and painters, but only dermatologists and photographers."[5]

That Mencken could make common cause with the party of reticence when it suited his purposes suggests that the civilized minority had surprising affinities with a sensibility that they had gone far to abuse and discredit. Nevertheless, the two sensibilities did come together in their hatred for the growing commercialization and vulgarization of culture and private life under a social regime of constant exposure. Both also disdained the one-dimensionality of didactic writing, holding that art and love existed in a realm beyond any simplistic attempt to capture them in matter-of-fact language. Along these lines, Mencken criticized the typical American novel for its "habit of reducing the unknowable to terms of the not worth knowing." This assessment applied with equal force to sex reformers and experts, and to the many commercial entertainments—newspapers, magazines, novels, movies, and plays—that exploited their findings. In praising the "harsh, unyielding, repellent" philosophy of Joseph Conrad's novels and the "sinister and abhorrent" quality of the "love-making" of his heroes, Mencken distinguished art from its commercial pretenders: "One cannot imagine [Conrad's heroes] in the moving pictures, played by tailored beauties with long eye-lashes." "The world fails to breed actors for such roles, or stage managers to penetrate such travails of the spirit, or audiences for the revelation thereof."[6]

The shallowness of mind that transforms the unknowable into the not-worth-knowing is precisely what Agnes Repplier too found so annoying about sex reformers. She was appalled by their simple-minded plan to distribute "crude, undigested knowledge, without limit and without reserve" to everyone, including children. "If knowledge alone could save us from sin," she observed knowingly, "the salvation of the world would be easy work." This appreciation of the unfathomable in life and love was expressed in the urbane, ironic style of exemplars of reticence and the best of the smart set. (Where smart-set urbanity all too often degenerated into mean-spirited debunking, the party of reticence, ever polite, did not display this nasty streak.) Their opponents, in contrast, were literally without the means to turn a phrase let alone polish an essay; their syntax and vocabulary, whether in its literature ("problem plays" and "novels of ideas") or in its clinical inflection (sex-hygiene material), had only the meager resources necessary for rooting out evils. As Mencken's impatience with their "deadly matter-of-factness" makes clear, this wing of the party of exposure possessed neither a sense of proportion nor a feel for the right ordering of things, and thus were bereft of elegance and wit. Here Repplier was in complete agreement with Mencken: "The lamentable lack of reserve is closely associated with a lamentable absence of humor. . . . We could clearly estimate the value of reform, if we were not so befuddled with the serious sensationalism of reformers."[7]

Repplier and Mencken, then, were alike in that they both had the highest regard for art, for culture, and for the privacy that makes intimate life possible. Where the party of reticence and the smart-set flank of the party of exposure definitively parted company, however, was in their capacity and willingness to divide moral from aesthetic judgment. Although Repplier was as adamant as Mencken in believing that art must never be used in the service of ideas, reform, or commerce (she had early professed a sympathy for Oscar Wilde's aestheticism), she never abandoned the belief that "taste is a guardian of morality." Born in 1857, she was of a generation who wore their moral seriousness as a badge of honor. In 1914, she was still able to write, without any self-consciousness, "Whether [art] deals with high and poignant emotions, or with the fears and the wreckage of life, she subdues these human elements into an austere accord with her own harmonious laws."[8] And it is precisely this moral gravity that Mencken's generation left behind. It is not for nothing that Mencken bragged he had rejected the sex-hygiene movement for aesthetic reasons alone. And it is precisely this flip, self-consciously smart tone that someone of Repplier's moral and aesthetic convictions could never adopt, which, in turn, left such a person vulnerable to the charge of priggishness.

Even though Repplier and Mencken were describing the disenchantment of the world through endless scrutiny of what had once been held sacred, neither entertained for a moment that this project and its discoveries were worth taking seriously. Neither one's faith in the value of love was disturbed in the least. For Repplier, there was no such thing as sex distinct from its moral dimensions of love or lust. For Mencken, sex deprived of its aesthetic—romance—simply did not merit consideration. Their confidence in this regard stands in sharpest relief to the darker ponderings of Walter Lippmann's *A Preface to Morals* and Joseph Wood Krutch's *The Modern Temper*, both published in 1929. They approached the disenchantment of love from the inside, as it were, having initially embraced the method of exposure in hopes of discovering higher truths about love. Like Repplier and Mencken, these critics asked: What have clinical discussions about sex done to the experience of love? Lippmann and Krutch explicitly set out the problem in fact-value terms: once science revealed that sex was a fact of biology and psychology, it also exposed love as a contingent value, dependent upon social conventions—courtship, romance, and marriage—which vary over time and place. This acknowledgment of relativism was of course what the sex reformers and opponents of obscenity law had advocated all along. If the conventions surrounding love were not rooted in nature or part of a sacred order, then they could be adjusted in accordance with human happiness. Once taboos were demolished, candid discussions and images of sex would be permitted to appear in public. But to their surprise and dismay, Lippmann and Krutch found that life lived in the open air was not so delightful or edifying as optimistic reformers had promised. For them the demystification of love was but one aspect, though perhaps the most devastating, of the larger existential problem of the modern condition. The defining feature of that condition, both critics argued, was the dissolution of all standards of authority.

That both writers devoted entire chapters to love in the modern age once again demonstrates the extraordinary importance that the moderns attached to that most fragile and cherished edifice of the private sphere—intimacy. "With no subject has the contemporary mind been more persistently busy [than love]," Krutch announced in a dramatic moment in his essay. He unwittingly drew attention to the unprecedented regard for intimacy and the concomitant devaluation of public life, when he insisted that the Victorian popular sentiment "Love is best" expressed a "faith" that "lies deeper than religious or political creeds." Lippmann, too, put intimacy at the very center of modern life:

> It is in the realm of sexual relations that mankind is being schooled amidst pain and worry for the novel conditions which modernity imposes. It is there, rather than in politics, business, or even in religion, that the issues are urgent, vivid, and inescapable. It is there that they touch most poignantly and most radically the organic roots of human personality. And it is there, in the ordering of their personal attachments, that for most men the process of salvation must necessarily begin.[9]

THE DISENCHANTMENT OF LOVE

In "Love in the Great Society," Lippmann explored the new domestic arrangements advocated by modern reformers. Why, he asked, had the old consensus about "civilized" sexual morality broken apart? His explanation of one contributing cause includes what had become a sociological truism by the 1920s: the forces of modernization, urbanization, and industrialization had dramatically transformed sexual relations by freeing women from the constant surveillance that used to be a prominent and stifling feature of small-town life. It was the anonymity of the modern city, above all, that undermined the Victorians' stringent code of sexual conduct. "The whole revolution in the field of sexual morals," observed Lippmann, "turns upon the fact that external control of the chastity of women is becoming impossible."[10]

The other major force that undid Victorian sexual morality was the growing availability of birth-control information and devices. Providing a broad outline of agitation for birth control, Lippmann summarized the arguments that eventually made open discussion of private matters not only necessary but also socially acceptable. That he could write this summary at all once again testifies to the victory of the party of exposure over the so-called conspiracy of silence. The need for birth control, he reported, was argued first on the grounds of "sound economic public policy for economic and eugenic reasons" and second, on the grounds of the "happiness of families, the health of mothers, and the welfare of children." And finally, birth control was demanded by those who had "a desire to enjoy sexual intercourse without social consequences." This last move was revolutionary, changing the very nature of sex: it was no longer regarded as "an impure means to a noble end" but rather as "inherently delightful."[11]

Lippmann had no doubts about the many achievements of the birth-control movement, and his catalogue of their successes helps explain why their project eventually won widespread acceptance, which, in turn, made the nineteenth-century understanding of sex education as obscene unintelligible to moderns. He praised contraception for "relieving men and women of some of the most tragic sorrows which afflict them"—unwanted children, economic hardship, and the ruined health of women. Moreover, contraception "offers them freedom from intolerable mismating, from sterile virtue, from withering denials of happiness." Where Lippmann did have profound doubts was in regard to the new relationships proposed by reformers—free love, trial marriage, companionate marriage, and free divorce—which, they argued, were more in keeping with the logic of birth control than were traditional marriages. For Lippmann, these proposed relationships were "really designed to cure notorious evils. They do not define the good life in sex; they point out ways of escape from the bad life."[12]

The trouble with the reformers' proposals, according to Lippmann, could be found in their central premise: "the obvious fact that by contraception it is possible to dissociate procreation from gratification." The reformers therefore concluded that sex for the continuation of the race could and should be treated separately from the newly discovered aim of pleasure. "They propose . . . to distinguish between parenthood as a vocation involving public responsibility, and love as an art, pursued privately for the sake of happiness." Furthermore, they wanted the state to recognize and help foster different kinds of union based on this different premise.[13]

"Parenthood as a vocation" made the welfare of the child paramount and required rigorous preparation of both men and women "in the care, both physical and psychological, of children," while "the art of love" was "designed to permit the freest and fullest expression of the erotic personality" and to ensure "the happiness of lovers." Lippmann was quick to make the point that "there are two arts of love and it makes a considerable difference which one is meant." The first, for which he had no sympathy, he associated with Casanova: "the art of seduction, courtship, and sexual gratification . . . which culminates in the sexual act." Its "aftermath" was "either tedium in middle age or the compulsive adventurousness of the libertine." The second, for which he had a bit more patience, he associated with Havelock Ellis, quoting him as saying that " 'the act of intercourse . . . [was] only an incident, and not an essential in love.' " It is an incident to an " 'exquisitely and variously and harmoniously blended' activity of 'all the finer activities of the organism, physical and psychic.' "[14]

Reformers, following the logic of birth control, came to believe that sexual intimacy could flourish outside the old convention of marriage in two ways: as a "harmless pleasure" or as "a sacrament signifying some great spiritual reality." In both cases, they contended, "sexual conventions should be revised to permit such unions without penalties and without any sense of shame." Employing a pastoral idiom that evokes the naturalness of sex and then ecstatically merges lovers not only with each other but with nature itself, they urged that all sexual relationships outside of marriage be free of stigmatizing conventions so that "they will become candid, wholesome, and delightful." Like those who argued that obscenity existed only in unclean minds, these reformers claimed that neither shame nor sin existed in sex; rather, they sprang from conventions that "poison the spontaneous goodness of such relationships."[15]

For Lippmann, who accepted the fact-value distinction in the realm of love, the crucial question was, Should the logic of birth control determine conventions surrounding love? To answer this question, he considered whether the separation of "parenthood as a vocation from love as an end in itself" could lead to happiness. Weighing the evidence from a generation "approaching middle age [who] have exercised the privileges which were won by the iconoclasts who attacked what was usually called the Puritan or Victorian tradition," Lippmann, himself of this generation and a leading iconoclast, made a startling discovery: "Instead of the gladness which they were promised, they seem . . . to have found the wasteland." Quoting at length from Krutch's despairing analysis of fiction about emancipated love, he concluded that a life dedicated to the pursuit of such love brings about "a generally devaluated world . . . in which nothing connects itself very much with anything else." Trying to understand this apparent miscarriage of the promise of emancipation, Lippmann asked, "If you start with the belief that love is the pleasure of a moment, is it really surprising that it yields only a momentary pleasure?"[16]

Ellis's idealized love also failed to bring about the expected delights: separating parenthood from erotic love impoverished both. In isolating "love from work and the hard realities of living," Lippmann observed, "you have separated it from all the important activities which it might stimulate and liberate. You have made love spontaneous but empty, and you have made home-building and parenthood efficient, responsible, and dull." Counseling a weightier approach to life, which holds that meaning evolves only from responsibilities inherited from the past and from commitments that last into the future, he concluded, "love cannot successfully be isolated from the business of living, which is the enduring wisdom of the institution of marriage."[17]

Where Lippmann's essay was a sober analysis, Krutch's was a heart-rending lament over the wretched condition of love under the pressure of unrelenting analysis. In contrast to many of his contemporaries, Krutch was an uneasy modern. He, too, had absorbed the astounding lessons of Darwin, Nietzsche, Freud, and Ellis, that transcendental standards simply did not exist. But for Krutch, this meant that mythology, religion, and philosophy had lost their venerated function as "interpret[ers] of experience in terms which have human values." To his distress, this was also true for ethics: "Anthropology is ready to prove that no consistent human tradition has ever existed. Custom has furnished the only basis which ethics have ever had, and there is no conceivable human action which custom has not at one time justified and at another condemned."[18]

For the party of exposure, once a custom or a convention was unmasked as contingent and lost its legitimacy, the way was paved for new freedoms. While Krutch did not deny this line of thought, he could not embrace its cheery conclusions. For him, once a value was exposed as relative, it was not only divested of its legitimacy, but the experience it had once informed was deprived of its meaning. "Standards are imaginary things," he ruefully admitted, "and yet it is extremely doubtful if man can live well, either spiritually or physically, without the belief that they are somehow real." For Krutch, a world whose values were merely contingent meant alienation and existential despair: "The universe revealed by science . . . is one in which the human spirit cannot find a comfortable home. That spirit breathes freely only in a universe where what philosophers call Value Judgments are of supreme importance."[19]

Nowhere were value judgments more crucial for Krutch than in the realm of intimacy. Even though he was alarmed by the way scientific categories were infiltrating that venerated realm, he was so inculcated in the modern habit of mind that dissociates experiences from their value that he could observe: "Of the infinitely complicated processes of life, in the biological sense, only a few are subject to that elaboration and poetization which make them even potentially a part of significant experience." What he had in mind here was how conscious bodily activities, like eating or sex, "can be made into one of the ceremonies by which life is elaborated and can pass as a symbol into poetry and philosophy"—as opposed to automatic physical functions like "the beating of the heart and the slow churning of the stomach" which remain below awareness. Because conscious bodily experiences always involve this doubleness, they have not only the potential for transcendence through philosophy and poetry—once the languages of eros—but also the potential for lowering. To see sex as a mere biological function meant, for Krutch—as it had for the party of reticence—that "man is dehumanized and life is made to sink back to a level nearer that of the animal, for whom life is a phenomenon in which there is no meaning except the biological urge."[20]

Krutch was concerned that the modern lover suffered from hyper-self-consciousness. He had become so familiar with the inner work-ings of his body through "the cynical wisdom of biology and psychology"—"the world of metabolism and hormones, repressions and complexes"—that he could no longer simply fall in love or ex-perience tender feelings without appearing faintly ridiculous in his own eyes. "And thus," according to Krutch, "he is reduced to mock-ing his torn and divided soul."

> Man *qua* thinker may delight in the intricacies of psychology, but man *qua* lover has not learned to feel in its terms; so that, though complexes and ductless glands may serve to explain the feelings of another, one's own still demand all those symbols of the ineffable in which one has long ceased to believe.[21]

This rendering of the fragility of love recalls the age-old under-standing of privacy as a sanctuary for the body at its most vulnerable. Just as the ancients venerated birth and death as mysteries command-ing awe and reverence, tribal societies surrounded bodily activities with highly charged taboos, and Victorians had once held that inti-mate life was sacred, Krutch's approach to erotic love points to this same imaginative configuration. What distinguishes sex from other sensory experiences is the incapacity of the uninitiated to grasp its significance: "Much that, as a child, he had heard without under-standing becomes suddenly meaningful to him, and he realizes that he is capable of participating in experiences which have hitherto been known to him only by the words applied to them." Revealing once again the deep structure in consciousness of the shameful and the sacred, Krutch observed that a person, once initiated, "will invest thoughts of that which had been, a short time before, both ridiculous and obscene with a religious awe."[22]

Yet Krutch was equally under the sway of modern habits of mind, and was thus able to assume an evolutionary approach to the value of love, insisting that it was only after centuries of attention and embellishment that it had reached its exalted position during the late nineteenth century. He took pains to show how what his generation experienced as unbearable repression—"civilized" sexual morality—was precisely what, for the Victorians, gave love its emotional intensity and metaphysical grandeur. It was because love was so elaborately tabooed that it held out the hope of transcendence. The Victorian system of taboo, he believed,

> looked with loathing and fear at any of the cruder manifestations of the sexual instincts, but when those instincts had been adorned with poetry, and submitted to the discipline of society, it regarded them as the source not only of the most admirable virtues but of the most intrinsically valuable of human experiences as well.[23]

Love was deemed so momentous, according to Krutch, that rebels like Havelock Ellis and H. G. Wells sought to liberate it from "irrational proscriptions" to usher in "an age in which men should love more freely, more fully, and more perfectly." To gauge the success of their emancipatory project, Krutch cast a searching eye to the work of contemporary writers—Aldous Huxley, Ernest Hemingway, D. H. Lawrence, T. S. Eliot, and James Joyce—and shrewdly observed that while these moderns easily shed both their inner inhibitions and outer social restraints, instead of enjoying a freer, fuller, and more perfect love, they seemed suspended in a condition resembling what Milan Kundera later called "the unbearable lightness of being." "The more advanced set of those who are experimenting with life" indulge their sexual passions frequently, "but they cannot transmute that simple animal pleasure into anything else. . . . Absorbed in the pursuit of sexual satisfaction, they never find love." Even more devastating from Krutch's perspective, "they are scarcely aware they are seeking [love]." More often than not, characters who too frequently traverse the border between taboo and desire pay the price of cheapening the experience to the point of either boredom on the one hand or "despair" and "a sense of the emptiness of life" on the other. When writers like Huxley dissolve the tension between "sentiment" and "physiology" exclusively on the side of the body, picturing "a romantic pair 'quietly sweating palm to palm,' " the whole thing, Krutch thought, degenerates into "a sort of obscene joke."[24] We return, then, to the age-old insight about the fragility of the body: if private experiences are not properly contained in social artifice, they quickly become banal, absurd, or obscene.

The ambitious project to liberate love from the burdens of individual guilt and social injunctions had, insofar as it succeeded, brought with it astonishing unintended consequences:

When the consequences of love were made less momentous, then love itself became less momentous too, and we have discovered that the now-lifted veil of mystery was that which made it potentially important as well as potentially terrible. Sex, we learned, was not so awesome as once we had thought; God does not care so much about it as we had formerly been led to suppose; but neither, as a result, do we. Love is becoming so accessible, so unmysterious, and so free that its value is trivial.[25]

CONTINGENCY OR DESPAIR

For Krutch, the modern temper was despair, and his own state of utter disillusionment, which led to a nervous collapse, suggests the cost of taking to heart the modern project of exposure. Krutch, a Southerner born in 1893, apparently was enough of a Victorian to still have illusions that he could lose and lament. Lippmann, in contrast, had definitively rejected all things Victorian when he wrote, fresh out of college, *A Preface to Politics* and *Drift and Mastery*. By the time he wrote *A Preface to Morals*, he was approaching middle age and counseling a mature pragmatism. While he accepted the inevitability of moral relativism—"the acids of modernity are dissolving the usages and the sanctions to which men once habitually conformed"—he still believed in the possibility of shared morals—to which the book was a "preface." "The true function of the moralist in an age when usage is unsettled," Lippmann insisted, "is what Aristotle who lived in such an age described it to be: to promote good conduct by discovering and explaining the mark at which things aim."[26]

Lippmann, who had embraced modern thinkers from Nietzsche and Bergson to Freud and Dewey early in his intellectual career, was perfectly at home in a world where values were not etched in stone. That is why as a young man he was so dismissive of those who continued to adhere uncritically to old-fashioned morals and manners, and why he thought the only remaining purpose of conventions was to bolster the waning authority of a dying social class. By the close of the 1920s, however, Lippmann had rethought this position. "A convention," he now argued, "is essentially a theory of conduct and all human conduct implies some theory of conduct." Keeping the contingency of conventions in the foreground, he praised their potential for flexibility, the way they were "adopted, revised, and debated." Conventions were not arbitrary social constructs that demanded blind allegiance, as he had once supposed; rather, they "embody the considered results of experience." And the total dissolution of authority in modern society had made conventions more necessary than ever before, especially for the inexperienced: "They cannot be so utterly open-minded that they stand inert until something collides with them. In the modern world, therefore, the function of conventions is to declare the meaning of experience. A good convention is one which will show the inexperienced the way to a happy existence." Of the convention of marriage, he noted appreciatively that it "will survive as the dominant insight into the reality of love and happiness, or it will not survive at all." "There will be no compulsion behind it," he assured his readers, "except the compulsion in each man and woman to reach a true adjustment of his life."[27]

Lippmann's new position was a rebuke to sex reformers who refused to recognize any limits to individual freedom. And it acknowledged the responsibility that older people bear for introducing the young to what society, in the fullness of time, has come to value. To leave the uninitiated and the inexperienced on their own is to leave them cruelly vulnerable to the vicissitudes of life. His appreciation of conventions recalls the premodern moral scheme that regarded virtues as a store of knowledge that enables a person to move successfully from human nature in its "untutored" state to "man as he could be if he realized his telos."[28] Where Lippmann parts company with this scheme is that he, along with other modern moral philosophers and ordinary people, had difficulty imagining, let alone agreeing to, what human nature in either its untutored or tutored state looks like. Lippmann thus neglects the first condition and for the second can only evoke fragments from various philosophical traditions—the utilitarian standard of happiness at one point in his argument and the pragmatic standard of "adjustment to life" at another, both of which were key features of the new therapeutic ethos.

And it was precisely this loss of a shared understanding of human nature and its ultimate ends that was expressed in the fact-value distinction that had emerged during the eighteenth century. As Alasdair MacIntyre has convincingly shown in *After Virtue*, the modern habit of separating fact from value would have been unintelligible from the standpoint of the classical, Aristotelian moral tradition that Lippmann himself evoked:

> Moral arguments within the classical, Aristotelian tradition—whether in its Greek or its medieval versions—involve at least one central functional concept of *man* understood as having an essential nature and an essential purpose or function. . . . Aristotle takes it as his starting-point for ethical inquiry that the relationship of "man" to "living well" is analogous to that of "harpist" to "playing the harp well."

This view is part of a tradition that predates Aristotle, as MacIntyre points out, and it rests on the premise that "to be a man is to fill a set of roles each of which has its own point and purpose: member of a family, citizen, soldier, philosopher, servant of God. It is only when man is thought of as an individual prior to and apart from all roles that 'man' ceases to be a functional concept."[29]

In their quest for personal freedom and individuality, moderns completely rejected this functional view of man and reinterpreted these pre-scripted, social roles as heavy, rusted chains that must be thrown off. It is doubtful, however, that the original architects of the fact-value distinction ever imagined that their quest for liberation would eventually reach into the most private regions of intimate experience. It is the distinguishing mark of twentieth-century Western society that its "most advanced set" ever dared imagine, let alone actually attempted, such probings. The ideal of the private sphere as the locus of freedom and individuality, and of intimacy as the source of meaning, is only as old as the eighteenth century, and it came to full flower only for a brief moment during the nineteenth. It is one of the bitterest of historical ironies that the means employed by modern reformers and cultural radicals to realize this cherished ideal exposed it to a kind of light that violated the privacy required to nurture it, which, in turn, stripped love of its value. Since our contemporary consumerist society offers little opportunity for meaning either in fulfilling, non-degraded work or in politics concerned with the public good rather than the administration of the economy, the trivialization of love through endless analysis is indeed catastrophic. Krutch recognized this when he mournfully observed, "We have grown used . . . to a Godless universe, but we are not yet accustomed to one which is loveless as well, and only when we have so become shall we realize what atheism really means."[30]

A less apocalyptic conclusion was suggested by Lippmann. He acknowledged that while the value of love was undeniably a frail creature of the imagination, so long as it was protected by the convention of marriage it would surely survive. From this vantage point, conventions—which are the tentative social work of fallible people and therefore open to elaboration and rethinking—are a gift in the cultural inheritance that one generation passes to the next and that lend support to the human endeavor of making a home of the world. Even though conventions are only fragile supports—their fragility, in fact, is what makes them precious—they furnish life with the potential for its deepest meanings and, for that reason, require the utmost care.

9

THE CONTROVERSY OVER
MASS CULTURE

During the next few decades, a new generation of critics loosely known as the "New York intellectuals" also unknowingly revived aspects of the language of reticence when they confronted what they believed to be one of the most powerful threats to civilization in their time—"mass culture." Beginning in the late 1930s and continuing for twenty years, leftist "little" magazines—notably *Partisan Review* (founded in 1937), *Politics* (1944–49), and *Dissent* (founded in 1954)—became home to a body of criticism that attacked the pernicious consequences of such new forms of mass entertainment as comics, movies, detective novels, radio, popular music, and advertising. While the New York intellectuals, in their enthusiasm for political radicalism and aesthetic innovation, were in some respects latter-day members of the party of exposure, in their suspicion of and distaste for commercial entertainment, they resembled no one so much as the nineteenth-century party of reticence when they first set out to battle the modern agencies of exposure they feared posed the greatest threat to civilization in their time—mass-circulation journalism, realist fiction, and sex-reform literature.

In retrospect, that body of criticism—especially the vigorous attack on invasive and sensational journalism—appears to be a prototype of the mass-culture critique. Just as proponents of reticence were mortified that the press was quickly deteriorating into a business enterprise with no higher aim than to entertain and titillate its readers, these new critics of mass culture deplored the rapid absorption and displacement of the fine arts by spurious forms of profit-driven entertainment. In each case, anguished critics spelled out the disastrous consequences of the application of commercial techniques to forms of public address that had previously been immune to them. And they were forced to make explicit the crucial tasks which the press in one instance and the arts in the other filled in the life of a civilized, democratic society. This mass-culture critique can best be understood as the mid-century installment of the controversy about which things belong in public.

The Alienated Intellectual
as Revolutionary

What distinguished this generation of cultural radicals from previous and subsequent ones was their experience with communism during the 1930s. During the Depression, many American intellectuals, buoyed by the seeming collapse of capitalism and the apparent triumph of the Soviet experiment, decided to cast their lot with the "enlightened proletariat" against the "decaying bourgeoisie." The project of creating a proletarian literary movement appealed to them because it promised to fuse literature with politics, help to spark class consciousness in the workers, and, at the same time, create a new artistic vanguard that its advocates sincerely imagined would rival past literary achievements. "Proletarian art appeared to overcome the problem of the artist who existed without a homeland," according to one of the most insightful historians of this period, James Gilbert, "for it promised a new country and a revolutionary sort of artist." By the middle of the decade, however, the revelations of the true nature of the Soviet government in the Moscow Trials, the horrors of the Spanish Civil War, and the abandonment of the proletarian literary movement in order to support the Popular Front dashed these hopes. Without the flesh-and-blood alternative of a thriving communist society and the financial and moral support of the Communist Party, some of the best of this generation felt compelled to rethink their commitment not only to proletarian culture but also to Stalinism.[1]

It was against this background of political disillusionment that Philip Rahv and William Phillips, editors of one of the more influential New York organs of the John Reed Club, the *Partisan Review*, renounced their earlier communist ties, temporarily halted publication of their magazine, regrouped, and brought out a refurbished *Partisan Review* in 1937, adding Dwight Macdonald, F. W. Dupee, and George L. K. Morris to their masthead. The avowed aim of the new journal was to establish, in the words of Rahv and Phillips, "a rapprochement between the radical tradition on the one hand and the tradition of modern literature on the other."[2] While this appears to be a restatement of the project of pre-World War I little magazines like *The Masses* and *The Seven Arts*, it differed in a number of significant ways. As we have seen, the prewar generation was in open revolt against the reticent sensibility. Their attacks on comstockery, the genteel tradition, and puritanism were all attempts to account for the pathetically meager quality of American culture. Above all else, they were in search of a usable past that would lay the grounds for a specifically American culture, as democratic as it was modern. The intellectuals of the *Partisan Review*, too, were concerned about the paltry condition of American culture, but they were more concerned with the work of the intellectual in promoting social change. They had begun their careers as committed Marxists, but the calamities of the 1930s forced them to rethink politics and art as well as the relation between the two. For them, the most pressing issue was the failure of Marxism, both as a blueprint for society and as a force in opposition to the mass movements of Nazism and fascism. In addition, the inability of proletarian literature to move beyond formulaic and crudely propagandistic stories, coupled with the constant meddling of Party officials, suggested that Marxism had also failed as a theory of literature and art.

Another important difference between the two groups of intellectuals concerned the kind of literature each endorsed. For the first generation, Dreiser was the master debunker of genteel pretensions and his novels represented the most promising fiction of the time. The New York intellectuals rejected realism wholesale in favor of "experimental" writing. Where Marxists had characteristically condemned theories of art for art's sake and experimental writing as bourgeois, decadent, and escapist, intellectuals associated with the *Partisan Review*, the more they broke with their earlier communist ties, began to embrace precisely such work. Not only did the new *Partisan Review* publish the modernist writers of the day—among the poets, Eliot, Auden, Lowell, Elizabeth Bishop, Allen Tate, and Gertrude Stein, and among the fiction writers, Kafka, Gide, and Delmore Schwartz—but in essay after essay they praised these writers, along with Dostoevsky, Joyce, Proust, and Yeats, for their unwitting and therefore authentic depiction of the alienated quality of life in modern bourgeois society (as opposed to the artificiality of Party-directed proletarian writing). In celebrating literature that exposed the dissolution of the autonomous self under modern conditions, they began to posit a new revolutionary class—the alienated intellectual. According to Gilbert:

> The estrangement of the artist from society, his special psychological problems, the difficulty of living two lives, citizen and artist, became

their chief concern. . . . Practical politics and art were entirely divorced, but literature and politics in a philosophic sense, as a moral stance toward the social context, remained intimate. . . . The alienated man became the radical man.[3]

THE DANGERS OF MASS CULTURE

During this highly charged moment of political and aesthetic re-alignments, criticism of mass culture was first articulated. Clement Greenberg, in his well-known essay "Avant-Garde and *Kitsch*" (1939), was one of the first to identify the new phenomenon and, in addition, to announce the apparent end of the avant-garde. For him, the avant-garde represented the only escape from "motionless Alexandrianism"—the "academicism" that inevitably plagues the arts of a decaying society. Even though the earliest avant-garde was "un-interested" in politics, their art, according to Greenberg, nonetheless drew its inspiration and courage from "the revolutionary ideas in the air about them." In a very sketchy paragraph, Greenberg argued that in their revolt against bourgeois society, the avant-garde "succeeded in 'detaching' itself from society," and in the end "repudiate[d] rev-olutionary as well as bourgeois politics." With that repudiation, avant-garde art came into its own; it became increasingly concerned with the processes of its own making: " 'Art for art's sake' and 'pure poetry' appear and subject matter or content becomes something to be avoided like a plague."[4]

For Greenberg, the defining feature of the avant-garde—painters like "Picasso, Braque, Mondrian, Miró, Kandinsky, Brancusi, even Klee, Matisse, and Cézanne," and poets like "Rimbaud, Mallarmé, Valéry, Eluard, Pound, Hart Crane, Stevens, even Rilke and Yeats" —was their effort to represent "the disciplines and processes of art and literature themselves," to "creat[e] something valid solely on its own terms." When he mentioned fiction, he pointed to Gide and Joyce as quintessential vanguardists, concerned primarily with the act of writing. Joyce, he believed, had reduced "experience to expression for the sake of expression, the expression mattering more than what is being expressed."[5] This understanding of Joyce—and of all avant-garde art, for that matter—differs sharply with that formulated by opponents of obscenity law during this same period. One need only recall Judge Woolsey's exoneration of *Ulysses* in primarily realist terms to see the distance separating those in the legal arena from those in the literary-art world.

Even though Greenberg granted that these new and largely abstract aesthetic forms had "estranged a great many of those who were capable formerly of enjoying and appreciating ambitious art and literature," he nonetheless insisted, though he did not develop this idea, that "by no other means is it possible today to create art and literature of a high order." He was concerned that without the support of an audience—"an elite among the ruling class of society"—no culture could develop or maintain itself, let alone flourish. "Since the avant-garde forms the only living culture we now have," warned Greenberg, "the survival in the near future of culture in general is thus threatened." But the terrible specter of the end of culture could not be attributed simply to the waning audience for "ambitious art and literature." Rather, Greenberg believed, something unprecedented was happening: "The avant-garde itself, already sensing the danger, is becoming more and more timid every day that passes. Academicism and commercialism are appearing in the strangest places." The greatest threat to the avant-garde came from a novel type of entertainment dependent on new technologies, what Greenberg called, borrowing from German, *"Kitsch"*—"popular, commercial art and literature with their chromeotypes, magazine covers, illustrations, ads, slick and pulp fiction, comics, Tin Pan Alley music, tap dancing, Hollywood movies, etc., etc."[6] It is striking that neither Greenberg nor any other critic at this time mentioned censorship as a potential threat, even though opponents of obscenity laws typically and repeatedly made this claim during this same period. Astute critics like Greenberg were, as early as 1939, already fearful that avant-garde art was coming to an end; in contrast, legal writers, who viewed the cultural scene from a distance and were uncritically attached to the idea of artistic progress, continued to mouth the old pieties about the sanctity of art that was before its time.

Having identified kitsch as the greatest menace to the survival of true culture, Greenberg provided a historical account of its emergence. First, he distinguished between "formal culture"—the culture of the wealthy, educated, leisured few—and "folk culture"—which he did not define except to say that it belonged to "peasants" whose "background was the countryside." This new distinction not only made Van Wyck Brooks's famous formulation of highbrow and lowbrow obsolete but also set the terms for all subsequent discussions. Greenberg was also quick to point out that kitsch was a recent development. Drawing on Marxist categories of interpretation, he laid out the circumstances of its birth: kitsch was "a product of the industrial revolution which urbanized the masses of western Europe and America and established what is called universal literacy." With the movement of peasants into the cities, and the increase of literacy and leisure for both the proletariat and the bourgeois, "the new urban masses set up a pressure on society to provide them with a kind of culture fit for their own consumption." Responding to this "new market," entrepreneurs devised a "new commodity"—"ersatz culture, kitsch, destined for those who, insensible to the values of genuine culture, are hungry nonetheless for the diversion that only culture of some sort can provide."[7]

Having introduced the economic vocabulary of markets and commodities, Greenberg went on to define kitsch in terms of commodification. And in this emphasis, his analysis resembles that of the party of reticence when they deplored the low quality of the mass-circulation newspaper once it was geared exclusively to profit:

> Kitsch is mechanical and operates by formulas. Kitsch is vicarious experience and faked sensations. Kitsch changes according to style, but remains always the same. Kitsch is the epitome of all that is spurious in our times. Kitsch pretends to demand nothing of its customers except their money—not even their time.

Not only was kitsch an inauthentic, unsatisfying, standardized form of entertainment, it also threatened to destroy formal culture through brazen imitation. It was parasitic; it "draws its life blood, so to speak, from [the] reservoir of accumulated experience" of formal culture, and opportunistically "loots" the avant-garde for "new 'twists,'" which are then watered down." Its promise of high economic returns constantly tempted artists and writers away from their true vocation, sapping the avant-garde at its root. As if that were not enough, kitsch also threatened to destroy folk culture not only in America but worldwide:

> Another mass product of Western industrialism, it has gone on a triumphal tour of the world, crowding out and defacing native cultures in one colonial country after another, so that it is now by way of becoming a universal culture, the first universal culture ever beheld. Today the Chinaman, no less than the South American Indian, the Hindu, no less than the Polynesian, have come to prefer to the products of their native art, magazine covers, rotogravure sections, and calendar girls.[8]

Where the party of reticence attributed the enthusiastic reception of invasive journalism to an insatiable curiosity about other people's lives and a desire to drag everyone down to the same low level, Greenberg attributed the wide appeal of kitsch to the lack of demands it placed upon its audience. With surprising echoes of Matthew Arnold's understanding of culture, which places striving toward one's "best self" at its center—surprising because this understanding had been caricatured to death by the first generation of cultural radicals—Greenberg insisted that the appreciation of art requires strenuous effort: the work of avant-garde painters like Picasso, for instance, requires reflection on the part of a "spectator sensitive enough to react sufficiently to plastic qualities." Kitsch, in contrast, asks nothing of anyone:

> Kitsch pre-digests art for the spectator and spares him effort, provides him with a short cut to the pleasure of art that detours what is necessarily difficult in genuine art. . . . The same point can be made with respect to kitsch literature: it provides vicarious experience for the insensitive with far greater immediacy than serious fiction can hope to do.[9]

Many later critics of mass culture elaborated on this distinction between art and kitsch, though perhaps none so elegantly as Leo Lowenthal. In his "Historical Perspectives of Popular Culture" (1950), he insisted upon the enormous divide between the "spurious gratification" offered by commercial entertainment and "genuine experience as a step to greater individual fulfillment (this is the meaning of Aristotle's *catharsis*)" provided by art. Lowenthal, echoing the party of reticence, linked the appreciation of the beautiful with a sense of awe and reverence for powerful, mythical experiences: "Men free themselves truly from the mythical relation to things by stepping back, so to speak, from that which they once worshiped and which they now discover as the Beautiful. To experience beauty is to be liberated from the overpowering domination of nature over men." In contrast, "in popular culture, men free themselves from mythical powers by discarding everything, even reverence for the Beautiful." In language that leaves no doubt that mass culture is a latter-day version of the party of exposure with its cult of hard, crude reality, Lowenthal observed, "They deny anything that transcends given reality."[10]

This understanding of art was also invoked in a different though closely related context in "Obscenity as an Esthetic Category" (1955) by the philosopher Abraham Kaplan. Where Greenberg and Lowenthal concentrated on the spectator's response to art so as to show by contrast the failings of kitsch, Kaplan discussed the aesthetic status of art and its difference from obscenity and pornography as things in the world. Yet because kitsch and obscenity share certain features—just as invasive journalism, realist fiction, and sex-reform literature did—the analytical categories that Greenberg and Lowenthal employed also appear in Kaplan's essay. Like them, though he makes his Kantian foundation more explicit, he maintained that "esthetic experience requires a kind of disinterest or detachment, a psychic distance." Genuine art, according to Kaplan, depends on distance, for space is needed for contemplative evocation of experience: "The work [of art] brings emotions to mind or presents them for contemplation. When they are actually felt, we have overstepped the bounds of art."[11]

No doubt one source of Kaplan's emphasis on disinterestedness is Kant's *Critique of Judgment*, which laid the foundation of modern aesthetics. But it is also significant that this concern coincides with the party of reticence's repeated attacks on invasions of privacy and the new familiarities, which for them were proof that the party of exposure was not observing the proper distance required by decorum, neither in manners nor in art. The distancing inherent in art, Kaplan maintained, differentiates it from things designed to excite immediate responses, such as advertising and propaganda. Pornography, too, was "essentially promotional": "It is the obscene responded to with minimal psychic distance. . . . It is not itself the *object* of an experience, esthetic or any other, but rather a stimulus *to* an experience not focussed on it." Pornography, by Kaplan's lights, was nothing more than narcissistic self-indulgence: "It serves to elicit not the imaginative contemplation of an expressive substance, but rather the release in fantasy of a compelling impulse." As for that genre of pornography that "masquerades as art" and calls itself "erotica," Kaplan tellingly dismissed it as "kitsch." So closely does his analysis of pornography resemble Greenberg on kitsch that one could replace the subject of his concluding remarks with "mass culture" and not change its meaning: "Hence the popularity of the merely pornographic: it makes so few demands. Genuine expression is replaced by a spurious consummation."[12]

The opening salvo of the mass-culture critique, then, was launched in defense of avant-garde art. The analysis acquired other important dimensions during and after World War II when this same group of anti-Stalinist left-wing intellectuals began to ponder why socialist revolution had failed to materialize. For some—Dwight Macdonald, Irving Howe, James T. Farrell, William Barrett, and, from a different direction, the German émigré theorists and sociologists of the Frankfurt School—mass culture was a primary suspect; its power as an agency of untold social control responsible for both false consciousness and conformism came under intense scrutiny.[13]

Macdonald—who broke with the *Partisan Review* in 1943 over the editors' support of the war and brought out his own magazine, *Politics*, the following year—developed this interpretation in a number of articles, the most influential being "A Theory of Popular Culture" (1944). This piece was widely acknowledged by his contemporaries as a founding article of the mass-culture debate. T. S. Eliot, for example, in his preface to his *Notes Toward a Definition of Culture* (1949), remarked, "Mr. Macdonald's theory strikes me as the best alternative to my own that I have seen." Likewise, Ernest van den Haag, in a well-known contribution to the debate, also paid tribute to Macdonald: "Some of the most cogent analyses of popular culture patterns are owed to Dwight Macdonald's lively pen. Indeed, he christened the concept, though he did not father it." And when the mass-culture critique came under fire, Macdonald was a primary target. The sociologist Edward Shils, for example, singled out Macdonald, "who as editor of *Politics* did more than any other American to bring this interpretation of mass culture to the forefront of the attention of the intellectual public."[14] Even though Macdonald continually reworked this seminal piece—different versions of it appeared as "A Theory of Mass Culture" in *Diogenes* (1953) and "Masscult and Midcult" in the *Partisan Review* (1960)—and, significantly, jettisoned precisely the sections that argued that mass culture was a capitalist conspiracy to manipulate the masses, his original article introduced ideas that continue to define the terms of the debate into our own time.

Macdonald's account of the history of popular culture is essentially the same story as Greenberg's: "Political democracy and universal education broke down the old upper-class monopoly of culture," and a new market for culture led to the mass production of cheap goods. He also borrowed from Greenberg's classifications of culture; in his typology, "Formal Culture" became "High Culture"—that which is "chronicled in the textbooks"; and "kitsch" became "Popular Culture"—that which is "manufactured wholesale for the mass market." So novel were the phenomena of the "new media"—"the movies, the radio, the comics, the detective story"—that critics like Macdonald had difficulty settling on terms that captured their particular character. In the 1953 version of his essay, Macdonald replaced "popular" with "mass." " 'Mass Culture,' " he explained, "[is] a more accurate term, since its distinctive mark is that it is solely and directly an article for mass consumption, like chewing gum."[15]

Like his contemporaries at the *Partisan Review*, Macdonald argued that "the genuine High Culture of this period [1890–1930] is pretty much identical with Avant-gardism." And, again following Greenberg, he voiced the fear that popular culture not only threatened high culture by competing with it, bastardizing and standardizing it, and luring away genuine artists, but also threatened to destroy folk art. Where Greenberg wanted to give a thorough account of the avant-garde, Macdonald was more interested in delineating the shape of popular culture. And it is in his contrast of popular culture to folk art that he made his most original contribution to the discussion: whereas folk art grew spontaneously from the people and was made by the people for themselves, "Popular Culture," Macdonald insisted, "is imposed from above." Employing a Marxist idiom, he emphasized the exploitation of the masses, cultural as well as economic: "It is manufactured by technicians hired by the ruling class and working within the framework of High Culture. It manipulates the cultural needs of the masses in order to make a profit for their rulers." Even more sinisterly, popular culture was an instrument of social control that produced false consciousness: "Popular Culture is an instrument of social domination, not only exploiting the masses as consumers but also integrating them into upper-class culture (in a debased form)."[16]

For Macdonald, Marxism had failed to account for recent historical events and, in consequence, the critic needed to turn to matters once held to be beyond the Marxist purview: "One of the reasons for the sterility of socialist politics since the last war is its too narrow conception of politics." Perhaps under the sway of the Frankfurt School, he widened the notion of politics to include culture and especially popular culture—a "culture-pattern stamped deep into the modern personality, much deeper than conscious political ideas." While this undoubtedly is the most original part of his essay, it is also the point at which he shares most with the party of reticence. Where they worried that longtime exposure to invasive journalism and obscenity would corrode standards of moral and aesthetic judgment, paving the way for a world both ugly and uncivil, Macdonald warned that "the deadening and warping effect of long exposure to movies, pulp magazines, and radio can hardly be overestimated."[17]

A final component of the early mass-culture critique that merits attention is the introduction of Freudian language into the debate. A good example is Irving Howe's "Notes on Mass Culture" (1948), with sections bearing such titles as "The Unconscious Urge to Self-Obliteration" and "The Dissociation of Personality." Drawing heavily from T. W. Adorno's study of popular music, Howe argued that mass culture was an agency of vast psychological control, "perpetuating passivity and shredding personality," its only aims being to provide "relief from work monotony without making the return to work too unbearable; it must provide amusement without insight, and pleasure without disturbance." Trying his hand at content analysis, Howe ominously concluded that "more movies than we know are comments on our experience and help us to 'adjust to it,' that is, to acquiesce to it. . . . The movies help us to remain at peace with ourselves by helping to suppress ourselves." When he turned to what many critics believed to be the most pernicious form of mass culture—the comics—he argued that they "dissociate personality by erasing distinctions between adulthood and childhood"; some comics "allow adults to sink, for the moment, into the uncomplicated ways of childhood," while others—"little more than schematized abstractions of violence and sadism"—"push children into premature adulthood."[18] Here again, the argument coincides with the fears voiced by the party of reticence that mass-circulation newspapers would "debauch" the intellect and make people "passive."

Both Greenberg and Macdonald raised the question, What is to be done? Both were convinced that the only salvation lay in a radical transformation of political, social, and economic conditions through socialism. "Today we no longer look toward socialism for a new culture—as inevitably as one will appear, once we do have socialism," declared Greenberg. "Today we look to socialism *simply* for the preservation of whatever living culture we have right now." For Macdonald, too, the problem of mass culture was "basically a political question." Because of his own democratic commitment, Macdonald rejected José Ortega y Gasset's solution—the rebuilding of class walls to restore "the old High Culture–Folk Art compartmentalization" (which he later reluctantly accepted as the only solution). What was needed, he insisted, was more popular participation, and he hoped that with the coming of socialism, a new vigorous culture would emerge: "The standard by which to measure Popular Culture is not the old aristocratic High Culture but rather a potential new *human* culture, in Trotsky's phrase, which for the first time in history has a chance of superseding the *class* cultures of the present and the past."[19] In later versions of both essays, these painfully optimistic sections would be deleted.

THE REGULATION OF "HARMFUL TRASH"

Questions about mass culture were also raised in other quarters. By 1955, Eric Larrabee, in a *Law and Contemporary Problems* symposium on obscenity and the arts, announced, "The point need scarcely be labored that the American popular culture is saturated with sexual images, references, symbols, and exhortations; this is a conclusion that both literati and philistines might well agree on, and they might agree that it reflects a condition of pervasive psychological disease." According to two influential legal writers, James C. N. Paul and Murray L. Schwartz, popular agitation for state regulation of mass culture exploded during the 1940s:

> The country, it was said many times over, from many varied sources, was being inundated by a flood of harmful trash. Distinguished church and lay leaders identified and deplored what seemed to be a steady erosion of moral values. Beginning in 1948, juvenile crime seemed to increase significantly in volume and became a major subject for news, editorial, TV, movie, and literary coverage. Mr. Hoover of the FBI warned the public frequently and vigorously that much of the salacious material that was readily available to immature or unstable people was producing sex criminals. Hundreds of other police chiefs, prosecutors, and civic leaders echoed this assertion. And in any event there were trends in the mass media which caused great concern among a great many sober-minded people. . . . It was said that over 29 million Americans read the paperbound works of Mickey Spillane; the obvious popularity of these and other "tough" detective tales so well larded with sex and sadism evoked disturbed comment from many quarters, including commentators who were vigorous opponents of censorship.[20]

In this overwrought atmosphere, private groups began to organize local boycotts and demand that state legislatures regulate the more extreme instances of published sex and violence by expanding the range of existing obscenity laws. Their target was different from that of the New York intellectuals, who objected not to obscenity per se but to the false vision of the good life presented by mass culture. Local groups, in contrast, stressed the bad effects of the new media on individual victims, in particular children. By the late 1930s, a number of state legislatures had introduced bills forbidding the sale of violent comic books to children under a specific age. Then, in 1943, a New York statute that prohibited publication and sale of the more bloodthirsty comic magazines of the detective and crime genre was challenged. In *New York* v. *Winters*, Winters, a New York bookseller, was convicted for offering for sale a magazine entitled *Headquarters Detective: True Cases from the Police Blotter*, specializing, as the court described it, in stories "embellished with pictures of fiendish and gruesome crimes, and . . . besprinkled with lurid photographs of victims and perpetrators. Featured articles bear such titles as 'Bargains in Bodies,' 'Girl Slave to a Love Cult,' and 'Girls Reformatory.' "[21]

The court pointed out that the defense made no claims of high literary merit for the contents.

Winters appealed, but his conviction was upheld in the New York State Supreme Court. Following the logic of obscenity law that banned material that would harm a specified victim, the court found that *Headquarters Detective* should not be allowed since graphic accounts of

> criminal deeds of bloodshed or lust unquestionably can be so massed as to become vehicles for inciting violent and depraved crimes against the person and in that case such publications are indecent or obscene in an admissible sense, though not necessarily in the sense of being calculated or intended to excite sexual passion.

In addition, the Court flatly rejected Winters's contention that the statute was unconstitutional because of its vagueness, though in a dissenting opinion Judge Lehman agreed that the statute "is so vague and indefinite as to permit punishment of the fair use of freedom of speech."[22]

In 1948, the case reached the U.S. Supreme Court, who sided with Judge Lehman, 6–3. In their reversal of the lower-court decision, they cleared the way for First Amendment protection of mass culture, which, in turn, would lend it the kind of prestige previously reserved only for material of high literary or scientific merit. While Justice Stanley Reed reiterated the Court's long-standing recognition of "the importance of the exercise of a state's police power to minimize all incentives to crime," he nonetheless gave precedence to the interest of free speech, insisting that the First Amendment was not limited only to "the exposition of ideas."

> The line between the informing and the entertaining is too elusive for the protection of that basic right. Everyone is familiar with instances of propaganda through fiction. What is one man's amusement teaches another's doctrine. Though we can see nothing of any possible value to society in these magazines, they are as much entitled to the protection of free speech as the best of literature.[23]

The Supreme Court's refusal to restrict First Amendment protection to socially valuable material crucial to public debate and its decision to extend it to lurid stories and graphic photographs of crimes marks a radical break with previous obscenity decisions. By giving priority to the First Amendment, it introduced into the obscenity discourse the same stumbling block that had stymied early right-to-privacy plaintiffs. Because First Amendment protection of the press is enshrined in the Constitution, courts were understandably reluctant to control even the most outrageous tabloids, but it is nonetheless surprising that the Supreme Court was willing to grant such latitude to sensational crime magazines, given its long-standing precedent of treating commercial entertainment as fundamentally different from material expressing ideas. Ever since movies first appeared, they had been screened in advance by local and state boards before being re-leased for general distribution, and the courts endorsed this form of pre-censorship since, according to an early Supreme Court decision, *Mutual Film Corp.* v. *Industrial Commission of Ohio* (1915), movies were a form of entertainment no different from "the theater, the circus, and all other shows and spectacles," and therefore not entitled to First Amendment protection. "It cannot be put out of view," de-clared the Court, "that the exhibition of pictures is a business, pure and simple, originated and conducted for profit, like other spectacles, not to be regarded . . . as part of the press of the country, or as organs of public opinion."[24]

Nevertheless, even as the courts were permitting more and more violent and sexually explicit material to appear in public during the 1940s and 1950s, popular opinion mostly opposed this material. The year the Supreme Court overturned the Winters decision, 1948, there was so much agitation against comics that the Association of Comic Magazine Publishers, following the Production Code of Hollywood, instituted a code of minimum editorial standards which emphasized the control of indecency as much as violence. But this halfhearted attempt at self-regulation did not stem cries for more aggressive state action. In 1949, responding to public pressure, a joint legislative com-mittee was created in New York to investigate and report on comics, paperback books, "girlie" magazines, mail-order materials, and, soon thereafter, movies. A number of states followed suit. For private watchdog organizations like the National Organization for Decent Literature (NODL), these state investigations did not go far enough. They demanded more aggressive action, applying so much pressure that the House of Representatives created a Select Committee on Current Pornographic Materials in 1952.

As mass culture proliferated, congressional committees multiplied to investigate. In quick succession there came Estes Kefauver's Senate Judiciary Subcommittee to Investigate Juvenile Delinquency, subtitled "Obscene and Pornographic Materials" (1954, 1955, 1956), and the Granahan Congressional Committee on Post Office and Civil Service (1959, 1960, 1961). Under the heading of obscenity, these com-mittees included paperback books with sexually suggestive covers, "girlie" picture magazines, lurid and violent comics, mail-order nudes, and pornography. Each committee reached the same conclusion: huge quantities of these materials were being distributed by highly organized and efficient businesses and such businesses were making tremendous profits. In 1959, the Granahan Committee published estimates that the total commerce in obscene materials had reached close to $1 billion a year.[25]

BALANCING THE INTERESTS: OBSCENITY AND FREE SPEECH

For some legal observers, the efforts of these private organizations and congressional committees were but the latest skirmish in the long battle of censorious Puritans against freedom-loving rebels. William B. Lockhart and Robert C. McClure, in an extremely influential article "Literature, the Law of Obscenity, and the Constitution" (1954), dismissed the findings of the Select Committee on Current Pornographic Materials in typical debunking fashion: "The committee . . . express[ed] a devout wish for return to the pious reserve of Puritan England and the literary restraint of the Victorian era." Their article played the same pathbreaking role in obscenity law as Brandeis and Warren's had played in privacy law. Just as Brandeis and Warren plumbed the relevant case law to establish a legal right to privacy, Lockhart and McClure examined not only the legal literature and sociological and anthropological investigations of obscenity but also recent free-speech decisions in their effort to establish constitutional protection for "significant literature that deals with vital sex problems in a restrained and intelligent way."[26]

Their article, according to one authority on obscenity law, Harry Clor, "had considerable influence on the course of judicial decisions, as well as on libertarian thought in this area." In an important lower appellate court decision, *United States* v. *Roth* (1956), Judge Jerome Frank cited it, and his dissenting opinion with its highly unorthodox, lengthy appendix on obscenity and the First Amendment, is, according to Clor, "widely regarded as a classic statement of the case against censorship of obscenity." Together, Judge Frank's opinion and Lockhart and McClure's article forced the First Amendment into the forefront of legal debate so that the Supreme Court could not avoid addressing it in *Roth* v. *United States* in 1957. Justice William O.

Douglas, in a dissent that made its way into later majority opinions and countless law reviews, cited Lockhart and McClure at key points in his argument. The article was also routinely invoked by judges in the most significant obscenity decisions during the early 1960s.[27]

Lockhart and McClure's article was a direct response to the activities of extra-legal agencies of censorship, most prominently the National Organization for Decent Literature, along with state boards of review and local police departments. They detailed the "surreptitious" maneuvers of censors who "intimidate" booksellers with threats of local blacklists and boycotts. Not only did they insinuate that such tactics were "undemocratic," they also employed what had by then become a staple of anti-censorship argument—they listed the banned books, predominantly paperbacks sold at newsstands and drugstores, to show the irrational and indiscriminate nature of censorship. "The titles of the books on the NODL list makes a strange collection," Lockhart and McClure observed. "They range all the way from something called *Hot Dames on Cold Slabs* to William Faulkner's *Pylon*, *Sanctuary*, and *Soldier's Pay*, with Mickey Spillane's tours in sadism and voyeurism sandwiched somewhere in between." The best antidote to extra-legal censorship, they insisted, was to establish a constitutional standard for obscenity that would be "uniform and liberal" and would put an end to "the present unsatisfactory system that permits one or a few states to control the reading of the nation."[28]

Preparing the way for their treatment of the constitutional issue, Lockhart and McClure provided a brief history of obscenity law, relying on H. L. Mencken's masterpiece of Puritan-baiting, "Puritanism as a Literary Force," and Heywood Broun and Margaret Leech's devastating psychobiography *Anthony Comstock, Roundsman of the Lord*. With this highly partisan material as their only historical source, they devoted a single paragraph in their 100-page article to the culture in which moral-reform movements took root. Contrasting the relative absence of obscenity regulation before the Civil War with the explosion of concern after, they argued that "financial scandals, the vulgar and lax social behavior, and the flagrant immorality of the years immediately after the war" were responsible for "a powerful social reaction." Then, quoting Broun and Leech, they established the alleged lineage of moral reform, thereby eliminating any need to take it seriously: " 'The voice of the reformer was heard in the land. The stage was set for a stern and rigorous revival of the spirit of the Puritan forefathers.' " And they predictably conjured the censor par excellence, Anthony Comstock: "This was the stage on which Anthony Comstock stepped to begin his 40-year campaign to purify the reading matter of the American public under the banner 'MORALS, Not Art or Literature.' "[29] With their Puritan-baiting and self-congratulatory tone, Lockhart and McClure enshrined in the legal record a stock but highly misleading account of early obscenity regulation. It is, of course, not so much history as polemic.

And when they tried to account for the recent spate of censorship activity, they resorted to debunking, which by overuse had become stale and predictable. "The same ignorance or disregard of the literary and other values of a book," the two writers condescendingly observed, "marks the censor's activities today as it has in the past, and the reasons for this are not hard to find." They then dredged up the psychological reductionism that had so marred the early party of exposure's case against their opponents:

> For the censor is seldom a person who appreciates esthetic values or understands the nature and function of imaginative literature. His interests lie elsewhere. Often an emotionally disturbed person, he sets out to look for smut and consequently finds it almost everywhere, oblivious of the context and the values of the book in which he finds what he seeks.[30]

By reducing the question of obscenity to the psychological pathology and aesthetic backwardness of an individual censor, this strategy effectively eliminated in advance the possibility that there might be good reasons for regulating obscenity—notably concern for the quality of the public realm and respect for privacy—and with it, the possibility of meaningful public debate. Equally devastating, this focus on styles of personality has made it virtually impossible to raise objections about obscenity without seeming philistine, backward, or repressed, even to oneself.

Lockhart and McClure also made the predictable claim that history was on their side, presenting the case law as a story of irresistible progress, marching forward to its present modern moment of liberalization. With the single exception of Judge Learned Hand's celebrated Kennerley decision of 1913, they dismissed the first sixty years of trials as a dark age of unremitting repression and prejudice. The most significant moment in their story was the glorious early 1930s, when the courts began reformulating the Hicklin Test. "Though routed, the Hicklin rule was not finally defeated," Lockhart and McClure regretfully admitted. "A battle against it had been won, not the whole war." It was their contention that the project of liberalizing obscenity law, while it had made important strides, was still unfinished, and it was their aim to complete it by ensuring constitutional protection for serious literature dealing with sex.[31]

Because their historical account is so selective, Lockhart and Mc-

Clure were forced to consign to footnotes those trials that did not fit their story of automatic progress. As earlier chapters in this book have suggested, however, when the issues raised in precisely those trials are taken seriously, the history of obscenity law emerges in an entirely different light. That history reveals not automatic progress, but rather the dissolution of shared moral and aesthetic standards, the subjectivization and trivialization of the faculties of taste and judgment, and the waning of the sense of shame—developments that, in turn, have given rise to a common world that is ugly, indecent, and uncivil. Perhaps the shape of this history can be clearly discerned only now that the battles for birth control and for literary freedom have long been won.

To establish the constitutionally protected status of obscenity, Lockhart and McClure scoured Supreme Court decisions concerning the First Amendment and obscenity for any mention of the relationship between the two. They found no formal statements, only "dicta" and "off-hand remarks," through which they painstakingly sifted. In this part of their argument, they mentioned trials that would be repeatedly cited as precedents in later decisions and law-review articles. The most important was *Chaplinsky* v. *New Hampshire* (1942), in which the Supreme Court found that "fighting" words—and, in the same sentence, "obscene," "profane," and "libelous" words—were not protected speech, and that the Court therefore need not consider the issues in the "clear and present danger" doctrine derived from *Schenck* v. *United States* (1919) regarding seditious speech during wartime. Like so many commentators arguing both for and against obscenity regulation after them, Lockhart and McClure quoted the Supreme Court's explanation for their exclusion: they "are no essential part of any exposition of ideas, and are of such slight social value as a step to truth that any benefit that may be derived from them is clearly outweighed by the social interest in order and morality."[32]

Lockhart and McClure set out to demonstrate that the Court did not mean what it had said when it placed obscenity in the same category as fighting, profane, and libelous words. Serious literature concerning sex *did* have important "social value": "Sex has always occupied too important and dominant a place in literature and in human interest and concern to be impliedly [sic] excluded from the broadly stated First Amendment freedoms." They offered excerpts from recent free-speech decisions, including the Winters decision, that established protection for "all matters of public concern," so that they could argue by analogy that literature treating sex was entitled to the same protection. Like apologists for invasive journalism who claimed they were simply giving people what they wanted, Lockhart and Mc-Clure made much of the public's enormous interest in "literature on sex problems, practices, and behavior" to justify its existence:

> It is common knowledge that in recent years there has been wide distribution and sale in this country of books and other publications dealing with many aspects of sex, sex problems, and sex behavior from a great many points of view—psychology, sociology, anthropology, education, birth control, marital relations, sex instruction, and sex techniques.[33]

Their claim that discussions and representations of intimate life were of public interest and therefore deserving of First Amendment protection leaves no doubt as to the disappearance of the line between public and private in the legal imagination. That they could apparently see no difference between literature dealing with that most private of experiences, sexual intimacy, and "literature dealing with other social and economic problems"—and of course they are not alone here—testifies to the success of the party of exposure's eighty-year project, bringing to mind Mencken's withering observation that sex reformers "reduc[ed] the unknowable to terms of the not worth knowing."

Once obscenity was recognized as a First Amendment issue, there still remained the important question as to whether it presented a "clear and present danger" to the public, which would then allow for its suppression. The salient point for judges was to "balance two significant interests—the public interest in preventing the supposed evil [of obscenity] and the public interest in preserving freedom of speech." Offering what would become the classic case against censorship, Lockhart and McClure argued that regulation not only makes publishers hesitant to publish unorthodox material but also causes authors to police their thoughts, which inhibits creativity—"and society," they warned, "may lose the values of important literary, scientific, and educational contributions."[34] This danger, however, was already something of an anachronism, given the enormous amount of sexual material already in open circulation. In addition, it flies in the face of an earlier comment of theirs: since the Dennett and *Ulysses* decisions, courts almost always ruled that literary, scientific, and educational values outweigh the potential threats of obscenity. Moreover, they overestimated the centrality of sex in modern literature. As the early criticisms of mass culture made clear by way of omission, the arts were threatened not by censorship but, rather, by mass culture luring the serious artist from his rightful work and crowding out, even as it absorbed, high and folk culture alike.

Having established the paramount value of free speech to their own satisfaction, Lockhart and McClure proceeded to analyze the " 'evils' claimed to justify obscenity censorship," and in each instance, unsurprisingly, found that the value of free speech outweighs the alleged harm. In their summation of almost eighty years of controversy, they settled upon two kinds of potential harm: offensiveness and the consequences of obscenity in relation to "changing community moral standards," individual thoughts, and individual behavior. This part of their argument is especially important because it set the terms of our contemporary debate, which has changed remarkably little in the intervening forty years.

Although offensiveness has become the primary standard for judging obscenity today, it made a relatively late appearance in the legal debate, and it did so as a kind of stand-in for aesthetic judgment, but a kind of aesthetic judgment that is so subjective as to be virtually worthless. This becomes clear when we contrast the role of offensiveness with that played by indecency in the early debate. Indecency, as judges always defined it, was that which was not fit to be seen or heard in public. It was not a matter of personal opinion or subjective taste but a quality that inhered in the object. It belonged to the world, not to the self. In sharpest contrast, offensiveness, according to Lockhart and McClure, was "the relatively minor harm that results from disturbing or shocking the sensitive soul," or "a temporary sense of shock, irritation, and outrage at worst."[35]

Because offensiveness was so insignificant a thing, Lockhart and McClure claimed that harm stemming from it, "if it is a harm, is relatively minor for two reasons," both of which continue to be offered today. The first demoted an entire range of issues that used to concern the public to a matter of individual choice: "Those who dislike or are offended by such literature need not, and ordinarily do not, read it." The second reduced the controversy to a need for tolerance on the part of the oversensitive few for the more robust tastes of the majority: "For the relatively few readers who will be offended by what they read, the shock to their sense of decency and propriety is really a very trivial harm, standing by itself." This drastic diminution in the scope of the harm allowed Lockhart and McClure to conclude triumphantly: "This infrequent and trivial offense to the sense of decency and propriety of relatively few readers cannot possibly outweigh the values of unrestricted freedom in literature, unless the author is writing only 'dirt for dirt's sake.' "[36] By the 1950s, then, judgments about the quality of the world had dropped out of the discussion altogether. This was due, in part, to the single-minded legal focus on victims and harm, which made it impossible to consider the physical condition of the world; indecency and ugliness, from this perspective, are either too amorphous or too subjective and, therefore, beyond the range not only of legal action but also of public deliberation.

The disappearance of the public dimension of the debate is also apparent in Lockhart and McClure's treatment of the threat that obscenity poses to "community moral standards." They reformulated the concept of public harm to be consonant with the legal need to have a victim if there was a crime. Did serious literature about sex, they demanded, literally lead to changed community moral standards, and if so, did that change present a clear and present danger to society? They confidently responded, "The causal relationship between such literature and a change in the general moral standards is far too tenuous to satisfy the constitutional standard of 'clear' or 'probable' danger."[37] This exclusive focus on actual harm was not new to the debate about obscenity, of course. What was new was their assertion that things that appear in public have no demonstrable consequences. But if no "causal relationship" exists between literature, the people who read it, and the world in which it is published, then such literature is obviously so trivial that its regulation can be of little importance to anyone. This way of formulating the issue inadvertently threatens to deprive the principle of free speech of its significance.

Such a conclusion was certainly not what these advocates of free speech would have wanted. Consequently, Lockhart and McClure, as well as all libertarians who have embraced this way of thinking, have been left in a muddle, arguing on the one hand that there is no empirical proof that literature concerning sex actually influences community moral standards, and on the other that such literature is so important that it is entitled to constitutional protection. Dedicated partisans in the battle for free speech, they have apparently been blinded by their uncritical assumption that open discussion always furthers social progress. Evoking John Stuart Mill, Lockhart and McClure made explicit the relation of free speech to democracy and progress, with the implicit criticism that to object to discussions of sex is to be against these liberal values: "Back of this fundamental freedom lies the basic conviction that our democratic society must be free to perfect its own standard of conduct and belief—political, economic, social, religious, moral—through the heat of unrepressed controversy and debate."[38]

This way of formulating the issue once again reveals that moderns have lost the capacity to recognize that intimate life is liable to become banal, laughable, or obscene when it is flooded by unmodulated light. Since Lockhart and McClure, like all enthusiasts of exposure, were loath to acknowledge limits to what is speakable for fear of closing off possibilities, they assimilated discussions and images of sex—except pornography—to the category of normal debate, and then insisted that "the remedy against those who attack currently accepted standards is spirited and intelligent defense of those standards, not censorship." Because they were insensible to subtler harms—in particular, to the way indiscriminate publicity wears away not only the aesthetic sense but also the sense of the sacred and the shameful—free speech, in their accounting, always emerged as the weightier value:

> When the faint risk that a book may, at some future and probably distant time, be a minor factor in a gradual change of the accepted moral standards is weighed against the incalculable harm that would result from suppressing literature that challenges or questions these standards, we can only conclude that this risk can never justify censorship.[39]

The "evils" of stimulating "libidinous" thoughts and inciting "sex conduct inconsistent with accepted moral standards" also turned out, in their account, to be of little consequence. To make their case, Lockhart and McClure offered the standard hygienic account of sex: the "creation of normal sexual desires is, in itself, neither immoral nor contrary to the accepted sex standards . . . sex thoughts are perfectly normal; without them men and women would be abnormal." After giving examples of the varied sources of sexual desire, including women's dresses, perfume, and dancing, they concluded that "the causal relationship between literature dealing with sex and the composite sex thoughts and desires of an individual is likely to be extremely tenuous."[40]

While they were adamant that the incitement of sexual thoughts was unlikely to present danger to individuals or society, the risk that obscenity might cause "anti-social behavior" was of a different order. If the causal connection could be conclusively demonstrated, they thought the state would have to intervene. But, they observed, "there is a great deal of talk and very little factual data upon which to base a fair judgment." On the one hand, the practical experience of those who actually dealt with sex criminals was "unscientific" and therefore irrelevant. But when it came to evidence gathered by social scientists, they were on no firmer ground. Sheldon and Eleanor Glueck's comprehensive study of the causes of juvenile delinquency had concluded that their subjects did not usually read so the role of obscenity was moot. The greatest authority on sexual behavior at the time, the Kinsey Reports, simply showed "the minor degree to which literature serves as a potent stimulant."[41]

While they acknowledged the need for more "factual data," Lockhart and McClure still reached the predictable conclusion that "the many other influences in society that stimulate sexual desire are so much more potent in their effect, that the influence of reading is likely, at most, to be relatively insignificant in the composite of forces that lead an individual into conduct deviating from the community sex standards." Such literature must, in the interest of free speech, be allowed.[42] That Lockhart and McClure wrote in the jargon of social science and expected that "factual data" would finally resolve the controversy signals the growing authority of social science in settling legal questions, but their faith that aesthetic experience and erotic emotion could be quantified in a meaningful way is remarkable for both its philistinism and naïveté. The expectation that experiments, surveys, and interviews could accurately determine the effects of obscenity is, more than anything else, responsible for the fruitlessness and interminability of our contemporary debate; both feminists who oppose pornography and free-speech absolutists now routinely summon experts and present "scientific" studies to make their opposing yet equally plausible cases.

In *Roth* v. *United States* (1957), decided together with *Alberts* v. *California*, the Supreme Court finally addressed the constitutional status of obscenity. The case that decided the issue did not concern a literary masterpiece or the work of an author of high standing, as Lockhart and McClure had hoped; rather, it centered on the mailing of obscene circulars and advertisements along with obscene books. Samuel Roth, a disreputable small-time publisher, dealer, and distributor of obscenity, had a long history of excerpting sexually charged passages from various sources and publishing them together in book form. In 1927, for example, he pirated three sexual episodes from *Ulysses* against Joyce's wishes. Joyce not only sued him but also spearheaded an international protest. Roth was also indicted for selling pirated versions of *Lady Chatterley's Lover* during the 1920s. In both cases, he was convicted and served short prison terms. At the time of his appeal before the Supreme Court in 1957, he had been arrested seven times for advertising and distributing obscenity and convicted four times. Roth bragged that he had sent out 10 million advertisements of his publications during his publishing career.[43]

Writing for the majority, Justice Brennan immediately dispensed with the argument that the First Amendment protected obscene speech: "Obscenity is not within the area of constitutionally protected freedom of speech or press—either (1) under the First Amendment, as to the Federal Government, or (2) under the Due Process Clause of the Fourteenth Amendment, as to the states." He made explicit the essentially political nature of the First Amendment: it "was fashioned to assure unfettered interchange of ideas for the bringing about of political and social changes desired by the people." After reviewing the history of obscenity law, he concluded, "It is apparent that the unconditional phrasing of the First Amendment was not intended to protect every utterance." Libel, blasphemy, profanity, and obscenity had long been exceptions. And at this point in his discussion Justice Brennan introduced the qualification of "redeeming social importance":

> All ideas having even the slightest redeeming social importance—unorthodox ideas, controversial ideas, even ideas hateful to the prevailing climate of opinion—have the full protection of the guaranties, unless excludable because they encroach upon the limited area of more important interests, but implicit in the history of the First Amendment is the rejection of obscenity as utterly without redeeming social importance.

That all civilized peoples restrained obscenity was made clear, according to the judge, in "the universal judgment . . . reflected in the international agreement of over 50 nations, in the obscenity laws of all the 48 states, and in the 20 obscenity laws enacted by the Congress from 1842 to 1956."[44]

While the Supreme Court rejected the claim that obscenity was entitled to constitutional protection, it did liberalize the law by overturning the Hicklin Test. Justice Brennan incorporated all the changes the courts had made since the early 1930s in formulating the new test: "The standard for judging obscenity . . . is whether, to the average person, applying contemporary community standards, the dominant theme of the material, taken as a whole, appeals to prurient interest." In Justice Brennan's formulation, the notoriously vague harm of inciting libidinous thoughts was at last dropped, only to be replaced by an equally elusive phrase about "prurient interest." To clarify this, he turned to the American Law Institute's Model Penal Code, which he quoted at length: " 'A thing is obscene if, considered as a whole, its predominant appeal is to prurient interest, i.e., a shameful or morbid interest in nudity, sex, or excretion, and if it goes substantially beyond customary limits of candor in description or representation of such matters.' "[45]

The Court split 6–3, and separate dissenting opinions from Justices Harlan and Douglas were at least as important as, if not more important than, the majority opinion. It is in these opinions that the influence of the Lockhart and McClure article is most apparent. In the opening of Justice Douglas's dissent, he referred to the work of "two outstanding authorities on obscenity," Lockhart and McClure, and quoted directly from their article, making their formulation of the balancing act between literary freedom and the dangers of obscenity the central issue.[46]

One of Justice Douglas's primary objections to the majority opinion was its formulation of "the common conscience of the community" as the new standard of judgment. His line of reasoning shows that he, like Lockhart and McClure, had lost the capacity to discern the difference once easily understood between things that were large enough to withstand public scrutiny and things that were too private and fragile. "Certainly that standard would not be an acceptable one if religion, economics, politics, or philosophy were involved. How does it become a constitutional standard when literature treating with sex is concerned?" His other objection was rooted in the sophisticate's conventional suspicion of "the community" as parochial, backward, complacent, and hostile to anything new. "Any test that turns on what is offensive to the community's standards is too loose, too capricious, too destructive of freedom of expression to be squared with the First Amendment," he insisted. "This is community censorship in one of its worst forms." Then—and his comment shows how domesticated claims for the avant-garde had become once a Supreme Court justice, the epitome of state power, could cleave to it—he admonished the Court: "It creates a regime where in the battle between the literati and the Philistines, the Philistines are certain to win."[47]

Justice Douglas also strenuously objected to the majority's pronouncement that obscenity was "utterly without redeeming social importance." By this time, the myth of the persecuted genius had such tremendous power that Justice Douglas was reduced to cliché: "The test that suppresses a cheap tract today can suppress a literary gem tomorrow. All it needs is to incite a lascivious thought or arouse a lustful desire."[48] While the introduction of First Amendment protection of obscenity is usually celebrated as a victory for progress, in the context of these remarks it is better understood as a marker of the disappearance of shared ideas about what constitutes obscenity and what constitutes art. Justice Douglas's position boils down to the proposition that since there is no general agreement about what obscenity or art is, everything should be permitted and future generations will sort it out.

The other major objection to Brennan's majority opinion revolved around the notoriously difficult problem of determining the consequences of obscenity. Justice Harlan rejected the Model Penal Code's definition of obscenity on the grounds that its underlying presumption—that "the distribution of certain types of literature will induce criminal or immoral social conduct"—was "a matter of dispute among critics, sociologists, psychiatrists, and penologists." In fact, he pointed out, "there is a large school of thought, particularly in the scientific community, which denies any causal connection between the reading of pornography and immorality, crime, or delinquency." Justice Douglas reached the same conclusion: "The absence of dependable information on the effect of obscene literature on human conduct should make us wary."[49]

THE KINSEY REPORT:
THE SOCIOLOGICAL APPROACH TO INTIMATE LIFE

That the linchpin of modern obscenity law turned out to be scientific study of sexual behavior is ironic, given that this had once been understood as a species of obscenity in its own right; sex-reform and birth-control materials were the prime suspects in obscenity prosecutions through the 1920s. As we have seen, critics ranging from nineteenth-century proponents of reticence to Mencken and Krutch accused science of robbing life of one of its most mysterious—and thus exalted and powerful—experiences. Yet, what those critics lamented as an irrevocable loss of depth, intensity, and meaning, the party of exposure celebrated as an unqualified gain for individual freedom. For sex reformers, the demystification of sex through scientific method had been both the animating vision and the missing link of their project, and with the publication of *Sexual Behavior in the Human Male* by Alfred C. Kinsey, Wardell B. Pomeroy, and Clyde E. Martin in 1948, their aspirations were finally realized. "The Kinsey Report has done for sex what Columbus did for geography," Morris Ernst and his co-author, David Loth, enthusiastically declared in *American Sexual Behavior and the Kinsey Report* (1948). So earth-shattering were its discoveries to Ernst that this inveterate popularizer felt it required a book-length exegesis for the general public. "It makes a successful scientific voyage to explore an unknown world which had been open only to speculation and suspicion—the sex life of human beings." The Kinsey Report's candor, unexpected findings, and enormous popularity ensured that "it will be impossible to go back to the old folkway of reticence about sex."[50]

While Ernst and Loth raised many of the same issues that would make their way into Lockhart and McClure's article six years later— the constitutional status of obscenity, the clear and present danger test, and the need for scientific proof of actual harm—the timing of the publication introduced a new and distinctive dialect into the legal discourse that has persisted into the present day. Although Ernst had already in the early 1930s drawn attention to the close relationship between censorship and fascism, by 1948 free speech, in his hands, came to stand for the American way of life itself. Due to the highly charged atmosphere of the cold war, the authors politicized two of the most cherished mechanisms of liberal society—free speech and the marketplace: "This book is dedicated to a people who, not under a dictator, can still work out their own salvation by the free spread of knowledge, and to Alfred C. Kinsey, Wardell B. Pomeroy, and Clyde E. Martin, who have enriched the marketplace of thought."[51]

In the ever-escalating ideological battle between East and West, such claims about the importance of the "free spread of knowledge" became increasingly extravagant. The anti-democratic idiom once used to discredit the party of reticence gained new life when retooled to fit the rhetorical specifications of the cold war:

> So perhaps the greatest achievement of the Kinsey Report is a reaffirmation of our freedom to talk; freedom for the individual to talk in confidence and have it respected, freedom for the scientist and the commentator to propound facts and interpretations which are deeply shocking to certain sections of the community.[52]

Whereas *épater les bourgeois* had been the rallying cry of the avant-garde, of bohemians, realists, anarchists, and birth-control champions alike, under the new dispensation of the cold war, opposition to middle-class complacency and conformism was miraculously converted into a sign of the moral superiority of the West. It is testimony to the elasticity of the imagination of cold war liberals that they could reformulate the once-radical project of sexual emancipation in the innocuous terms of "shocking . . . certain sections of the community," and testimony to their hubris that they could then parade this emasculated rebellion as evidence of the American values of freedom and tolerance. That this implausible conversion was accomplished so effortlessly shows that the forces arrayed against puritanism and comstockery had carried the day; by the time the Kinsey Report had been published, the party of exposure was involved in a simple mop-up operation.

Ernst, a decorated veteran of the most spectacular censorship battles of the 1920s and 1930s, could not help noting the difference between those early turbulent days and the calmer 1940s and, in typical Whig fashion, saw it as a sign of progress: "In some respects, the publication of this sober, scientific work marks the culmination of an era in literature. At the beginning of the era of emancipation from the Victorian taboos in regard to sex, there was a positive rash of books and stories around the theme of rebellion against parental authority." Fortunately, times had changed; there was now "comparative freedom from restraint," which, in turn, "has borne mellower fruit." Just as Clement Greenberg and Dwight Macdonald had drawn attention to the apparent end of the avant-garde, Ernst and Loth made a similar observation about the waning of the social avant-garde, though they saw this development as a victory rather than a defeat. The line of rebellion that had begun with the rambunctious idealism of sex radicals in the nineteenth century, gathered force and venom with the youthful cultural radicals at the turn of the century, now apparently culminated with the "sober" and bloodless jargon of sociologists working out of Indiana University in the 1940s: "Professor Kinsey and his associates are representatives of this kindlier age. With a wealth of data which would have given narrower minds a handle to strip the hide from human complacency, they have chosen the less sensational role."[53] This coming together of unlikely company once again draws attention to the values shared by "the new class" of experts, social scientists, social reformers, lawyers, professors, intellectuals, writers, and artists, who also were typically members of what I have called the party of exposure.

Where Ernst and Loth's celebration of the Kinsey Report as a paean to free speech and tolerance is representative of the party of exposure during the cold war, Lionel Trilling's famous attack on the Kinsey Report in the *Partisan Review* (1948), reprinted in his *The Liberal Imagination* (1950), stands as a good example of what remained of the reticent sensibility at mid-century, though Trilling was a long distance from the nineteenth-century sensibility. What he continued to share with it was his enduring commitment to humanism. That his first book was a study of Matthew Arnold suggests the genesis of that commitment, and it was made even clearer in "Some Notes for an Autobiographical Lecture" (1971). Speaking of his education at Columbia University in the late 1920s, he praised the General Honors course for introducing him to what would become one of the key faiths of his criticism, the practice of "intelligence"—the activity of mind that is always ready "to confront and deal with difficulty and complexity." By linking the man who instituted the Great Books course, John Erskine, with Charles Eliot Norton, Trilling declared his own heritage:

> Erskine had been the pupil at Columbia of George Edward Woodberry, who at Harvard had been the pupil of Charles Eliot Norton, who had been the friend of Carlyle, Ruskin, and Matthew Arnold. This lineage makes clear the provenance of the idea that was at the root of the General Honors course—the idea that great works of art and thought have a decisive part in shaping the life of a polity.[54]

Trilling's embrace of this tradition, however, was not uncritical. He declared his allegiance to the best iconoclastic thinkers of his youth —Van Wyck Brooks, Lewis Mumford, and Randolph Bourne (Mencken is conspicuously missing)—and the progressive journals of the time—*The Nation, The New Republic,* and the *Freeman.* He also spoke of his debt to the "two commanding, preeminent minds, Marx and Freud," whom he characterized as the greatest "unmaskers." Trilling was well aware of the danger of humanism deteriorating into the "inert and passionless" genteel tradition, and his own writings are a sustained attempt to bring the faculties of judgment and taste to bear not only on literature but also on contemporary cultural events.[55]

While Trilling had many objections to the best-selling Kinsey Report that coincide with what I have characterized as the reticent sensibility, they were not rooted in a reluctance to discuss intimate matters publicly, but rather in what he saw as the limitations of the behaviorist framework—"a science as simple and materialistic as the subject can possibly permit . . . a science of statistics and not of ideas." He advocated a Freudian approach to sex, and his argument against the Report is also an argument about psychology. It is instructive to recall that Krutch, a more reluctant and ambivalent modern, blamed "the cynical wisdom of biology *and* psychology" for stripping love of its moral, aesthetic, and cosmic values. Trilling, an avowed Freudian, was critical of the Report because of its psychological crudeness: it is "resistant to the possibility of making any connection between the sexual life and the psychic structure. This strongly formulated attitude of the Report is based on the assumption that the whole actuality of sex is anatomical and physiological; the emotions are dealt with very much as if they were a 'superstructure.' " One of his most devastating criticisms was that because the Report "is a study of sexual behavior in so far as it can be quantitatively measured," it yielded only one conclusion: "Frequency is always a sign of robust sexuality," even if, as Trilling suggests, following the psychoanalysts, it might also plausibly be interpreted as a sign of anxiety or compulsiveness.[56]

Trilling's essay gives the impression that he believed he was the first person ever to address the condition of love in a world where the scientific perspective reigns supreme, even though, as I have tried to show, a controversy over precisely this question had been raging for more than a half century. One of the signal accomplishments of the party of exposure was to relegate to the trash heap of history the discourse of the party of reticence, thereby forcing anyone who is not a direct descendant of Comstock but nonetheless objects to indecency and invasions of privacy to gather up the fragments of that discarded language as best one can. Trilling, like earlier critics, argued that clinical pictures of sexual intimacy ultimately flatten the experience: "Professor Kinsey and his coadjutors drag forth into the light all the hidden actualities of sex so that they may lose their dark power and become domesticated among us." He also noted the way scientific objectivity devalues love: as opposed to the older usages of "love" or "lust," the invention of the term "sex" "implied scientific neutrality, then vague devaluation, for the word which neutralizes the mind of the observer also neuterizes the men and women who are being observed."[57]

At this point in our story, the criticism of the behaviorist approach to sex coincides with the mass-culture critique, and once again we see how much the two seemingly disparate kinds of public address share. In his "Theory of Mass Culture" (1953), Macdonald echoed Trilling when he castigated "scientific and artistic technicians of our Mass Culture" for

> degrad[ing] the public by treating it as an object, to be handled with the lack of ceremony and the objectivity of medical students dissecting a corpse. . . . When one hears a questionnaire-sociologist talk about how he will "set up" an investigation, one feels he regards people as a herd of dumb animals, as mere congeries of conditioned reflexes, his calculation being which reflex will be stimulated by which question.[58]

Although the study of sexual behavior was supposed to free people from ignorance, misconception, and guilt (and also provide conclusive evidence as to the consequences of obscenity), for Trilling the very act of observation violated privacy and betrayed a lack of respect for the dignity of others: "There is something repulsive in the idea of men being studied for their own good. The paradigm of what repels us is to be found in the common situation of the child who is *understood* by its parents." Behind this paradigm was a manipulative motive, and it, in turn, deformed the idea of what it is to be an individual; Trilling pointed out that the carefully watched and analyzed child eventually "yield[s] to understanding as never to coercion, [and] does not develop the mystery and wildness of spirit which it is still our grace to believe is the mark of full humanness. The act of understanding," he concluded, "becomes an act of control."[59]

The clinical method of exposing, dissecting, and tallying the most fragile activities of intimate life has the same consequences, for Trilling, as those described by earlier opponents of exposure: when intimate experiences are detached from a person's larger life story, they are deprived of their emotional depth and significance, which on the one hand makes them light and laughable and on the other cheapens the tone of public conversation. The Report, wrote Trilling, was

> snickered at and giggled over and generally submitted to humor: American popular culture has surely been made the richer by the Report's gift of a new folk hero—he already is clearly the hero of the Report —the "scholarly and skilled lawyer" who for thirty years has had an orgasmic frequency of thirty times a week.

Trilling, remarking on how the Report "draw[s] sexuality apart from the general human context," noted a strange omission: "It is striking how small a role woman plays in *Sexual Behavior in the Human Male.* We learn nothing about the connection of sex and reproduction."[60] Once again we see the irony at the root of the scientific approach toward sex: the more it succeeds in its avowed aim of turning sex into an observable fact, the more it divests intimacy of its potential for meaning. In consequence, the Kinsey Report as well as its numerous successors tell us nothing interesting about sex—why it evokes the sweetest tenderness, the most ecstatic pleasures, and the most excruciating jealousy. Though scientific studies have been and continue to be heralded as sacred oracles in obscenity law, their inherent inadequacies require us to ask whether they are in fact at all useful to the obscenity debate.

Trilling did not broach this question, but he did introduce a related issue concerning judgment and its role in democracy. He criticized the researchers' naïve use of the "natural" behavior of animals—that is, whatever animals happened to do—as the standard for human sexual conduct. For Trilling, this "zoological" approach was woefully misplaced in human relations since what was "natural" for animals was often bestial or perverse from the perspective of civilized society. But it was not only a problem of giving precedence to the so-called natural over the civilized, which risked reducing people to the base equality of the condition of having a body. In Trilling's view, this "non-judgmental" stance went to the core of American life. While he acknowledged the generous "impulse toward acceptance and liberation," the "broad and general desire for others that they be not harshly judged," and not be rejected as "sexually aberrant," he also insisted that it betrayed something pernicious, "an almost intentional intellectual weakness." Drawing attention to the way judgment and, with it, distinction and discrimination—all key words of the discourse of reticence—had been reduced to synonyms for social injustice, Trilling observed, this "generosity of mind . . . goes with a nearly conscious aversion from making intellectual distinctions, almost as if out of the belief that an intellectual distinction must inevitably lead to a social discrimination or exclusion." This attitude of general acceptance—which, Trilling noted, was firmly established in American universities and in foundations supporting intellectual work—is distinctly at odds with the smart set's passion for making distinctions between the civilized few and the "booboisie." Where Ernst and Loth had pointed to this shift in temper when they praised Kinsey and his fellow researchers as "kindlier" rebels, Trilling decried the inherent evasiveness of the sociological style:

> We might say that those who most explicitly assert and wish to practice the democratic virtues have taken it as their assumption that all social facts—with the exception of exclusion and economic hardship—must be *accepted*, not merely in the scientific sense but also in the social sense, in the sense, that is, that no judgment must be passed on them, that any conclusion drawn from them which perceives values and consequences will turn out to be "undemocratic."[61]

Where the activity of judging had previously been understood as a way of participating in the world with others by imaginatively taking the standpoints of others, the reluctance to judge for fear of undemocratic consequences signals not only the subjectivization of judging but also its relentless politicization. The non-judgmental stance is the flip side of unmasking—and both grow directly out of the emotivist moral position underlying all emancipatory projects of exposure, which holds that judgments express nothing but private whims and subjective preferences, and, as they belong to the individual, are always self-interested and manipulative. Liberal judgment thus defined can never rise above an anemic version of tolerance; essentially defensive, it is leery of judging others for fear of being judged and subjected to the unrestrained will of another. All relationships, from this perspective, are sheer power struggles, and judgment, distinction, and discrimination are modes of domination. (This sheds some light on the myopia of many academic debunkers today, who see all transactions, past and present, as exercises of exclusion based on race, class, gender, or sexual preference.)

It is significant that Trilling's discussion of judgment takes place in an essay on the Kinsey Report. Nowhere does he question the propriety of public discussions about sexual intimacy or suggest that public talk of this nature might be shameful or obscene. A sophisticated modern himself, he was indiffferent to this aspect of the reticent sensibility, even though he was acutely sensitive to related matters of taste and judgment; indeed, he was so dedicated to the activity of judging that he could seriously entertain the prospect of judging other people's most intimate affairs. Thus he was irritated by the Kinsey Report's virtual refusal to judge—and, by extension, the failings of liberal judgment. He objected to the implication that "there can be only one standard for judgment of sexual behavior—that is, sexual behavior as it actually exists; which is to say that sexual behavior is not to be judged at all, except, presumably, in so far as it causes pain to others."[62] Trilling's insistence that sexual behavior should or could be judged resembles Lockhart and McClure's insistence that public discussions of sex are no different in kind from any other discussions. It is not surprising that those who speak the legal language of rights and interests display little moral or aesthetic subtlety, since their analytical categories make it virtually impossible to do so, but it *is* surprising that even the heir apparent to Norton and Arnold seemed not to appreciate that sexual conduct, because of its essentially private nature, can never appear before strangers, let alone be subjected to their judgment, without suffering severe deformation. This suggests that by mid-century, the common knowledge of the party of reticence had been lost to even the most refined and cultivated critics of the time.

Without this respect for the limits as to what can be spoken, private and public had collapsed into one another, leaving in their wake a strange new realm, at once as noisy and promiscuous as a circus and as sterile and solemn as a laboratory. In this new world, the protection afforded by cultural conventions such as privacy and modesty no longer held sway. An amorous couple could be wrenched from each other's arms and dragged naked before the court of public opinion, where they would be asked by experts in white coats, laboriously taking down their every word, to describe every detail of their erotic life. And "the human male" does not protest that his privacy is violated or that it is a breach of fidelity to speak of those moments that belong exclusively and completely to his loved one and himself; instead, he enthusiastically tells all.

10

THE STALLED DEBATE
ABOUT THE PUBLIC SPHERE

For almost a half century, the debate about the quality and character of our common world has stalled, and in recent years it has become all too clear that it is running on empty. This is due, in large part, to the predominance of the law in controversies concerning what may or may not be done or shown in public. Because the legal language of individual victims, harm, rights, and interests lacks the resources to address matters of taste and judgment, the most pressing questions of how the world should look, which manner of thing and action should appear in it, cannot be raised. The resort to the law, however, is not the only reason for the impoverishment of our public conversation and the debasement of our common world. They are also the consequence of a striking change in the thinking of many contemporary intellectuals—most of whom have found a home in institutions of higher learning and the arts—who apparently believe it no longer possible, necessary, or valuable to make distinctions between mass culture and art, or between what is obscene and what is decent. In the case of mass culture, an uncritical attachment to an alleged democracy of taste has led, on the one hand, to claims that efforts to introduce people to traditional canons of art and literature are acts of cultural imperialism and, on the other, to celebrations of the most debased and manipulated forms of consumer culture—most recently, rap music—as the authentic voice of oppressed peoples. In the case of obscenity—whether the writing of the Marquis de Sade or specific photographs of Robert Mapplethorpe—because they believe there are no limits to what a searching individual can know or experience, they refuse to abide by the old wisdom that some things are simply unspeakable, in the sense that language, except in the hands of the most extraordinary artists, almost always fails before them.

Mass Culture, Mass Society,
and the Cold War

As we have seen throughout this study, even some of the most discerning writers on the side of exposure—Howells, Bourne, and
Mencken, for example—were critical of indiscriminate talk about intimate life and of the proliferation of commercial entertainment. This
hostility toward commercial entertainment reached a crescendo in the
1940s and 1950s in essays written by the New York intellectuals, who
were also the first to notice the waning of the avant-garde as a vital
cultural force. At the very moment they were making their dire fore-
casts about the end of culture, a new kind of institution was taking
shape that would soon replace the ailing avant-garde—the postmodern academy. The Kinsey Reports on "human sexual behavior" suggest the demeanor of this new vanguard, as does a collection of essays
entitled *Mass Culture: The Popular Arts in America*, published in 1957.
In the opening sentence of their preface, Bernard Rosenberg and David Manning White set forth the essentially academic nature of their
project: "This book is the result of a need . . . which both editors
personally experienced in trying to teach courses where no traditional
source books were available."[1] They came at the subject from opposite
sides: Rosenberg, a close associate of Irving Howe at Brandeis University and a founding member of *Dissent*, made the case against mass
culture; White, a sociologist, distinguished himself as one of its earliest
apologists.

To justify the need for a college reader in a contemporary subject
that had once been considered to fall beneath the threshold of formal
instruction, Rosenberg and White observed that "the interplay between the mass media and society" had gained "substantial attention"
from "scholars in the humanities, English and American literature,
American civilization, journalism, the communication arts of radio,
television and cinema, as well as in sociology, psychology, economics,
and anthropology." Anticipating the academic vogue that goes under
the name of "cultural studies" in our own time, they expressed their
hope "that this Reader will be a step in the creation of an interdis-
ciplinary focus on problems common to everyone who takes a serious
interest in what is happening to this aspect of modern civilization."
In proper academic fashion—and here they parted company with
both the avant-garde and cultural critics of the past—they insisted
they were not trying to "prove any individual point of view the 'right'
one, but rather to examine the phenomena as fully as possible,"

though they admitted that there had been more "excoriators of mass culture than defenders."[2] This opinion would soon shift, however, partly as a consequence of their volume.

The only historical materials in the collection were excerpts from Tocqueville's *Democracy in America* and Whitman's *Democratic Vistas*. With the exceptions of a chapter from José Ortega y Gasset's *The Revolt of the Masses* (1930) and Clement Greenberg's "Avant-Garde and *Kitsch*" (1939) (minus his original call for socialism), all the other contributions were no more than a decade old; a number of them were commissioned for the book. The most vigorous attacks were Greenberg's piece, Howe's "Notes on Mass Culture," and Macdonald's revised "A Theory of Mass Culture" (1953). Equally influential and critical were contributions from writers associated with the Frankfurt School, including Leo Lowenthal and T. W. Adorno. From different quarters, Ernest van den Haag's "Of Happiness and Despair We Have No Measure" (1957) was an especially devastating indictment. In defense of mass culture, selections from the work of Gilbert Seldes, Marshall McLuhan, and Leslie Fiedler were included. The largest part of the book was given over to studies of the content of mass culture or the role of the market in their production, and they were treated under separate headings of mass literature, motion pictures, television and radio, divertissement, and advertising.

The picture that emerged from the more theoretical essays—with which I am concerned here—was dire. Products of mass culture, the critics repeatedly pointed out, shared nothing with genuine art; they had all the marks of mass-produced goods, "standardization, stereotypy, conservatism, mendacity," as Lowenthal put it. These critics were especially concerned with the menace mass culture posed to the durability of the public sphere: because of its rapaciousness, it threatened to scavenge the bodies of both high and folk art, and because of its astounding capacity to proliferate, it threatened to crowd out all other forms of public address and display. While this was disastrous from the point of view of the survival of culture in general, critics also deplored the psychological effects. Repeatedly they observed that mass culture offered consolation to exploited laborers even while it promised them spurious happiness in the form of commodities. "The message of . . . popular culture," according to van den Haag, "is 'you, too, can be happy' if you only buy this car or that hair tonic; you will be thrilled, you will have adventure, romance, popularity—you will no longer be lonely and left out if you follow this formula." This empty therapeutic vision was matched by a sinister one, as when Adorno described mass culture as "a medium of undreamed of psychological control." "The repetitiousness, the self-sameness, and the ubiquity of modern mass culture," he observed, "tend to make for automatized reactions and to weaken the forces of individual resistance." The worst fears were voiced by Rosenberg in language approaching the apocalyptic: "At its worst, mass culture threatens not merely to cretinize our taste, but to brutalize our senses while paving the way to totalitarianism."[3]

Edward Shils's review of this book, "Daydreams and Nightmares: Reflections on the Criticism of Mass Culture," which appeared in *Sewanee Review* (1957), restates much of the emerging defense of mass culture, and Shils soon became the figure most closely associated with that stance. In 1960, in a special issue of *Daedalus* devoted to "Mass Culture and Mass Media," his "Mass Society and Its Culture," a more elaborate version of his position, was put at the center of the debate. Hannah Arendt and Ernest van den Haag, among others, responded. In later discussions, both Dwight Macdonald and Irving Howe singled out Shils—"the Pangloss of the sociological approach," in Macdonald's words—as a leading debunker of the critics.[4]

More than anything else, the mass-culture debate became a referendum, cold-war style, on Western consumer society. Critics of mass culture found themselves in a position similar to that of Charles Eliot Norton at the end of his life when he tried to weigh material against moral progress in order to judge the quality of American democracy. Following the horrors of World War II, intellectuals struggled with many agonizing questions: How had the people of modern, industrialized Germany so thoroughly embraced the barbarism of Nazism? How had the promise of the Soviet experiment deteriorated into totalitarianism? What accounted for the widespread conformism of American society? Erich Fromm's *Escape from Freedom* (1941), George Orwell's *1984* (1949), Adorno's *The Authoritarian Personality* (1950), David Riesman's *The Lonely Crowd* (1950), and Arendt's *The Origins of Totalitarianism* (1951) were among the most influential attempts to describe and account for these terrible miscarriages of history. Many avowed friends of democracy began to wonder whether the very successes of modern consumer society had not, ironically, destroyed such cherished ideals of liberalism as personal freedom, individuality, autonomy, and privacy. Repeatedly, critics tallied the balance sheet, noting that more people than ever before in history enjoyed a higher standard of living, the benefits of education and high levels of literacy, and unheard-of amounts of leisure time. Yet these conditions—measured against the tragic events of recent history and the emptiness of modern life—had obviously not led to general enlightenment. Not surprisingly, these larger concerns about mass society found their way into criticisms of mass culture. Van den Haag's balance-sheet approach to progress is typical of the tenor of the debate:

> While immensely augmenting our comforts, our conveniences and our leisure, and disproportionately raising the real income of the poor, industry has also impoverished life. Mass production and consumption, mobility, the homogenization of taste and finally of society were among the costs of higher productivity. They de-individualized life and drained each of our ends of meaning as we achieved it.[5]

It was this assessment to which Shils took the greatest exception, and his reflections on the mass-culture critique were, first and foremost, an impassioned restatement of the liberal faith in progress and an affirmation of American consumer society. In his account, mass culture, vulgar and ugly, was a regrettable side effect of democracy, and to be hostile to it was to be hostile to democracy itself. In this uneasy balancing act, he echoed the early apologists for invasive journalism who maintained that journalistic excesses were the price of democracy, and using every weapon at the disposal of the party of exposure, he set out to discredit the enemies of mass culture on every front. First, relying on the anti-democratic idiom, he took obvious pleasure in revealing the surprising alliance of left and right in matters of culture, linking contemporary critics to Wyndham Lewis, José Ortega y Gasset, and the Leavises, whom he characterized as "aristocratic and aesthetic in their outlook." "The new critique of mass culture," he announced, "takes over many of the aristocratic and aesthetic arguments and the anti-bourgeois attitudes of nineteenth-century Europe."[6]

Playing the elitist card had in earlier phases of this debate ensured easy victory—especially when done in tandem with Puritan-baiting —and in the politically charged atmosphere of the cold war it offered new opportunities for impugning the character of an opponent. Red-baiting quickly took the place of Puritan-baiting. Thus Shils indicted his opponents, one by one, for their "Marxian socialist" affinities: Dwight Macdonald, "a former Trotskyite communist"; Max Horkheimer, "an apolitical Marxist whose Hegelian sociological terminology obscures his Marxism"; T. W. Adorno and Leo Lowenthal, "leading adherents of the school in which a refined Marxism finds its most sophisticated expression"; and Irving Howe and Bernard Rosenberg, "socialists in the tradition of Trotsky and moving spirits of *Dissent*." Then, in a deft mixing of bugaboos, Shils observed, "Nothing shows the persistence of puritanical Marxism in the writings critical of popular culture as much as the idea that popular culture is 'escapist.' "[7]

Just as critics of obscenity law had lost track of the public consequences of obscenity the more they focused on rooting out the puritanism and philistinism of their opponents, Shils skirted any real engagement with the issues raised by critics of mass culture by drawing undue attention to their personal psychology, notably to their alleged disillusionment with the working classes who had failed to fulfill their revolutionary role: "Part of the preoccupation with mass culture is the obsessiveness of the disappointed lover who, having misconceived his beloved when their love was blooming, now feels that she deceived him and he has no eye for anything but her vices and blemishes."[8] So intent was Shils on unmasking pathologies and ulterior motives that he misread an attack clearly aimed at the *purveyors* of mass culture and turned it into an assault on the *audience*. In his zeal to demolish his enemies, the embattled condition of the world, which was the reason for the mass-culture criticism in the first place, receded to the point of vanishing.

Shils, anxious to display his own credentials as a sophisticated modern, lost no time declaring his agreement with his opponents' overall judgment of mass culture: "It would, of course, be frivolous to deny the aesthetic, moral, and intellectual unsatisfactoriness of much of popular culture or to claim that it shows the human race in its best light." But he took issue with the critics' "romantic" assessment of the past: "The critical interpretation of mass culture rests on a distinct image of modern man, of society, and of man in past ages. This image," he announced triumphantly, "has little factual basis." Because Shils worshipped at the liberal cult of progress, he was unable to meet head-on any appreciation of the past that cast a shadow on the present, and was thus reduced to sputtering a string of esoteric invective: "It is a product of disappointed political prejudices, vague aspirations for an unrealizable ideal, resentment against American society, and, at bottom, romanticism dressed up in the language of sociology, psychoanalysis, and existentialism."[9]

Instead of addressing the critics' most penetrating insights concerning what was new and pernicious about mass culture—its commodification of culture, its imperiousness, the threat it posed to both high and folk arts as well as to the durability of the world— Shils treated mass culture as virtually identical to the folk cultures of the past and, further, insisted that if not exactly an improvement over the past, it was certainly no worse: "The present pleasures of the working and lower-middle classes are not worthy of profound aesthetic, moral, or intellectual esteem but they are surely not inferior to the villainous thing which gave pleasure to their European ancestors from the Middle Ages to the nineteenth century." Stone deaf to the slightest nuances of the criticism of mass culture, he lectured his opponents on the depravity of times past:

> The culture of these strata [the lower classes], which were dulled by labor, illness, and fear, and which comprised a far larger proportion of the population than they do in advanced societies in the twentieth century, was a culture of bear-baiting, cock-fighting, drunkenness, tales of witches, gossip about the sexual malpractices of priests, monks, and nuns, stories of murders and mutilations.

The high culture of the past fared no better: "Only a very small minority of the upper classes of the first four centuries of the modern era read a great deal, and a great deal of what they read was worthless from any point of view except that much of it was harmless." For Shils, "the root of the trouble lies not in mass culture but in the intellectuals themselves." "The readiness of university teachers and literary publicists to lower their own standards in their teaching and writing," Shils berated his opponents, "is more pernicious in its effects on high culture than Hollywood or the radio industry."[10]

THE END OF IDEOLOGY AND THE END OF VANGUARDS

This campaign against the critics of mass culture, with its cold-war Red-baiting, charges of elitism, romanticism, and nostalgia, and, perhaps most effective of all, its imputation that to be critical of mass culture was to be against progress itself, quickly carried the day. As Arendt noted in the opening sentence of her contribution to the *Daedalus* symposium on Mass Society and Mass Media (1960):

> Mass culture and mass society (the very terms were still a sign of reprobation a few years ago, implying that mass society was a depraved form of society and mass culture a contradiction in terms) are considered by almost everyone today as something with which we must come to terms, and in which we must discover some "positive" aspects—if only because mass culture is the culture of a mass society. And mass society, whether we like it or not, is going to stay with us into the foreseeable future.[11]

The search to find something "positive" in mass culture which mystified Arendt marks a crucial change in the long-standing controversy about what should appear in public. Prior to this moment during the cold war, no self-respecting intellectual had ever found anything to praise in the commercial products of the mass-entertainment industry. And this newfound receptivity was accompanied by two equally astounding developments—the embrace of avant-garde culture by the academy and by society in general, and the renunciation of radical politics by leftist intellectuals. Just as cold-war liberals optimistically viewed mass culture as bearing the first fruits of a democratized culture, they interpreted the end of the old aesthetic and political vanguards as a harbinger of a new, pluralistic, consensus-oriented age. Where Shils put himself forward as the no-nonsense defender of mass culture, Daniel Bell played the same role in regard to mass society, confidently announcing "the end of ideology" in his well-known book of the same title, published in 1960. Bell attributed the "exhaustion" of political ideologies to recent historical "calamities"—"the Moscow Trials, the Nazi-Soviet pact, the concentration camps, the suppression of the Hungarian workers"—that had exposed Stalin's Soviet Union as a totalitarian society as vicious and repressive as Nazi Germany's, thereby chastening would-be revolutionaries and discrediting once and for all their "blueprints" for total social change. Bell also argued that "such changes as the modification of capitalism [and] the rise of the Welfare State" indicated that Western societies were reforming themselves. Given the choice between Soviet totalitarianism wrought from overheated ideology on the one hand and consumerist capitalism that could deliver a generalized state of security and comfort on the other, Bell observed that "a rough consensus among intellectuals on political issues" had emerged: "the acceptance of a Welfare State; the desirability of decentralized power; a system of mixed economy, and of political pluralism."[12]

For the enthusiast of pluralism and consensus, one of the most promising signs of the coming moderate era was the disappearance of an identifiable enemy to oppose. In his essay "The Mood of Three Generations," Bell testified to the end of the modern revolt against Victorianism that took shape at the turn of the century (mistakenly tracing its first act to the 1920s):

> The problem of the [younger] generation is . . . an inability to define an "enemy." One can have causes and passions only when one knows against whom to fight. The writers of the twenties—Dadaist, Menckenian, and nihilist—scorned bourgeois mores. The radicals of the thirties fought "capitalism," and later, fascism, and for some, Stalinism. Today, intellectually, emotionally, who is the enemy that one can fight? The paradox is that the generation wants to live a "heroic" life but finds the image truly "quixotic." This is, as for Cervantes' Don, the

end of an age. For the younger generation, as for all intellectuals, there is this impasse. It is part of the time which has seen the end of ideology.[13]

This remarkable passage reveals that the myth of generational revolt had become so deeply ingrained that each new generation believed their very identity and potential for creativity were possible only to the extent that they slayed their predecessors. It also reveals how completely political, cultural, and aesthetic revolt had merged into one amorphous category.

Not only did Bell believe that political radicalism, "with the lesson of totalitarianism and bureaucracy in mind," had given way to "moderation in social politics," but he also believed that "cultural radicalism" was becoming obsolete, since whatever was called radical or avant-garde in culture was almost instantly accepted and acclaimed. To Bell, these changes were "a feature of the absorption of radicalism into society," which he praised as one more piece of progress:

> Just as managerial society is shared, in part, by the unions, and political power is shared, in part, with the ethnic and labor groups, so the culture, too, in part has been transformed. Many of the new cultural arbiters (Clement Greenberg and Harold Rosenberg in painting, Lionel Trilling and Alfred Kazin in literature) were part of the *ancien* Left, and their tastes have affected not only the serious painters and novelists but the standards of the larger public as well.[14]

While many of Bell's contemporaries also noticed that political and cultural vanguards had come to a halt, not all of them were so sanguine about its meaning. Dwight Macdonald rehearsed a similar historical sequence—"the depression, the rise of Nazism, the Spanish Civil War, the Moscow Trials, the Nazi-Stalin Pact, the war itself, Hitler's extermination of six million Jews, Stalin's murderous forced-labor camps, Truman's atomic bombings"—to account for his withdrawal from politics, explaining that radicals like himself had expected to find "drastic solutions" to these terrible events, just as they had expected "revolutionary situations" to develop after the war. But neither the solutions nor the situations materialized, which left would-be radicals in a wretched position. In a famous debate with Norman Mailer at Mount Holyoke College in 1952, he voiced what he believed was the only position left to responsible people at the time: "I prefer an imperfectly living, open society to a perfectly dead, closed society." In a postscript penned in the shadow of the Korean War, he wrote that the Nazi threat had been replaced by a menace just as terrible—communism; in consequence, he had no choice but to ally himself with the West, even though, as he was forced to admit, "the results of the Korean war have been disastrous, especially for the Korean people." The great iconoclast, not surprisingly, had a hard time stomaching his new allegiance to the West, justifying it as "a 'lesser evil' choice," to which he could not resist immediately adding, "The pages and pages of argumentation I have written exposing the illogic and immorality of this position!" In one of his most dispirited moments, he confessed, "This is one reason I am less interested in politics than I used to be."[15]

A number of intellectuals were not so hopeful as Bell about the meaning of the end of the avant-garde either. As early as 1954, Irving Howe, in a searing indictment "This Age of Conformity," warned that "American radicalism exists only as an idea, and that barely. The literary avant-garde—it has become a stock comment for reviewers to make—is rapidly disintegrating, without function or spirit, and held together only by an inert nostalgia." He went on to speculate that "today . . . the danger is that the serious artists are not scorned enough. Philistinism has become very shrewd: it does not attack its enemies as much as it disarms them through reasonable cautions and moderate amendments." By 1967, the adversary position of the avant-garde had so deteriorated that Howe could declare, "Bracing enmity has given way to wet embraces, the middle class has discovered that the fiercest attacks upon its values can be transposed into pleasing entertainments, and the avant-garde writer or artist must confront the one challenge for which he has not been prepared: the challenge of success."[16]

The rise of the avant-garde to new heights of respectability led to two further developments which no doubt would have astonished the original avant-garde and which have certainly had dire consequences for the arts ever since: the vibrant experimentalism of modernism in both form and content has hardened into an academic genre; and the rebellious spirit of the avant-garde has been routinized into increasingly theatrical and empty gestures made by self-proclaimed rebels who, misconstruing the aesthetic components in the "shock of the new," have made a style of shock for its own sake. One of the first writers to note this stunning involution of the avant-garde was Delmore Schwartz in a lecture before the Library of Congress in 1958. "What was once a battlefield has become a peaceful public park on a pleasant summer Sunday afternoon," he pungently observed, "so that if the majority of new poets write in a style and idiom which takes as its starting point the poetic idiom and literary taste of the generation of Pound and Eliot, the motives and attitudes at the heart of the writing possess an assurance which sometimes makes their work seem tame and sedate."[17]

Speaking of a recently published anthology of work by younger poets, *New Poets of England and America*, Schwartz marveled at their "trained and conscious skill, a sophisticated mastery of the craft of versification," though he also remarked on their "tameness" and "constrained calm," which he attributed to their being "teachers of literature." This fact—that poets, novelists, critics, and public intellectuals were more and more finding a home in colleges and universities—was perhaps the single most significant reason for the hobbled condition of the avant-garde, since historically the academy and the avant-garde had always been at odds. Almost everyone who wrote about the dissolution of the avant-garde during the 1950s spoke not only of the unprecedented growth of higher education in the United States after World War II but also of the strangeness of the new situation in which obstreperous freethinkers and quirky writers were becoming respectable professors. The poet as a teacher, observed Schwartz, "is a useful and accepted member of society and not a peculiar and strange being, since the writing of poetry is clearly a pursuit for the teacher of literature." The once defiantly independent avant-garde, amazing as it seemed, was being welcomed and absorbed by its natural enemy. "But," as Howe warned, "no one who has a live sense of what the literary life has been and might still be . . . can accept the notion that the academy is the natural home of intellect."[18]

For Schwartz, the academic quality of the younger poets was also apparent in their choice of subject matter—the stuff of prosaic and intimate life—which showed how they were domesticating once-explosive material:

> One poem is about a toothache; and one poem is about a vacuum cleaner; and in general, the objects and experiences of daily life, which in previous generations were either supposed to be outside the realm of poetry or were introduced into poetry with a conscious daring and defiance, now appear in poem after poem in the most matter-of-fact way, as if their poetic quality had never been denied, questioned or regarded as outrageous. In a like way, there is an explicitness about sexual experience without the self-consciousness or the assertive Bohemianism which characterized the poetry written during the first postwar period.[19]

Literary transgression had become such an empty ritual that the new poets no longer remembered the icons they were shattering; yet without the imposing authority of the classical hierarchy of genres against which to rebel, their poetry about toothaches and vacuum cleaners and sex was simply that and nothing more. When Schwartz dismissed their efforts as "tame" and "sedate"—undoubtedly the worst insult imaginable for those who march under the banner of the avant-garde—he also announced the disappearance of an entire range of experience: in a culture of exposure, nothing was shocking.

The only "counter-tendency" to academic modernism that Schwartz could discern was "the San Francisco circle of poets who, under the leadership of Kenneth Rexroth, have recently proclaimed themselves super-Bohemians and leaders of a new poetic revolution." But this coterie, whom he christened "the San Francisco Howlers," was also stuck in a cul-de-sac. Academic modernists failed to see that their formulaic transgressions had sapped the dynamism from experimental writing, and similarly the Beatniks did not see that they had trivialized the bohemian revolt against the bourgeoisie, so that all too often it became a battle for personal style consisting in the right to wear "a turtleneck sweater, slacks, and a sports coat" instead of a gray flannel or Brooks Brothers suit. "The San Francisco Howlers" were, in Schwartz's shriveling assessment, "imaginary rebels since the substance of their work is a violent advocacy of a non-conformism which they already possess and which requires no insurrection whatsoever, since non-conformism of almost every variety had become acceptable and respectable and available to everyone." He made the telling point that where bohemians of the past had genuine enemies—"the dominant Puritanism and Victorianism of respectable society . . . the censorship of books, Prohibition, and a prudery enforced by the police"—the new non-conformists were "unopposed and permitted to exist in freedom." "The new rebel," he concluded, "bears a great deal of resemblance to a prize fighter trying to knock out an antagonist who is not in the ring with him." Given Schwartz's undisguised loathing for this preposterous situation, it is stunning that Bell approvingly quoted these same remarks to demonstrate the progress American society had made in fostering individual freedom and non-conformity.[20]

Whether writers cheered these developments as portents of an age of consensus and pluralism or cursed them for their deadening effects on politics and the arts, by the end of the 1950s, influential writers, in and out of the academy, agreed that political and aesthetic vanguards had seen their day. And by the middle of the next decade, obituaries about related public-sphere controversies began appearing everywhere. With the 1966 Supreme Court decision that the eighteenth-century English novel *Fanny Hill* was not obscene, many observers agreed with Charles Rembar, the attorney who had defended the book, that "in its traditional, its time-dishonored sense—the impermissible description of sex in literature—the legal concept of obscenity was at an end. This was the meaning of the *Fanny Hill* case. Literary censorship was gone." And with the flourishing of mass culture and unapologetic celebrations of it by a number of younger intellectuals, many observers concluded that the mass-culture critique was also at an end. Irving Howe observed in 1968 that "almost as if by common decision, the whole subject of mass culture was dropped. For years hardly a word could be found in the advanced journals about what a little earlier had been called a crucial problem of the modern era."[21]

Howe offered a number of reasons for its sudden disappearance: the power of Shils's charge that it was "elitist" to attack mass culture; intellectuals' apparent inability to develop the critique any further; the inherent triviality of "the commercial pseudo-arts," which made it difficult to sustain interest in them; the "ingenuity and resourcefulness" that movies and television had begun to show, which went beyond "the severe notions advanced by Greenberg and Macdonald"; and the turbulence of the 1960s, which opened the possibility that political criticism was once again possible and, in consequence, "the appetite for cultural surrogates became less keen." Howe also pointed to a new generation of writers who found "that the whole approach of these men was heavy and humorless." Making clear that nothing less than the capacity for judgment was at stake—and by extension, the durability of the world—he set out the contours of "the new sensibility":

> Susan Sontag has proposed a cheerfully eclectic view which undercuts just about everything written from the Greenberg-Macdonald position. Now everyone is to do "his thing," high, middle, or low; the old puritan habit of interpretation and judgment, so inimical to sensuousness, gives way to a programmed receptivity; and we are enlightened by lengthy studies of the Beatles.[22]

With the appearance of the new sensibility and the new left in the 1960s, radical politics and avant-garde art were momentarily revived. Yet it is clear, at least in retrospect, that the major cultural battles of the moderns against the Victorians had been virtually won by the 1930s and definitively so by the 1950s and that it took the 1960s' youth revolt to translate these victories into the popular culture at large in their "life style" of "sex, drugs, and rock 'n' roll." The habit of generational rebellion acquired during this long march, however, was far more difficult to give up. Celebrants of the new sensibility set forth to shock bourgeois society out of its famous complacency, even though by now they were up against a bourgeoisie who had, in Dwight Macdonald's words, "developed a passion for being shocked."[23] Under these virtually unprecedented circumstances, they landed upon two unlikely surrogates for the avant-garde: kitsch—once regarded as hopelessly banal, manipulative, and exploitative; and pornography—once considered the most vile and degrading form of obscenity. These self-conscious and rather desperate attempts at provocation, however, make clear the debt the new sensibility owes to the modern one, notably the way the former takes one of the latter's distinguishing features—the capacity to regard all aspects of the human condition without passing moral judgment or flinching—and pushes it to the outermost limits in the name of shock alone.

THE AESTHETICIZATION OF KITSCH

A harbinger of this new style of effrontery, which delivers its shock with a simple inversion of expected hierarchies, had been Leslie Fiedler's "The Middle Against Both Ends" (1955). In order to stay one step ahead of his much-needed opponents—who, however, were failing to play their pre-scripted role in the cultural drama of philistine vs. literati—Fielder jauntily assumed the mantle of philistine to show up the educated middle class's cultural pretensions and, at the same time, to show off his superior aestheticism. Flaunting his rebellion against high culture, which, as a member of the educated class, he was supposed to hold sacred, Fiedler gleefully confessed, "I am surely one of the few people pretending to intellectual respectability who can boast that he has read more comic books than attacks on comic books. I do not mean that I have consulted or studied the comics— I have read them, often with some pleasure."[24]

The exemplar of the new sensibility in the 1960s was Susan Sontag, whom Howe singled out as its most influential "publicist." In her celebrated piece "Notes on 'Camp'" (1964), she offered kitsch as a candidate for expanding the range of aesthetic experience. "One cheats oneself, as a human being," Sontag coyly chided her readers, "if one has respect only for the style of high culture, whatever else one may do or feel on the sly." And the way *not* to cheat oneself as a human being was not to shackle oneself to "moralistic" high culture with its defining values, according to Sontag, of "truth, beauty, and seriousness." Instead, in keeping with the spirit of abundance of modern consumer society, she informed her readers that there were two other "creative sensibilities" and that they were also "valid": the sensibility of "extreme states of feeling . . . whose trademark is anguish, cruelty, derangement"; and "camp . . . the sensibility of failed seriousness, of the theatricalization of experience . . . the consistently aesthetic experience of the world."[25] With great verve, Sontag treated her audience to a series of delectable examples of camp, each outdoing the last in extravagance, exaggeration, artifice, glamour, and style— all key words of the camp sensibility. At their best, her exuberant jottings were a commonsensical rejoinder to the more apocalyptic critics of mass culture that some things are simply fun. But they were also more—and worse.

Unlike earlier defenders of mass culture—apologists for mass-circulation newspapers who claimed their publications were democratic because they gave the people what they wanted, or liberal sociologists who admitted the poverty of mass culture but insisted it was a small price to pay for democracy—Sontag did not speak in the name of democracy. Instead, she offered her notes on camp as the last word in sophisticated taste, and they can best be understood as an up-to-date rendition of Mencken's smart-settism. Strewn with epigrams from Oscar Wilde (to whom she dedicated it), her essay presented the aficionado of camp as the modern-day dandy. "Camp is the answer to the problem: how to be a dandy in the age of mass culture."[26] With this lighthearted formulation, Sontag simply waved away the problem of mass culture, which, for its most searching critics, concerned the survival of culture in a world overrun with standardized, commercial forms of exploitative entertainment. For Sontag, the only question raised by mass culture was the fate of the would-be snob in a world quickly losing the range of leisure-time activities and the variety of consumable objects that had previously provided occasions for distinguishing oneself from the mob.

Sontag's singular interest in mass culture was to show that, when viewed from the vantage point of the camp sensibility, it furnished abundant opportunities for parading a highly polished ironic style. In a dazzling display of cultural one-upmanship, she regaled her readers with the news that the modern-day dandy could relish "the coarsest, commonest pleasures in the arts of the masses" with as much gusto as the old dandy relished "Latin poetry and rare wines and velvet jackets." With the disappearance of society's shared judgment of how the world should look, the self, bereft of resources to regard and conduct itself as a citizen of the world, swells to fill the void. Thus, Sontag, like all debunkers, cast everything in terms of the self and its manipulative relation to people and things. Just as the sociologist

Edward Shils saw intellectual debate and principled criticism of mass culture as nothing more than assertions of will, the consuming aesthete missed no opportunity to use mass culture to show off an updated sophistication that was more hard-boiled than refined: "The new-style dandy, the lover of Camp, appreciates vulgarity. . . . [He] sniffs the stink and prides himself on his strong nerves."[27]

Eager to display the complexity of the camp sensibility the better to bolster her claims for its high level of sophistication, Sontag insisted that "camp doesn't reverse things. It doesn't argue that the good is bad, or the bad is good." Rather, it "offer[s] for art (and life) a different—a supplementary—set of standards." Yet a few pages later she characterized camp in a way that threatened to make her claim of its supplementary status empty: "The whole point of Camp is to dethrone the serious. Camp is playful, anti-serious." Since she had already made seriousness a defining feature of high culture, it is hard to see how camp taste could remain "supplementary" and not, instead, destroy the appreciation of, along with respect for, the serious as it "dethrones" it. But she did not acknowledge this obvious tension. Rather, Sontag took refuge in the alleged complexity of the situation: "Camp involves a new, more complex relation to 'the serious.' One can be serious about the frivolous, frivolous about the serious."[28] With her reliance on the complexity alibi and the substitution of wordplay for reasoned argument, Sontag introduced a style of writing that is characteristic of the postmodern academy.

As a world-weary sophisticate, Sontag exhibited a kind of detachment that is so thoroughgoing she could even see through the sensibility she had just been celebrating. With a wink to the cognoscenti, she confessed, "Every sensibility is self-serving to the group that promotes it. Jewish liberalism is a gesture of self-legitimation. So is Camp taste, which definitely has something propagandistic about it." Having identified homosexuals as the virtuosos of camp, she unapologetically unmasked their ulterior motive: "Homosexuals have pinned their integration into society on promoting the aesthetic sense. Camp is a solvent of morality. It neutralizes moral indignation, sponsors playfulness." Sontag's transformation of camp into a tactic for gaining social acceptance for homosexuals coincided with what Trilling had said about the evasion of judgment in the Kinsey Report: the liberal's non-judgmental stance, while expressing a generous "impulse toward acceptance and liberation," also betrayed a fear that "intellectual distinction must inevitably lead to a social discrimination or exclusion." While the open-mindedness and receptivity to different "sexual behavior" of the Kinsey Report shared much with the permissive attitude that Sontag urged, what was different about camp was that it allowed its devotees to be both non-judgmental about the world and snobbish about their fellow citizens at the same time. They generously embraced "the coarsest, commonest pleasures in the arts of the masses," yet turned this alleged generosity against the masses who consumed kitsch uncritically and, even more deliciously, against intellectuals who insisted on making invidious distinctions between genuine art and mass culture. The capacity to "appreciate vulgarity," to aestheticize kitsch, was, after all, what gave the dandy his or her only claim to distinction in a world of homogenized mass culture.[29]

PORNOGRAPHY AS THE LAST VANGUARD

Where camp lends the would-be dandy a new lease on life, pornography serves the same purpose for another tired war-horse of the avant-garde—the heroic truth-seeker. It is striking that by the mid-1960s pornography could be offered as the last outpost of advanced art and adventurous taste by cultural figures as different as Susan Sontag and Maurice Girodias, publisher of Olympia Press and the first to publish not only Nabokov's *Lolita* and Beckett's *Watt* but also so-called high pornography, including works by Henry Miller, William Burroughs, and Jean Genet, *Fanny Hill, The Story of O*, Terry Southern and Mason Hoffenberg's *Candy*, Frank Harris's *Life and Loves*, J. P. Donleavy's *The Ginger Man*, and Lawrence Durrell's *The Black Book*, as well as more pedestrian varieties of the genre. It is also striking that the novel claim for the vanguard status of pornography rested on two of the most exhausted truisms of avant-garde lore: that the artist's only responsibility is to "tell the truth about life," no matter how indecent, unseemly, or ugly—a rallying cry of American realists since the time of William Dean Howells; and that artists as heroic seers and cultural outlaws deserve special dispensation from society—a piece of legal wisdom since the *Ulysses* trial.

In his introduction to *The Olympia Reader* (1965), which featured forty-one selections from his list, Girodias portrayed himself as persecuted hero in the long-running cultural drama of literati vs. philistines, relating in tedious detail his financial and legal troubles as the premier publisher of "d.b.'s"—his glib shorthand for "dirty books." In contrast to Sontag's persona as sophisticate, he saw himself as a sincere light-bringer in the old reformer mold of Theodore Schroeder or Morris Ernst. Pornography, he insisted, was not merely a means to pleasure for the reader or to monetary gain for the writer but the final fulfillment of the long revolt against gentility: "Writing d.b.'s was generally considered a professional exercise as well as a necessary participation in the fight against the Square World—an act of duty." Girodias tried earnestly to define "the Square World," and unwittingly showed how fugitive the enemy had become, how predictable and feeble generational revolt itself was once it was simply "an act of duty":

> What the Square World exactly was, nobody could have explained with any precision: but the notion was very strong, indeed; and it was not the usual routine of a new generation picking a quarrel with the old, it was a much stronger and deeper protest; not a protest against war or hunger, or against the bomb, but beyond that, a protest against the mental weakness, the poverty of spirit, and the general lack of genius and generosity of a rich and sclerotic society.[30]

The more Girodias tried to distinguish the pornographer's revolt against "the Square World" from earlier generational rebellions, the more his argument resembled—in degenerate form—precisely the earliest claims advanced against the genteel tradition by George Santayana, Van Wyck Brooks, and Randolph Bourne at the turn of the century. But where they had hoped that the democratic poetry of Whitman or the realist fiction of Dreiser might establish "a genial middle ground" between the otherworldly vision of the Puritan and the crass "catchpenny realities" of the businessman, Girodias's boastful account of the new avant-garde once again revealed that it was running on empty: "The colorful banner of pornography was as good as any other to rally the rebels: the more ludicrous the form of the revolt, the better it was, as the revolt was against ordinary logic, and ordinary good taste, restraint, and current morals."[31] The revolt of Girodias's band of pornographers against the Square World, then, was purely reactive, its only aim being shock.

In her famous essay "The Pornographic Imagination" (1967), Sontag showed herself to be as devoted as Girodias to keeping the avant-garde alive. Where Girodias's blind dedication to the myth of the avant-garde was of a piece with his uncritical belief in progress and his pleasure in provocation, it is startling that Sontag, who prided herself on ironic detachment, ended up making the most earnest claims yet for the avant-garde status of some pornography. "Some pornographic books are interesting and important works of art," she confidently announced, and, trying to lift the subject above mere prurient interest, chided her readers: "We might be able to regard [them] (in the role of connoisseur, rather than client) with more sympathy or intellectual curiosity or aesthetic sophistication." Her candidates for this distinction came from "the French literary canon" that included Sade, Apollinaire, Georges Bataille, *The Story of O*, and *The Image*. Modern artists were "freelance explorer[s] of spiritual dangers," she claimed, and praised them for "making forays into and taking up positions on the frontier of consciousness (often very dangerous to the artist as a person) and reporting back what's there." Yet, so remote was the possibility of a genuine avant-garde that Sontag dredged up the old bogey of the earliest American realists—the long-discredited genteel tradition—to boost the alleged advances made by her candidates for vanguard honors: "His job is inventing trophies of his experiences—objects and gestures that fascinate and enthrall, not merely (as prescribed by older notions of the artist) edify or entertain."[32]

Having diminished the radicality of avant-garde art to simply a theatrical display of the artist's personal experiences, another species of dandyism, Sontag, like Girodias, was unwittingly disclosing the self-defeating trajectory of an avant-garde so narrowly conceived: "His principal means of fascinating is to advance one step further in the dialectic of outrage. He seeks to make his work repulsive, obscure, inaccessible; in short, to give what is, or seems to be, *not* wanted." The artistic pornographer is thus companion to the enthusiast of camp as well as the belligerent child: each obligingly does the opposite of what is expected in the name of defining the self through rebellion. Sontag did not question how art that is supposed to be radical had deteriorated into this essentially reactive position—a formulaic game of "the dialectic of outrage" played with a willing and eager audience. Without a touch of irony, she persisted in the familiar myth of the romantic artist: "The exemplary modern artist is a broker in madness."[33]

It is not only the clichéd quality of these claims—a sorry caricature of Arthur Rimbaud's feverish image of himself as a deranged outlaw —that raises doubts about her project; it is also telling that she made no argument for the innovativeness of pornography as an artistic form, though this kind of innovation had been the distinguishing mark of modern fiction from Proust to Joyce to Beckett. Instead, Sontag devoted close to half her essay to readings of Sade's *120 Days of Sodom*, *The Story of O*, *The Image*, and Bataille's *Histoire de l'Oeil* and *Madame Edwarda*, complete with old-fashioned plot summaries, character analyses, and comparisons with other works. Her concluding remarks on *The Story of O* are representative:

O's quest is neatly summed up in the expressive letter which serves her for a name. "O" suggests a cartoon of her sex, not her individual sex but simply woman; it also stands for a nothing. But what *Story of O* unfolds is a spiritual paradox, that of the full void and of the vacuity that is also a plenum.[34]

The problem before Sontag was the same one that confronted the first American realists who wanted to depict everyday life without producing banal art, and early sex radicals who wanted to speak the truth about sex without descending into the illicit region of obscenity, but hers was more daunting: how to make a serious argument for "pornography as an art form" without reproducing its language or effects. Sontag's solution was to give her subject a philosophical tone. But, since she was treating representations of sexual perversities involving brutality, mutilation, and humiliation, the grandeur of her ambitions overwhelmed the smallness and nastiness of her subject, producing her inflated almost camp style.

In the end, Sontag's argument for pornography as an art form rested on the claim she made for "its peculiar access to some truth." "What pornographic literature does is precisely to drive a wedge between one's existence as a full human being and one's existence as a sexual being—while in ordinary life a healthy person is one who prevents such a gap from opening up." Here she distanced herself both from therapeutic proponents of exposure, like the Kinsey researchers, who saw sex primarily in terms of health and pleasure, and from liberationists like Girodias's pornographers, who saw pornography not only as a healthy release from repression but as both the foundation and the expression of freedom.[35] In contrast, Sontag's perspective shared something with those people and societies who appreciate that sexual experience can be degrading or transcendent, for she emphasized how pornography compels the essential doubleness of sex into consciousness. The similarity, however, ends there. Rather than viewing pornography as an invasion of privacy that turns the most sublime and tender aspects of love into mere bodily functions, detached and bizarre, Sontag celebrated it, and especially representations of the "demonic forces" of sex, for revealing "the voluptuous yearning for the extinction of one's consciousness, for death itself." The pornography of "the French literary canon" was to be appreciated for revealing "something beyond good and evil, beyond love, beyond sanity; . . . a resource for ordeal and for breaking through the limits of consciousness."[36]

What is at stake here is not only our judgment about which kinds of aesthetic experience are worth having but, more fundamentally, the limits of knowledge and the limits of representation. For what I have called the party of reticence, sex is a mystery and, therefore, as unrepresentable as it is unapproachable; to speak of it is to try to deprive it of its power. For Sontag, too, sex is a mystery, but one that can be approached, represented, and "participated in," and the kind of pornography she had in mind "capitalizes on that mystery; it isolates the mystery and makes the reader aware of it, invites him to participate in it."[37] In the end, Sontag's receptivity to *all* experiences, her refusal to close off any possibilities in art or life, spoke—ironically—to the continued hold of liberal habits of mind even on those who vociferously rejected its tradition.

And while Sontag presented her version of pornography as a breathtaking advance in sophisticated taste, the pornographic imagination, in fact, resembles an old and well-worn commodity, the kind of reporting that was once the hallmark of late-nineteenth-century invasive journalism. Critics then quoted popular aphorisms to show that the spirit animating invasive journalism was located deep in consciousness: "We take a secret pleasure in the misfortunes of our best friends"; "Old Cato is as great a rogue as you." At bottom, there burns a hatred of distinction and, with it, a rage to violate privacy, revel in baseness, and extinguish consciousness of difference. Invasive journalists, pornographers—"high" and "low"—and their rapacious audiences want to drag everyone down—not just the high and mighty or the accomplished few, but also themselves—to the equality of the condition of having a body, where no one can escape the pull of biological necessity.

THE LEGAL VINDICATION OF "LITERARY" PORNOGRAPHY

A similar, if not so urbane, defense of pornography was simultaneously being waged by First Amendment lawyers, Supreme Court justices, English professors, and literary critics. In 1965, three obscenity cases came before the Supreme Court. Two convictions—in *Ginzburg* v. *United States* and *Mishkin* v. *New York*, both concerning commercial pornography exploiting homosexuality, sadomasochism, and fetishism—were upheld; while the prosecution victory in *A Book Named "John Cleland's Memoirs of a Woman of Pleasure" et al.* v. *Attorney General of Massachusetts* was overturned on the grounds that the novel in question, *Fanny Hill*, had "literary, historical, and social importance" and was therefore not "utterly without redeeming social value."[38]

Sontag relegated *Fanny Hill* to a lower "rank as literature" than the classics of French pornography, but the appellant's attorney, Charles Rembar, did his best to demonstrate the solid literary standing of *Fanny Hill*, and he had a cadre of experts—mainly English professors—to attest to its literary values. Almost all of them praised the book as "well-written." One went so far as to declare the character Fanny Hill an "intellectual"—"someone who is extremely curious about life and who seeks . . . to record the details of the external world, physical sensations, psychological responses." Another told the court that it was "widely accredited as the first deliberately dirty novel in English."[39]

What emerged in the majority opinion, written by Justice Douglas, was a recalibrated version of the test developed in *Roth* v. *United States.* A work is obscene, according to Justice Douglas, if it has three characteristics: "the dominant theme of the material taken as a whole appeals to a prurient interest in sex"; "the material is patently offensive because it affronts contemporary community standards relating to the description and representation of sexual matters"; and "the material is utterly without redeeming social value." The first two conditions restated the test developed in *Roth*, but the third condition had not been a part of the original Roth test. In his dissent, Justice Clark declared that "such a condition rejects the basic holding of Roth and gives the smut artist free rein to carry on his dirty business."[40]

While the other two decisions upholding the convictions kept open the possibility that the legal concept of obscenity still had a role to play in society, that there were fourteen separate opinions handed down in these three cases suggests the extent of the disagreement about both the meaning of obscenity and its continued viability as a legal concept. This extraordinary number of opinions both reflected and added to the growing confusion about what was fit to appear in public during the 1960s. And it is in the dissenting opinions that the terms of our contemporary disputes about obscenity were given their now familiar form, enshrining both moral relativism and the primacy of free speech into the law.

What is perhaps most surprising about these dissents, in particular Justice Douglas's, is that in their role as the voice of the state—the voice of patriarchal, repressive authority—they resemble no one so much as Sontag, the voice of the new, hip, receptive sensibility. The Supreme Court dissenters do nothing less than codify 1960s permissiveness. Where Sontag made claims for the commonality of sadomasochism when she asserted that "everyone has felt (at least in fantasy) the erotic glamour of physical cruelty and an erotic lure in things that are vile and repulsive," Justice Douglas observed that some publications that have been found obscene appeal to "the masochistic yearning that is probably present in everyone and dominant in some." Douglas, however, lacked Sontag's philosophical ambitions. When he defined masochism, he did not speak, as she did, of "the voluptuous yearning for the extinction of one's consciousness, for death itself," but rather in prosaic, if more direct, terms: masochism was "a desire to be punished or subdued. . . . The desire may be expressed in the longing to be whipped and lashed, bound and gagged, and cruelly treated."[41]

Justice Douglas was anxious, as he was in his Roth dissent, to present himself as the most liberated, non-judgmental Supreme Court justice. Thus, he asked provocatively, "Why is it unlawful to cater to the needs of this [masochistic] group?" Where Sontag claimed that French writers of pornography were heroic outlaws on the edge of consciousness and, by extension, that those who appreciated their labors were courageous, sophisticated, aesthetic adventurers, Justice Douglas, again in more prosaic terms, made a similar claim, observing that Ginzburg's clientele was "somewhat offbeat, nonconformist, and odd." And just as Sontag called for a more generous approach to both pornography and kitsch, the judge, too, called for open-mindedness. Yet, in his hands, the position of open-mindedness deteriorated into an abdication of judgment, which, in turn, led to the utter trivialization of the faculty of taste: "We are not in the realm of criminal conduct, only ideas and tastes. Some like Chopin, others like 'rock and roll.' Some are 'normal,' some are masochistic, some deviant in other respects, such as the homosexual."[42]

This complete leveling of experiences is as much a consequence of the limitations of legal discourse as of the relativization of taste and judgment. As we have seen, the legal imperative to locate actual victims who suffer tangible harm had forced opponents of obscenity regulation into the precarious position of asserting that things which appear in public have no consequences inasmuch as they do not actually lead to "antisocial behavior." This was one source of Justice Douglas's denigration of ideas and of the faculty of taste; another lay in his refusal—or, perhaps, incapacity—to discern the difference between genuine art and commercial entertainment, or between public and private activities. This was evident in his deliberate pairing of Chopin with rock and roll, and his further pairing of both with clinical categorizations of sexual conduct. By treating these fundamentally different kinds of things as if they were equivalent, he acted as if the only difference to be found between them lay not in the experience or activity itself—its scale, its location in the world, its traditions and practices—but rather in individual taste.

Yet, in the end, for Justice Douglas, the question of pornography was a First Amendment issue. Where legal critics of obscenity law such as Lockhart and McClure had insisted that "literature dealing with sex problems and behavior" was as entitled to constitutional protection as "literature dealing with other social and economic problems," Justice Douglas reworked this argument so it would encompass pornography exploiting sexual perversions. Thus, he made a series of moves that have since become the common currency of the party of exposure. First, in keeping with the interest-group pluralism advocated by political scientists and sociologists of the time, he reconceptualized the public sphere as a conglomeration of competing groups or communities, each with its own set of ideas, tastes, and values, and further, that every group deserves First Amendment protection for any of its "expressions":

> Why is freedom of the press and expression denied [deviant groups]? Are they to be barred from communicating in symbolisms important to them? . . . Why is not a minority "value" cognizable? The masochistic group is one; the deviant group is another. Is it not important that members of those groups communicate with each other? . . . If the communication is of value to the masochistic community or to others of the deviant community, how can it be said to be "utterly without any redeeming social importance"? "Redeeming" to whom? "Importance" to whom?[43]

Next, and most ingeniously, he recast pornography that "caters to the taste of the most unorthodox amongst us" as the latest example of the expression of an embattled minority threatened by suppression at the hands of the majority.[44] Justice Douglas's provocative use of the word "unorthodox"—a key word in First Amendment literature—was calculated to dissociate pornography from smut and miraculously turn it into a species of dissident speech. His project was the political counterpart to Sontag's effort to elevate French pornography to the status of "risky," advanced art. In addition, by characterizing Ginzburg's pornography as appealing to "unorthodox" tastes, he was deliberately playing on Justice Brennan's declaration in Roth that the First Amendment does not protect libel, blasphemy, profanity, and obscenity. Justice Brennan's remarks bear repeating in this context:

All ideas having even the slightest redeeming social importance—unorthodox ideas, controversial ideas, even ideas hateful to the prevailing climate of opinion—have the full protection of the guaranties, unless excludable because they encroach upon the limited area of more important interests, but implicit in the history of the First Amendment is the rejection of obscenity as utterly without redeeming social importance.[45]

It is also worth recalling that in Roth, Justice Brennan had given special emphasis to the essentially political purpose of the First Amendment: it "was fashioned to assure unfettered interchange of ideas for the bringing about of political and social changes desired by the people." As we have seen, this traditional understanding had already been weakened in *Winters* v. *New York* (1948), the case concerning violent crime stories and graphic pictures in a magazine called *Headquarters Detective: True Cases from the Police Blotter*, where the Supreme Court admitted that even though it could "see nothing of any possible value to society in these magazines," they nonetheless were "as much entitled to the protection of free speech as the best of literature."[46]

In his dissent in Ginzburg, Justice Stewart expressed similar sentiments, further dissolving the political purpose of the First Amendment and, in so doing, trivializing this most cherished liberal right. He began by saying, "Personally, I have a hard time discerning any [artistic and social merit]. Most of the material strikes me as vulgar and unedifying." But then, introducing a rhetorical device that would be repeatedly employed into our own time, which demonstrates that the writer is so devoted to absolute free speech that he will not be swayed—not even by his own taste and judgment—to regulate anything, he announced, "But if the First Amendment means anything, it means that a man cannot be sent to prison merely for distributing publications which offend a judge's esthetic sensibilities, mine or any other's."[47]

Given the dismal history of the infringement of the First Amendment—in particular, the arrests made during World War I of those who courageously spoke out against the war, most famously, the imprisonment of Eugene V. Debs and the deportation of Emma Goldman—it is astounding to see Supreme Court justices making pornography a litmus test of the First Amendment. Yet for Justice Stewart—and he was not alone—the First Amendment had shed its fundamentally political associations. He described its purpose as "protect[ing] coarse expression as well as refined, and vulgarity no less than elegance." This distinction recalls the one judges were struggling to make in the 1920s and 1930s when attempting to come to terms with the literary style appropriate to realism and modernism. But it is also important to remember that they never imagined vulgar language to be a First Amendment issue, which again reveals by contrast how far dissenting voices on the Supreme Court in the 1960s had moved from the earlier understanding of protected speech.

When Justice Stewart offered his vision of a "free society," it was essentially a vision of private individuals exercising their right to choose in matters of personal consumption. And when he discussed the relation of the First Amendment to a free society, he had nothing to say about spirited public debate among citizens about common, though disputed, ideals and projects; he spoke only of competing personal tastes and preferences that require tolerance on the part of "neighbors." "A book worthless to me may convey something of value to my neighbor," he observed. "In the free society to which our Constitution has committed us, it is for each of us to choose for himself."[48]

By the mid-1960s, there were no traces in legal discourse of the reticent sensibility with its appreciation of the fragility of private activities and experiences, which, almost a century earlier, had provided the grounds for obscenity legislation in the first place. This was also true of a related branch of law that emerged at the same time and was involved in demarcating many of the same boundaries as obscenity law—the right to privacy. Louis Brandeis and Samuel Warren's understanding of the pressing need to protect privacy for the sake of both individual dignity and the durability of the public sphere was, by the 1960s, typically greeted with derision and condescension. William L. Prosser's extremely influential essay "Privacy" (1960), which challenged the idea of privacy as an overriding interest in this area of tort law, set the tone. Circulating what turned out to be a false rumor about the motive behind Brandeis and Warren's famous article—that the "Brahmin" Warren had become "annoyed" "when the newspapers had a field day on the occasion of the wedding of a daughter" —Prosser belittled Warren's reaction: "It was an annoyance for which the press, the advertisers, and the entertainment industry of America were to pay dearly over the next seventy years."[49]

Alan Westin's debunking approach toward theorists of the right to privacy in his authoritative study *Privacy and Freedom* (1967) is also representative: "The movement begun by Godkin's and Warren-Brandeis's essays was essentially a protest by spokesmen for patrician values against the rise of the political and cultural values of 'mass society.'" Also typical of the legal commentators was their dismissal of mental anguish as merely an artifact of an overly fastidious age. Harry Kalven, a leading First Amendment scholar, condescendingly declared, "There is a curious nineteenth-century quaintness about the grievance, an air of injured gentility. . . . One may wonder if the tort is not an anachronism, a nineteenth-century response to the mass press which is hardly in keeping with the more robust tastes and mores of today." Paul Freund put the matter to rest once and for all in 1971: "At best this tort is a bourgeois value, deserving only a low priority among the pressing concerns of the law. . . . In its original form, the right of privacy is trivial and rather outdated."[50]

11

THE LAST STAND
OF RETICENCE

By the 1960s, the most "advanced" legal commentators and judges, English professors and cultural critics were at one not only in their embrace of the new sensibility but also in their contempt for those who were troubled by it. They dismissed such people as repressed and overly serious or accused them of wanting simply to inculcate bourgeois values in the masses. But their opponents, another generation of writers and commentators to be mortified anew by what appeared to be a final repudiation of the values they cherished, responded with vigor. "Civilization, and humanity, nothing less," declared Irving Kristol in 1971, was at stake:

> The idea that "everything is permitted," as Nietzsche put it, rests on the premise of nihilism and his nihilistic implications. . . . We are here confronting the most fundamental of philosophical questions, on the deepest levels. But that is precisely my point, and that the matter of pornography and obscenity is not a trivial one, and that only superficial minds can take a bland and untroubled view of it.[1]

This would be the last time a principled argument was made against the party of exposure by critics who were not easily brushed off with charges of prudery, lack of sophistication, or elitism. This body of criticism, while it has almost completely fallen into oblivion today, is singular not only in its passion and elegance but in its willingness to consider the crucial relationship between what is said or done in public and the cultural and political life of a democracy. In contrast to the most vocal critics of pornography today—whether politicians and public figures of the Jesse Helms variety, who grandiosely don the mantle of comstockery, or legal feminists, who are straitjacketed by the narrow legal categories of harm and victims—they were the last, though unknowing, inheritors of the reticent sensibility in its most universal aspects—notably its respect for the limits of knowledge and, in turn, the limits of representation. Irving Howe, for example, in "The Idea of the Modern" (1967), criticized epigones of modernism in precisely such terms: "The traditional values of decorum, in both the general ethical sense and the strictly literary sense, are overturned. Everything must now be explored to its outer and inner limits; but more, there may be no limits."[2]

Where their nineteenth-century predecessors had been arrayed against invasive journalism, realist fiction, and sex-reform literature, and their immediate precursors against mass culture, now they were forced to confront pornography—both "high" and "low." As the levels of public violence, lewdness, and indecency required to incite shock rose ever higher, the insight of the party of reticence was once again affirmed: repeated exposure to indecency ultimately inures people and threatens to make all of society shameless, in the precise sense that it considers nothing sacred. The brazen appearance of pornography in places where it had not been seen before—in over-the-counter books and magazines, on movie screens, on the stage, and on the streets—was so outrageous and its crass commercial spirit so different from that of early targets of censorship that even some of the most distinguished free-speech advocates began to ponder the wisdom of their lifelong commitment. In 1964, Donald Friede, publisher of suppressed novels such as Radclyffe Hall's *Well of Loneliness* and Theodore Dreiser's *An American Tragedy* voiced his second thoughts: "When I see some of the books published today, I cannot . . . but wonder if our fight against censorship in the twenties was really wise. . . . *Fanny Hill* in paper! And *Naked Lunch* in any form! . . . But I suppose there are some people still willing to play the piano in the literary brothel. Certainly the pay is good."[3]

On January 5, 1970, the *New York Times* reported that "Morris Ernst, the noted civil liberties lawyer and long-time opponent of censorship, declared yesterday that he would not choose 'to live in a society without limits to freedom.' " This was indeed a dramatic turnaround. Apparently, even Ernst—dedicated proponent of free speech, free love, and nudism—could not stomach the "present display of sex and sadism on the streets and on the stage." He was stunned by the spread of "four-letter words out of context," by the performance of "sodomy on the stage or masturbation in the public area." Surely his lifelong project had miscarried when purveyors of pornography could claim they were completing the movement begun by his own brilliant defense of *Ulysses*, where, as he put it, he had "legitimatized a four-letter word." "I deeply resent the idea," sniffed the newly chastened Ernst, "that the lowest common denominator, the most tawdry magazine, pandering for profit, to use the Supreme Court's word, should be able to compete in the marketplace with no constraints."[4]

It was not only these confessions of doubt by decorated veterans of censorship battles that indicated something had gone terribly wrong. The argument for free expression itself was so hackneyed that critics easily noted its predetermined form. That they could set out the positions of both sides in advance testifies to the interminability and fruitlessness of the discussion. Yet, because commentators largely identified with the progressive values of the party of exposure, they did not vigorously challenge the caricature of those who would regulate obscenity. Instead, they acknowledged, in the words of C. Herman Pritchett, that "the intellectual debate over the handling of obscenity has been a highly unequal combat." Four features of the standard caricature of "Victorians" and "Puritans" were given prominence: their legendary parochialism, self-righteousness, and moralism; their twisted psychology of sexual repression and prurient prudery; their incapacity to appreciate avant-garde art; and their propensity for censorship and their authoritarian leanings, which, in cold-war terms, raised Orwell's specters of "Big Brotherism" and *1984*. On the other side, the party of exposure had successfully positioned itself at the forefront of battles for individual freedom and free expression. The English novelist Storm Jameson, irritated with these paltry choices, complained, "There is little to choose in self-righteousness and irrationality between the outraged moralist and the dogmatic liberal. Because he is fighting a losing battle the first is possibly less of a bore, but it is a near thing."[5] But these rigid stances proved remarkably impervious to criticism; against all odds, they continue to determine the range and outcome of our disputes about the character of our common world.

Even worse than the risk of being summarily dismissed as Victorian or Puritan was the unavoidable inner tension which plagued the modern sophisticated intellectual who had been raised believing in the twin myths of the avant-garde and of progress. Since these intellectuals, like their opponents, held personal freedom and free expression in the highest esteem, they found it awkward to criticize those who pushed their own commitments into areas they had never anticipated. Reflecting upon liberals' ironclad attachment to absolute free speech, the political philosopher Walter Berns summed up the problem of those who would take a principled stance in favor of obscenity regulation: "To be a liberal is to be against censorship or it is to be nothing." Irving Howe noted comparable difficulties facing writers who had always ardently championed advanced art but now found themselves "not quite enchanted with the current scene":

Given the notorious difficulties in making judgments about contemporary works of art, how can they be certain that Kafka is a master of despair and Burroughs a symptom of disintegration, Pollock a pioneer of innovation and Warhol a triviality of pop? The capacity for self-doubt, the habit of self-irony which is the reward of decades of experience, renders them susceptible to the simplistic cries of the new.[6]

A publisher of risky books, a civil libertarian, a political theorist, and a champion of literary modernism and socialism—these were by no stretch of the imagination latter-day Victorians or Puritans, yet in their distaste for the excesses of the new sensibility, they found themselves playing the role historically reserved for foes of free expression and advanced art. The most impassioned effort to understand this strange turn of events is Howe's "The New York Intellectuals" (1968), an essay that was both an elegy for his own generation, who had "come too late" to participate firsthand in either political radicalism or modernist literature, and a scathing attack on those who rejected wholesale his generation's aspirations and principles.

THE WILLFUL SHALLOWNESS
OF THE NEW SENSIBILITY

One of the most illuminating distinctions Howe drew between the new sensibility—whose "high priests" were Norman O. Brown, Herbert Marcuse, and Marshall McLuhan, its leading "publicists" Susan Sontag and Leslie Fiedler, and its most noted novelist the "literary swinger" Norman Mailer—and the modern sensibility associated with the New York intellectuals and *Partisan Review* concerned the underlying "moral psychology" of each and their respective relation to a particular literary tone. In the liberated 1960s, to raise the question of "moral psychology" was to risk the epithets "square," "old-fashioned," and "moralistic." Howe, himself a modern sophisticate, was forced into a confessional mode the better to disarm his critics in advance: "I feel a measure of uneasiness, as if it were bad form to violate the tradition of antinomianism in which we have all been raised." Then he moved into forbidden territory:

> What, for "emancipated" people, is the surviving role of moral imperatives, or at least moral recommendations? . . . Are we still to give credit to the idea, one of the few meeting points between traditional Christianity and modern Freudianism, that there occurs and must occur a deep-seated clash between instinct and civilization, or can we

now, with a great sigh of collective relief, dismiss this as still another hang-up, perhaps the supreme hang-up, of Western civilization?[7]

In his confession of Freudian faith, with its conviction that "a high order of culture" and "a complex civilization" depend on the irremediable conflict between instinct and civilization, Howe set himself and his generation apart both from champions of the new sensibility and from the first rebels against Victorian morality. "Now even those of us raised on the premise of revolt against the whole system of bourgeois values," he continued with a great show of self-consciousness, did not "imagine ourselves to be exempt from the irksome necessity of regulation, even if we had managed to escape the reach of the commandments. Neither primitive Christians nor romantic naifs, we did not suppose that we could entrust ourselves entirely to the beneficence of nature, or the signals of our bodies, as a sufficient guide to conduct."[8]

In their reliance upon "the beneficence of nature" as "a sufficient guide" to moral life, proponents of the new sensibility resembled early radicals such as Moses Harman and Ezra and Angela Heywood. Celebrants of an essentially pastoral version of exposure, these first rebels had merged an extravagant assessment of the powers of science with a utopian spirit of social reform, promising equality and freedom in intimate life and the elevation of erotic love to a higher spiritual plane. From their rhapsodic perspective, sex was pure and natural; only superstition, religious dogma, and hypocritical social conventions had perverted it and made it obscene. They believed that the universe was created for human happiness and that the psyche was innocent and good or, at the very least, endlessly pliable. And their counterparts in realist fiction held the same assumptions: if evils—domestic and social—were unveiled, people of good conscience would act to save the world.

Then, in subsequent decades, birth-control champions had determined to dismantle "the conspiracy of silence" and cultural radicals to explode "the genteel tradition," to force the great repressed theme of sex into the open. They demanded that the traditional union of moral and aesthetic judgment be dissolved: the functions of the body needed to be considered apart from the values of love, fidelity, chastity, modesty, or shame; and the artistry of the novel needed to be appreciated apart from its moral lessons. By the late 1920s, however, some reluctant moderns were alarmed by the very successes of the party of exposure. Joseph Wood Krutch expressed dismay at the quality of life—and in particular, love—in a society dedicated to relentless scrutiny of all things. The larger story of demystification that Krutch told had profound reverberations: once science unmasked social practices as bound by place and time, then all values were exposed as relative. And for Krutch, the contingency of values meant despair.

Howe's analysis of modernism takes as its starting point Krutch's recognition of the power of doubt to shatter meaning. But, for Howe, doubt was also a wellspring of creativity. Literary modernism, he declared, "provides a vocabulary through which the most powerful imaginations of the time can act out a drama of doubt." The strenuousness of this drama, the need for "nerves of iron," accounts for the complexity, difficulty, and experimentalism of modernist literature, and this is why Howe ascribed heroic dimensions to it. Here Howe differed from both the sex radicals who hoped to release the tension between civilization and instinct completely on the side of benevolent instinct and from critics like Krutch who saw a world vacated by God, love, and art as a desperately lonely and hopeless place. Howe put nihilism at the core of modernism, acknowledging that it was a force "the writer must subdue or by which he will surely be destroyed."

> Nihilism lies at the center of all that we mean by modernist literature, both as subject and symptom, a demon overcome and a demon victorious. For the terror which haunts the modern mind is that of meaninglessness and eternal death. . . . Heroically, the modern sensibility struggles with its passion for eternal renewal, even as it keeps searching for ways to secure its own end.[9]

Howe believed it was a profound failure to evade this crucial "confrontation and struggle with the demons of nihilism." With nothing less than the practices, principles, and aspirations of modernism hanging in the balance, he charged his extraordinary intellectual and moral energies with fiery vitriol, conjuring a devastating portrait of the new sensibility:

> The new sensibility is impatient with ideas. It is impatient with literary structures of complexity and coherence, only yesterday the catchwords of our criticism. It wants instead works of literature—though literature may be the wrong word—that will be as absolute as the sun, as unarguable as orgasm, and as delicious as a lollipop. It schemes to throw off the weight of nuance and ambiguity, legacies of high consciousness and tired blood. It is weary of the habit of reflection, the making of distinctions, the squareness of dialectics, the tarnished gold of inherited wisdom. It cares nothing of the haunted memories of old Jews. It has no taste for the ethical nail-biting of those writers of the left who

suffered defeat and could never again accept the narcotic of certainty.
. . . It breathes contempt for rationality, impatience with mind, and a
hostility to the artifices and decorums of high culture. It despises liberal
values, liberal cautions, liberal virtues.

Disgusted by what amounted to a perverse dedication to shallowness,
Howe launched one last searing salvo: "The new American sensibility
does something no other culture could have aspired to: it makes nihilism seem casual, good-natured, even innocent."[10]

PORNOGRAPHY: THE ULTIMATE INVASION OF PRIVACY

Where Howe took up arms against the cheerful nihilism of the new
sensibility, other critics sounded the alarm against its nastier, though
equally shallow, incarnation in pornography. One of the most famous
attempts to think critically about pornography is George Steiner's
searching essay "Night Words" (1965), a review of Maurice Girodias's
The Olympia Reader, published in *Encounter* and anthologized many
times over. Steiner, another sophisticated modern, was quick to distinguish himself from prudes and squares who were shocked by such
writing. Eager to demonstrate that he was a connoisseur of the "classics of erotica," Steiner expertly escorted the reader through a grand
tour of the terrain, visiting many of the same sights that Sontag was
later to stake out as "avant-garde." For Steiner, however, pornography
did not represent the last frontier of advanced sensibility. To the
contrary, he complained—in a smart-set style that rivals Sontag's and
outdoes the liberationism of Girodias—that after fifty pages of *The
Olympia Reader*, "the spirit cries out, not in hypocritical outrage, not
because I am a poor Square throttling my libido, but in pure, nau-
seous *boredom*. Even fornication can't be as dull, as hopelessly predictable as all that!"[11]

Having furnished the obligatory proof of his own sophistication,
Steiner then took on the far more important task of judging Girodias's
"assertion about freedom, about a new and transforming liberation of
literature through the abolition of verbal and imaginative taboos."
Steiner set out to assess *The Olympia Reader* according to how well
it satisfied Girodias's vaunted claims for it. In his description of what
freedom for writers consists in, Steiner shares much with Howe's
appreciation of the complexity and nuance of the modern sensibility:
"The sensibility of the writer is free where it is most humane, where

it seeks to apprehend and reenact the marvelous variety, complication, and resilience of life by means of words as scrupulous, as personal, as brimful of mystery of human communication, as the language can yield." And just as Howe deplored the new sensibility for its obstinate attachment to the surface of things, Steiner criticized "high pornography" for the same reasons: "The very opposite of freedom is cliché, and nothing is less free, more inert with convention and hollow brutality than a row of four-letter words."[12]

A new and compelling aspect of Steiner's treatment of pornography was his placing the author's respect both "for the imaginative maturity of his reader, and in a very complex but central way, for the wholeness, for the independence and quick of life, in the personages he creates" at the center of the creative project. Respect, of course, is a key word of the reticent sensibility; it is the outward recognition of the integrity and dignity of other people, which involves the acceptance of limits concerning not only what can be known, seen, or heard about them but also what can be *done* to them both in actuality and in imagination. Steiner found the pornographer utterly incapable of respect:

> There is no real freedom whatever in the compulsive physiological exactitudes of present "high pornography," because there is no respect for the reader whose imaginative means are set at nil. . . . And there is none for the sanctity of autonomous life in the characters of the novel, for that tenacious integrity of existence which makes a Stendhal, a Tolstoy, a Henry James tread warily around their own creations.[13]

The pornographer's incapacity for respect, either for actual readers who exist in the world or for fictional characters who exist in his or her imagination, had, for Steiner, the most diabolical implications: "The novels being produced under the new code of total statement shout at their personages: strip, fornicate, perform this or that act of sexual perversion. So did the S.S. guards at rows of living men and women." His linking "the 'total freedom' of the uncensored erotic imagination and the total freedom of the sadist" was not simply an exaggeration of the well-known argument that obscenity causes "antisocial behavior," nor was it merely an inversion of the claim that censorship irresistibly leads to totalitarianism, though it did take the political high ground away from free-speech absolutists. Rather, it raised the terrible specter that once there are no limits to what is imaginable, then there are no limits to what is possible in the world. This is precisely the point Arendt had made in *The Origins of Totalitarianism*, where she argued that one of the defining characteristics of the "authentically totalitarian structure" is the belief that "everything is possible." And just as Arendt also argued that totalitarianism not only depended on but also accelerated the collapse of public and private, Steiner observed that Nazism and the uncensored erotic imagination "are both exercised at the expense of someone else's humanity, of someone else's most precious right—the right to a private life of feeling."[14]

Steiner's argument once again returns us to the nineteenth-century reticent sensibility, which understood obscenity and invasions of privacy to be one and the same thing, and which invented the legal concepts of sexual obscenity and the right to privacy to protect individuals and the common world from indecent representations. It also returns us to the promise originally offered by liberal society: that the private sphere would provide the requisite space for the flourishing of individuality and personal freedom. This promise of private happiness came in a series of historical trade-offs: eighteenth-century Scottish Enlightenment thinkers, grappling with the rise of a market economy, had calculated that a higher standard of living, along with cosmopolitanism, refinement, politeness, and diversification of personality, would more than compensate for any loss of civic virtue and the practice of self-rule among equals; and when nineteenth-century liberals discovered that industrial society and mass democracy had not delivered on those promises and were instead twin forces of conformity, they turned inward, insisting that the private realm guaranteed the necessary mental and physical conditions for freedom, autonomy, individuality, and creativity. Steiner, then, spoke as a liberal who held privacy—and not the public realm—to be the locus of individuality and freedom and, furthermore, held that people have a "right" to their "private life of feeling." He also spoke as an emancipated modern who equated privacy not primarily, as Mill had, with "the inward domain of consciousness," of thought and feeling, opinion and sentiment, tastes and pursuits, but with sexual experience, which he placed at the core of one's identity: "It is in sexual experience that a human being alone, and two human beings in that attempt at total communication which is also communion, can discover the unique bent of their identity."[15]

One of the reasons that the controversy about pornography had acquired so much significance is that emancipated moderns, who had renounced the elaborate artifices of domesticity that had lent erotic love much of its emotional intensity in the first place, put extraordinary, if not impossible, expectations upon sex in its own right as a source of identity. Faced with an outpouring of clichéd representations of that "last, vital privacy," Steiner found himself in a position similar to that of the critics of mass culture, who had pinned their hopes for individual fulfillment and social progress on leisure-time activities that were, however, undergoing a process of standardization as ruthless as that which had regulated the workplace and deskilled and degraded the worker. In both instances, instead of freedom and meaning, overly hopeful moderns found conformism and emptiness.

In his attack on pornographers for "do[ing] our imagining for us," Steiner resembles critics of mass culture who characterized kitsch as predigested fare which starved the imagination, and nineteenth-century writers who criticized invasive journalism for robbing personal life of its emotional resonance. The new pornographers "take away the words that were of the night and shout them over the roof-tops, making them hollow. The images of our love-making, the stammerings we resort to in intimacy, come pre-packed." Sex, especially in America, he thought, was "passing more and more into the public domain. This is a profoundly ugly and demeaning thing whose effects on our identity and resources of feeling we understand as little as we do the impact on our nerves of the perpetual 'sub-eroticism' and sexual suggestion of modern advertisement." This was precisely the old argument: that repeated exposure to obscenity threatened to cheapen the most precious aspects of intimate life and coarsen the tone of public conversation. "The power to feel, to experience and realize the precarious uniqueness of each other's being, can . . . wither in a society." "Where everything can be said with a shout," Steiner warned his readers, "less and less can be said in a low voice."[16]

OBSCENITY, PUBLIC MORALITY, AND DEMOCRACY

There was still another set of urgent concerns that attracted the attention of political writers. After the Supreme Court's legalization of *Fanny Hill* in 1966, a number of people felt compelled to articulate the consequences for democracy of this dramatic abrogation of society's right to regulate its environment. In an admirable, if neglected, study, *Obscenity and Public Morality: Censorship in a Liberal Society* (1969), Harry M. Clor, a political philosopher, formulated the issue in essentially political terms:

> The problem of obscenity involves far-reaching questions about the nature of our community—the ends and values by which this civil society should be governed—and it also involves the most delicate and

personal interests of individual human beings. The way of life of "We, the People" and the relation between public and private spheres of life are, ultimately, at issue.[17]

Clor had three aims: to define obscenity, to make an argument as to how its free circulation threatens democracy, and finally, to offer a program for legally regulating it. And he wanted to accomplish these tasks without resorting to long-discredited formulations or introducing legal remedies that would threaten free speech.

To accomplish his first task, Clor provided an extensive review of leading legal, sociological, and psychological definitions of obscenity, only to find them all lacking. For Clor, the concept of obscenity was not exhausted by pornography with its explicit sexual content; it also encompassed subject matter that had been at the heart not only of the nineteenth-century party of reticence's attack on exposure but also of the more recent attack on mass culture—tabloid newspapers' lurid portrayals of accidental deaths and "scenes of intense private grief," sensational crime novels like those written by Mickey Spillane, and occasions when too much attention was paid to private bodily functions, such as eating or bathing. In each of these instances, Clor detected the same mechanisms at work:

> 1) Obscenity consists in making public that which is private; it consists in an intrusion upon intimate physical processes and acts or physical-emotional states; and 2) it consists in a degradation of the human dimension of life to a sub-human or merely physical level.[18]

The crucial point here is the awareness of the irreducible doubleness of bodily experiences: on the one hand, because we are part of the biological life cycle, we are always confronted with its futility, as Arendt had made clear; on the other hand, the cultural elaborations of poetry, art, philosophy, religion, manners and morals offer the potential for meaning, as both Krutch and Lippmann had argued. "To the participants, the act of eating, or of sex, can have important personal and supra-biological meanings," observed Clor. "But the outside observer cannot share the experience of these meanings; what he sees is simply the biological process." Recognizing the fragility of this kind of private activity, he appreciated the way "moral attitudes, aesthetic proprieties, and social forms" surround them and serve as "barriers" against their reduction "to a collection of physical properties and reactions."[19] That Clor reached these conclusions—as Krutch and Lippmann had—apparently without recourse to a specific moral tradition once again suggests their deep roots in consciousness. But his sensitive rendering of the fragility of private experiences also

shows the extent to which the modern individual has become estranged from any coherent moral tradition. Whereas members of
tribal societies cleave to pollution rules because those rules are inscribed in the very structure of their universe, the best that alienated
moderns can do is acknowledge, self-consciously, the way biological
necessity threatens to reduce us to the status of a mere body and then
embrace—both critically and gratefully—the cultural artifices that
lend our lives their only possible meanings.

In 1970, Clor elaborated upon how obscenity, as an invasion of
privacy, threatens dignity and, in turn, individuality. Here, like
Steiner, he returns us to the liberal cult of privacy as the locus of
individuality and freedom. In addition, we see once again how liberal
society, because it places such an enormous premium on individuality,
must vigilantly maintain the border between public and private so as
to keep those aspects of existence that have the potential to level us
hidden away from sight:

> It is unlikely that any of us would ever become "individuals" if we
> had to do all of our acts, and particularly all of our physical acts, in
> public. For the physical is that aspect of each man which is the least
> individual, the least unique. Social proprieties render the purely phys-
> iological things less obtrusive in our lives, enabling us to concentrate
> upon the things that distinguish us as individuals. Thus, paradoxical
> as it may seem, the restraints of social convention make a contribution
> to the development of individuality.[20]

It is striking that Edward J. Bloustein, the only modern legal writer
to defend Brandeis and Warren's understanding of the right to privacy
as the protection of "inviolate personality," also invoked "the individual's independence, dignity, and integrity." "I believe," declared
Bloustein, "that what provoked Warren and Brandeis to write their
article was a fear that a rampant press feeding on the stuff of private
life would destroy individual dignity and integrity and emasculate
individual freedom and independence."[21]

With this emphasis on the way that obscenity reduces a dignity-
bearing individual to the condition of being simply an exposed body,
Clor and other critics introduced the notion of objectification, especially the objectification of women, into the debate. After chronicling
violence against and degradation of women in pornographic movies,
Clor hazarded his most complete definition of obscenity: "In the most
general terms, obscenity is that kind of representation which makes a
gross public display of the private physical intimacies of life, and
which degrades human beings by presenting them as mere objects of

impersonal desire or violence." This issue—the demeaning representation of women as things to be used sexually—has become a crucial component of the feminist argument against pornography, and it is important to note that objectification was a central feature of almost all critiques of pornography at this time. For instance, in "The Retreat from the Pleasure Principle," Storm Jameson characterized pornography as "essentially reductive, an exercise in the nothing-but mode, a depersonalizing of the human beings involved, a showing-up of human lust as nothing but an affair of the genitals." Ernest van den Haag's "Is Pornography a Cause of Crime?" also made good use of the objectification argument: "By definition, pornography deindividualizes and dehumanizes sexual acts; by eliminating all the contexts it reduces people simply to bearers of impersonal sensations of pleasure and pain." Anticipating Catharine MacKinnon's analysis of pornography as hate speech directed at women, van den Haag made this same powerful point in a more encompassing way: "Pornographic and finally sadistic literature is anti-human. Were it directed against a specific human group—e.g., Jews or Negroes—the same libertarian ideologues who now oppose censorship might advocate it." The "anti-human" quality of pornography is more compelling as an argument against it, in my judgment, than the current feminist focus on the victimization of women. This is not to deny the particularly cruel and vicious exploitation of women that is at the core of pornography, but to say that the emphasis on the harm inflicted on women alone makes for an overly narrow characterization of obscenity.[22]

Just as this understanding of obscenity is broader and deeper than characterizations offered by later critics, so was Clor's understanding of the consequences of obscene representations in "books, magazines, newspapers, advertising, and motion pictures." As he noted, some researchers insisted that obscenity caused juvenile delinquency, sex crimes, and perversion, while others claimed there was no conclusive proof of a cause-and-effect relation between obscenity and "anti-social behavior," even going so far as to argue that obscenity might work a positive good in society, as a "safety valve" for potentially dangerous behavior. But to Clor, the dangers posed by obscenity, though dire, were too elusive to be captured by the gross measurements of social scientists. Employing terms that uncannily recall the nineteenth-century discourse of reticence, he observed, "The most socially significant issues concern the more subtle and long-term influences of obscenity upon mind and character—its moral effects. Obscenity can contribute to the debasement of moral standards and ultimately of character." And, he thought, one could "become desensitized" when "assaulted by prurient and lurid impressions." Both fueling and accompanying this desensitization was the weakening of the faculties that decide how the world should look—taste and judgment: "Obscenity promotes the grosser passions; its corroding effect is upon the higher or more refined feelings—those upon which ethical and aesthetic discrimination depend."[23]

In his description of the ultimate harm caused by obscenity, Clor evoked the Aristotelian political tradition, introducing a set of concerns that had not appeared in the debate before: "Liberal democracy and the constitutional system of government depend, for their vitality if not for their sheer survival, upon the character of citizens." And it was obscenity—here Clor used the word as a shorthand for the values of "sexual revolution" promoted by the new sensibility—that threatened the character of citizens. Against the position of sexual liberationists "which deemphasizes moral considerations, and which maximizes considerations of personal taste, personal choice, and personal satisfaction," and the view of libertarians that democracy is "the maximization of individual liberty in every area of life," he argued that citizens who are excessively absorbed in their sensual pleasures lack the discipline upon which "self-control and social responsibility" depend. What Clor had in mind here is the republican idea of the polis that relies on citizens' willingness and capacity "to sacrifice immediate satisfaction to long-term ends." This single-minded pursuit of pleasure, in his view, worked against public-spiritedness, which, in turn, made democracy increasingly remote. "A people devoted exclusively to the satisfaction of sensual appetites is not, strictly speaking, a citizen body at all. It is a collection of private individuals, each concerned with his private gratifications."[24]

Clor's account of the erosion of civic virtue by obscenity is important for showing that celebrants of the new sensibility were resourceless when it came to imagining a public sphere, but it exaggerates the role obscenity plays in promoting self-indulgence. For Clor's penetrating criticism to be cogent, he would need to make the point that self-indulgence—along with self-absorption, narcissism, immediate gratification, and personal happiness—is actively promoted as an end in itself not only by obscenity but also by liberal individualism, consumer capitalism, advertising, post-Freudian psychotherapy, mass culture, and the postmodern academy. From this perspective, the state's relegation of obscenity to the private realm of individual choice is not so much the primary cause of rampant self-involvement as one of its most feverish symptoms.

The Supreme Court's extreme reluctance to regulate obscenity also signified something more. By the mid-1960s, the new-sensibility credo, "do your own thing" had made its way into legal discourse through the concept of "victimless crimes": private activities between "consenting adults" that depart from community standards of morality but do not interfere with the rights of others—e.g., obscenity, pornography, prostitution, homosexuality, drugs, gambling—and therefore should not be regulated by the state.[25] This formulation completely deprived obscenity of any public, moral, or aesthetic dimension and rendered it utterly trivial. Moreover, the notion of a victimless crime is tautological: since individual "victims" are in fact consenting to the activity in question, there can be no crime; this is the logical outcome of the legal hunt for victims and it reveals once again the resourcelessness of liberal jurisprudence in the face of harms suffered by the public at large.

A crucial component of Clor's project was to make a case against this extremely minimalist formulation of the law, and he did so most effectively by contrasting it with the Aristotelian understanding of law as not only educative but also embodying the highest ideals of a polity. Against the victimless-crime mentality, which sees obscenity censorship as legislating private morality, Clor appealed to the public good: "Government may concern itself with morality, not in order to promote the virtuous character of individuals, but in order to prevent such a degree of vice as is incompatible with the health of society and the security of government." To justify the legitimacy of censorship in a liberal democracy, he set out an argument "concerning the need for public standards designed to maintain the minimal moral requisites of decency, social responsibility, and citizenship." Here he brought to the fore aspects of American social life that were once central to the nineteenth-century vision of the good life but had disappeared from disputes not only about obscenity and free speech but also about democracy. "The enterprise of self-government requires mutual respect and certain capacities of self-restraint, or, as these things used to be called, 'civility.'" In another context, he argued, "Civil society has an interest in the maintenance of, at least, that level of moral sensibility that is implied in the term 'decency.'" As for libertarians and sexual liberationists who made "personal taste, personal choice, and personal satisfaction" the only aims of democracy, Clor pointedly reminded them, "Our country is not only liberal—it is also democratic; it is also constitutional; it is also civilized. Our country is a liberal democracy, but it is also a civil society subject to the needs and purposes of civil life."[26]

The salient point here is that modern, laissez-faire, capitalist society was never conceived exclusively in libertarian terms of doing as one pleases so long as no one else is hurt. As we have seen, civility and decency had been envisioned as essential components of the good life since the birth of commercial society in the eighteenth century. The pursuit of civility through the exercise of good manners became an alternative to the pursuit of civic virtue: diversification of personality, sociability, refinement, and culture would be the rewards of commercial society and they would redeem the loss of civic virtue that was its price.[27] What is more, politeness, civility, and common decency would smooth relations not only between strangers in the new market society but also among friends and family in the newly discovered realm of intimacy. Without these social arts, life would not be worth living. Henry James's famous words bear repeating here: "There are decencies that in the name of the general self-respect we must take for granted, there's a kind of rudimentary intellectual honor to which we must, in the interest of civilization, at least pretend."[28]

That James felt compelled to make this announcement—and he did so to justify the seemingly unrealistic responses of some of his own fictional characters to publicity in his time—indicates that by his time the earlier vision of a society at once commercial, civil, polite, and refined, had largely vanished. This is implicit in Charles Eliot Norton's tortured attempt to balance material and moral progress. Material progress, from his perspective, entailed both a widespread coarsening of morals and manners and a decline in the quality of the arts. "The 'put money in thy purse' doctrine," as one critic of the new journalism put it, "[operated] without the slightest regard to the feelings or rights of others to truth, manhood, honor, or common decency."[29]

And while the profit motive had a corrosive effect on those values, an equally potent threat came from an unlikely source—avowed friends of personal freedom and individuality who attempted to translate these liberal ideals into life. Heirs to the Enlightenment project of spreading light into dark places, they repeatedly argued that the progressive values promoted by their projects of exposure took precedence over politeness and gentility. Apologists for invasive journalism, like later apologists for mass culture, insisted that vulgarity and incivility were a small price to pay for the benefits of free expression. Champions of sex education assured their audiences that the truth gained from scientific discoveries would more than compensate for any loss of delicacy or feelings of shame arising from violations of reticence. And Reginald Wright Kauffman's taunt, "If it is right to tell the truth, every place is the right place to tell it," vividly expresses

the impetus behind the new literary candor.[30] The younger generation's fight for personal freedom, individuality, and social justice demanded an active assault on "the genteel tradition"; from their
vantage point, decency and civility were simply other names for hypocrisy. Thus it is that the story of how reticence got a bad name
also accounts for how civility and decency disappeared from debates
about obscenity, free speech, and democracy. But their absence guarantees that these debates will be repetitive, shallow, and shrill.

The Need for Judgment
and Taste

What, then, was to be done about the menace posed by the new
sensibility? Steiner flatly rejected censorship, calling it "stupid," "repugnant," and unworkable, yet in the same breath maintained, "This
is entirely different from saying that pornography doesn't in fact deprave the mind of the reader, or incite to wasteful or criminal gestures." Clor patiently and carefully put forward a rational program of
censorship suited to a liberal, democratic, civil society. "If the circulation of obscenity is to be controlled at all," he insisted, "then drawing the line requires the exercise of political judgment in the broadest
and deepest sense." In his description of what political judgment consisted in, Clor emphasized its inherent difficulty: "It is never an easy
matter to acquire, and to combine, theoretical and practical wisdom,
to reason rightly about fundamental principles, *and* to apply principles
with intelligent sensitivity to changing circumstances."[31]

For Howe, who never raised the possibility of censorship in his
discussion of the new sensibility, the rigorous exercise of judgment
and taste was the only antidote. But the "tradition of the new" gave
a clear advantage to those who claimed modernist status for the new
sensibility, even if from Howe's point of view the claim was intellectually evasive, if not outright dishonest: "The effort to assimilate new
cultural styles to the modernist tradition brushes aside problems of
value, quality, judgment. It rests upon a philistine version of the theory of progress in the arts: all must keep changing, and change
signifies a realization of progress." Howe's insight into the uncritical
but successful connection of the avant-garde with novelty and change,
and the further automatic link of change with progress in the arts,
applies with equal force to the position of free-speech absolutists.
Libertarians, as Clor rightly pointed out, while deeply skeptical about

moral standards and truth, nonetheless have boundless faith in discussion and debate about them. "The only standard of value" about which they are not skeptical, according to Clor, is " 'change.' " Offering Morris Ernst as the exemplar of this position, he observed, "In Ernst's writings, change—the erosion of old values and their replacement by new ones—is always presented, not only as inevitable, but as unquestionably desirable." For libertarians—and here they resemble not only champions of the avant-garde but also Hollywood, Madison Avenue, and the fashion industry—" 'new' is synonymous with 'good.' "[32]

It was not only that publicists of the new sensibility had progress on their side. Howe also pointed to "the notorious difficulties in making judgments about contemporary works of art," and he knew that the hard-won "capacity for self-doubt, the habit of self-irony" that were the among the most valued accomplishments of sophisticated intellectuals left them "susceptible to the simplistic cries of the new." To the question, how could they be certain of their low estimation of the work of new-sensibility masters like Burroughs and Warhol, Howe had a no-nonsense answer: "There can be no certainty: we should neither want nor need it. One must speak out of one's taste and conviction, and let history make whatever judgments it will care to."[33]

Yet, as we have seen throughout this book, taste was among the first casualties of the devastating cultural war waged against nineteenth-century reticence. Taste has become as empty and relativized as its associated concepts such as judgment, which is generally understood as "judgmental," and discrimination, which means little more than "social discrimination" these days. Nevertheless, critics of the new sensibility in the 1960s *did* have the courage of their convictions to challenge the most extreme wing of the party of exposure with its hoarse battle cry that nothing is sacred and everything is permitted. What they were confronting were exaggerated, sometimes perverse expressions of many of their own principles and ideals. The new aesthetic which valued both mass culture and the "classics" of French pornography as the last word in advanced sensibility and the new legal framework which pictured obscenity as a victimless crime took familiar arguments, once advanced by birth-control champions and by supporters of Dreiser and Joyce, and pressed them to their outermost reaches.

In this way, the new sensibility had the same relation to the postwar party of exposure as comstockery had to the nineteenth-century party of reticence: they are deformed offshoots of their respective parties.

Comstockery intersected with reticence in its insistence that moral and aesthetic judgment were part of the same continuum and that private matters could not be indiscriminately paraded in public. But they were worlds apart in tone: politeness, tact, civility, and cosmopolitanism were the keynotes of the party of reticence, all of which the Comstocks lacked; their range was severely limited by their prejudice, overwrought moralism, religious zeal, and their singular inability to appreciate that some private matters, if miraculously transformed by art, could properly appear in public.

The new sensibility intersected with the postwar party of exposure in its insistence that aesthetic and moral questions were questions of individual taste, and that private matters, in the name of personal freedom and individuality, must see the light of day; they most significantly differed in the blanket refusal on the part of libertarians and members of the postmodern academy to make distinctions between genuine art on the one hand and mass culture or pornography on the other. In their prejudice, dogmatism, and self-righteousness, as well as in their uncritical allegiance to conventional habits of mind, their refusal to engage their opponents directly, and their automatic reliance on name-calling and debunking, the new sensibility and comstockery are brothers under the skin. And in their absolutism in matters of censorship, both positions betray a deep-seated fear that neither unfettered speech nor censorship is containable, that neither can be tempered by judgment or taste.

What became unbearable about the Comstocks for the younger generation was their refusal to recognize that "the conspiracy of silence" had not only deformed intimate life and established a hypocritical double standard but also had stunted the American imagination, making artistic excellence impossible and culture provincial and third-rate. But, where the younger generation could scoff and laugh at their opponents' antics, today's critics no longer have that luxury. Today it is not a question of Comstock ludicrously trying to stop the Art Students' League from mailing a pamphlet with reproductions of studio nudes. Instead, it is libertarians with the full machinery of the state behind them fighting for the rights of neo-Nazis to march in Skokie, the rights of the Ku Klux Klan to burn crosses, the rights of bigots to scream racial slurs, and the rights of pornographers to their exploitative trade in women. And just as the nineteenth-century party of reticence had been unable or unwilling to discipline the Comstocks, what remains of the postwar party of exposure today appears to be in a similar predicament. The failure, or inattentiveness, of the party of reticence set the stage for the grand cultural battle between moderns and Victorians (or at least their caricature of Victorians); the parallels with our present cultural moment are too obvious to ignore. The libertarian position that permits pornography and uncivil speech is under intense fire not only from legal feminists led by Catharine MacKinnon but also from a related group of legal scholars associated with "Critical Race Theory." Both groups are trying to demonstrate that pornography and racial epithets are actually instances of "hate speech" that require state intervention; they are demanding that the right of equal protection receive priority over the right of free speech.[34] Recent controversies over speech codes on college campuses and "date rape" are further evidence that a younger generation is beginning to find their elders' liberationist position unbearable.

It is striking that the most powerful challenges to the ideology of liberationism are coming from within the legal profession. This strenuous rethinking of the law has gone far in discrediting the trivial notion of victimless crimes and restoring obscenity and other forms of incivil speech to their rightful status as issues of great public concern. But because these critics speak the language of liberal jurisprudence, they, like their opponents, continue to be straitjacketed by the constricting categories of victims and harm, rights and interests. It has been the purpose of this study to argue that liberal jurisprudence has failed to address what is really at stake in controversies about obscenity, mass culture, and avant-garde art—the quality and character of our common world and the fragility of intimacy—and, furthermore, to argue that if we are going to live in a civilized, democratic society worthy of the name, we shall have to enlarge the range of debate by going beyond the legal discourse.

This will entail moving moral and aesthetic judgment out of the shadowy realm of private choice and into the full light of the world which we all inhabit together. While this is no easy task, the effort to escape our present stalemate would at the very least reveal that even though ideas about which things are suitable for public appearance are open to dispute, the possible positions available to us are not so various as people like to think. In fact, I would argue, they boil down essentially to two. Since the discoveries and arguments of Darwin, Nietzsche, Havelock Ellis, and Freud have made the traditional continuity of fact-value judgments impossible for us to maintain—and this appears to be an irrevocable development at least thus far—we are all confronted with the doubleness of bodily experience. Those who consider conventions to be artificial and oppressive will argue for more exposure to reveal the true nature of humanity; for one wing of this party, it is important that we witness, even perhaps revel in, abject experiences like those documented in Robert Mapplethorpe's photographs of extreme sexual brutality and humiliation; for others more pastorally inclined, dualisms must be dissolved so we can live in a non-hierarchical region of bodies, pure and simple. On the other hand, there are those who acknowledge that conventions, though artificial, are not always oppressive and should be accepted with gratitude even while they are rethought, since vital conventions preserve the best wisdom acquired so far concerning what makes life worth living. For this latter-day party of reticence, there must be limits to thought and imagination, to discussion and representation, because they appreciate that the scale of private and intimate activities guarantees they will become banal or obscene if displayed in public, unless they are miraculously transfigured through the grace of art.

These two positions on the limits of knowledge and the limits of representation have their counterparts in modes of intimacy and general dispositions toward life; Milan Kundera, the great novelist of intimate life in our time, has aptly called them lightness and weight. Lightness is essentially an aesthetic temper, where a person tries to lose himself or herself in the immediacy of present experience; the aim of sexual intimacy is pleasure; the mode of erotic engagement is an endless stream of affairs. To live in the perpetual present is to endure the "unbearable lightness of being," in Kundera's memorable phrase, where one is unencumbered by the past and free to imagine any number of possible futures. Yet, living in and for the present moment means that experience is necessarily disjointed and, in consequence, no event can amass larger significance. The competing disposition toward life is ethical in nature. When being is weighted, living is burdened by the past, made heavy by responsibilities that determine the course of the future. Yet, at the same time, this weight gives life its distinctive shape as an unfolding, coherent narrative. Marriage as a state of enduring commitment and heartfelt obligation is its purest expression. Lightness pervades the temper of the liberationist as weight pervades the temper of the reticent person.[35] Lightness or weight—there is no other alternative. And so it is with the quality of public life: either we recognize that certain activities and experiences require privacy to give our lives ballast, or the common world becomes literally shameless and our shared existence without consequence.

NOTES

INTRODUCTION: TASTE AND THE COMMON WORLD

1. Hannah Arendt, "The Crisis in Culture," reprinted in *Between Past and Future* (New York: Penguin Books, 1968, 1985), p. 222.
2. Ronald Dworkin, "Liberty and Pornography," *New York Review of Books*, August 15, 1991, p. 13.
3. "Senate Passes Compromise on Arts Endowment," *New York Times*, October 25, 1990, p. C28.
4. Quoted in Anna Quindlen, "Grand Juries," *New York Times*, October 25, 1990.

I. THE TOPOGRAPHY OF THE HUMAN CONDITION: PUBLIC AND PRIVATE

1. Hannah Arendt, *The Human Condition* (Chicago: University of Chicago Press, 1958), pp. 50, 55.
2. Ibid., pp. 72, 62–63. See also pp. 30–46.
3. Mary Douglas, "Preface," *Implicit Meanings* (London: Routledge & Kegan Paul, 1975), p. xv. "Pollution," reprinted in *Implicit Meanings*, p. 51. See also Douglas, *Purity and Danger: An Analysis of the Concepts of Pollution and Taboo* (London: Routledge, 1966, 1985).
4. Douglas, "Pollution," p. 55. Malinowski quoted in Carl D. Schneider, *Shame, Exposure, and Privacy* (Boston: Beacon Press, 1977), p. 50. Franz Steiner, *Taboo* (London: Pelican Books, 1956, 1967), p. 116.
5. Helen Merrell Lynd, *On Shame and the Search for Identity* (New York: Harcourt, Brace, 1958), p. 27. For an excellent overview of twentieth-century psychoanalytic and anthropological approaches to shame and their contemporary political implications, see Christopher Lasch, "In Defense of Shame," *New Republic*, August 10, 1992, pp. 29–34. For an excellent discussion of obscenity and shame, see Harry M. Clor, *Obscenity and Public Morality* (Chicago: University of Chicago Press, 1969), especially Chapter 6.
6. See Arendt, *The Human Condition*, p. 51, for an account of the radical subjectivity of pain. Cf. Elaine Scarry, *The Body in Pain: The Making and Unmaking of the World* (New York: Oxford University Press, 1985), especially pp. 1–50.
7. Norbert Elias (Edmund Jephcott, trans.), *The Civilizing Process* (New York: Urizen Books, 1939, 1978), p. 120. For a good social history of the civilizing process, see John F. Kasson, *Rudeness and Civility: Manners in Nineteenth-Century Urban America* (New York: Hill and Wang, 1990).
8. Clifford Geertz, "Deep Play: Notes on the Balinese Cockfight," *Daedalus* 101 (1972), p. 7.

9. Douglas, "Social and Religious Symbolism of the Lele," reprinted in *Implicit Meanings*, pp. 9, 11–12.

10. Douglas, "Environments at Risk," reprinted in *Implicit Meanings*, p. 247.

11. *Olmstead* v. *U.S.*, 277 U.S. 438 (1928).

12. Arendt, Part II, "The Public and the Private Realm," in *The Human Condition*.

13. Ibid., p. 46.

14. See Harry Braverman, *Labor and Monopoly Capital: The Degradation of Work in the Twentieth Century* (New York: Monthly Review Press, 1974).

15. Hannah Arendt, *Between Past and Future* (New York: Penguin Books, 1961, 1985), p. 150. John Pocock and others have persuasively argued that this was not the interpretation of events held by those living through these changes. Instead, thinkers, at least in the eighteenth century, saw the division of labor as allowing for more wealth for all and a growing diversification and variety of individual personality. Though they were concerned about the durability of a commercial republic that was undergirded by self-interest rather than by civic virtue, they were guardedly optimistic about the future. See J. G. A. Pocock, *Virtue, Commerce, and History* (Cambridge: Cambridge University Press, 1985); and Istvan Hont and Michael Ignatieff (eds.), *Wealth and Virtue* (Cambridge: Cambridge University Press, 1983).

16. I am deeply indebted for my understanding of the Scottish Enlightenment to the work of J. G. A. Pocock, especially *The Machiavellian Moment: Florentine Political Thought and the Atlantic Republican Tradition* (Princeton: Princeton University Press, 1975), Part III; Pocock, *Virtue, Commerce, and History*; and Hont and Ignatieff, *Wealth and Virtue*.

17. Pocock draws out this threat in great detail in *The Machiavellian Moment*, especially Chapter 14. According to Pocock: "If the arts proved to have been built up through a process of specialization, then culture itself was in contradiction with the ethos of the *zoon politikon*; and if it were further argued . . . that only specialization, commerce, and culture set men free enough to attend to the goods of others as well as their own, then it would follow that the polis was built up by the very forces that must destroy it" (p. 499).

18. Pocock, "Virtues, Rights, and Manners: A Model for Historians of Political Thought," in *Virtue, Commerce, and History*, p. 49. Pocock, "Cambridge Paradigms and Scotch Philosophers," in Hont and Ignatieff, *Wealth and Virtue*, p. 243.

19. Pocock, "Virtues, Rights, and Manners," p. 50.

20. Arendt, *The Human Condition*, p. 39.

21. Max Lerner (ed.), "On Liberty," in *Essential Works of John Stuart Mill* (New York: Bantam Books, 1961), p. 266.

22. Ibid., p. 265.

23. E. L. Godkin, "The Rights of the Citizen: To His Own Reputation," *Scribner's Magazine* (July 1890), p. 65.

24. Ibid.

25. Ibid. Elizabeth Stuart Phelps, "The Décolleté in Modern Life," *Forum* 9 (1890), pp. 671, 670. Louis Brandeis and Samuel Warren, "The Right to Privacy," *Harvard Law Review* 4 (1890), p. 195.

26. Oswald Garrison Villard, *Fighting Years: Memoirs of a Liberal Editor* (New York: Harcourt, Brace, 1939), p. 82.

27. Henry James, *Notes on Novelists* (New York: Biblo and Tannen, 1969, originally published in 1914), p. 421. CEN to C. C. Stillman, April 10, 1899, in Sara Norton and M. A. DeWolfe Howe (eds.), *Letters of Charles Eliot Norton* (Boston: Houghton Mifflin, 1913), Vol. 2, pp. 282–83.

28. Norton quoted in Kermit Vanderbilt, *Charles Eliot Norton: Apostle of Culture*

(Cambridge: Harvard University Press, 1959), p. 220. CEN to S. G. Ward, November 28, 1897, pp. 255–56. See also CEN to J. R. Lowell, September 8, 1889, pp. 192–93.

29. CEN to Sir Mountstuart E. Grant-Duff, September 10, 1889, pp. 193–94. CEN to E. L. Godkin, August 2, 1899, pp. 287–88. For more about the changed conditions of Cambridge, see CEN to S. G. Ward, September 19, 1900, pp. 300–1: "There is no atmosphere of letters. Our scholars are men of learning in the modern sense, and of very little literature . . . No, the Cambridge of today is a town of prose, and the College is given over to athletics." Also see Nicholas Phillipson, "Adam Smith as Civic Moralist," in Hont and Ignatieff, *Wealth and Virtue*, esp. pp. 184–90, for the roots of this appreciation of conversation and friendship in Adam Smith's philosophy.

30. CEN to Edward Lee-Childe, April 10, 1896, p. 243. For more on society and the qualities of a gentleman, see CEN to S. G. Ward, November 5, 1901, pp. 315–16; CEN to S. G. Ward, February 4, 1904, quoted in Vanderbilt, p. 220; CEN to Eliot Norton, April 4, 1908, pp. 398–99; and Arthur Sedgwick's "Words of a Contemporary," in Norton and Howe, *Letters*, Vol. 2, pp. 441–42.

31. For more on the tension between democracy and "the social accomplishments and arts," see CEN to Sir Mountstuart E. Grant-Duff, November 8, 1895, p. 235.

32. CEN to S. G. Ward, August 8, 1900, p. 298. See also CEN to S. G. Ward, September 19, 1900, pp. 300–1; and CEN to W. L. Mackenzie King, January 26, 1903, pp. 330–33. For the effects of material progress on spiritual belief, see CEN to L. P. Jacks, April 29, 1905, p. 354; and CEN to S. G. Ward, April 14, 1901, pp. 304–5. For more on the bad effects of materialism, see Norton's letters on the condition of England in 1900, which had come to closely resemble America, CEN to E. L. Godkin, July 21, 1900, p. 294; and CEN to S. G. Ward, July 23, 1900, pp. 294–95.

33. CEN to Sir Mountstuart E. Grant-Duff, April 19, 1896, p. 242. See also CEN to S. Weir Mitchell, March 5, 1904, pp. 339–40.

34. CEN to S. G. Ward, April 26, 1896, pp. 243–44. For another bitter denunciation of democracy in America along the same general lines, see CEN to Leslie Stephen, January 8, 1896, pp. 236–37. For early letters about his fears about democracy (but still hopeful), see CEN to J. B. Harrison, July 23, 1882, p. 135; and CEN to J. R. Lowell, November 16, 1884, p. 166. For examples of his "bitter disillusionment in regard to the country I have loved and hoped for," see CEN to S. G. Ward, December 15, 1904, p. 352; CEN to Leslie Stephen, March 20, 1896, p. 241; CEN to Edward Lee-Childe, June 28, 1897, pp. 252–53; CEN to S. G. Ward, October 10, 1898, p. 274; and CEN to S. G. Ward, March 13, 1901, pp. 303–4.

35. CEN to Edward Lee-Childe, September 29, 1883, pp. 156–57.

36. CEN to S. G. Ward, April 26, 1896, p. 244. See also CEN to Edward Lee-Childe, June 26, 1898, pp. 272–73; and CEN to S. G. Ward, August 8, 1900, p. 299.

37. CEN to S. G. Ward, August 8, 1900, p. 298. See also CEN to S. G. Ward, July 1897, p. 253. For an excellent account of the cult of material progress, see Christopher Lasch, *The True and Only Heaven: Progress and Its Critics* (New York: W. W. Norton, 1991).

38. Charles Eliot Norton, "The Intellectual Life of America," *New Princeton Review* 6 (November 1888), p. 313. Norton, "Some Aspects of Civilization in America," *Forum* 20 (February 1896), p. 644.

39. Norton, "The Intellectual Life of America," p. 321. "Some Aspects of Civilization in America, p. 647. For more criticisms of the newspapers, see "The Intellectual Life of America," p. 318.

40. Norton, "The Intellectual Life of America," p. 323, 321–22. For a similar list of virtues, see "Some Aspects of Civilization in America," p. 651.
41. F. R. Leavis (ed.), *Mill on Bentham and Coleridge* (London: Chatto & Windus, 1950), p. 85. Raymond Williams, *Keywords* (New York: Oxford University Press, 1976, 1983), p. 113. For more on the need for leadership by the best and the threats posed to democracy by the widespread "indifference to distinction," see E. L. Godkin, *Unforeseen Tendencies of Democracy* (Boston: Houghton Mifflin, 1898), pp. 30–46. For a denunciation of "fake culture," see Godkin, "Chromo-Civilization," reprinted in *Reflections and Comments, 1865–1895* (New York: Charles Scribner's Sons, 1895), especially pp. 201–2. For good historical accounts of the suspicion of "aristocratic" culture in the nineteenth century, see Kenneth Cmiel, *Democratic Eloquence: The Fight over Popular Speech in Nineteenth-Century America* (New York: William Morrow, 1990); and Kasson, *Rudeness and Civility*. Thorstein Veblen's *Theory of the Leisure Class* (1899) remains the classic text on refinement as a form of snobbery.
42. Norton, "The Intellectual Life of America," p. 324. Norton's "Educational Review" quoted in editor's narrative in Norton and Howe, *Letters*, Vol. 2, pp. 8–9. For more on Norton's ideas about the fine arts, see Vanderbilt, *Charles Eliot Norton*, pp. 124–25. See Richard Hofstadter, *The Age of Reform* (New York: Vintage Books, 1955), especially pp. 135–66, for his well-known theory of "status anxiety"; and Jackson Lears, *No Place of Grace* (New York: Pantheon Books, 1981), especially pp. 3–58, for his account of "the crisis of cultural authority during the late nineteenth century." See also Daniel Walker Howe, "Victorian Culture in America," and David D. Hall, "The Victorian Connection," in Daniel Walker Howe (ed.), *Victorian America* (Philadelphia: University of Pennsylvania Press, 1976); and Thomas Bender, *New York Intellect* (Baltimore: Johns Hopkins University Press, 1987), Chapter 5.
43. Raymond Williams, *Culture and Society: 1780–1950* (New York: Columbia University Press, 1958, 1983).
44. Pocock, "Virtues, Rights, and Manners," p. 50. See, for example, David Hume, "Of the Rise and Progress of the Arts and Sciences," in his *Essays: Moral, Political, and Literary* (Eugene F. Miller, ed.) (Indianapolis: Liberty Classics, 1985).
45. Norton worries about anarchy in "Some Aspects of Civilization in America," p. 651. See also Stow Persons, *The Decline of Gentility* (New York: Columbia University Press, 1973) pp. 301–2.
46. Some of the most important contributions to the cult of domesticity include Nancy Cott, *The Bonds of Womanhood* (New Haven: Yale University Press, 1977); Barbara Leslie Epstein, *The Politics of Domesticity* (Middletown, Conn.: Wesleyan University Press, 1981); Catherine Kish Sklar, *Catherine Beecher* (New York: W. W. Norton, 1973); and Ann Douglas, *The Feminization of American Culture* (New York: Avon, 1977).
47. See Christopher Lasch, *Haven in a Heartless World* (New York: Basic Books, 1977), for a complete account of this development, and his "Woman as Alien" in *The New Radicalism in America* (New York: Vintage Books, 1965, 1967), pp. 38–68.
48. Arendt, *The Human Condition*, pp. 70, 50.
49. Charlotte Perkins Gilman, *The Home: Its Work and Influence* (New York: McClure, Phillips, 1903), pp. 32, 64–65.
50. See *U.S.* v. *Smith*, 11 Fed. Rep. 663 (1882); *Swearingen* v. *U.S.*, 161 U.S. 446 (1896); *People* v. *Eastman*, 188 N.Y. 478 (1907). For summaries of the history of obscenity, see Martha Alschuler, "Origins of the Law of Obscenity," *The Technical Report of the Commission on Obscenity and Pornography*, Vol. 2: *Legal Analysis* (1972), pp. 65–79; Morris L. Ernst and William Seagle, *To the Pure . . . A Study of Obscenity and the Censor* (New York: The Viking Press, 1928), pp. 140–71; Leo M. Alpert,

"Judicial Censorship of Obscene Literature," *Harvard Law Review* 52 (1938), pp. 41–76; Sidney Grant and S. E. Angoff, "Massachusetts and Censorship," *Boston University Law Review* 10 (1930), pp. 36–60; Norman St. John-Stevas, *Obscenity and the Law* (London: Secker and Warburg, 1956), pp. 1–28.

2. THE RETICENT SENSIBILITY AND THE VALUE OF PRIVACY

1. Elizabeth Stuart Phelps, "The Décolleté in Modern Life," *Forum* 9 (1890), p. 676. Charles Dudley Warner, "Editor's Study II," *Harper's New Monthly Magazine* 94 (May 1897), p. 970. For similar declarations about the widespread attack on newspapers, see George T. Rider, "The Pretensions of Journalism," *North American Review* 135 (June 1882), p. 471; James Parton, "Newspapers Gone to Seed," *Forum* 1 (March 1886), p. 15; Joseph Bishop, "Newspaper Espionage," *Forum* 1 (August 1886), p. 529; W. S. Lilly, "The Ethics of Journalism," *Forum* 7 (July 1889), p. 505; Charles Dudley Warner, "Newspapers and the Public," *Forum* 9 (April 1890), p. 197; and Editors, "A Newspaper Symposium," *Dial* 15 (August 16, 1893), p. 79.

2. E. L. Godkin, "Newspapers Here and Abroad," *North American Review* 150 (February 1890), p. 202. See Condé Benoist Pallen, "Newspaperism," *Lippincott's Monthly Magazine* 38 (1886), p. 471, for the way the newspaper has displaced "the forum, the pulpit," and even "the hearthstone"; and Richard Watson Gilder (interviewed by Clifton Johnson), "The Newspaper, the Magazine, and the Public," *Outlook* 61 (February 4, 1899), p. 317, for the way that the newspaps "wield a wider influence than the pulpit, and perhaps even the schools."

3. J. N. O. Gilmer Speed, "Do Newspapers Give the News?" *Forum* 15 (August 1893), p. 709. Aline Gorren, "The Ethics of Modern Journalism," *Scribner's Magazine* 19 (April 1896), p. 508. See Hazel Dicken-Garcia, *Journalistic Standards in Nineteenth-Century America* (Madison: University of Wisconsin Press, 1989), for criticism of journalism before 1890, and Marion Tuttle Marzolf, *Civilizing Voices: American Press Criticism, 1880–1950* (New York: Longman, 1991) for later criticisms. See Frank Mott for analysis of journalism in general. See also James L. Crouthamel, "James Gordon Bennett, "*The New York Herald* and the Development of Newspaper Sensationalism," *New York History* 54 (July 1973), pp. 294–316.

4. Rider, "The Pretensions of Journalism," p. 472. Also see Anonymous, "The Ethics of Interviewing," *New Princeton Review* 3 (1887), p. 131.

5. Richard Grant White, "The Pest of the Period: A Chapter of the Morals and Manners of Journalism," *Galaxy* 10 (June 1870), p. 102. W. H. H. Murray, "An Endowed Press," *Arena* 2 (October 1890), p. 555. For more examples, see White, "The Pest of the Period," p. 102; William H. Bushnell, "Journalistic Barbarism," *The Inland Printer* 3 (January 1886), p. 201. For a vivid account of the press's relentless pursuit of President Cleveland and his bride, see Bishop, "Newspaper Espionage," pp. 529–534. F. O. Matthiessen and Kenneth B. Murdock (eds.), *The Notebooks of Henry James* (New York: Oxford University Press, 1947), November 17, 1887, pp. 82, 83; April 8, 1883, p. 47. For an account of the incidents that inspired *The Reverberator*, see Henry James, *The Novels and Tales of Henry James, vol. 13* (New York: Charles Scribner's Sons, 1908), pp. vii–xii. Also see James's description of the late nineteenth century as "the age of newspapers and telegrams and photographs and interviewers" in *The Aspern Papers* (1888), Willard Thorp (ed.), *The Turn of the Screw and Other Short Novels* (New York: Signet, 1962), p. 157.

6. Louis Brandeis and Samuel Warren, "The Right to Privacy," *Harvard Law Review*, 4 (1890), p. 195. Bushnell, "Journalistic Barbarism," p. 201. Rider, "The Pretensions of Journalism," p. 477. Anonymous, "The Ethics of Interviewing," pp. 128–

29. Sir Edward Coke's well-known dictum, "A man's house is his castle and fortress as well as his defense against injury and violence as for his repose," was often the starting point of these criticisms. For examples, see also Bushnell, "Journalistic Barbarism," p. 201; O. B. Frothingham, "The Interviewer," *Forum* 1 (1886), p. 190; and E. L. Godkin, "The Rights of the Citizen: To His Own Reputation," *Scribner's Magazine* (July 1890), p. 65.

7. Brandeis and Warren, "The Right to Privacy," p. 196. Letter dated September 28, 1888, quoted in Kermit Vanderbilt, *Charles Eliot Norton: Apostle of Culture in a Democracy* (Cambridge: Harvard University Press, 1959), p. 170. It is interesting that Norton's daughter chose to include Ruskin's portrait of that first meeting in her collection of his letters, though she omitted Norton's response to it. See Sara Norton and M. A. DeWolfe Howe (eds.), *Letters of Charles Eliot Norton* (Boston: Houghton Mifflin, 1913).

8. Letter quoted in Bishop, "Newspaper Espionage," p. 535. For another good example of this sense of insult, see Pallen, "Newspaperism," p. 475.

9. Henry James, *The Reverberator* (London: Rupert Hart-Davis, 1949, originally published in 1888), p. 188. James was concerned about where to locate the story. He considered England only to reject it because "publicity is far too much, by this time, in the manner of society for my representation to have any verisimilitude here" (*Notebooks*, p. 84).

10. Godkin, "The Rights of the Citizen," p. 61. Georg Simmel (Kurt H. Wolff, trans.), *The Sociology of Georg Simmel* (Glencoe, Ill.: The Free Press, 1950), p. 321. James, *The Reverberator*, pp. 190, 194. In the original 1888 version, the phrase read: "sense of desecration, of pollution" (p. 199).

11. Godkin, "The Rights of the Citizen," p. 67. Also see Wilbur Larremore, "The Law of Privacy," *Columbia Law Review* 12 (1912): "The average person likes to see his picture in a newspaper upon any pretext" (p. 702). E. L. Godkin, "The Right to Privacy," *The Nation* (December 25, 1890), p. 497. White, "The Pest of the Period," p. 106. Norton to Edward Lee-Childe, August 18, 1874, reprinted in Norton and Howe, *Letters of Charles Eliot Norton*, Vol. 1, p. 47. Also see Anonymous, "The Taste for Privacy and Publicity," *Spectator* 61 (1888), pp. 782, 783.

12. Anonymous, "The Defence of Privacy," *Spectator* 66 (1891), p. 200. Edith Wharton, *The House of Mirth* (New York: Macmillan, 1987, originally published in 1905). See Leo Braudy, *The Frenzy of Renown: Fame and Its History* (New York: Oxford University Press, 1986); Daniel Boorstin, *The Image: A Guide to Pseudo-Events in America* (Atheneum: New York, 1961), especially Chapters 1 and 2; and Richard Schickel, *Intimate Strangers: The Cult of Celebrity* (New York: Doubleday, 1985), pp. 1–55.

13. Charles Eliot Norton (ed.), *Letters of James Russell Lowell*, Vol. 1 (New York: Harper & Brothers, 1894), pp. iii–iv.

14. Charles Eliot Norton (ed.), *Letters of John Ruskin to Charles Eliot Norton*, p. x. See John Lewis Bradley and Ian Ousby (eds.), *The Correspondence of John Ruskin and Charles Eliot Norton* (Cambridge: Cambridge University Press, 1987), p. 8, where they criticize Norton's edition of Ruskin's letters: "The chief value of Norton's edition is as a model of the censorship which the Victorians often thought it necessary to impose on the private papers of their great contemporaries."

15. Charles Eliot Norton, "James Russell Lowell," *Harper's New Monthly Magazine* 86 (May 1893), p. 847.

16. CEN to Ruskin, April 2, 1873, in Bradley and Ousby (eds.), *The Correspondence*, p. 285.

17. Ibid., p. 286.

18. Norton, *Letters of James Russell Lowell*, Vol. 1, p. iii. CEN to Mrs. Alexander Carlyle,

July 5, 1882, p. 136. For a similar perspective on the shamefulness of publishing authors' private letters, see Edith Wharton's novel on the subject, *The Touchstone* (1900). Charles Eliot Norton (ed.), *Early Letters of Thomas Carlyle, 1814–1826* (London: Macmillan, 1886), pp. vii–viii. For more on the Froude affair, see Vanderbilt, *Charles Eliot Norton*, p. 168.

19. CEN to John Ruskin, April 3, 1882, p. 146.
20. James Fitzjames Stephen, *Liberty, Equality, and Fraternity* (Cambridge: Cambridge University Press, 1967, originally published in 1873), pp. 160–62. For more recent accounts of the vulnerability of the experiences of the sphere of intimacy to the outside world, see Hannah Arendt, *The Human Condition* (Chicago: University of Chicago Press, 1958), especially pp. 22–78; Charles Fried, "Privacy," *Yale Law Journal* 77 (1968), pp. 475–93; and Christopher Lasch, *Haven in a Heartless World* (New York: Basic Books, 1977).
21. Godkin, "The Rights of the Citizen," p. 66. Rider, "The Pretensions of Journalism," p. 479.
22. Hamilton Wright Mabie, "A Typical Novel," *Andover Review* 4 (November 1885), reprinted in George L. Becker (ed.), *Documents of Modern Literary Realism* (Princeton: Princeton University Press, 1963), pp. 302–3. See also William R. Thayer, "The New Story-Tellers and the Doom of Realism," *Forum* 18 (December 1894), p. 477; H. E. Scudder, "Mr. Howells's Literary Creed," *Atlantic Monthly* 68 (October 1891), pp. 566–69; and Henry Clay Vedder, *American Writers of To-day* (New York: Silver, Burdett, 1894), pp. 53–54. For a good summary of the various charges of triviality of the new realism, see Helen McMahon, *Criticism of Fiction: A Study of Trends in the Atlantic Monthly, 1857–1898* (New York: Bookman Associates, 1952), especially pp. 23–27.
23. Vedder, *American Writers of To-day*, p. 56.
24. Mabie, "A Typical Novel," p. 303. Vedder, *American Writers of To-day*, pp. 56–57.
25. Emile Zola, "The Experimental Novel" (1880), reprinted in Becker, *Documents of Modern Literary Realism*, p. 196.
26. Thayer, "The New Story-Tellers and the Doom of Realism," p. 476. Also see Mabie, "A Typical Novel," p. 302. For a general survey of the criticisms that realism took too much from scientific method, see McMahon, *Criticism of Fiction*, pp. 94–98.
27. Henry James, "Nana" (1880), reprinted in Becker, *Documents of Modern Literary Realism*, pp. 239, 240–41. For a later, more appreciative review of Zola, see James, "Emile Zola" (1903), reprinted in Becker, pp. 506–34. In this essay, James praises Zola's lack of taste: "Paradoxical as the remark may sound, this accident [of having no taste] was positively to operate as one of his greatest felicities" (p. 515). Cf. Phelps on Tolstoy's "unpardonable fault . . . of literary taste," in her "The Décolleté in Modern Life," p. 683.
28. Thayer, "The New Story-Tellers and the Doom of Realism," p. 476 (his emphasis). For more descriptions of the dehumanizing effects of the scientific method applied to literature, see Anonymous, "Novel-Writing as a Science," *Catholic World* 42 (November 1885), pp. 274–80; and Maurice Thompson, "The Analysts Analyzed," *Critic* 6 (July 1886), pp. 19–22.
29. Murray, "An Endowed Press," pp. 553–54. E. L. Godkin, "Editorial Perspective," *The Nation* 10 (January 27, 1870), p. 55. Bushnell, "Journalistic Barbarism," p. 201. Also see Augustus A. Levey, "The Newspaper Habit and Its Effects," *North American Review* 143 (1886), p. 311. Brandeis and Warren, "The Right to Privacy," p. 196. Also see Rider, "The Pretensions of Journalism," p. 478; Gorren, "The Ethics of Modern Journalism," p. 508; J. H. Crooker, "Daily Papers and Their Readers: A Suggestion" (letter to the editor), *Dial* 15 (October 1, 1893), p. 179; and Frothingham, "The Interviewer," pp. 182–83.

30. White, "The Pest of the Period," p. 106. E. L. Godkin, "Opinion-Moulding," *The Nation* 9 (August 12, 1869), p. 126. Also see Frothingham, "The Interviewer," p. 185. Crooker, "Daily Papers and Their Readers," p. 179.

31. W. H. Mallock, "The Relation of Art to Truth," *Forum* 9 (March 1890), pp. 44–45.

32. Agnes Repplier, "Fiction in the Pulpit," *Atlantic Monthly* 64 (October 1889), p. 536. James, "Nana," p. 242.

33. *U.S.* v. *Bennett*, 16 Blatchford (1879), pp. 364, 355, 368. Also see *U.S.* v. *Beebout*, 28 Fed. Rep. 524 (1886).

34. Charles Dudley Warner, "The Novel and the Common School," *Atlantic Monthly* 65 (June 1890), p. 723. Pallen, "Newspaperism," p. 476. For a social-scientific version of the bad effects of the "newspaper habit," see Delos F. Wilcox, "The American Newspaper: A Study in Social Psychology," *American Academy of Political and Social Science, Annals* 16 (July 1900), pp. 56–92.

35. Levey, "The Newspaper Habit and Its Effects," pp. 309, 310. William Dean Howells, (Clara Marburg Kirk and Rudolph Kirk, eds.), *Criticism and Fiction and Other Essays* (New York: New York University Press, 1959), p. 46.

36. Godkin, "Newspapers Here and Abroad," p. 203. Cf. Godkin, *Unforeseen Tendencies of Democracy* (Boston: Houghton Mifflin, 1898), pp. 199–200.

37. Howells, *Criticism and Fiction*, pp. 53, 54.

38. Editors, "A Newspaper Symposium" (1893), p. 79. E. L. Godkin, "Responsibility for Yellow Journalism," *The Nation* 73 (Sept. 26, 1901), p. 238. Also see Editors, "An Endowed Newspaper," *Dial* 14 (January 16, 1893), pp. 36–37; Warner, "Newspapers and the Public," p. 197; and Gorren, "The Ethics of Modern Journalism," p. 508.

39. James, *The Reverberator*, p. 158. In the original 1888 version, this sentence read: " 'Perhaps they had got case-hardened,' Francie said to herself; 'perhaps they had read so many bad things that they had lost the delicacy of their palate, as people were said to do who lived on food too violently spiced' " (p. 165). Parton, "Newspapers Gone to Seed," pp. 16–17.

40. Godkin, "The Rights of the Citizen," p. 67. Pallen, "Newspaperism," pp. 474, 476. Cf. Warner, "Newspapers and the Public," p. 206.

41. *U.S.* v. *Harmon*, 45 Fed. Rep. (1891), pp. 423, 418. Though the defendant's name was Moses Harman, the Federal Reporter lists the case as Harmon.

42. Mabie, "A Typical Novel," pp. 304, 307.

43. Thayer, "The New Story-Tellers and the Doom of Realism," p. 472. For examples of the sacred quality of privacy, see Pallen, "Newspaperism," pp. 475, 476; Bishop, "Newspaper Espionage," pp. 531, 533; and Bushnell, "Journalistic Barbarism," p. 201.

44. Pallen, "Newspaperism," p. 473. Cf. p. 474. For a similar list, see White, "The Pest of the Period," pp. 102–3. Also see E. L. Godkin, "Judges and Witnesses," in *Reflections and Comments, 1865–1895* (New York: Charles Scribner's Sons, 1895), pp. 219–26, in which he criticizes the cross-examination as "not the eliciting of a certain number of facts bearing on the question in court, but a complete revelation of the whole private life of a family" (p. 219). For more examples of the use of the metaphors of contamination and sewers, see Editors, "An Endowed Newspaper," p. 37; Rider, "The Pretensions of Journalism," p. 477, and Bushnell, "Journalistic Barbarism," p. 212. Franz Steiner, *Taboo* (London: Pelican Books, 1956, 1967), p. 115.

45. White, "The Pest of the Period," p. 102. Bushnell, "Journalistic Barbarism," p. 202. Rider, "The Pretensions of Journalism," pp. 476–77.

46. Thayer, "The New Story-Tellers and the Doom of Realism," p. 479. Mallock, "The Relation of Art to Truth," p. 36. Vedder, *American Writers To-day*, pp. 82–83.

47. *People* v. *Muller*, 96 N.Y. 413 (1884). *Rosen* v. *U.S.*, 161 U.S. 37 (1896). For more examples of the pollution metaphor, see *U.S.* v. *Bennett*, p. 339; *U.S.* v. *Harmon*, p. 414; *U.S.* v. *Foote*, 25 Fed. Cas. 1141 (1876); *Dunlop* v. *U.S.*, 16 Sup. Ct. 376 (1897); and *State* v. *McKee*, 73 Conn. 18 (1900).

48. Mary Douglas, "Pollution," in her *Implicit Meanings* (London: Routledge & Kegan Paul, 1975), p. 58.

49. Edith Wharton (Cynthia Griffin Wolff, ed.), *The Touchstone* (New York: Harper Perennial, 1991, originally published in 1900), p. 90. For another fictional account of the attempt to publish the letters of a famous deceased poet, see Henry James, *The Aspern Papers* (1888). James Russell Lowell, "Chapman," in *Latest Literary Essays and Addresses* (Boston: Houghton Mifflin, 1891), pp. 264, 266. For more examples of the degradation that comes with reading shameful material, see Vedder, *American Writers To-day*, pp. 82–83; Editorial, "The Decay of American Journalism," *Dial* 22 (April 16, 1897), p. 237; and *U.S.* v. *Harmon*, p. 423.

50. Godkin, "The Right to Privacy," p. 497. For more on the role of curiosity in the popularity of journalism, see Gilder, "The Newspaper, the Magazine, and the Public," p. 320. For good accounts of the meaning of democracy, see Gordon Wood, *The Creation of the American Republic, 1776–1787* (New York: W. W. Norton, 1969), and Raymond Williams, definition of "Democracy," pp. 93–98, in *Keywords* (New York: Oxford University Press, 1976, 1983).

51. Anonymous, "The Defence of Privacy," *Spectator* 66 (1891), p. 200. In fact, the hatred of publicity could be used as subject matter for a story. When Mrs. Luna in James's *The Bostonians* objects to Matthias Pardon's badgering of her, "If you have the impertinence to publish a word about me, or mention my name in print, I will come to your office and make such a scene!" Pardon replies "enthusiastically," "Dearest lady, that would be a godsend!" (p. 410). Also see Daniel Boorstin's account of Charles Lindbergh's refusal to grant interviews about his child's kidnapping becoming the subject of news (*The Image*, p. 69).

52. White, "The Pest of the Period," p. 102. Godkin, "The Rights of the Citizen," pp. 65–67. Warner, "Newspapers and the Public," pp. 101–102, also refers to Rochefoucauld's maxim. For explanations blaming "morbid" and/or "prurient" curiosity, and the love of gossip and scandal, see Richard Grant White, "The Morals and Manners of Journalism," *Galaxy* 8 (December 1869), p. 840; White, "The Pest of the Period," p. 102; Bushnell, "Journalistic Barbarism," p. 201; Parton, "Newspapers Gone to Seed," p. 17; Levey, "The Newspaper Habit and Its Effects," p. 309; and Gorren, "The Ethics of Modern Journalism," p. 509.

53. Lilly, "The Ethics of Journalism," p. 512.

54. Gorren, "The Ethics of Modern Journalism," p. 510. For more examples of leveling, see Godkin, "Opinion-Moulding," pp. 126–127; and White, "The Pest of the Period," p. 102.

55. Matthew Arnold, "Civilization in the United States" (1888) in Kenneth Allott (ed.), *Five Uncollected Essays of Matthew Arnold* (Liverpool: University Press of Liverpool, 1953), pp. 56, 57. For more on Arnold's impressions of the American press during his tour, see George W. E. Russell (ed.), *Letters of Matthew Arnold*, Vol. 2: *1848–1888* (New York: Macmillan, 1896), pp. 267, 273.

56. James, *The Bostonians*, p. 139. Matthiessen and Murdock (eds.), *The Notebooks of Henry James*, November 17, 1887. Godkin, "The Rights of the Citizen," p. 66.

57. Henry James, "The Lesson of the Master," in *The Art of the Novel* (Boston: Northeastern University Press, 1934, 1984), p. 222. Simmel, *The Sociology of Georg Simmel*, p. 131.

58. W. S. Lilly, "The New Naturalism," *Fortnightly Review* 38 (August 1, 1885). Also see O. B. Frothingham, "The Morally Objectionable in Literature," *North American Review* 15 (1882), pp. 328–29.
59. Mabie, "A Typical Novel," p. 306.

3. THE DISCOURSE OF EXPOSURE AND THE VALUE OF PUBLICITY

1. O. B. Frothingham, "The Interviewer," *Forum* 1 (1886), p. 189. Condé Benoist Pallen, "Newspaperism," *Lippincott's Monthly Magazine* 38 (1886), p. 474. Anonymous, "The Defence of Privacy," *Spectator* 66 (1891), pp. 200–1.
2. Henry James, "The Reverberator," in *The Art of the Novel* (Boston: Northeastern University Press, 1934, 1984) p. 191. James, *The Reverberator* (London: Rupert Hart-Davis, 1949; originally published in 1888), pp. 151–52, 183.
3. Stanton and Jacobi quoted in William Leach, *True Love and Perfect Union: The Feminist Reform of Sex and Society* (New York: Basic Books, 1980), pp. 150, 40. Lester Ward, *Dynamic Sociology*, Vol. 1 (New York: D. Appleton, 1883, 1926), p. 624. For other studies of the sex-reform movements, see Sidney Ditzion, *Marriage, Morals, and Sex in America* (New York: W. W. Norton, 1953, 1969); Victor Robinson, *Pioneers of Birth Control* (New York: Voluntary Parenthood League, 1919); Hal Sears, *The Sex Radicals: Free Love in High Victorian America* (Lawrence: Regents Press of Kansas, 1977); and Taylor Stoehr (ed.), *Free Love in America: A Documentary History* (New York: AMS Press, 1979).
4. Sears, *The Sex Radicals*, p. 78. For accounts of Comstock and his battles against obscenity, see Heywood Broun and Margaret Leech, *Anthony Comstock: Roundsman of the Lord* (New York: Literary Guild of America, 1927); Sears, *The Sex Radicals*, especially pp. 1–74; and Richard C. Johnson, *Anthony Comstock: Reform, Vice, and the American Way* (Ph.D. dissertation, University of Wisconsin, 1973).
5. Andrews quoted in Broun and Leech, *Anthony Comstock*, p. 77.
6. "Degeneration," review of Max Nordau's *Degeneration, Harper's Weekly* (April 13, 1895), reprinted in William Dean Howells (Clara Marburg Kirk and Rudolph Kirk, eds.), *Criticism and Fiction and Other Essays* (New York: New York University Press, 1959), p. 160.
7. Boynton quoted in Leach, *True Love and Perfect Union*, p. 51. Heywood quoted in Sears, *The Sex Radicals*, p. 177. Purity reformers discussed in Nathan G. Hale, *Freud and the Americans: The Beginnings of Psychoanalysis in the United States, 1876–1917* (New York: Oxford University Press, 1971), pp. 252–54. See also Bryan Strong, "Ideas of the Early Sex Education Movement in America, 1890–1920," *History of Education Quarterly* 12 (1962); David J. Pivar, *Purity Crusade: Sexual Morality and Social Control, 1868–1900* (Westport, Conn.: Greenwood Press, 1973); and Sears, p. 116, where he describes the organ of the National Purity Association, *Christian Life*, and the *Woman's Journal*, "which generally lauded the efforts of the vice societies."
8. Howells, *Criticism and Fiction*, pp. 9, 51. Brander Matthews, "Mr. Howells as a Critic," *Forum* 32 (January 1902), p. 629: "To many placid creatures of habit, the publication of this little book was very like the explosion of a bomb in a reading room."
9. Early restrictive state legislation included Vermont (1821), Connecticut (1834), Massachusetts (1835), Pennsylvania (1860), and New York (1861).
10. Ezra Heywood, *Cupid's Yokes or The Binding Forces of Conjugal Love* (Princeton: Cooperative Publishing, n.d.), p. 5. Sexual abuses appeared on p. 9 and birth-control information on p. 20. Heywood quoted in Sears, *The Sex Radicals*, p. 160. According

to Sears, 50,000 to 200,000 copies of *Cupid's Yokes* were sold between its publication in 1876 and the trial (Sears, p. 159).

11. Howells, *Criticism and Fiction*, p. 73.
12. D. H. Meyer, "American Intellectuals and the Victorian Crisis of Faith," in Daniel Walker Howe (ed.), *Victorian America* (Philadelphia: University of Pennsylvania Press, 1976), p. 62. Pillsbury quoted in Leach, *True Love and Perfect Union*, p. 136. Also see D. M. Bennett, *Anthony Comstock: His Career of Cruelty and Crime* (New York: Da Capo Press, 1971, originally published in 1878), p. 1118.
13. Ward, *Dynamic Sociology*, Vol. 1, p. 611. Emile Zola, "The Experimental Novel" (1880), reprinted in George L. Becker (ed.), *Documents of Modern Literary Realism* (Princeton: Princeton University Press, 1963), p. 189.
14. Howells, *Criticism and Fiction*, p. 9.
15. Joseph Wood Krutch, *The Modern Temper* (New York: Harcourt, Brace, 1929, 1957) pp. 66–67. My observations in this paragraph are indebted to Krutch.
16. Anonymous, *Alpha*, May 1, 1878, quoted in Leach, *True Love and Perfect Union*, p. 26. Ward, *Dynamic Sociology*, Vol. 1, p. 632. Heywood quoted in Sears, *The Sex Radicals*, p. 177.
17. Ward, *Dynamic Sociology*, Vol. 1, p. 636. I am indebted to Richard Tristman for this understanding of the pastoral.
18. See Howells, *Criticism and Fiction*, pp. 47, 48; "Problems of Existence in Fiction," *Literature* (March 10, 1899), reprinted in Kirk and Kirk, p. 337; and the remarks made by the Reverend Sewell in Howells, *The Rise of Silas Lapham*, in Henry Steele Commager (ed.), *Selected Writings of William Dean Howells* (New York: Random House, 1950), p. 176.
19. Howells, "A Case in Point," review of Frank Norris's *McTeague*, *Literature* (March 24, 1899), reprinted in Kirk and Kirk, pp. 279–82.
20. Ward, *Dynamic Sociology*, Vol. 1, p. 601. Ward notes that the Latin quotation comes from Bacon's *Novum Organum*.
21. *U.S. v. Bennett*, 16 Blatchford 355 (1879). Cf. p. 356.
22. L.R. 3 Q.B. 36. This passage from the Hicklin decision is referred to or quoted directly in *U.S. v. Bennett*, pp. 339, 365 (1879); *People v. Muller*, 96 N.Y. 411 (1884); *U.S. v. Clarke*, 38 Fed. Rep. 732 (1889); *U.S. v. Harmon*, 45 Fed. Rep. 414 (1891); *U.S. v. Kennerley*, 209 Fed. 120 (1913); *People v. Seltzer*, N.Y. Misc. 330 (1924).
23. *U.S. v. Bennett*, pp. 361, 338, 362–68. See also *People v. Muller*, p. 409; *U.S. v. Clarke*, p. 732; *U.S. v. Harmon*, p. 414.
24. *U.S. v. Harmon*, p. 414. Though the defendant's name was Moses Harman, the Federal Reporter lists the case as Harmon. The letter is reprinted in Sears, *The Sex Radicals*, p. 110. For examples of other letters that got Harman in trouble with the law, see the pamphlet he published entitled *The Kansas Fight for Free Press: The Four Indicted Articles* (Kansas: Lucifer Publishing, n.d.).
25. *U.S. v. Harmon*, pp. 415, 423. He included such examples as a woman convicted of polygamy when she had remarried under the honest belief that her first husband was dead; a man convicted for admitting a minor to his billiard room because he honestly believed he was of age; a magistrate convicted for performing a marriage ceremony of a minor believing that the minor was of age (pp. 420–21). Diggs quoted in Sears, *The Sex Radicals*, pp. 148–49.
26. Howells, *Criticism and Fiction*, pp. 49, 38.
27. William Dean Howells, "Novel-Writing and Novel-Reading, an Impersonal Explanation" (1899), reprinted in William M. Gibson (ed.), *Howells and James: A Double Billing* (New York: New York Public Library, 1958), pp. 8, 20. Also see Howells, *Criticism and Fiction*, p. 49; "The Philosophy of Tolstoy" from *The Library of the*

World's Best Literature (1897) and "Pleasure from Tragedy," review of Hardy's *Jude the Obscure, Harper's Weekly* (December 7, 1895), both reprinted in Kirk and Kirk; and W. H. Mallock, "The Relation of Art to Truth," *Forum* 9 (March 1890).

28. Howells, *Criticism and Fiction*, p. 86. Also see "Emile Zola," *North American Review* (1902) and "Zola's Naturalism," review of *La Terre, Harper's Monthly* (March 1888), both reprinted in Kirk and Kirk.

29. Frothingham, "The Interviewer," p. 190. Also see Charles Dudley Warner, "Newspapers and the Public," *Forum* 9 (1980), p. 204. Junius Henri Browne, "Newspaperism Reviewed," *Lippincott's Monthly Magazine* 38 (1886), p. 728.

30. James, *The Reverberator*, p. 70 (his emphasis). See, for example, Editors, "A Newspaper Symposium," *Dial* 15 (August 16, 1893), p. 80; and J. H. Crooker, "Daily Papers and Their Readers: A Suggestion," *Dial* 15 (October 1, 1893), p. 179.

31. William Dean Howells, *A Modern Instance* (1881), in Henry Steele Commager (ed.), *Selected Writings* (New York: Random House, 1950). Cf. Charles Dudley Warner's "Newspapers and the Public," *Forum* 9 (1890), where he cautioned critics against concluding that Americans are "attracted to a newspaper because it is sensational and vulgar." Rather, he argued, Americans' love of such newspapers is in keeping with their love of the new, the quick, the "snappy" (pp. 202, 203).

32. Howells, *A Modern Instance*, p. 551. See also John Henderson Garnsey, "The Demand for Sensational Journals," *Arena* 18 (1897), p. 681: "This protest [against sensational journalism] has reached such a volume that . . . it is met by a majority of the editors and managers with the statement that 'sensationalism is what the people want.' "

33. William H. Bushnell, "Journalistic Barbarism," *The Inland Printer* 3 (January 1886), p. 201. Criticism of the moneymaking spirit of modern journalism appeared in almost every article on journalism. See Joseph Bishop, "Newspaper Espionage," *Forum* 1 (1886), p. 535. For two early examples, see E. L. Godkin, "Opinion-Moulding," *The Nation* 9 (August 12, 1869), p. 127, and Richard Grant White, "The Morals and Manners of Journalism," *Galaxy* 8 (December 1869), p. 847.

34. E. L. Godkin, "Newspapers Here and Abroad," *North American Review* 150 (February 1890), p. 203. Also see James Parton, "Newspapers Gone to Seed," *Forum* 1 (1886), p. 17. W. H. H. Murray, "An Endowed Press," *Arena* 2 (October 1890), p. 556. Bishop, "Newspaper Espionage," p. 535. Also see Pallen, "Newspaperism," p. 474. He dismissed the excuse that invasive journalism is responding to public demand as unconvincing since "an agent for brothels" also caters to "a vicious public taste." For more on the commercialization of newspapers and the marked deterioration of the practice of journalism, see Editors, "A Newspaper Symposium" (1893), p. 79; and Editors, "An Endowed Newspaper," *Dial* 14 (January 16, 1893), pp. 35–36.

35. Howells, "The Man of Letters as a Man of Business," *Scribner's*, October 1893, reprinted in Kirk and Kirk, pp. 298–309. For another criticism of the way "the making of novels has become a process of manufacture," see Charles Dudley Warner, "The Novel and the Common School," *Atlantic Monthly* 65 (June 1890), pp. 724–25.

36. See *Criticism and Fiction*, Sections XVII, XXII, and XXVII. There are many other sources of Howells's commitment to democracy and a democratic literature. See, for examples, his "The Man of Letters as a Man of Business"; "The Romantic Imagination," review of Bellamy's *Looking Backward, Atlantic Monthly* (August 1898), reprinted in Kirk and Kirk, pp. 250–55; Thomas Sergeant Perry, "William Dean Howells," *Century Magazine*, March 1882; Henry James, "William Dean Howells," *Harper's Weekly* 30 (June 1886), pp. 394–95; Hamlin Garland, "Sanity in Fiction," *North American Review* 176 (March 1903), pp. 336–48.

37. Ralph Waldo Emerson, "The American Scholar," reprinted in *Essays and Lectures* (New York: The Library of America, 1983), p. 69. See Howells's *The Rise of Silas Lapham*, p. 179, for further discussion of the importance of the commonplace. Howells, "Professor Barrett Wendell's Notions of American Literature," review of Wendell's *A Literary History of America*, *North American Review* (April 1901), reprinted in Kirk and Kirk, pp. 330–31. For a defense of Howells's invocation of Whitman, see Hamlin Garland, "Mr. Howells's Latest Novels," *New England Magazine* 2 (May 1890), pp. 243–50. Howells, *Criticism and Fiction*, p. 15.
38. Howells, *Criticism and Fiction*, p. 40.
39. Ibid., p. 87. For another early example of the anti-democratic idiom used in the name of realist fiction, see Frank Norris, "Novelists of the Future" in *The Responsibilities of the Novelist* (1903), p. 277.
40. Howells, *Criticism and Fiction*, p. 66.
41. Ibid., pp. 87, 67, 85. Also see Stephen Crane, "Fears Realists Must Wait" (interview with Howells), *New York Times*, October 28, 1894, p. 20.
42. Howells, *The Rise of Silas Lapham*, p. 104. Howells, *Criticism and Fiction*, pp. 85, 86.
43. Browne, "Newspaperism Reviewed," pp. 721, 725, 727.
44. Godkin, "Opinion-Moulding," pp. 126–27. For the same kind of name-calling in the realist war, see William R. Thayer, "The New Story-Tellers and the Doom of Realism," *Forum* 18 (December 1894), p. 477. Browne, "Newspaperism Reviewed," p. 726. For more on hypocrisy, see Howells, *A Modern Instance*, p. 493; Warner, "Newspapers and the Public," p. 203; and C. R. Miller, "A Word to the Critics of Newspapers," *Forum* 15 (August 1893), pp. 713–17.
45. B. O. Flower, "The Postmaster-General and the Censorship of the Mails," *Arena* 2 (October 1890), p. 543 (his emphasis).
46. Ibid., p. 552.
47. Howells, *Criticism and Fiction*, pp. 12, 15, 27, 24.
48. See Jean-Christophe Agnew, "The Consuming Vision of Henry James," in Jackson Lears and Richard Fox (eds.), *The Culture of Consumption* (New York: Pantheon Books, 1983), for an excellent analysis of this aspect of James's work.

4. THE DEFEAT OF THE "CONSPIRACY OF SILENCE"

1. Mabel Dodge Luhan quoted in James Gilbert, *Writers and Partisans: A History of Literary Radicalism in America* (New York: Columbia University Press, 1968, 1992), p. 26. David M. Kennedy, *Birth Control in America: The Career of Margaret Sanger* (New Haven: Yale University Press, 1970), pp. 12–13. For good descriptions of Dodge's salon, see Margaret Sanger, *An Autobiography* (New York: Dover, 1971, originally published in 1938), Chapter 6; and Martin Green, *New York 1913: The Armory Show and the Paterson Strike Pageant* (New York: Charles Scribner's Sons, 1988), pp. 47–61.
2. Agnes Repplier, "The Repeal of Reticence," *Atlantic Monthly* 113 (1914), p. 298. Also see her "The Virtuous Victorians," in her *Points of Friction* (Boston: Houghton Mifflin, 1920), pp. 149–66. She observes, "There are no more taboos, no more silent or sentimental hypocrisies" (p. 165). William Trufant Forster, "The Social Emergency" (letter to the editor), *The Nation* 98 (January 22, 1914), p. 81.
3. Repplier, "The Repeal of Reticence," pp. 300, 298, 303. Forster, "The Social Emergency," p. 81.
4. See, for examples, Barbara and John Ehrenreich, "The Professional-Managerial Class," in Pat Walker (ed.), *Between Labor and Capital* (Boston: South End Press, 1979); and Alvin Gouldner, *The Future of Intellectuals and the Rise of the New Class*

(New York: Seabury Press, 1979). For a good overview of this literature, see Jean-Christophe Agnew, "A Touch of Class," *Democracy* 3 (1983), pp. 59–72.

5. Repplier, "The Repeal of Reticence," pp. 297, 298, 301.
6. Ibid., pp. 298, 297. Editorial, "Raw Material," *Dial* 52 (January 16, 1912), p. 40. H. W. Boynton, "Ideas, Sex, and the Novel," *Dial* 60 (April 13, 1916), p. 361.
7. Emma Goldman, "The Hypocrisy of Puritanism" (1910) in her *Anarchism and Other Essays* (New York: Dover, 1969, originally published in 1917), p. 170. Theodore Schroeder, *"Obscene" Literature and Constitutional Law* (New York: Privately printed, 1911), p. 60. See also pp. 8, 59, 61, 122, 124. All the Schroeder essays cited hereafter are in this volume. Maurice Bigelow, *Sex-Education* (New York: American Social Hygiene Association, 1916, 1936), pp. 11–12.
8. Cited in Victor Robinson, *Pioneers of Birth Control* (New York: Voluntary Parenthood League, 1919), pp. 101–2. See Sanger's accounts of the suffering and deaths of poor women seeking abortions, in *An Autobiography*, pp. 88–90. See also Goldman, "The Hypocrisy of Puritanism," pp. 172–73.
9. Goldman, "The Hypocrisy of Puritanism," pp. 173–74. Margaret Sanger, *The Pivot of Civilization* (New York: Brentano's, 1922), p. 246. Schroeder, "Obscenity, Prudery, and Morals," pp. 126, 127.
10. Jacobi quoted in Robinson, *Pioneers of Birth Control*, pp. 75, 76.
11. Sigmund Freud, " 'Civilized' Sexual Morality and Modern Nervousness" (1908), in Joan Rivière (trans.), *Collected Papers*, Vol. 2 (New York: Basic Books, 1959), pp. 76, 80, 89, 77, 90. Freud notes that the phrase " 'civilized' sexual morality" comes from Ehrenfels (p. 76). For commentary on "civilized" sexual morality, see Nathan G. Hale, *Freud and the Americans: The Beginnings of Psychoanalysis in the United States, 1876–1917* (New York: Oxford University Press, 1971), pp. 24–46; William L. O'Neill, *Divorce in the Progressive Era* (New Haven, Conn.: Yale University Press, 1967), especially "Origins of the New Morality," Part 1 and Part 2; and Kennedy, *Birth Control in America*, pp. 66–71.
12. Freud, " 'Civilized' Sexual Morality and Modern Nervousness," pp. 92, 93. "The intellectual inferiority of so many women can be traced to that inhibition of thought necessitated by sexual suppression" (p. 94).
13. Ibid., pp. 89, 90, 96, 97.
14. Philip Rieff, *Freud: The Mind of the Moralist* (Chicago: University of Chicago Press, 1959, 1979), p. 317.
15. Freud, " 'Civilized' Sexual Morality and Modern Nervousness," pp. 82, 91, 88.
16. Walter Lippmann, *A Preface to Politics* (New York: Macmillan, 1913, 1933), pp. 49–51, 148–51. Sanger, *The Pivot of Civilization*, pp. 200, 229. Cf. Goldman, "The Hypocrisy of Puritanism," pp. 171–72, where she cites Freud.
17. Schroeder, *"Obscene" Literature*, p. 7. For examples of Schroeder's influence, see James F. Morton, "Our Foolish Obscenity Laws," *Case and Comment* 23 (1916), p. 23; and Morris L. Ernst and William Seagle, *To The Pure . . . A Study of Obscenity and the Censor* (New York: The Viking Press, 1928), p. 106. Sanger describes her relation to Schroeder and his infatuation with psychoanalysis in *An Autobiography*, pp. 112–13.
18. Schroeder, *"Obscene" Literature*, pp. 258, 103. See also pp. 25, 30, 43, 103, 253.
19. Schroeder, "On the Adverse Emotional Predisposition," p. 27.
20. Schroeder, "Obscenity, Prudery, and Morals," pp. 113–14. "Varieties of Official Modesty," p. 324. "Psychologic Study of Modesty and Obscenity," p. 275. Cf. H. L. Mencken's similar portrait of "the Golden Age of euphemism" in "Puritanism as a Literary Force," *A Book of Prefaces* (New York: Alfred A. Knopf, 1917), p. 228.
21. Schroeder, "On the Adverse Emotional Predisposition," pp. 25, 28.

22. See ibid., pp. 29, 30. See also "The Reasons Underlying Our Constitutional Guarantee of a Free Press, Applied to Sex Discussion" (1906), pp. 74–100.
23. Schroeder, "On the Adverse Emotional Predisposition," pp. 28–29; "The Reasons Underlying Our Constitutional Guarantee of a Free Press, Applied to Sex Discussion," pp. 83–84. For Schroeder's treatment of ethnography, see "Science versus Judicial Dictum: A Statement of Novel Contentions and a Plea for Open-mindedness," pp. 240–57. For an account of Havelock Ellis's popularity and influence in America, especially in the period 1890–1920, see Hale, *Freud and the Americans*, pp. 259–68.
24. Schroeder, "Science versus Judicial Dictum," pp. 241–50, 251. Since the 1920s, legal writers have typically acknowledged the relativity of morals to undercut obscenity law. See, for early examples, Ernst and Seagle, *To the Pure*, pp. 251–62; Sidney S. Grant and S. E. Angoff, "Massachusetts and Censorship," *Boston University Law Review* 10 (1930), p. 36; and Alpert, "Judicial Censorship of Obscenity Literature," *Harvard Law Review* 52 (1938), pp. 74–75.
25. Schroeder, "The Reasons Underlying Our Constitutional Guarantee of a Free Press, Applied to Sex Discussion," pp. 74–75. See also pp. 77–81.
26. *New York Tribune* quoted in Kennedy, *Birth Control in America*, p. 86. Schroeder, "The Etiology and Development of Our Censorship of Sex-Literature, p. 43.
27. Harman quoted in Hal Sears, *The Sex Radicals* (Lawrence: Regents Press of Kansas, 1977), p. 79.
28. Robinson, *Pioneers of Birth Control*, p. 90. Sanger, *An Autobiography*, p. 110.
29. Hippolyte Havel, "Biographic Sketch," in Goldman, *Anarchism and Other Essays*, p. 19. Among her powerful high-society friends, Sanger could count on Mrs. Amos Pinchot, who appealed directly to the governor of New York to commute Ethel Byrne's sentence (*An Autobiography*, pp. 188–91).
30. Sanger, *An Autobiography*, pp. 232, 306. For more on Sanger's arrest and its aftermath, see pp. 302–10, and *The Pivot of Civilization*, pp. 10–21. Sanger's statement about being gagged is quoted in Kennedy, *Birth Control in America*, p. 82.
31. Sanger, *An Autobiography*, pp. 221, 255, 309. For more on Sanger's views on publicity, see pp. 189, 192, 206.
32. See Mary Ware Dennett, *The Sex Side of Life* (privately published, 1928, 18th printing), pp. 1–14.
33. The *Free Press* quoted in Morris L. Ernst and Alexander Lindey, *The Censor Marches On* (New York: Doubleday, 1940), p. 40. For more on this trial, see Paul S. Boyer, *Purity in Print* (New York: Charles Scribner's Sons, 1968), pp. 238–42. For descriptions of Dennett's career, see Kennedy, *Birth Control in America*, pp. 75–77, 222–25.
34. *U.S. v. Dennett*, p. 565.
35. Ibid., p. 566.
36. Ibid.
37. Ibid., pp. 566, 567.
38. Ibid., p. 567.
39. Ibid., p. 568.
40. Ibid., p. 569.
41. Anonymous, "The Enforcement of Laws Against Obscenity in New York," *Columbia Law Review* 28 (1928), p. 950. *U.S. v. Dennett*, p. 568.
42. *U.S. v. Dennett*, p. 569. For early sociological analyses of this "revolution," see Freda Kirchwey (ed.), *Our Changing Morality: A Symposium* (New York: Albert and Charles Boni, 1924), especially the introduction by Kirchwey and the articles by the anthropologist Elsie Clews Parsons and the psychiatrist Beatrice M. Hingle. Cf. Han-

nah M. Stone, "Birth Control and Population," in Harold E. Stearns (ed.), *America Now* (New York: Literary Guild of America, 1938).
43. Ernst and Seagle, *To the Pure*, p. 282.
44. Schroeder, "Obscenity, Prudery, and Morals," p. 102; "Psychologic Study of Modesty and Obscenity," p. 276.
45. Sanger, *An Autobiography*, p. 412.

5. The Defeat of Gentility

1. Sinclair Lewis, "The American Fear of Literature" (1930), reprinted in Harry Maule and Meville H. Cane (eds.), *The Man from Main Street: A Sinclair Lewis Reader* (New York: Random House, 1953), pp. 3–17.
2. Ibid., p. 8. For more on the myth of Dreiser as a beleaguered genius, see H. L. Mencken, "Theodore Dreiser," in his *A Book of Prefaces* (New York: Alfred A. Knopf, 1917), pp. 98–101, 140–45.
3. Lewis, "The American Fear of Literature," p. 7.
4. Goldman quoted in Hal Sears, *The Sex Radicals* (Lawrence: Regents Press of Kansas, 1977), p. 128.
5. Theodore Dresier on *Sister Carrie*, *St. Louis Post-Dispatch*, (January 26, 1902), p. 4, reprinted in Donald Pizer (ed.), *Sister Carrie* (New York: W. W. Norton, 1970), p. 458.
6. Theodore Dreiser, "True Art Speaks Plainly," *Booklover's Magazine* 1 (February 1903), p. 129, reprinted in Pizer, pp. 473, 474.
7. William Dean Howells (Clara Marburg Kirk and Rudolph Kirk, eds.), *Criticism and Fiction and Other Essays* (New York: New York University Press, 1959), p. 62.
8. Ibid., pp. 70, 71.
9. Dreiser, "True Art Speaks Plainly," p. 473.
10. Reginald Wright Kauffman, "The Drama and Morality," *Forum* 51 (January 1914), p. 672.
11. H. G. Wells, "The Contemporary Novel," *Atlantic Monthly* 109 (1912), p. 11. See Editorial, "Raw Material," *Dial* 52 (January 16, 1912), pp. 39–40, for criticism of Wells's position. See Christopher Lasch, "The Education of Lincoln Steffens," in *The New Radicalism in America* (New York: Vintage Books, 1965, 1967), for more on the young rebel's delight in discovering unpalatable truths.
12. Randolph Bourne, "Chivalry and Sin" (ms.), in Olaf Hansen (ed.), *The Radical Will: Randolph Bourne, Selected Writings, 1911–1918* (New York: Urizen Books, 1977), p. 487. For an excellent account of Bourne and his milieu, see Casey Nelson Blake, *Beloved Community* (Chapel Hill: University of North Carolina Press, 1990). For more on the "young intellectuals," see Thomas Bender, *New York Intellect* (Baltimore: Johns Hopkins University Press, 1987, 1988), pp. 228–41.
13. Mencken, "Theodore Dreiser," p. 88.
14. H. L. Mencken, "Joseph Conrad," in *A Book of Prefaces*, p. 19. The quotes from Arthur Symons on Conrad appear in *The Forum* for May 1915. For more on the stance of moral neutrality, see Mencken, pp. 31–32.
15. Stuart P. Sherman, "The Naturalism of Mr. Dreiser," *The Nation*, December 8, 1915, reprinted in George J. Becker (ed.), *Documents of Modern Literary Realism* (Princeton: Princeton University Press, 1963), p. 453. Sherman would change his critical assessment of Dreiser in 1927 when he praised his *An American Tragedy*.
16. Bourne, "The Art of Theodore Drieser" in Randolph Bourne (Van Wyck Brooks, ed.), *History of a Literary Radical and Other Essays* (New York: B. W. Huebsch, 1920), pp. 198, 197. Also see Mencken, "Theodore Dreiser," p. 96.
17. Bourne, "The Art of Theodore Dreiser," p. 197.

18. Ibid., p. 198. For Bourne's most fully realized analysis of "conglomerate American-ism," see "Transnational America," in Brooks, pp. 266–99.

19. Bourne, "This Older Generation," *Atlantic Monthly*, September 1915, in Brooks, p. 123. Bourne, "Pageantry and Social Art," in Hansen, p. 516. See also *Commonwealth v. Fried*, 271 Mass. 318 (1930), where *An American Tragedy* was found obscene.

20. Bourne, "The Art of Theodore Dreiser," pp. 198–99. See also Edmund Wilson, "Signs of Life: *Lady Chatterley's Lover*" (1929) in Wilson, *The Shores of Light: A Literary Chronicle of the 20s and 30s* (New York: Farrar, Straus and Young, 1952). Wilson calls for a language appropriate to sexual love: "We have only, on the one hand, colloquial words that will deeply offend some people and no doubt be un-intelligible to others, and on the other hand, the technical words in works on biology and medicine. Neither kind goes well in a love scene intended to generate an illusion of charm or romance" (pp. 406–7).

21. Bourne, "The Art of Theodore Dreiser," pp. 199–200.

22. See *Besig* v. *U.S.*, 208 Fed. 2nd 142 (1953), regarding Miller's *Tropic of Cancer* and *Tropic of Capricorn*: "It is claimed that they truthfully describe a base status of society in the language of its own iniquities. And that, since we live in an age of realism, obscene language depicting obscenity in action ceases to be obscene" (p. 145).

23. For some good examples, see Malcolm Cowley, "Foreword," *After the Genteel Tra-dition* (Gloucester: Peter Smith, 1959); Henry May, *The End of American Innocence* (New York: Alfred A. Knopf, 1959), pp. 340–45; Daniel Aaron, *Writers on the Left* (New York: Harcourt, Brace & World, 1961), pp. 8–15; James Gilbert, *Writers and Partisans* (New York: John Wiley & Sons, 1968); and Warren Susman, "Uses of the Puritan Past," in *Culture as History* (New York: Pantheon Books, 1984), pp. 39–50.

24. Mary Alden Hopkins, "Birth Control and Public Morals: An Interview with An-thony Comstock," *Harper's Weekly* 60 (May 22, 1915), p. 489. H. L. Mencken, "Puritanism as a Literary Force," in *A Book of Prefaces*, p. 260. Morris L. Ernst and William Seagle, *To the Pure . . . A Study of Obscenity and the Censor* (New York: The Viking Press, 1928) p. 105. Edward De Grazia, "Obscenity and the Mail: A Study of Administrative Restraint," *Law and Contemporary Problems* (1955), p. 619. Robert W. Haney, *Comstockery in America* (Boston: Beacon Press, 1960).

25. Sears, *The Sex Radicals*, p. 72; and Richard C. Johnson, *Anthony Comstock: Reform, Vice, and the American Way* (Ph.D. dissertation, University of Wisconsin, 1973). Hopkins, "Birth Control and Public Morals: An Interview with Anthony Com-stock," p. 489. Comstock quoted in Heywood Broun and Margaret Leech, *Anthony Comstock: Roundsman of the Lord* (New York: Literary Guild of America, 1927), pp. 15–16.

26. For examples of nineteenth-century attacks on Comstock, see Sears, *The Sex Radicals*, p. 37; Ezra Heywood, *Cupid's Yokes: The Binding Forces of Conjugal Love* (Princeton: Co-operative Publishing, n.d.), pp. 11, 12; D. M. Bennett, *Anthony Comstock: His Career of Cruelty and Crime* (New York: Da Capo Press, 1971, originally published in 1878), pp. 1018–1106; and O. B. Frothingham, "The Suppression of Vice," *North American Review* 135 (June 1882), pp. 489–95. Theodore Schroeder, *"Ob-scene" Literature and Constitutional Law* (New York: Privately printed, 1911), pp. 103, 102. For more direct attacks on Comstock, see pp. 101, 124, 225. Comstock never received a salary for his work.

27. Shaw quoted in Morris L. Ernst and Alexander Lindey, *The Censor Marches On* (New York: Doubleday, 1940), p. 60. Broun and Leech, *Anthony Comstock*, p. 235. For more on Shaw's discussions of comstockery in America, see Sears, *The Sex Radicals*, pp. 264–66. H. L. Mencken, while he freely adopted Shaw's expression, dismissed him: "Shaw, a highly dexterous dramaturgist, smothers his dramaturgy in

a piffish iconoclasm that is no more than a disguise for Puritanism." Mencken, "Joseph Conrad," p. 26.

28. H. L. Mencken, "The Emperor of Wowsers" (review of Heywood Broun and Margaret Leech, *Anthony Comstock: Roundsman of the Lord*, 1927) in James T. Farrell (ed.), *H. L. Mencken, Prejudices: A Selection*, p. 239.
29. This incident is recounted in Broun and Leech, pp. 216–20, and also in Anthony Comstock (Robert Bremner, ed.), *Traps for the Young* (Cambridge: Belknap Press, 1967, originally published in 1883), p. xxviii.
30. The *New York Sun*, October 13, 1906, quoted in Sears, *The Sex Radicals*, p. 263. See Theodore Schroeder's account of the meeting in his *"Obscene" Literature and Constitutional Law*, p. 327.
31. Hopkins, "Birth Control and Public Morals: An Interview with Anthony Comstock," p. 489. H. L. Mencken, "Puritanism as a Literary Force," in *A Book of Prefaces*, pp. 197–283.
32. Mencken, "Puritanism as a Literary Force," pp. 276, 270.
33. Ibid., pp. 230, 232.
34. Ibid., pp. 242, 244, 243, 255. Mencken's discussion of the expert's prominent position in these reform organizations points to the complexity of the history of the new class and the malleability of its methods. Although Progressive reformers had developed scientific management with its reliance on experts to promote their chief goal, efficiency, Mencken's linkage of experts with the old-fashioned project of moral improvement suggests that Puritan reformers were able to successfully modify modern techniques to further their own seemingly outdated aims.
35. Louis Kronenberger, "H. L. Mencken," in Cowley, *After the Genteel Tradition*, p. 103.
36. Mencken, "Puritanism as a Literary Force," p. 228.
37. Ibid., pp. 101–2, 207.
38. Ibid., p. 199.
39. Ibid., pp. 200, 225.
40. Ibid., p. 28.
41. Mencken, "James Huneker," in *A Book of Prefaces*, p. 156. "Puritanism as a Literary Force," pp. 275–76. Also see "The Dean," in *Prejudices: First Series* (Alfred A. Knopf, 1919), pp. 52–58. An excellent anthology of attacks on Howells is Kenneth E. Eble (ed.), *Howells: A Century of Criticism* (Dallas: Southern Methodist University Press, 1962).
42. Broun and Leech, *Anthony Comstock*, pp. 244, 270, 275.
43. Randolph Bourne, "H. L. Mencken," *Dial* 64 (March 1918), in Hansen, pp. 472–74; "Traps for the Unwary," *New Republic* 3 (May 1915), in Hansen, p. 480; "The Light Essay," *New Republic* 6 (April 1916), in Hansen, p. 509.
44. Walter Lippmann, *A Preface to Politics* (New York: Macmillan, 1913, 1933), p. 5. H. W. Boynton, "Ideas, Sex, and the Novel," *Dial* 60 (April 13, 1916), p. 359. Bourne, "An Examination of Eminences," *New Republic*, April 1915, in Hansen, pp. 489, 490. For insightful criticism of "the historic complacency" which had settled on the reigning interpretation of the "revolt against gentility and repression" in American studies by the 1940s, see the preface to Alfred Kazin's *On Native Grounds* (New York: Harcourt Brace Jovanovich, 1942, 1982). Kazin criticized this point of view for applying "mechanically Santayana's well-worn phrase, the 'Genteel Tradition,' to everything Mencken's iconoclastic generation disliked in late-nineteenth-century life" (p. xiv). Cf. Malcolm Cowley's introduction in *After the Genteel Tradition*. Also see Edwin Harrison Cady, *The Gentleman in America* (Syracuse: Syracuse University Press, 1949). He points out the limitations of understanding modernity as a revolt against gentility (pp. 23–27).

45. R.E.R., "The Young Modern and the Puritan," *New Republic* 16 (August 17, 1918), p. 84. See Alasdair MacIntyre, *After Virtue* (Notre Dame: University of Notre Dame Press, 1981), pp. 8–10, 68, for an excellent discussion of the character of modern moral disputes.
46. Walter Lippmann, *Drift and Mastery* (Madison: University of Wisconsin Press, 1985), p. 92. Bourne, "An Examination of Eminences," in Hansen, p. 489. For an excellent analysis of the role of generational conflict in Bourne's thought, see Christopher Lasch's "Randolph Bourne and the Experimental Life," pp. 69–103, in his *The New Radicalism*.
47. Lippmann, *A Preface to Politics*, p. 37. See Franz Steiner, *Taboo* (London: Pelican Books, 1956, 1967), p. 51, for the Victorian roots of the concept of taboo, and MacIntyre, *After Virtue*, pp. 105–7, for a penetrating discussion of taboos.
48. Bourne, "Old Tyrannies," *Untimely Papers* (1919), in Hansen, pp. 172–73.
49. MacIntyre, *After Virtue*, pp. 11 (his emphasis), 107.
50. Bourne, "This Older Generation," in Brooks, pp. 120–21.
51. Bourne, "The Puritan's Will to Power," *New Republic*, April 1917, in Brooks, pp. 180, 184, 182, 185. Mencken quoted this essay approvingly in his "Puritanism as a Literary Force," p. 237. See MacIntyre, *After Virtue*, pp. 66–69, for an extensive discussion of how "unmasking the motives of arbitrary will and desire" has become "one of the most characteristically modern of activities."
52. Van Wyck Brooks, *America's Coming-of-Age* (New York: B. W. Huebsch, 1915). See Douglas L. Wilson's introduction to Santayana, *The Genteel Tradition* (Cambridge: Harvard University Press, 1967), pp. 20–21, for a detailed analysis of Brooks's indebtedness to Santayana.
53. George Santayana, "The Genteel Tradition in American Philosophy" (1911) in Wilson (ed.), *The Genteel Tradition*, pp. 39, 38, 40. Brooks, *America's Coming-of-Age*, pp. 14, 7.
54. Santayana, "The Genteel Tradition," p. 41.
55. Ibid., pp. 42, 43, 44, 51. Brooks located the source of the lowbrow in the "practical shifts of Puritan life, becoming a philosophy in Franklin, passing through the American humorists, and resulting in the atmosphere of our contemporary business life" (p. 9).
56. Brooks, *America's Coming-of-Age*, pp. 9, 110.
57. George Santayana, "The Academic Environment," in *Character and Opinion in the United States* (New York: W. W. Norton, 1967), p. 44. Brooks, *America's Coming-of-Age*, p. 111. Cf. pp. 17–29. Mencken also employed this anti-feminine idiom, missing no opportunity to sneer at feminized culture. See his "Puritanism as a Literary Force," pp. 213–16.
58. Geoffrey Blodgett, "Reform Thought and the Genteel Tradition," in H. Wayne Morgan (ed.), *The Gilded Age* (Syracuse: Syracuse University Press, 1963, 1973), p. 56.
59. Christopher Lasch, "Woman as Alien," in *The New Radicalism*, p. 65. Also see his "Jane Addams: The College Woman and the Family Claim," pp. 3–37.
60. For a good account of intellectuals' feelings of "overrefinement," see Lasch, *The New Radicalism*. See also T. J. Jackson Lears, *No Place of Grace* (New York: Pantheon, 1981), pp. 3–58.
61. Lionel Trilling, "Reality in America" (1940, 1946), in *The Liberal Imagination* (New York: The Viking Press, 1950), p. 13. Richard Hofstadter, *The Age of Reform* (New York: Vintage Books, 1955), p. 201. See, for example, Howells's review of Frank Norris's *McTeague*, reprinted in *Criticism and Fiction and Other Essays*, pp. 279–82. Cf. Charles Dudley Warner, "Modern Fiction," *Atlantic Monthly* 51 (April 1883),

pp. 464–74. He questions how the representation of the "shady and seamy side of life" came to be identified with realism.
62. Cowley, *After the Genteel Tradition*, p. 20. For another excellent example of this position, see F. O. Matthiessen, *Theodore Dreiser* (New York: William Sloane Associates, 1951), p. 62.
63. Trilling, "Reality in America," pp. 12, 15.
64. Cf. Lasch's chapter "The Anti-Intellectualism of the Intellectuals" in *The New Radicalism*, pp. 286–349. For an insightful account of the historical shift that devalued thought and contemplation and glorified labor and action, see Hannah Arendt, "Tradition and the Modern Age," pp. 17–41, in *Between Past and Future* (New York: Penguin Books, 1961, 1985), and *The Human Condition* (Chicago: University of Chicago Press, 1958), pp. 289–304. See Gilbert, *Writers and Partisans*, pp. 9–15, for the romance with the tramp and proletcult writers' infatuation with virile workers. "The effeminate intellectual concerned only with the workings of his own mind and committed to a theory of art vs. the tough, virile worker determined to remake the world" (p. 75). Also see Martin Green, *New York: 1913* (New York: Charles Scribner's Sons, 1988), pp. 148–67, for a picture of the virile Wobbly.

6. The Legal Debate about the Right to Privacy

1. E. L. Godkin, "The Rights of the Citizen: To His Own Reputation," *Scribner's Magazine* 8 (1890), p. 61. Cf. Anonymous, "The Defense of Privacy," *Spectator* 66 (1891): "Nobody can be horsewhipped today for asking why a man changed his faith, what his income is, or why he married his wife" (p. 200).
2. Editorial, "The Decay of American Journalism," *Dial* 22 (1897), pp. 238, 239. J. H. Crooker, "Daily Papers and Their Readers: A Suggestion," *Dial* 15 (October 1, 1893), p. 179. Richard Watson Gilder (interviewed by Clifton Johnson), "The Newspaper, the Magazine, and the Public," *Outlook* 61 (1899), p. 321. Also see William H. Bushnell, "Journalistic Barbarism," *The Inland Printer* 3 (January 1886), p. 202; E. L. Godkin, "The Right to Privacy," *The Nation* (December 25, 1890), pp. 496–97, and E. L. Godkin, "Responsibility for Yellow Journalism," *The Nation* 73 (September 26, 1901), p. 238.
3. Editorial, "A Newspaper Symposium," *Dial* 15 (August 16, 1893), p. 80. Editors, "An Endowed Newspaper," *Dial* 14 (January 16, 1893), p. 36. Also see W. H. H. Murray, "An Endowed Press," *Arena* 2 (October 1890), pp. 556–59.
4. Murray, "An Endowed Press," p. 555. Also see Richard Grant White, "The Pest of the Period: A Chapter of the Morals and Manners of Journalism," *Galaxy* 9 (June 1870), p. 112; George T. Rider, "The Pretensions of Journalism," *North American Review* 135 (June 1882), p. 476; Condé Benoist Pallen, "Newspaperism," *Lippincott's Monthly Magazine* 38 (1886), p. 475; Charles Dudley Warner, "Newspapers and the Public," *Forum* 9 (1890), p. 205; and George W. Alger, "Sensational Journalism and the Law," *Atlantic Monthly* 91 (February 1903), pp. 145–51.
5. Pound quoted in Alpheus T. Mason, *Brandeis: A Free Man's Life* (New York: The Viking Press, 1946), p. 70. Louis Brandeis and Samuel Warren, "The Right to Privacy," *Harvard Law Review* 4 (1890), pp. 195, 196. For examples of recent legal discussions of the right to privacy that evoke Brandeis and Warren, see Harry Kalven, "Privacy in Tort Law—Were Warren and Brandeis Wrong?" *Law and Contemporary Problems* 31 (1966), pp. 326–41; Edward J. Bloustein, "Privacy, Tort Law, and the Constitution: Is Warren and Brandeis's Tort Petty and Unconstitutional As Well?" *Texas Law Review* 46 (1968), pp. 611–29; and Diane L. Zimmerman, "Requiem for a Heavyweight: A Farewell to Warren and Brandeis's Privacy Tort," *Cornell Law Review* 68 (1982–83), pp. 291–367.

6. J. G. A. Pocock, "Virtues, Rights, and Manners: A Model for Historians of Political Thought" in *Virtue, Commerce, and History* (Cambridge: Cambridge University Press, 1985), pp. 50, 49.
7. Brandeis and Warren, "The Right to Privacy," p. 175. For examples of "sociological jurisprudence, see Brandeis and Warren, "The Right to Privacy," pp. 192–95; Roscoe Pound, "Interests of Personality," *Harvard Law Review* 28 (1915), pp. 343–65, 445–56; and R. Jeffrey Lustig, *Corporate Liberalism* (Berkeley: University of California Press, 1982), pp. 176–83.
8. Brandeis and Warren, "The Right to Privacy," pp. 195, 197. This phrase is taken from Judge Cooley's influential *Torts* (1888). This definition is later expanded by Archibald W. McClean in "The Right of Privacy," *The Green Bag* 15 (1903): "Would it not give a new meaning to our boasted liberties, by opening, enlarging, and guarding a sphere where individuality might grow and mature, conscious of a right to be let alone?" (p. 497). They cite Godkin's piece twice, on p. 195 n. 6 and p. 217 n. 14.
9. Brandeis and Warren, "The Right to Privacy," p. 198.
10. Ibid., pp. 198–99, 205.
11. Ibid., p. 213. Cf. p. 213 n. 1: "The cases referred to above show the common law has for a century and a half protected privacy in certain cases, and to grant the further protection now suggested would be merely another application of an existing rule."
12. Ibid., p. 219.
13. Ibid., pp. 214–16.
14. Ibid., pp. 219–20. See Mary Ann Glendon, *Rights Talk: The Impoverishment of Political Discourse* (New York: The Free Press, 1991), for an excellent discussion of the limiting language of the right to privacy.
15. After 1919, no new issues were raised even with the introduction of new technological means of spying and of computers.
16. *Schuyler* v. *Curtis*, 19 N.Y.S. 264 (1891), 42 N.E. 22 (1895).
17. *Schulman* v. *Whitaker*, 117 La. 704 (1906); *Itzkovitch* v. *Whitaker*, 117 La. 708 (1906); *Hodgeman* v. *Olsen*, 86 Wash. 435 (1915).
18. *Murray* v. *Gast Lithographic and Engraving Co.*, 28 N.Y.S. 271 (1894); *Munden* v. *Harris*, 153 Mo. App. 652 (1911). In *Douglas* v. *Stokes*, 149 S.W. 850 (1912), Douglas's wife had given birth to Siamese twins born together from the shoulders and down to the end of their bodies. They died, and after their death, the plaintiff employed Stokes, a photographer, to take a photograph of the babies nude. The defendant agreed to make twelve photographs for the plaintiff. Contrary to the agreement, however, the defendant made several more photographs, one of which he filed in the U.S. Copyright Office, which then issued a copyright to him. The judge found on behalf of the plaintiff, asserting that the plaintiff's right of privacy of the bodies of his dead children had been violated.
19. Elbridge Adams, "Right of Privacy and Its Relation to the Law of Libel," *American Law Review* 39 (1905), pp. 38–39. John Henderson Garnsey, "The Demand for Sensational Journals," *Arena* 18 (1897), p. 681. *New York Times*, August 23, 1902, p. 8. For another description of violations of privacy, see Samuel W. Pennypacker, "Sensational Journalism and the Remedy," *North American Review* 190 (November 1909), pp. 587–93.
20. Godkin, "The Right to Privacy," pp. 496–97. Pallen, "Newspaperism," p. 475. Murray, "An Endowed Press," p. 556. The editors of *The Atlantic Monthly* 67 (1891), pp. 428–429, also met Brandeis and Warren's call for a new protection of privacy and their evolutionary view of law with skepticism and derision.

21. *Vassar College* v. *Loose-Wiles Biscuit Co.*, 197 Fed. 985 (1912). Brandeis and Warren, "The Right to Privacy," pp. 215–16.
22. *Roberson* v. *Rochester Folding Box Co.*, 171 N.Y. (1902), 542–43.
23. Ibid., p. 543. For an earlier example of this attitude, see *Schuyler* v. *Curtis*, 42 N.E. 22 (1895), where the judge, finding against the plaintiff, remarked, "It is wholly incredible that any individual could dwell with feelings of distress or anguish upon the thought that, after his death, those whose welfare he had toiled for in life would inaugurate a project to erect a statue in token of their appreciation of his efforts, and in honor of his memory. This applies to the most refined and retiring woman as to a public man" (p. 25). "Feelings that are thus easily and unnaturally injured and distressed under such circumstances are much too sensitive to be recognized by any purely earthly tribunal" (p. 26).
24. *Roberson* v. *Rochester Folding Box Co.*, pp. 550, 545, 540. Cf. Roscoe Pound, "Interests of Personality," *Harvard Law Review* 28 (1915). Pound claimed that the two major problems facing the right to privacy were that the interest of the right to privacy is mental and subjective, which makes it difficult to prove; and that it is often in conflict with "social interests in free speech and dissemination of news" (p. 347).
25. Ibid., pp. 560, 561.
26. Ibid., pp. 561–62. See also Percy L. Edwards, "Rights of Privacy and Equity Relief," *Central Law Journal* 35 (1902): "Equity, the progressive part of the law, moves toward ethical perfection. . . . The proposition that equity will protect rights other than property is a distinct advance in equitable doctrine, and proves the progressiveness of this side of the law" (p. 123).
27. Ibid., p. 562. This claim is made repeatedly. See, for example, *Schuyler* v. *Curtis*, 42 N.E. 25 (1895), where the dissenting opinion asserted that the "sacred" right of privacy protects "not only the person of the individual, but every personal interest which he possesses and is entitled to regard as private." For a long view of this perspective, see Richard Tuck, *Natural Rights Theories: Their Origin and Development* (Cambridge: Cambridge University Press, 1979), and James Tully, *A Discourse on Property: John Locke and His Adversaries* (Cambridge: Cambridge University Press, 1980). By the close of the nineteenth century, discussions about property became acute largely on account of debates about socialism, the influence of neo-Hegelians such as Bernard Bosanquet and T. H. Green, and the increase of trusts and monopolies, whose multiple ownership began to separate personality from property and property from power. Likewise, a burgeoning literature about "corporeal" vs. "incorporeal" property entered the law journals. In 1913, confusion about the meaning of property had become so great that a legal scholar, Wesley Hohfield, declared, "Both with lawyers and laymen [property] has no definite or stable connotation." He observed that "a similar looseness of thought and expression lurks in the supposed (but false) contrast between 'corporeal' and 'incorporeal' property." In Hohfield's account, all legal interests were "incorporeal" because they necessarily represent abstract legal relations. Moreover, he drew attention to the many ambiguities embodied in the idea of "right"—its complicated association with property, interest, power, prerogative, immunity, and privilege. Wesley N. Hohfield, "Some Fundamental Legal Conceptions as Applied in Judicial Reasoning," *Yale Law Review* 23 (1913), pp. 21, 24.
28. *Roberson* v. *Rochester Folding Box Co.*, p. 564. This proprietary claim to the value of one's features was made in other cases as well. See *Edison* v. *Edison Polyform and Manufacturing Co.*, 73 N.J. Eq. 141, where the judge asserted that a person's name and features are one's property and that "its pecuniary value, if it has one, belong to its owner rather than to the person seeking to make an unauthorized use of it";

Munden v. *Harris*, 153 Mo. App. 660, where the judge concluded "that one has an exclusive right to his picture, on the score of its being a property right of material profit." Cf. *Murray* v. *Gast Lithographic and Engraving Co.*, p. 272 where the judge decided against issuing an injunction against the reproduction of a photograph of the Murrays' daughter because the father could not bring suit on a portrait that was the property of his wife. See C. B. Macpherson, *The Political Theory of Possessive Individualism* (Oxford: Oxford University Press, 1962).

29. *American Law Review* quoted in Morris L. Ernst and Alan U. Schwartz, *Privacy: The Right to Be Let Alone* (New York: Macmillan, 1962), p. 143. *New York Times*, August 23, 1902, p. 8. *Yale Law Journal* 12 (1902–3), pp. 37–38. Cf. McClean, "The Right of Privacy": "Does not the license of yellow publicity suggest the absolute need of establishing the principle and righteousness of privacy?" (p. 494).

30. Denis O'Brien, "The Right of Privacy," *Columbia Law Review* 2 (1902), pp. 437–48.

31. Chapter 132 of *New York Laws* (1903). It was later amended, Section 51 and 52 of "Civil Rights Law of New York," Chapter 14 of *New York Laws* (1909).

32. Brandeis and Warren, "The Right to Privacy," p. 198.

33. *Pavesich* v. *New England Mutual Life Insurance Co.*, 122 Ga. 190 (1904).

34. Ibid., pp. 213, 220, 220–21, 202–5.

35. Ibid., pp. 193–98.

36. Ibid., p. 196.

37. Ibid., p. 201.

38. Ibid., p. 220.

39. *Mackenzie* v. *Soden Mineral Springs Co.*, 18 N.Y. Supp. 241 (1891). For other cases that exploit experts, see *Corliss* v. *E. W. Walker*, 57 Fed. Rep. 435 (1894), where the widow of a famous inventor brought suit to prevent the publication of an unauthorized biography of her husband containing his portrait and photograph; *Edison* v. *Edison Polyform and Manufacturing Co.*, p. 136 (1907), where the inventor Thomas Edison's name was used without his permission to sell a medicinal preparation intended to relieve neuralgic pains that Edison had compounded and sold in 1879; *D'Altomonte* v. *New York Herald Co.*, 154 App. Div. 453 (1913), where the defendant published an article of a sensational nature, describing an absurd and improbable adventure written in the first person and falsely attributing its authorship to the plaintiff, who was a traveler, writer, and lecturer of recognized ability, "whereby he was held up to public scandal, disgrace, and ridicule."

40. *Foster-Milburn Co.* v. *Chinn*, 134 Ky. 424, 425 (1909). For other cases that exploit public figures, see *Atkinson* v. *Doherty*, 80 N.W. 288 (1899), where the widow of a well-known lawyer and politician wanted to restrain the use of the name and likeness of her husband on a label to sell cigars named after him; *Von Thodorovich* v. *Franz Josef Beneficial Association*, 154 Fed. 911 (1907), where the use of the name of the Emperor of Austria-Hungary to advertise an insurance company was found to defraud his countrymen, to whom the name and portrait was meant to appeal. See also *Vassar College* v. *Loose-Wiles Biscuit Co.*, p. 983, for an example of the exploitation of the name and insignia of a public institution to sell chocolates.

41. For other cases that exploit private persons, see *Hart* v. *Woodbury*, 98 N.Y.S. 1000 (1906), where the defendant "maliciously composed and published" an advertisement of the plaintiff demonstrating that her skin, scarred by smallpox, had been improved by his treatments; *Henry* v. *Cherry and Webb*, 73 Atl. 98 (1909), where a mercantile company published a picture of the plaintiff as part of an advertisement to sell automobile coats; *Munden* v. *Harris*, p. 654, where a child's picture was used in an advertisement to sell jewelry; *Peck* v. *Tribune Co.*, 214 U.S. 188 (1909), where a portrait of a woman dressed as a nurse and false testimony were used to sell Duffy's

Pure Malt Whiskey as an "invigorating, life-giving laxative"; *Kunz v. Allen and Bayne*, 102 Kan. 883 (1918), where the plaintiff's photograph was displayed in a moving-picture theater advertising a dry-goods store.

42. *Binns* v. *Vitagraph Co.*, 147 App. Div. 783, 786.

43. *Kunz v. Allen and Bayne*, p. 883.

44. *Pavesich* v. *New England Mutual Life Insurance Co.*, p. 202. Richard F. Hixson's *Privacy in a Public Society: Human Rights in Conflict* (New York: Oxford University Press, 1987), a recent example, is almost entirely devoted to the interminable problem of balancing the individual's right to privacy with the freedom of the press.

45. Brandeis and Warren, "The Right to Privacy," pp. 214–15. For criminal cases, see *Schulman* v. *Whitaker*, 117 La. 704; *Itzkovitch* v. *Whitaker*, 117 La. 708; *Hodgeman* v. *Olsen*, 86 Wash. 615.

46. Brandeis and Warren, "The Right to Privacy," p. 116. *Corliss* v. *E. W. Walker*, 57 Fed. Rep. 435 (1894). Paul M. Brice, "Newspaper Ethics," *Editor and Publisher* (July 29, 1905), p. 7, quoted in Marion Tuttle Marzolf, *Civilizing Voices: American Press Criticism, 1880–1950* (New York: Longman, 1991), p. 71.

47. *Atkinson* v. *Doherty*, 80 N.W. 288 (1899). *Roberson* v. *Rochester Folding Box Co.*, p. 555.

48. *Munden* v. *Harris*, 153 Mo. App. 652 (1911). Wilbur Larremore, "The Law of Privacy," *Columbia Law Review* 12 (1912). *Hillman* v. *Star Publishing Co.*, 117 Pac. 594 (1911).

49. *Commonwealth* v. *Herald Publishing Co.*, 128 Ky. 429, 434, 435. Cf. Editorial, "Newspapers' Sensations and Suggestion," *The Independent* 62 (February 21, 1907): "Since so many people are deeply interested in the [court] proceedings, it must be beneficial to them to have the opportunity to read them" (p. 410).

50. *Commonwealth* v. *Herald Publishing Co.*, pp. 436, 437. For other examples of obscenity cases concerning newspapers publishing trials and crime stories, see *In Re Banks*, 56 Kan. 242 (1895); *State* v. *Van Wye*, 136 Mo. 227 (1896); *Strohm* v. *People*, 160 Ill. 582 (1896); and *State* v. *McKee*, 73 Conn. 18 (1900).

51. Editorial, "What the Public Wants," *Dial* 47 (December 16, 1909), p. 500. *U.S.* v. *Journal Co.*, 197 Fed. 419 (1912). See Pennypacker, "Sensational Journalism and the Remedy," p. 593, where he insists that sensational journalism "has no part in the liberty of the press any more than sewerage has place in the streams." See Will Irwin, "The American Newspaper: A Study of Journalism in Its Relation to the Public," a series of articles that appeared in *Collier's* (January–July 1911), for a good summary of the battle over mass-circulation journalism.

52. *Corliss* v. *E. W. Walker*, p. 435. *Marks* v. *Jaffa*, 26 N.Y. Supp. 909 (1893). *Pavesich* v. *New England Mutual Life Insurance Co.*, pp. 202, 219.

53. *Jeffries* v. *New York Evening Journal Publishing Co.*, 124 N.Y. Supp. 781 (1910). Cf. *Moser* v. *Press Publishing Co.*, 109 N.Y. Supp. 963 (1908), where the judge ruled that the New York law "has no application to and does not prevent the publication of a person's photograph without his consent in a daily newspaper in connection with items of news not in any way libelous"; *Almina* v. *Sea Beach Railway*, 141 N.Y. Supp. 842 (1913), where a railway used pictures of passengers entering and leaving a car in order to teach passengers the proper and safe way to do so. The court asserted, "While the picture was not used for 'trade purposes,' the element of gain being too remote, it was used for 'advertising purposes,' which is not limited to matters of vocation, or even avocation, but includes advertisements essentially for unselfish purposes"; *Humiston* v. *Universal Film Manufacturing Co.*, 178 N.Y. Supp. 752 (1919), where the judge found that the New York law did not prohibit the publication of a person's picture or name without his consent "in a single set of films of actual events" which are a matter of current news.

54. *Colyer* v. *Richard K. Fox Publishing Co.*, 162 App. Div. 299 (1914).
55. Merle Thorpe (ed.), *The Coming Newspaper* (New York: Henry Holt, 1915), pp. 2, 3. This symposium provides good examples of the continued invasive methods of journalism.
56. Mitchell Dawson, "Paul Pry and Privacy," *Atlantic Monthly* 150 (October 1932), p. 393.
57. Frederick Seaton Siebert, *The Rights and Privileges of the Press* (New York: D. Appleton-Century, 1934), pp. 249, 250. Also see Silas Bent, *Ballyhoo: The Voice of the Press* (New York: Horace Liveright, 1927), p. 63.
58. See Thorpe, *The Coming Newspaper*, especially Barrat O'Hara, "A State Licence for Newspapermen"; Bent, *Ballyhoo*, pp. 371–72; Dawson, "Paul Pry and Privacy," p. 394; and Marzolf, *Civilizing Voices*.
59. Bent, *Ballyhoo*, p. 369.
60. Oswald Garrison Villard, "Tabloid Offenses," *Forum* 77 (1927), p. 486. Also see Bent, *Ballyhoo*, pp. 363–64; Dawson, "Privacy and Paul Pry," p. 391; Marzolf, *Civilizing Voices*, p. 84. For a good discussion of the explosion of sensational journalism during the 1920s, see Paul S. Boyer, *Purity in Print* (New York: Charles Scribner's Sons, 1968), pp. 154–61.
61. Bent, *Ballyhoo*, pp. 371, xvi, 378. Villard, "Tabloid Offenses," pp. 485, 488. John Macy, "Journalism," Harold E. Stearns (ed.), *Civilization in the United States* (New York: Harcourt, Brace, 1922), p. 44.
62. Dawson, "Paul Pry and Privacy," p. 385. Villard, "Tabloid Offenses," pp. 485, 486. For a description of further offenses published in magazines, see Oswald G. Villard, "Sex, Art, Truth, and Magazines," *Atlantic Monthly* 137 (1926), pp. 388–98.
63. Dawson, "Paul Pry and Privacy," p. 387.
64. Macy, "Journalism," p. 51. Stearns concluded after examining the volume that the only place for a civilized person was Paris, to which he immediately set off. Villard, "Tabloid Offenses," p. 485. Dawson, "Paul Pry and Privacy," pp. 387, 394.
65. Martin Weyrich, "The Why of Tabloids," *Forum* 77 (1927), p. 492.
66. Ibid., pp. 494, 496, 497, 499.
67. Boyer, *Purity in Print*, pp. 94, 193. For Villard's anti-censorship position, see Villard, "Sex, Art, Truth, and Magazines," pp. 397–98.
68. Richard Burton, "Good Manners in Literature," *Forum* 77 (1927), p. 231.
69. Ibid., pp. 231–32.
70. Ibid., pp. 232, 230, 232.
71. Ibid., p. 234.

7. THE LEGAL DEBATE ABOUT OBSCENITY

1. See *U.S.* v. *Loftis*, 12 Fed. Rep. 671 (1882), and *U.S.* v. *Wilson*, 58 Fed. Rep. 768 (1893).
2. See *Worthington Co.*, 30 N.Y.S. (1894), and *Commonwealth* v. *McCance*, 164 Mass. 162 (1895).
3. *People* v. *Seltzer*, 122 N.Y. Misc. 332 (1924). *People* v. *Muller*, 90 N.Y. 411 (1884). *U.S.* v. *Harmon*, 45 Fed. Rep. 417 (1891). *U.S.* v. *Clarke*, 38 Fed. Rep. 734 (1889). The importance of trial by jury was also stressed in *U.S.* v. *Bennett*, 16 Blatchford 351 (1879); *U.S.* v. *Harmon*, pp. 414, 418; *Commonwealth* v. *Buckley*, 200 Mass. 346 (1908); *U.S.* v. *Kennerley*, 209 Fed. 121 (1913). For accounts of the history of the rise to prominence of experts, see, for example, Burton Bledstein, *The Culture of Professionalism* (New York: W. W. Norton, 1978); Robert Wiebe, *The Search for Order* (New York: Hill and Wang, 1967), especially Chapter 5; Thomas Haskell,

The Emergence of Professional Social Science (Urbana: University of Illinois Press, 1977).

4. *U.S.* v. *Bennett*, pp. 364, 368. See also *U.S.* v. *Bebout*, 28 Fed. Rep. 524 (1886). *U.S.* v. *Clarke*, p. 733. *State* v. *Brown*, 27 Vt. 619. Cf. *Commonwealth* v. *Buckley*, 200 Mass 346 (1908).

5. *U.S.* v. *Bennett*, pp. 355, 368, 365. *People* v. *Eastman*, 188 N.Y. 485 (1907). *U.S.* v. *Bebout*, p. 524.

6. Comstock Act of March 3, 1873, 17 Stat. at L., 598. *Regina* v. *Hicklin*, L.R. 3 Q.B. 36 (1868).

7. For examples of the importance of "influence" in the nineteenth century, see Ann Douglas, *The Feminization of American Culture* (New York: Alfred A. Knopf, 1976); and Karen Haltunnen, *Confidence Men and Painted Women* (New Haven: Yale University Press, 1982).

8. Alasdair MacIntyre's remarks are suggestive in this context: "Deprive children of stories and you leave them unscripted, anxious stutterers in their actions as in their words." *After Virtue* (Notre Dame: University of Notre Dame Press, 1981) p. 201.

9. *Dunlop* v. *U.S.*, 171 Sup. Ct. 380 (1897).

10. Anonymous, "The Enforcement of Laws Against Obscenity in New York," *Columbia Law Review* 28 (1928), p. 951. *U.S.* v. *Harmon*, pp. 419, 417. *People* v. *Muller*, p. 413. Also see *People* v. *Seltzer*, p. 335; and *Ex Parte Jackson*, 96 U.S. 727 (1878).

11. *U.S.* v. *Bennett*, p. 343; *U.S.* v. *Harmon*, p. 415.

12. *U.S.* v. *Bennett*, pp. 358, 359, 360.

13. *U.S.* v. *Harmon*, p. 416.

14. Ibid.

15. *People* v. *Muller*, p. 423.

16. *U.S.* v. *Clarke*, pp. 732, 734.

17. Quoted in Paul S. Boyer, *Purity in Print: The Vice Society Movement and Book Censorship in America* (Charles Scribner's Sons, 1968), p. 46.

18. *U.S.* v. *Kennerley*, pp. 120–21. For praise of the decision, see Sidney S. Grant and S. E. Angoff, "Massachusetts and Censorship," *Boston University Law Review* 10 (1930), p. 156; and Harry M. Clor, *Obscenity and Public Morality* (Chicago: University of Chicago Press, 1969). Clor characterized Judge Hand's remarks as "the most influential paragraph in the history of the subject between Kennerley and Roth" (p. 19).

19. E.R.K., "Criminal Law—Meaning of Obscenity Federal Statute," *Illinois Law Review* 9 (1914–15), p. 193. James F. Morton, "Our Foolish Obscenity Laws," *Case and Comment* 23 (1916), pp. 23, 24.

20. For fully developed accounts of the "unencumbered self," see Alasdair MacIntyre, *After Virtue*, and Michael J. Sandel, *Liberalism and the Limits of Justice* (Cambridge: Cambridge University Press, 1982).

21. "The Enforcement of Laws against Obscenity in New York," p. 953. Grant and Angoff, "Massachusetts and Censorship," pp. 188, 157. Morris L. Ernst and William Seagle, *To the Pure . . . A Study of Obscenity and the Censor* (New York: The Viking Press, 1928), p. 192. Ernst represented Radclyffe Hall's *The Well of Loneliness*, Mary Ware Dennett, the two publications by Stopes, and James Joyce's *Ulysses*, to name a few of the most important trials.

22. Quoted in Boyer, *Purity in Print*, p. 234.

23. Ernst and Seagle, *To the Pure*, p. 234.

24. Ibid., pp. 234, 235.

25. Ibid., pp. 239–49.

26. Ibid., pp. 197, 198.

27. "Who's Obscene?" *The Nation* 130 (February 26, 1930), p. 236; Arthur Garfield

Hays, *Let Freedom Ring* (New York: Boni & Liveright, 1928), pp. 163–64; Mary Ware Dennett, *Publishers Weekly* 117 (May 31, 1930), p. 2735—all quoted in Boyer, *Purity in Print*, p. 150.

28. *People* v. *Friede*, 133 N.Y. Misc. 612 (1929), p. 614. See Boyer, *Purity in Print*, pp. 132–35, for a full account of the controversy over *The Well of Loneliness*.

29. *U.S.* v. *Dennett*, 39 Fed. 2nd 569 (1930). *U.S.* v. *One Obscene Book Entitled "Married Love,"* 48 Fed. 2nd 824 (1931).

30. *U.S.* v. *One Book Entitled "Contraception,"* 51 Fed. 2nd 528 (1931). For other trials in which the defendant was found not guilty according to the Hicklin Test, see *Dysart* v. *U.S.*, 47 Sup. Ct. Rep. 234 (1926), where Justice McReynolds found that an advertisement of a lying-in retreat to enable unmarried women to conceal their "missteps," even though written in "a coarse and vulgar style," did not fall within the scope of the statute, and was not obscene within the meaning of the law; and *Duncan* v. *U.S.*, 48 Fed. 2nd 129 (1931), where the court found that a radio broadcast that insulted public officials was not obscene even though the defendant made "use of extremely abusive and objectionable names, and use of rough, abusive, vulgar, and unseemly language."

31. *Commonwealth* v. *Friede*, 271 Mass. 318, pp. 319, 320, 322. See also *Dreiser* v. *John Lane Co.*, 171 N.Y.S. 605 (1918), where Dreiser sued his publisher for refusing to publish his novel *The Genius* or advertise it further once the New York Society for the Suppression of Vice had deemed the book obscene. The court found that John Lane had not made a breach of contract since "it was a fact that [the book] was obscene."

32. *People* v. *Pesky*, 243 N.Y. Supp. (1930), pp. 196, 197. Cf. Ernst and Seagle's remarks in *To the Pure* on the belief of "common folk" that the literati have "poor character" and are "perverse" (p. 222). For a parallel attack on "high brows who are so fond of . . . European literature" that took place in Congress during debates over tariff restrictions in 1930, see Boyer, *Purity in Print*, p. 232.

33. *People* v. *Pesky*, p. 199.

34. Ernst and Seagle, *To the Pure*, pp. 43, 55–56.

35. Ibid., p. 75. For a good account of the role played by customs officials in censorship, see Boyer, *Purity in Print*, Chapter 8; and Morris Ernst and Alexander Lindey, *The Censor Marches On* (New York: Doubleday, 1940), pp. 15–16.

36. Ernst and Seagle, *To the Pure*, p. 4.

37. Ibid., pp. 271, 272. Leo M. Alpert, "Judicial Censorship of Obscene Literature," *Harvard Law Review* 52 (1938), pp. 74–75.

38. Grant and Angoff, "Massachusetts and Censorship," pp. 159, 160.

39. Silas Bent, *Ballyhoo: The Voice of the Press* (New York: Horace Liveright, 1927), pp. 362, 363–64. Marion Tuttle Marzolf, *Civilizing Voices: American Press Criticism, 1880–1950* (New York: Longman, 1991), p. 84.

40. Ernst and Seagle, *To the Pure*, pp. 36, 163.

41. Ibid., pp. 8, 13–14. Alpert, "Judicial Censorship of Obscene Literature," pp. 74–75.

42. Richard Burton, "Good Manners in Literature," *Forum* 77 (1927), p. 232.

43. For accounts of these controversies, see Alfred Kazin, *On Native Grounds* (New York: Harcourt, Brace, 1942, 1982); James Gilbert, *Writers and Partisans* (New York: Columbia University Press, 1968, 1992); and Jeffrey Segall, *Joyce in America* (Berkeley: University of California Press, 1933), Chapters 1–3. The leading New Humanist manifesto is Norman Foerster (ed.), *Humanism and America: Essays on the Outlook of Modern Civilization* (New York: Farrar and Rinehart, 1930). The leading manifesto against the New Humanists is C. Hartley Grattan (ed.), *The Critique of Humanism: A Symposium* (New York: Kennicart Press, 1930). Also see Ernst and Seagle,

To the Pure, pp. 212–18, for a description of the relativism plaguing American aesthetic theory and its consequences for obscenity law.

44. *People v. The Viking Press*, 264 N.Y. Supp. 534 (1933), pp. 537, 538. *People v. Friede*, p. 615. Cf. *People v. Seltzer*, p. 334, where the judge also rejects testimony from literary experts.

45. *People v. The Viking Press*, pp. 539, 534, 535. *People v. Friede*, p. 625.

46. *People v. The Viking Press*, pp. 536, 538. Cf. Ernst and Seagle, *To the Pure*: "It is plainly silly to attempt to derive the permissible sexiness of a novel from a judgment as to the degree in which sex actually pervades life" (pp. 202–3).

47. *People v. Wendling*, 258 N.Y. (1932), pp. 451, 452, 453.

48. Ibid., pp. 453, 454.

49. *Halsey v. New York Society for the Suppression of Vice*, 136 N.E. 223 (1922).

50. *People v. Seltzer*, p. 334. For a description of Thomas Seltzer's other legal troubles, especially as publisher of D. H. Lawrence's *Women in Love*, see Edward De Grazia, *Girls Lean Back Everywhere: The Law of Obscenity and the Assault on Genius* (New York: Vintage Books, 1992), pp. 71–84.

51. *People v. Pesky*, p. 198.

52. Boyer, *Purity in Print*, p. 256. Conflicting accounts of the history of the banning of *Ulysses* are presented by Ernst and Lindey, *The Censor Marches On*, pp. 21–22; Robert W. Haney, *Comstockery in America* (Boston: Beacon Press, 1960, 1974), pp. 26–27; and Boyer, *Purity in Print*, pp. 84–84, 253–54. The relevant passages of the Tariff Act (1930) can be found in 19 U.S. Code, Section 1305 (a). For a good summary of the events that led up to this legislative action and of the congressional debate surrounding it, see Boyer, pp. 208–38.

53. *U.S. v. One Book Called "Ulysses,"* 5 Fed. Supp. 183 (1933).

54. Ibid., p. 184.

55. Ibid., pp. 183–84. Ernst and Seagle, *To the Pure*, p. 201. Also see p. 218: "Literary dictatorship is a thing of the past, and impressionism is the prevailing mood of modern criticism. When it comes to explaining the 'obscene' and the 'aesthetic sense,' a modern critic has nothing more than his intuitions to go upon. The formula offered more frequently nowadays is that it is all a matter of 'taste.' "

56. *U.S. v. One Book Called "Ulysses,"* p. 184. The precedents Woolsey cited for this definition were *U.S. v. Dennett*, both Stopes trials, over which he himself had presided, and the *Frankie and Johnnie* decision. It is significant that instead of referring to the two landmark trials of the nineteenth century—*U.S. v. Bennett* and *U.S. v. Harmon*—he cited only two rather inconsequential ones—*Swearingen v. U.S.*, 161 U.S. 450 (1896), concerning a political slur, and *Dunlop v. U.S.*, 17 Sup. Ct. (1897), involving indecent ads for "massage treatments."

57. Ibid., p. 185.

58. Ernst's foreword appears in James Joyce, *Ulysses* (New York: Modern Library, 1934, 1942), pp. viii, vii. The ACLU quoted in Boyer, *Purity in Print*, p. 257. Sumner quoted in Ernst and Lindey, *The Censor Marches On*, p. 22.

59. *U.S. v. One Book Entitled "Ulysses,"* 72 Fed. 2nd (1934), pp. 706, 705, 707.

60. Ibid., pp. 706, 707, 708. Alpert, "Judicial Censorship of Obscene Literature," p. 75 (his emphasis).

61. The question whether obscene speech is protected by the First Amendment was not addressed by the Supreme Court until *Roth v. U.S.*, 354 U.S. 476 (1957), when the court ruled that "obscenity is not within the area of constitutionally protected freedom of speech or press." Although Theodore Schroeder had raised the issue in 1911 in his *"Obscene" Literature and Constitutional Law* his work was the exception. According to Harry Kalven, "The Metaphysics of the Law of Obscenity," *Supreme Court Review* (1960): "The law of obscenity regulation seems to have had a kind of

'sleeper' development outside the main stream of decisions dealing with the problems of freedom of speech" (p. 2).

62. Bailey quoted in Boyer, *Purity in Print*, p. 203. See Boyer, pp. 203–7, for a brief summary of the ACLU's position on obscenity laws.

63. *U.S.* v. *One Book Entitled "Ulysses,"* pp. 709, 710.

64. Ibid., p. 711.

65. Elgas quoted in Ernst and Lindey, *The Censor Marches On*, pp. 34–35. See Boyer, *Purity in Print*, p. 251, for a good summary of the final demise of the vice-society movement by the late 1930s.

66. Margaret Sanger, *An Autobiography* (New York: Dover, 1971, originally published in 1938), p. 412. Mencken quoted in Boyer, *Purity in Print*, p. 249.

67. Ben Ray Redman, "Obscenity and Censorship," *Scribner's Magazine* 95 (May 1934), pp. 341, 344, 343. Ernst makes the same argument in *The Censor Marches On*, p. 189.

68. Redman, "Obscenity and Censorship," p. 344.

8. Reticence Restated

1. Paul S. Boyer, *Purity in Print: The Vice Society Movement and Book Censorship in America* (New York: Charles Scribner's Sons, 1968), especially Chapter 6, "The Latter 1920s."

2. H. L. Mencken, "The Unblushful Mystery" in *Prejudices, First Series* (New York: Alfred A. Knopf, 1919), pp. 195, 196, 197. Randolph Bourne, "Theodore Dreiser" reprinted in Olaf Hansen (ed.), *The Radical Will* (New York: Urizen Books, 1977), p. 461.

3. Mencken, "The Unblushful Mystery," pp. 198, 199.

4. Ibid., p. 199.

5. Ibid., pp. 199–200. For Mencken's negative assessment of novels dedicated to "petty jousts of sex," see his "Joseph Conrad" in *A Book of Prefaces* (New York: Alfred A. Knopf, 1919), pp. 34–35. See W. R. Thayer, "The New Story-Tellers and the Doom of Realism," *Forum* 18 (December 1894), where this earlier critic of realism also coupled photography and skin to express his repugnance for the "dehumanized" realism.

6. Mencken, *A Book of Prefaces*, pp. 69, 58, 59; cf. p. 35.

7. Agnes Repplier, "The Repeal of Reticence," *Atlantic Monthly* 113 (1914), pp. 298–99, 300, 303.

8. Ibid., pp. 298, 304. For her assessment of Wilde, see "Mr. Wilde's *Intentions*," in her *Essays in Miniature* (Boston: Houghton Mifflin, 1895), pp. 121–28.

9. Joseph Wood Krutch, *The Modern Temper: A Study and a Confession* (New York: Harcourt, Brace, 1929, 1957), pp. 65, 59. Walter Lippmann, *A Preface to Morals* (New York: Time-Life Books, 1964, originally published in 1929), p. 292.

10. Lippmann, *A Preface to Morals*, p. 269. For early sociological analyses in this vein, see Freda Kirchwey (ed.), *Our Changing Morality: A Symposium* (New York: Albert and Charles Boni, 1924), especially the introduction by Kirchwey and the articles by the anthropologist Elsie Clews Parsons and the psychiatrist Beatrice M. Hingle; and V. F. Calverton and S. D. Schmalhausen (eds.), *Sex in Civilization* (New York: Garden City Publishing, 1929).

11. Lippmann, *A Preface to Morals*, pp. 272, 273.

12. Ibid., pp. 287, 288.

13. Ibid., p. 274. For a sociological analysis of many of the same questions, see Willard Waller, *The Old Love and the New: Divorce and Readjustment* (New York: Horace Liveright, 1930).

14. Lippmann, *A Preface to Morals*, pp. 274, 276, 277.
15. Ibid., p. 278.
16. Ibid., pp. 280, 281, 283, 285.
17. Ibid., pp. 286, 288, 289.
18. Krutch, *The Modern Temper*, p. 9.
19. Ibid., pp. 9, xi.
20. Ibid., pp. 76, 75, 77. Lippmann also makes a similar point about eating, p. 285.
21. Ibid., pp. 11–12. See Lippman on the role of psychoanalysis in matters of sex and love, p. 287.
22. Ibid., p. 62.
23. Ibid., pp. 59, 58.
24. Ibid., pp. 66, 67, 68.
25. Ibid., p. 69.
26. Lippmann, *A Preface to Morals*, pp. 298, 299.
27. Ibid., pp. 281, 292.
28. Alasdair MacIntyre, *After Virtue* (Notre Dame: University of Notre Dame Press, 1981), p. 52.
29. Ibid., p. 56.
30. Krutch, *The Modern Temper*, p. 78. Also see pp. 73–74.

9. The Controversy over Mass Culture

1. James Gilbert, *Writers and Partisans: A History of Literary Radicalism in America* (New York: John Wiley & Sons, 1968), p. 121. My discussion of the political context of the early *Partisan Review* is indebted to Gilbert's study in general. Also see Irving Howe, "This Age of Conformity," *Partisan Review* 21 (1954), and Dwight Macdonald, "Introduction: Politics Past," *Memoirs of a Revolutionist* (New York: Farrar, Straus and Cudahy, 1957), for firsthand accounts of this period.
2. William Phillips and Philip Rahv, "In Retrospect: Ten Years of *Partisan Review*," in *The Partisan Reader* (New York: Dial Press, 1947), p. 683.
3. Gilbert, *Writers and Partisans*, p. 186. For a good account of this shift of emphasis from political to artistic vanguards, see Christopher Lasch, "Modernism, Politics, and Philip Rahv," *Partisan Review* 47 (1980), pp. 183–94.
4. Clement Greenberg, "Avant-garde and *Kitsch*," *Partisan Review* 4 (1939), reprinted in his *Art and Culture* (Boston: Beacon Press, 1961), pp. 4–5.
5. Ibid., pp. 7, 8.
6. Ibid., pp. 7–9.
7. Ibid., pp. 9–10.
8. Ibid., pp. 10, 12.
9. Ibid., p. 15.
10. Leo Lowenthal, "Historical Perspectives of Popular Culture," *American Journal of Sociology* 55 (1950), reprinted in Bernard Rosenberg and David Manning White (eds.), *Mass Culture: The Popular Arts in America* (Glencoe, Ill.: The Free Press, 1957), p. 51.
11. Abraham Kaplan, "Obscenity as an Esthetic Category," *Law and Contemporary Problems* 20 (Autumn 1955), p. 548.
12. Ibid., pp. 549, 550.
13. For good examples of the social-control thesis, see Dwight Macdonald, "A Theory of Popular Culture," *Politics* (February 1944), pp. 20–22; James T. Farrell, "The Language of Hollywood" (1944), in his *The League of the Frightened Philistines* (New York: Vanguard Press, 1945), p. 177; William Barrett, "The Resistance," *Partisan*

Review 12 (1946), p. 481; and Irving Howe, "Notes on Mass Culture," *Politics* 5 (1948), pp. 120–23.

14. T. S. Eliot, *Notes Toward a Definition of Culture* (New York: Harcourt, Brace, 1949). Ernest van den Haag, "Of Happiness and Despair We Have No Measure" (1957), in Rosenberg and White, *Mass Culture*, p. 524 n. 46. Edward Shils, "Daydreams and Nightmares: Reflections on the Criticism of Mass Culture," *Sewanee Review* 65 (1957), pp. 586–608, in *The Intellectuals and the Powers and Other Essays* (Chicago: University of Chicago Press, 1972), p. 249.

15. Macdonald, "A Theory of Popular Culture," p. 20. Macdonald, "A Theory of Mass Culture," in Rosenberg and White, *Mass Culture*, p. 59. He did not acknowledge Greenberg in the first version, but cited him in the 1953 version.

16. Macdonald, "A Theory of Popular Culture," pp. 21, 20.

17. Ibid., p. 22. Macdonald did not acknowledge any of the writers associated with the Frankfurt School until the 1953 version, when he cited T. W. Adorno's "On Popular Music." According to Irving Howe: "In the essays of writers like Clement Greenberg and Dwight Macdonald, more or less influenced by the German neo-Marxist school of Adorno-Horkheimer, there were the beginnings of a theory of 'mass culture.' " Howe, "The New York Intellectuals" (1968), reprinted in his *The Decline of the New* (New York: Harcourt Brace Jovanovich, 1970), p. 226.

18. Howe, "Notes on Mass Culture," pp. 120, 121, 122.

19. Greenberg, "Avant-garde and *Kitsch*," p. 21 (his emphasis). Macdonald, "A Theory of Popular Culture," p. 22 (his emphasis).

20. Eric Larrabee, "The Cultural Context of Sex Censorship," *Law and Contemporary Problems* 20 (Autumn 1955), p. 683. James C. N. Paul and Murray L. Schwartz, *Federal Censorship: Obscenity in the Mail* (New York: The Free Press of Glencoe, 1961), pp. 83, 84. Also see Leslie Fiedler, "The Middle Against Both Ends," *Encounter* 5 (1955), reprinted in Rosenberg and White, *Mass Culture*, pp. 538–39.

21. *New York* v. *Winters*, reprinted in Morris L. Ernst and Alan U. Schwartz, *Censorship: The Search for the Obscene* (New York: Macmillan, 1964), p. 173.

22. Ibid., pp. 172, 173.

23. *Winters* v. *New York*, 333 U.S. 507 (1948), p. 510.

24. *Mutual Film Corp.* v. *Industrial Commission of Ohio*, 236 U.S. 230 (1915).

25. Paul and Schwartz, *Federal Censorship*, pp. 80–90; and Harry M. Clor, *Obscenity and Public Morality: Censorship in a Liberal Society* (Chicago: University of Chicago Press, 1969), pp. 4–6.

26. William B. Lockhart and Robert C. McClure, "Literature, the Law of Obscenity, and the Constitution," *Minnesota Law Review* 38 (1954), pp. 308, 356.

27. Clor, *Obscenity and Public Morality*, p. 117. Clor (ed.), *Censorship and Freedom of Expression: Essays on Obscenity and the Law* (Chicago: Rand McNally, 1971), p. 1n. Lockhart and McClure's article was cited, for example, by Justice Harlan in his Manual Enterprises opinion (*Manual Enterprises, Inc.* v. *Day*, 370 U.S. 478 (1961), and by the Massachusetts Supreme Court in *Attorney General* v. *The Book Named "Tropic of Cancer,"* 345 Mass. 11 (1962). The article also helped to establish Lockhart's reputation as an authority in both obscenity and constitutional law. In 1968, Lockhart, then dean of the University of Minnesota Law School, was appointed chairman of the National Commission on Obscenity and Pornography.

28. Lockhart and McClure, pp. 317, 348.

29. They cite Ernst's *To the Pure* (1928) and *The Censor Marches On* (1940) on p. 324 note 199, and also include Zechariah Chafee, *Government and Mass Communication* (1947), and Alpert, "Judicial Censorship" (1930) in their citation of important legal studies. (*To the Pure* was co-authored by William Seagle and *The*

Censor Marches On was co-authored by Alexander Lindey.) Broun, Leech, and Mencken are cited on p. 325 notes 203, 204.

30. Ibid., p. 320. Cf. pp. 343–44.
31. Ibid., pp. 326–28. Quoted passage on p. 328.
32. Ibid., pp. 353–54. *Chaplinsky* v. *New Hampshire*, 315 U.S. 568 (1942), pp. 571–72.
33. Lockhart and McClure, pp. 359, 361.
34. Ibid., pp. 367, 373.
35. Ibid., p. 377.
36. Ibid., pp. 377, 378.
37. Ibid., p. 374.
38. Ibid., pp. 374–75.
39. Ibid., pp. 375, 376.
40. Ibid., p. 381.
41. Ibid., pp. 383, 386. Justice Douglas cited the Gluecks and the Kinsey Report in his dissenting opinion in *Roth* v. *U.S.* For a good discussion of sociological studies of the effects of obscenity during the 1950s, see Clor, *Obscenity and Public Morality*, Chapter 4.
42. Lockhart and McClure, p. 386. Cf. pp. 332–33.
43. Edward De Grazia, *Girls Lean Back Everywhere: The Law of Obscenity and the Assault on Genius* (New York: Random House, 1992), pp. 277–78.
44. *Roth* v. *U.S.*, 354 U.S. 476 (1957), pp. 484, 483, 484.
45. Ibid., pp. 489, 487.
46. Ibid., pp. 509–10.
47. Ibid., pp. 511, 512. See the concurring opinion of Judge Jerome Frank in the lower appellate court decision of *U.S.* v. *Roth*, 237 Fed. 2nd 796 (1956) for a more detailed account of the importance of literary values in the language of the avant-garde.
48. *Roth* v. *U.S.*, p. 514.
49. Ibid., pp. 513, 501, 511.
50. Morris L. Ernst and David Loth, *American Sexual Behavior and the Kinsey Report* (New York: Greystone Press, 1948), p. 187. For other extravagant assessments of the Kinsey Report, see Dr. Robert L. Dickinson's, p. vii, and Bruce Bliven's, p. 11.
51. Ibid., dedication. For Ernst's early denunciations of fascism and its link with censorship, see Paul S. Boyer, *Purity in Print* (New York: Charles Scribner's Sons, 1968), pp. 264–74; and Morris L. Ernst and Alexander Lindey, *The Censor Marches On* (New York: Doubleday, 1940), pp. viii, ix, 263, 264.
52. Ernst and Loth, *American Sexual Behavior*, p. 186. For more on the marketplace of ideas and the democratic value of controversy and dissent, see pp. 173–74.
53. Ibid., p. 187.
54. Lionel Trilling, "Appendix: Some Notes for an Autobiographical Lecture" (1971) in Diana Trilling ed., *The Last Decade: Essays and Reviews, 1965–1975* (New York: Harcourt Brace Jovanovich, 1978), pp. 230, 233. For his broader definition of humanism, see p. 234.
55. Ibid., pp. 229–30, 236, 234.
56. Lionel Trilling, "The Kinsey Report" (1948), reprinted in *The Liberal Imagination* (New York: The Viking Press, 1950), pp. 224, 232, 231. For an excellent analysis of sexology that pushes many of Trilling's insights even deeper, see Leslie H. Farber, "Sex in Bondage to the Modern Will," reprinted in David Holbrook (ed.), *The Case Against Pornography* (New York: Library Press, 1973), pp. 83–102.
57. Trilling, "The Kinsey Report," pp. 229, 228.

58. Dwight Macdonald, "A Theory of Mass Culture," in Rosenberg and White, *Mass Culture*, p. 70.
59. Trilling, "The Kinsey Report," pp. 226–27.
60. Ibid., pp. 227, 238.
61. Ibid., pp. 236–37, 241–42.
62. Ibid., p. 242.

10. THE STALLED DEBATE ABOUT THE PUBLIC SPHERE

1. Bernard Rosenberg and David Manning White (eds.), *Mass Culture: The Popular Arts in America* (New York: The Free Press of Glencoe, 1957), p. v.
2. Ibid.
3. Leo Lowenthal, "Historical Perspectives of Popular Culture," p. 55; Ernest van den Haag, "Of Happiness and Despair We Have No Measure," p. 535; T. W. Adorno, "Television and the Patterns of Mass Culture," p. 476; Bernard Rosenberg, "Mass Culture in America," p. 9.
4. Edward Shils, "Mass Society and Its Culture," *Daedalus* 89 (1960), 288–314. Dwight Macdonald, "Preface," *Against the American Grain* (New York: Da Capo Press, 1983, originally published in 1962), p. 10. Also see "Masscult and Midcult" (1960), p. 70. Irving Howe, "The New York Intellectuals," *Commentary* 46 (1968), reprinted in *Selected Writings, 1950–1990* (New York: Harcourt Brace Jovanovich, 1990) p. 249. For other examples of Shils's influence, see Daniel Bell, *The End of Ideology: On the Exhaustion of Political Ideas in the Fifties* (New York: The Free Press, 1962), pp. 13–14, 21–38, and p. 412 n. 13, where he praises Shils's essay as "brilliant"; Raymond A. and Alice H. Bauer, "America, 'Mass Society,' and Mass Media," *Journal of Social Issues* 16 (1960), pp. 3–56; Leon Bramson, *The Political Context of Sociology* (Princeton: Princeton University Press, 1961), Chapter 6; E. V. Walter, "Mass Society: The Late Stages of an Idea," *Social Research* 31 (1964), pp. 391–410; and Herbert Gans, *Popular Culture and High Culture: An Analysis and Evaluation of Taste* (New York: Basic Books, 1974).
5. Ernest van den Haag, "Of Happiness and Despair We Have No Measure," p. 531.
6. Edward Shils, "Daydreams and Nightmares: Reflections on the Criticism of Mass Culture," *Sewanee Review* 65 (1957), pp. 586–608, reprinted in his *The Intellectuals and the Powers and Other Essays* (Chicago: University of Chicago Press, 1972), p. 249. A number of contributors to the Mass Culture Reader noted the convergence of right and left in the criticism of mass culture. For examples, see Rosenberg, "Mass Culture in America," pp. 3–4; and Melvin Tumin, "Popular Culture and the Open Society," p. 548.
7. Shils, "Daydreams and Nightmares," pp. 249, 250. He also places Erich Fromm, Karl Bednarik, Czeslaw Milosz, and Richard Hoggart in this camp (p. 250). His comments on "puritanical Marxism" were, surprisingly, relegated to a note on p. 252.
8. Ibid., p. 252.
9. Ibid., pp. 261, 255, 257. The Frankfurt School comes in for particular abuse in this connection, pp. 257–59. See Bell, *The End of Ideology*, pp. 27–38, for a similar assessment of the flaws of the mass-society theory.
10. Shils, "Daydreams and Nightmares," pp. 262, 261, 262, 263, 264. For more of this kind of analysis, see David Manning White, "Mass Culture in America: Another Point of View" in *Mass Culture*, p. 14.
11. Hannah Arendt, "Society and Culture," *Daedalus*, p. 278.
12. Daniel Bell, "The End of Ideology in the West: An Epilogue" (1961), in his *The End of Ideology*, pp. 402–3. For a more critical account of these same developments,

see Irving Howe, *A Margin of Hope* (New York: Harcourt, Brace, 1982), pp. 170–73.

13. Bell, "The Mood of Three Generations" (different sections were written in 1955, 1957, and 1959), in *The End of Ideology*, p. 301.
14. Ibid., pp. 312–13.
15. Dwight Macdonald, *Memoirs of a Revolutionist* (New York: Farrar, Straus and Cudahy, 1957), pp. 5, 200, 201. Also see the self-deprecatory sentences on p. 31.
16. Irving Howe, "This Age of Conformity," pp. 46, 47; "The Idea of the Modern," p. 151 in *Selected Writings*. Also see Dwight Macdonald, "Masscult and Midcult," pp. 50–58, for the widespread acceptance and domestication of the avant-garde.
17. Delmore Schwartz, "The Present State of Poetry" (1958), reprinted in Donald A. Dike and David H. Zucker (eds.), *Selected Essays of Delmore Schwartz* (Chicago: University of Chicago, 1970), p. 44.
18. Ibid., p. 36; Howe, "This Age of Conformity," p. 32. Also see Howe, *A Margin of Hope*, pp. 170–73; Bell, *The End of Ideology*, p. 314; Macdonald, "Masscult and Midcult," p. 58; and Russell Jacoby, *The Last Intellectuals: American Culture in the Age of Academe* (New York: Noonday, 1987).
19. Schwartz, "The Present State of Poetry," pp. 47–48.
20. Ibid., pp. 44, 45. Bell, "America as a Mass Society: A Critique," in *The End of Ideology*, pp. 35–36.
21. Charles Rembar in Harry M. Clor, *Obscenity and Public Morality* (Chicago: University of Chicago Press, 1969), p. 28. Howe, "The New York Intellectuals," p. 249. For other announcements of the end of censorship, see Irving Kristol, "Is This What We Wanted?" in Hal Holbrook (ed.), *The Case Against Pornography* (New York: The Library Press, 1972), pp. 187, 188; and Walter Berns, "Beyond the (Garbage) Pale, or Democracy, Censorship and the Arts," in Holbrook, p. 276.
22. Howe, "The New York Intellectuals," pp. 249–50.
23. Macdonald, "Midcult and Masscult," p. 57.
24. Leslie Fiedler, "The Middle Against Both Ends" (1955), reprinted in Rosenberg and White (eds.), *Mass Culture*, p. 537. Howe singled out Fiedler as a publicist for the new sensibility in "New York Intellectuals," p. 277.
25. Susan Sontag, "Notes on 'Camp'" (1964), reprinted in *Against Interpretation* (New York: Farrar, Straus and Giroux, 1965), pp. 286, 287.
26. Ibid., p. 288.
27. Ibid., p. 289.
28. Ibid., pp. 286, 288.
29. Ibid., pp. 290, 291.
30. Maurice Girodias (ed.), *The Olympia Reader* (New York: The Grove Press, 1965), p. 23.
31. Ibid.
32. Susan Sontag, "The Pornographic Imagination" (1967), reprinted in *A Susan Sontag Reader* (New York: Farrar, Straus and Giroux, 1982), pp. 207, 232, 212.
33. Ibid., pp. 212–13.
34. Ibid., p. 220.
35. See Girodias, *The Olympia Reader*, p. 29.
36. Sontag, "The Pornographic Imagination," pp. 232, 222.
37. Ibid., p. 223.
38. *A Book Named "John Cleland's Memoirs of a Woman of Pleasure" et al.* v. *Attorney General of Massachusetts*, 383 U.S. 413 (1965), pp. 414, 413.
39. Sontag, "The Pornographic Imagination," p. 203. Rembar quoted in Edward De Grazia, *Girls Lean Back Everywhere: The Law of Obscenity and the Assault on Genius* (New York: Vintage Books, 1992), p. 438. *Memoirs* v. *Mass.*, pp. 445–46, 449. In

his dissenting opinion, Justice Clark took the professors to task for their testimony, pp. 441–49.

40. *Memoirs v. Mass.*, pp. 418, 441.
41. Sontag, "The Pornographic Imagination," p. 221; cf. p. 222. *Ginzburg* v. *U.S.*, 383 U.S. 463 (1966), p. 489.
42. *Ginzburg* v. *U.S.*, p. 489.
43. Ibid., pp. 489–90.
44. Ibid., p. 491. This move was used to good advantage most recently by defenders of the public exhibits of Robert Mapplethorpe's photographs.
45. *Roth* v. *U.S.*, 354 U.S. 476, p. 484 (1957).
46. *Winters* v. *New York*, 333 U.S. 507 (1948), reprinted in Morris L. Ernst and Alan U. Schwartz, *Censorship: The Search for the Obscene* (New York: Macmillan, 1964), pp. 174–75.
47. *Ginzburg* v. *U.S.*, p. 498.
48. Ibid.
49. William L. Prosser, "Privacy," *California Law Review* 48 (1960), p. 338. See Diane Zimmerman, "Requiem for a Heavyweight: A Farewell to Warren and Brandeis's Privacy Tort," *Cornell Law Review* 68 (1983), p. 337 n. 244, for an updated version of the right to privacy as a form of social control. The only legal writer to take Brandeis and Warren's position seriously and to defend it consistently is Edward J. Bloustein. See "Privacy as an Aspect of Human Dignity," *New York University Law Review* 39 (1964), pp. 962–1007; and "The First Amendment and Privacy: The Supreme Court Justice and the Philosopher," *Rutgers Law Review* 28 (1974), pp. 41–95.
50. Alan Westin, *Privacy and Freedom* (New York: Atheneum, 1967), p. 348. Harry Kalven, "Privacy in Tort Law—Were Warren and Brandeis Wrong?" *Law and Contemporary Problems* (symposium on privacy) 31 (1966), p. 329. Paul A. Freund, "Privacy: One Concept or Many," in J. Roland Pennock and John Chapman (eds.), *Privacy* (New York: Atherton Press, 1971), p. 190.

ii. The Last Stand of Reticence

1. Irving Kristol, "Is This What We Wanted?" published originally in the *New York Times* as "Pornography, Obscenity, and the Case for Censorship" (1971), reprinted in Hal Holbrook (ed.), *The Case Against Pornography* (New York: The Library Press, 1972), p. 191.
2. Irving Howe, "The Idea of the Modern" (1967), reprinted in *Selected Writings, 1950–1990* (New York: Harcourt Brace Jovanovich, 1990), p. 158.
3. Friede quoted in Paul S. Boyer, *Purity in Print* (New York: Charles Scribner's Sons, 1968), p. 134. Critics repeatedly objected to the crudeness and explicitness of the novels of William Burroughs and Norman Mailer. See Storm Jameson, "The Retreat from the Pleasure Principle," in Holbrook, pp. 208, 211–13; George Steiner, "Night Words" (1965), in Holbrook, p. 231; and Howe, "The New York Intellectuals" (1968), in *Selected Writings*, pp. 272, 275, 277.
4. "Censors' Foe Sees Needs for Limits to Freedom," *New York Times* (January 5, 1970), p. 46. Walter Berns took special pleasure in debunking the amazing change of heart displayed by Ernst and the *New York Times* editorial, "Beyond the (Garbage) Pale" (April 1, 1969, p. 46). See Berns, "Beyond the (Garbage) Pale, or Democracy, Censorship, and the Arts," pp. 275–76. See Irving Kristol's similar tack in "Is This What We Wanted?" p. 187. Both are reprinted in Holbrook.
5. C. Herman Pritchett, introduction to Harry M. Clor, *Obscenity and Public Morality: Censorship in a Liberal Society* (Chicago: University of Chicago Press, 1969), p. x.

Jameson, "The Retreat from the Pleasure Principle, p. 218. For other examples of this kind of characterization of the obscenity debate, see Clor, *Obscenity and Public Morality*, p. 6; Holbrook, p. 1, *The Case against Pornography*, and Pamela Hansford Johnson, "Peddling the Pornography of Violence, p. 195, and Berns, "Beyond the (Garbage) Pale," pp. 273–74. Also see Willard M. Gaylin, "Obscenity Is More Than a Four-Letter Word," in Harry M. Clor (ed.), *Censorship and Freedom of Expression: Essays on Obscenity and the Law* (Chicago: Rand McNally, 1971), p. 154.

6. Berns, "Beyond the (Garbage) Pale," p. 277. Howe, "The New York Intellectuals," p. 277.
7. Howe, "The New York Intellectuals," pp. 274, 276–77, 275, 270.
8. Ibid., p. 271.
9. Howe, "The Idea of the Modern," pp. 155, 163, 165.
10. Howe, "The New York Intellectuals," pp. 276, 273, 274.
11. George Steiner, "Night Words," p. 232 (his emphasis). For more on the boring and trivial aspect of pornography, see Steiner, pp. 227–31, and Jameson, "Beyond the Pleasure Principle," pp. 211, 217, 224, 225. Sontag mischaracterizes Steiner's essay in "The Pornographic Imagination," p. 206, as defending "society's right and obligation to censor dirty books."
12. Steiner, "Night Words," pp. 232, 233.
13. Ibid., p. 233.
14. Hannah Arendt, *The Origins of Totalitarianism* (New York: Harcourt Brace Jovanovich, 1951; 1973), p. 440. Steiner, "Night Words," p. 233.
15. John Stuart Mill, "On Liberty," in Max Lerner (ed.), *Essential Works of John Stuart Mill* (New York: Bantam Books, 1961), p. 265. Steiner, "Night Words," pp. 234–35.
16. Steiner, "Night Words," pp. 235, 236.
17. Clor, *Obscenity and Public Morality*, pp. 3–4.
18. Ibid., pp. 224, 225.
19. Ibid., p. 226. For more on the doubleness of bodily experiences and the importance of social conventions, see Harry M. Clor, "Obscenity and Freedom of Expression," in Clor, *Censorship and Freedom of Expression*, p. 103.
20. Clor, "Obscenity and Freedom of Expression," p. 104.
21. Edward J. Bloustein, "Privacy as an Aspect of Human Dignity," *New York University Law Review* 39 (1964).
22. Clor, "Obscenity and Freedom of Expression," p. 102; also see pp. 99–101. Storm Jameson, "The Retreat from the Pleasure Principle," p. 211. Ernest van den Haag, "Is Pornography a Cause of Crime?" p. 164. For more examples of this emphasis on objectification and degradation, see Holbrook, "Introduction," p. 8; Ian Robinson, "Pornography," p. 183; Irving Kristol, "Is This What We Wanted?" pp. 189, 190–91. For a representative sample of the early feminist argument against pornography, see Laura Lederer (ed.), *Take Back the Night: Women on Pornography* (New York: William Morrow, 1980). With the exception of an excerpt from Susan Brownmiller's *Against Our Will: Men, Women, and Rape* (1975), all of the other articles date from the late 1970s. For a representative work of Catharine MacKinnon, see her *Only Words* (Cambridge: Harvard University Press, 1993).
23. Clor, *Obscenity and Public Morality*, pp. 167, 174, 171. See also Clor, "Obscenity and Freedom of Expression," p. 106.
24. Clor, "Obscenity and Freedom of Expression," p. 109. Clor, *Obscenity and Public Morality*, pp. 198, 187, 200. For a similar view of the dangers posed to civic virtue by obscenity, see Berns, "Beyond the (Garbage) Pale."
25. Clor discusses the idea of victimless crimes in his analysis of the "Wolfenden Report on Homosexual Offenses and Prostitution" and the famous debate between

H. L. A. Hart and Patrick Devlin in *Obscenity and Public Morality*, pp. 175–80.

26. *Obscenity and Public Morality*, pp. 186, 190, 200, 207. "Obscenity and Freedom of Expression," p. 110.

27. J. G. A. Pocock, "Virtues, Rights, and Manners: A Model for Historians of Political Thought," in *Virtue, Commerce, and History* (Cambridge: Cambridge University Press, 1985), pp. 37–50, and Pocock, "Cambridge Paradigms and Scotch Philosophers," in Istvan Hont and Michael Ignatieff (eds.), *Wealth and Virtue* (Cambridge: Cambridge University Press, 1983), pp. 235–52.

28. Henry James, "The Lesson of the Master," in *The Art of the Novel* (Boston: Northeastern University Press, 1934, 1984), p. 222.

29. William H. Bushnell, "Journalistic Barbarism," *The Inland Printer* 3 (January 1886), p. 201.

30. Reginald Wright Kauffman, "The Drama and Morality," *Forum* 51 (January 1914), p. 672.

31. Steiner, "Night Words," p. 233. Clor, *Obscenity and Public Morality*, p. 11 (his emphasis).

32. Howe, "The New York Intellectuals, p. 276. Clor, *Obscenity and Public Morality*, p. 126.

33. Howe, "The New York Intellectuals," p. 277.

34. See Mari J. Matsuda et al., *Words That Wound: Critical Race Theory, Assaultive Speech, and the First Amendment* (Boulder, Colo.: Westview Press, 1993); and Laura Lederer and Richard Delgado (eds.), *The Price We Pay* (New York: Hill and Wang, 1994).

35. I am indebted here to MacIntyre's discussion of Kierkegaard's *Either/Or*, particularly the fine contrasts he draws between the aesthetic and moral life. Alasdair MacIntyre, *After Virtue* (Notre Dame: University of Notre Dame Press, 1981), p. 39.

INDEX